English Grammar Without Tears

English Grammar Without Tears

By

VISHWANATHAN NAIR
M.A. (English)
Diploma in Journalism
Cochin, Kerala

CHANDRIKA A
M.A. (English), M.Ed.,
P.G. Diploma in Journalism
English Teacher in
S.N. Higher Sec. School
Cochin, Kerala

UNIVERSITY SCIENCE PRESS

(An Imprint of Laxmi Publications Pvt. Ltd.)

BANGALORE • CHENNAI • COCHIN • GUWAHATI • HYDERABAD
JALANDHAR • KOLKATA • LUCKNOW • MUMBAI • PATNA
RANCHI • NEW DELHI

Published by :

UNIVERSITY SCIENCE PRESS

(An Imprint of Laxmi Publications (P) Ltd.)

113, Golden House, Daryaganj,
New Delhi-110002

Phone : 011-43 53 25 00
Fax : 011-43 53 25 28

www.laxmipublications.com
info@laxmipublications.com

First Edition : 2012

OFFICES

© **Bangalore**	080-26 75 69 30	© **Kolkata**	033-22 27 43 84
© **Chennai**	044-24 34 47 26	© **Lucknow**	0522-220 99 16
© **Cochin**	0484-237 70 04, 405 13 03	© **Mumbai**	022-24 91 54 15, 24 92 78 69
© **Guwahati**	0361-251 36 69, 251 38 81	© **Patna**	0612-230 00 97
© **Hyderabad**	040-24 65 23 33	© **Ranchi**	0651-220 4464
© **Jalandhar**	0181-222 12 72		

UEG-9642-325-ENG GRAMM WITHOUT TEARS-NAI **C—**

Typeset at : Goswami Associates, Delhi.

Printed at: Repro Knowledgecast Limited, Thane

Contents

1. Parts of Speech 1

1.1 Noun 1
1.2 Pronoun 2
1.3 Adjective 2
1.4 Verb 2
1.5 Adverb 3
1.6 Preposition 3
1.7 Conjunction 3
1.8 Interjection 4

2. Sentences, Phrases and Clauses, Subject and Predicate 5

2.1 The Sentence 5
2.2 Sentence Elements 5
2.3 Kinds of Sentences 6
2.4 Subject and Predicate 9
2.5 Phrases and Clauses 9
2.6 Classification of Phrases 10
2.7 Clauses 12
2.8 Different Kinds of Clauses 12
2.9 The Adverb Clause 12
2.10 The Adjective Clause 16
2.11 The Noun Clause 19

3. The Noun 23

3.1 Proper Noun 23
3.2 Common Noun 24
3.3 Collective Noun or Group Noun 24

3.4 Mass Nouns or Non-Count Nouns 25
3.5 Material Noun 28
3.6 Abstract Noun 28
3.7 The Noun-Gender 29
3.8 The Noun-Case 32
3.9 The Noun-Number 37

4. The Pronoun 54

4.1 Personal Pronouns 54
4.2 Reflexive Pronouns or Compound Personal Pronouns 59
4.3 Relative Pronouns 61
4.4 Reciprocal Pronouns 70
4.5 Distributive Pronouns 71
4.6 Demonstrative Pronouns 72
4.7 Indefinite Pronouns 73
4.8 Compound Pronouns 74
4.9 Interrogative Pronouns 74
4.10 Exclamatory Pronouns 77

5. The Verb 78

5.1 Finite and Non-Finite Forms of Verbs 79
5.2 Modal Auxiliaries or Modals: 82
5.3 Defective Verbs 85
5.4 Regular Verbs and Irregular Verbs 89
5.5 Dynamic Verbs and Static Verbs 90
5.6 Conjugation of Verbs 92
5.7 Transitive Verbs Used as Intransitive 95
5.8 Intransitive Verbs Used as Transitive 97
5.9 Strong and Weak Verbs 99
5.10 Mood 101
5.11 Non-finite Verbs 106
5.12 The Infinitive 106
5.13 The Participle or Verbal Adjective 116
5.14 The Gerund (Verbal Noun) 118

6. Agreement of the Verb with the Subject 137

7. The Adjective 144

7.1 Kinds of Adjectives 144
7.2 Uses of Adjectives 148
7.3 Position of Adjectives 151
7.4 Comparison of Adjectives 152
7.5 Adjectives Used as Nouns 156

8. The Adverb 161

8.1 Simple Adverbs 163
8.2 Interrogative Adverbs 165
8.3 Relative Adverbs 166
8.4 Sentence Adverbials 168
8.5 Comparison of Adverbs 177

9. Prepositions 182

9.1 Positions of Prepositions 183
9.2 Kinds of Prepositions 183
9.3 Relations Denoted by Prepositions 186
9.4 Use of Some Important Prepositions 189
9.5 Prepositions Used with Transitive and Intransitive Verbs 209
9.6 Omission of Prepositions 210
9.7 Prepositions and Prepositional Phrases 211

10. Conjunctions 214

10.1 Coordinating (Co-ordinating) Conjunctions 215
10.2 Subordinating Conjunctions 217
10.3 Correlative Conjunctions 219
10.4 Compound Conjunctions 220
10.5 Correct use of Some Important Conjunctions 221

11. Tenses 237

11.1 The Present Tense 239
11.2 The Past Tense 249
11.3 The Future Tense 255

12. The Sequence of Tenses 267

12.1 Tense and Events (General) 267
12.2 Sequence of Tenses 268

13. Degrees of Comparison 271

13.1 Comparison of Adjectives or Adverbs 271
13.2 Interchange of Degrees of Comparison 274

14. Transformation of Simple, Complex, Compound and Multiple Sentences 282

14.1 Transformation of Sentences 282
14.2 Simple, Complex, Compound and Multiple Sentences 285

15. Active and Passive Voice 290

16. Direct and Indirect Speech 303

16.1 Conversion of Statements into Indirect Speech or Narration 309
16.2 Conversion of Questions into Indirect Speech 311
16.3 Conversion of Imperatives [Commands and Requests] into Indirect Speech 313
16.4 Conversion of Exclamations into Indirect Speech 314

17. Articles 320

18. Punctuation 352

19. Question Tags or Tag Questions 363

20. Comprehension 370

20.1 Comprehension—Exercise 370

21. Precis-writing 381

21.1 Specimen 382
21.2 Functions of Democracy 382

22. Indianism 386

22.1 Common Mistakes Committed by Indian Speakers in English 386

23. Words Confused and Misused 390

24. Miscellaneous 417

24.1 Difference between FAIRLY and RATHER 420

25. Corrections 434

25.1 Miscellaneous Corrections 434

26. Story Writing 448

26.1 Complete Story 449

26.2 Complete Story 449

27. Letter Writing 451

27.1 General Form of A letter 451

27.2 The Superscription 455

27.3 Informal Letters/ Personal Letters 464

FOREWORD

With books on grammar flooding the literary market, one more might seem a superfluity. Mr. Viswanathan Nair's book, however, is unique in every respect, refreshingly different from the lot. Most of the books deal either traditional or modern grammar. Though not overtly stated, one can watch the path English grammar has trodden from the beginning to date. The advocates of Modern Grammar are inclined to scoff at Traditional Grammarians with statements like 'The Adverb is a literary ragbag into which words that cannot be classified are thrown'. Just as T.S. Eliot requires every new aspirating poet to have an awareness of the history of poetry from Homer to the present day, Sri Nair has conclusively established that English Grammar is an overflowing stream and that Modern Grammar is a supplement to and not a substitute for Traditional Grammar.

An outstanding characteristic of the author is that he has given us the proper term for every grammatical feature. Further they are also profusely illustrated (Mr. Nair is allergic to terms like etc., so on which writers usually employ when their stock is exhausted) with examples drawn from all fields of life which make enjoyable reading as if one is perusing a novel. I consider this book by a grammatical savant a monumental work which will be cherished by all lovers of the English language.

Prof. N. Madhukar Rao
Retd. Professor of English
Maharaja's College,
Ernakulam.

PREFACE

This book has been written with a view to providing a simple grammar book for all those who want to learn English, the language used world over. It does not claim any originality excepting for its highly user - friendly treatment of the subject. Written in simple language with numerous examples, this book , it is hoped , will amply help the readers understand the essentials of English Grammar with ease and without the help of a master.

We greatfully acknowledge our deep indebtness to Prof.N.Madhukar Rao, Rtd.Prof.of English, Maharaja's College, Ernakulam for his valuable advice and guidance in the preparation of this book.

Authors

Chapter 1 PARTS OF SPEECH

According to their use, words are classified into different kinds called **parts of speech**. They are eight in number:

1. Noun
2. Adjective
3. Pronoun
4. Verb
5. Adverb
6. Preposition
7. Conjunction
8. Interjection

Since a word may belong to different parts of speech it is easy to identify the part/s of speech to which it belongs if we see that word in a sentence.

For Example:

Smell the flower. (Here the word 'smell' is a verb)

The flower has sweet *smell.* (Here the word 'smell' is a noun)

Thus the word *'smell'* is **verb** in the first sentence and **noun** in the second.

1.1 NOUN

A word used for naming anything is called a **noun.**

For Example:

Raju, bus, smell, student, policy, rose, skin, anger, car, colour, white, red, man, beauty, honesty, danger, Mumbai, etc.

- *Raju* is a *student.*
- *Honesty* is the best *policy.*
- *Beauty* is *skin* deep.
- He went by *bus.*
- The *rose* has sweet *smell.*
- *Red* indicates *danger.*

1.2 PRONOUN

A word that is used instead of a noun is called a **pronoun**.

For Example:

he, she, it, they, that, me, them, etc.

For Example:

Raju is a good boy. *He* is very hard working.

(Here, the word 'He' stands for the noun Raju. Hence it is a pronoun.)

I am a student. (Here 'I' is a pronoun which stands for the speaker)

We are students. ('We' stands for the speaker/s.)

This is Helen. *She* is my neighbour. ('She'-pronoun standing for the noun Helen.)

Raju, Ram and Sita are students. *They* are friends.

('They'- pronoun standing for the nouns Raju, Ram and Sita.)

We eat egg because *it* is good for health. ('it'-pronoun standing for the noun egg.)

1.3 ADJECTIVE

A word used to qualify a noun or pronoun is called an **adjective**. (It adds something to the meaning of a noun or pronoun)

For Example:

The rose is a *beautiful* flower. (The adjective 'beautiful' describes or qualifies the noun 'flower'. It tells us what kind of flower it is.)

Sita is *smart*. She is *intelligent* too.

In the above examples the words 'beautiful', 'smart' and 'intelligent' qualify (add to the meaning of) the nouns *Rose* and *Sita*, and the pronoun *she* respectively and hence they are adjectives.

1.4 VERB

A word used to express an action, an event, or a state is called a **verb**.

For Example:

Ramu *slept* in the class. (The word 'slept' expresses an action)

He *happened* to fall. (The word 'happened' expresses an event.)

Water *exists* in three forms. (The word 'exists' expresses a state)

Note. The predicate of a sentence must be a verb or it must at least contain a verb.

1.5 ADVERB

A word used to modify or describe (add something to the meaning of) a verb, an adjective or another adverb is called an **adverb**.

For Example:

Ramu did his work *efficiently*. (Here 'efficiently' modifies or describes the verb 'did'. Hence the word 'efficiently' is an adverb.)

Ramu is a *very* efficient worker. ('very' is an adverb as it modifies or describes the adjective 'efficient'.)

Ramu did his work *very* efficiently. (The word 'very' further modifies or describes the adverb 'efficiently' and hence is an adverb.)

1.6 PREPOSITION

A word used with a noun or pronoun to indicate the relation of the noun or the pronoun with something else. Preposition means pre (before) + position as it is placed before a noun or a pronoun which is the object of the sentence.

(At, about, after, before, in, on, for, to, since, etc are some of the commonly used prepositions.)

For Example:

The book is *on* the table. (The word *'on'* shows the relation between the book and the table and hence it is a preposition. The sentence without the preposition 'on' is meaningless.)

The box is *under* the seat. (The word *'under'* shows the relation between the box and the seat and hence it is a preposition.)

He has gone *to* Delhi. (Here the preposition *'to'* indicates the connection between 'He has gone' and the proper noun 'Delhi')

1.7 CONJUNCTION

A word used to join words, phrases or clauses together is called a **conjunction**.

For Example:

and, but, as, etc are conjunctions.

For Example:

She is clever *and* attractive. (joining two words)

Ramu is clever, *but* he is honest. (joining two clauses)

As he was ill, he could not attend the class.

They greeted her with *big applause* and *full of energy*. (joining two phrases)

Here, the words 'and', 'but' and 'as' are conjunctions. And, or, nor, either....or, neither...nor, both... and, as well as, so, that, whether, if, when, why, how, since, etc. are some of the commonly used conjunctions.

1.8 INTERJECTION

A word expressing some feelings of the mind is called an **interjection**. It is actually a sound used while expressing some emotion of the mind.

(Alas, oh, wow, good heavens, what a sight, etc are commonly used interjections.)

For Example:

Alas ! I was cheated. ('Alas' shows that the speaker is sad.)

O! my country men. ('O' is used for addressing someone or something.)

Oh, what a wonderful sight! ('Oh'- expresses surprise)

Wow, what a wonderful catch! ('Wow'-expresses great surprise)

Ah, this is the kind of thing I wanted to posses. ('Ah'-expresses satisfaction, contentment, etc.)

What a sight! (What a sight it is!) (Exclamation)

How stupid! (How stupid it is!) (Exclamation)

EXERCISE

Name the part of speech of each underlined word in the following sentences.

1. Ramu is a clever boy.
2. The river flows into the sea.
3. The boys are playing on the ground.
4. He and his brother are living together.
5. He ran quickly.
6. Sometimes we have to take quick decisions.
7. He still works in that office.
8. This is the house he lives in.
9. They ran after the thief.
10. The city buses were off the roads last Monday.
11. Chandni is an intelligent girl. She is always first in the class.
12. You must do your homework before you go to bed.
13. Good heavens!

Chapter **2**

Sentences, Phrases and Clauses, Subject and Predicate

2.1 THE SENTENCE

A group of words that makes complete sense is called a sentence.

A sentence begins with a Capital Letter.

For Example:

He gave me a gift.

John went to Delhi.

Seeta is going to school.

From the above examples it may be seen that the meaning is clear if and only if something is said about something else in a sentence.

2.2 SENTENCE ELEMENTS

There are five elements of sentence structure.

They are: *Subject(S), Verb(V), Complement(C), Object(O)* and *adverbial(A)*

All these elements or some of them may be used in sentence construction.

For Example:

The members(S) unanimously(A) elected(V) him(O) (the) President(C).

The bird(A) flew(V) away(A).

Rivers(S) flow(V).

2.3 KINDS OF SENTENCES

(*a*) The Assertive or declarative sentence.

(*b*) The Interrogative sentence

(*c*) The Imperative sentence

(*d*) The Optative sentence

(*e*) The Exclamatory sentence.

(*a*) **The Assertive sentence.** A sentence that simply makes a statement or assertion is called an Assertive or a Declarative sentence.

For Example:

Ramu is a clever boy.

He did not go to school yesterday.

Note: An Assertive sentence ends with a Full Stop.

(*b*) **The Interrogative sentence.** A sentence that asks a question is called an Interrogative sentence.

For Example:

Where is Ramu going ?

Is he going to Mumbai?

There are two types:

(*i*) **Verbal questions:** These are questions that may be answered with *Yes* or *No*

For Example:

Are you going Home?

Is your mother at home?

'If'/'whether' is used in 'yes or no' interrogative sub-clauses.

For Example:

Do you know if/whether they are coming?

(Here only one of the two answers 'yes or no' is possible.)

'If…or / whether…or' is used in alternative question.

For Example:

It is immaterial if/whether you are affected or not.

Note: We can use 'or' immediately after 'whether' only.

For Example:

It is immaterial whether or not you are affected.(not: if or not)

(*ii*) **Pronominal Questions:** These are questions that cannot be answered with *Yes* or *No*. They begin with Interrogative pronouns, Interrogative adjectives, or Interrogative adverbs.

For Example:

Who knocked at the door? ('Who' – Interrogative pronoun)

What picture is this? ('What' – Interrogative adjective)

Where do you stay? ('Where' – Interrogative adverb)

Note: An Interrogative sentence ends with a Question Mark.

Note: Positive questions are sometimes asked in the form of statement by raising the tone of the question assuming an ' Yes' answer.

For Example:

You are going home?

You have got something to read?

Negative questions can also be asked in statement form assuming a 'No' answer.

For Example:

You didn't come yesterday?

She couldn't meet him?

Note: There are questions with more than two 'question words' (what, who, why, etc)

For Example:

Who is doing what?

When and how did you escape?

When did you go there, and why?

Note: Polite questions are asked by using 'please' 'could you tell', 'would you mind', etc.

What is your address, please?

Could you tell me your name?

Would you mind giving me your pen?

Could I have your address, please?

May I know your name, please?

Note: Short questions can be used in response to statements when more information is required by the hearer.

For Example:

Speaker: The officer was asking for you.

Hearer: Which officer?/When? etc. can be some of the short questions.

Speaker: I have gone to the police station.

Hearer: Which police station?/What for? etc.

Note: If the hearer wants the speaker to repeat part of what he has said as a clarification, he uses *echo* questions.

For Example:

1. *Speaker:* I don't subscribe to your views.

   Hearer: Do you mean that you don't subscribe to my views?

   Or

   You don't subscribe to my views?

2. *Speaker:* I am going to Chennai.

   Hearer: Where are you going?

3. *Speaker:* I am going to Delhi.

   Hearer: Pardon? (I beg your pardon?)/Sorry?/Excuse me?/What? etc.

(*c*) **The Imperative sentence.** A sentence that contains some command or request is called an Imperative sentence. The subject 'you' is usually understood in such sentences.

For Example:

Don't talk in the class. (command) (You don't........)

Please give me your pen. (request) (You please........)

Note: An Imperative sentence ends with a Full Stop

(*d*) **The Optative sentence :** A sentence that expresses a wish is called an Optative sentence.

For Example:

May God bless you.

May you live long.

Note: An Optative sentence ends with a Full Stop.

(*e*) **Exclamatory sentence.**_A sentence that expresses some sudden feeling or emotion such as surprise, pleasure or anger is called an exclamatory sentence.

For Example:

What a sight it is !

How wonderful it is!

Note: An Exclamatory sentence ends with an Exclamation Mark.

(*f*) **Aphoristic sentence.** An aphoristic sentence is a short statement that says something wise and true, usually found in some proverbs.

For Example:

The earlier, the better.

Well begun, half done.

Note: An Aphoristic sentence ends with a Full Stop.

2.4 SUBJECT AND PREDICATE

Every sentence must have a subject and a predicate, a *subject* to be spoken about and a *predicate* to speak something about that subject.

Every sentence therefore must have two parts:

(*a*) The Subject - The part that names the person or thing about whom or which something is spoken.

(*b*) The Predicate - The part that tells something about the subject.

Examine the following sentence:

The sun rises in the east.

'The sun' is the subject of the sentence (This part names the subject.)

and *'rises in the east'* is its predicate (This part tells something about the sun which is the subject)

He stands first in the class.

He – Subject (Name of the person about whom something is spoken)

Stands first in the class – Predicate. (It tells something about the subject 'He')

Note: (*a*) The subject of a sentence usually comes first, but sometimes it is placed after the predicate.

For Example:

Here comes the hero. (The hero comes)

(*b*) In imperative sentences the subject is omitted.

For Example:

Stand up. (*You* stand up.)

Come. (*You* come – example of a single word sentence.)

(*c*) In exclamatory sentences sometimes the subject and part of the predicate are omitted.

For Example:

What a beautiful sight !- Exclamation- meaning 'It is a beautiful sight'. Here the subject and part of the predicate (It is) are understood.

It- subject; 'is a beautiful sight' - predicate

2.5 PHRASES AND CLAUSES

There are phrases and clauses other than sentences.

A phrase is a group of words which makes some sense but not complete sense.

Phrases

Examine the following sentences:

He sat on the bench.

They went through the tunnel.

He stood in the corner.

There is a garden in front of the house.

In the above sentences the groups of words underlined are Phrases.

A phrase has no predicate or finite verb. It normally forms part of a sentence.

2.6 CLASSIFICATION OF PHRASES

1. Noun Phrase: This does the work of a noun in a sentence.

   For Example:

   (*a*) I do not know *what to tell.*

   The phrase 'what to tell' is the object of the verb 'know'.

   Hence 'what to tell' is a noun phrase.

   (*b*) *Viewing TV for a long time* is not good for the eyes.

   Here the underlined phrase is the subject of the verb 'is'.

   Hence it is a noun phrase.

2. Adjective Phrase: This does the work of an adjective.

   For Example:

   (*a*) This shelf *in the kitchen* is very old.

   The phrase 'in the kitchen' qualifies the 'shelf'. Hence it does the work of an adjective. It is therefore an adjective phrase.

   (*b*) This bottle is full of water.

   (The phrase 'full of water' does the work of an adjective. Hence it is an adjective phrase.)

3. Adverb Phrase: This does the work of an adverb.

   For Example:

   (*a*) He went into the room. (The phrase 'into the room' modifies the verb 'went'. That is, it does the work of an adverb. It is therefore an adverb phrase.)

   (*b*) He spoke a few words.(' a few words' is an adverb phrase.)

Note: Absolute phrase: A phrase that is grammatically independent of the rest of the sentence is called an absolute phrase.

For Example:

He being rich, I requested him to lend me some money.

(The absolute phrase ' He being rich' means 'As (or Because) he is rich' and does the work of an adverb clause. The pronoun 'He' stands alone before the participle 'being'. It (He) is neither the subject nor the object of any finite verb. Hence 'He being rich' is an absolute phrase.

Other examples:

This said, he went off. (*i.e.,* After he had said this, he went off.)

To tell (you) the truth, I don't like him.(If I tell (you) the truth, I don't like him)

Types of phrases

There are four types of phrases. They are:

1. A phrase introduced by a preposition.

   For Example:

   He slept *for* eight hours.

   He kept the bag *under* the table.

   It is *beyond* my imagination.

   He is *above* suspicion.

2. A phrase introduced by a participle (both present and past participles) .

   For Example:

   Crossing the road, he met with an accident (present participle).

   Having finished his work, he left the office (perfect participle).

   The tree is *laden with fruit.*

   Driven by anger, he beat his son.

3. A phrase introduced by an infinitive.

   For Example:

   To go to Chennai by road is very difficult.

   He wants *to go to Chennai by air.*

4. A phrase introduced by an adverb.

   For Example:

   He finished the work *very quickly indeed.*

   We reached *early in the morning.*

   He did the work *in no time.*

Note: While participal, prepositional and infinitive phrases may be used with subjects, objects and predicates, adverb phrases can be used only with predicates.

2.7 CLAUSES

Examine the following sentence:

As John was tired, he took rest.

In this sentence there are two parts:

(*a*) 'As John was tired'..............(*i*)

(*b*) 'he took rest'.......................(*ii*)

In part (*ii*) above 'he' is the subject and 'took rest' the predicate. It makes complete sense and exists independently. Such a group of words as part (*ii*) above is called a main or principal clause.

In part (*i*) above 'John' is the subject and 'was tired' the predicate, but it does not make complete sense nor can it exist independently. It can make complete sense only with the help of the main clause at. (*ii*) Such a group of words as part (*i*) above is called a subordinate clause.

Now examine the following sentence:

He is the man *who came here yesterday.*

In the above sentence the part 'He is the man' is the main clause and 'who(the man) came here yesterday' is the subordinate clause.

A subordinate clause is part of a sentence. It cannot exist independently. It has a distinct subject and predicate, but does not make complete sense.

For Example:

The girl who stood first in the class has left the school.

'Who stood first in the class' is the subordinate clause forming part of the sentence, the main clause being 'The girl has left the school'.

2.8 DIFFERENT KINDS OF CLAUSES

There are three kinds of clauses:

(*a*) *The Adverb Clause:* This does the work of an adverb in a complex sentence.

(*b*) *The Noun Clause:* This does the work of a noun in a complex sentence.

(*c*) *The Adjective Clause:* This does the work of an Adjective in a complex sentence.

2.9 THE ADVERB CLAUSE

Examine the following complex sentence:

When I reached the station, the train had left.

The clause 'when I reached the station' modifies the verb 'had left' and therefore does the work of an adverb. Hence it is an adverb clause.

Other examples:

As I was ill, I could not attend the class.

Here 'As I was ill' is an adverb clause because it modifies the verb 'could not attend' . It is therefore an adverb clause.

That is why he did not come.

Here the clause 'why he did not come' is an adverb clause as it does the work of adverb. (It modifies the verb 'is')

He went where his parents waited for him.

The clause 'where his parents waited for him' is an adverb clause which modifies the verb 'went'.

Classification of Adverb Clauses

1. Adverb Clause of Time
2. Adverb Clause of Place
3. Adverb Clause of Cause or Reason
4. Adverb Clause of Purpose
5. Adverb Clause of Condition
6. Adverb Clause of Concession or Supposition
7. Adverb Clause of Result or Consequence
8. Adverb Clause of Comparison.

1. **Adverb Clause of Time.** An Adverb Clause of Time indicates the time of an action and is introduced by a subordinating conjunction of time like *as, since, before, after, while, until, till, when, whenever, as soon as, as long as* etc.

   For Example:

   1. When he reached the station, the train left.

      The clause 'when he reached the station' tells us the time at which the train left. It is therefore an Adverb Clause of time.
   2. As they were crossing the road, the accident occurred.
   3. I have not seen him since he retired.
   4. He is asked to wait till the Minister returns.
   5. We have to reach the station well before the train starts.
   6. He came after his brother (had) left.
   7. Don't move until I come back.
   8. Whenever he comes he brings his wife too.
   9. We will start as soon as my friend comes.
   10. This arrangement will continue as long as there is scarcity.
   11. No sooner had he heard about the accident than he rushed to the spot.

2. **Adverb Clause of Place**

An Adverb Clause of Place indicates the place of an action and is introduced by conjunctions like *where, wherever* and *whence.*

For Example:

(*i*) Ask them to wait where they are.

The clause 'where they are' modifies the verb 'wait' and is therefore an Adverb Clause.

(*ii*) Nobody knows whence he came.

(*iii*) I will meet him wherever he is.

3. **Adverb Clause of Cause or Reason**

An Adverb Clause of Cause or Reason indicates the cause or reason of an action. It is introduced by the subordinating conjunctions *because, as, since, that*.

For Example:

(*i*) I like him because he is a gentleman.

The clause 'because he is a gentleman' modifies the verb 'like' and indicates the reason for my liking.

(*ii*) She helped him because he was poor.

(*iii*) As he was ill, he did not attend the office.

(*iv*) Since he has gone to Mumbai, you cannot meet him today.

(*v*) He is happy that he has been elected president. (that=because)

4. **Adverb Clause of Purpose**

An Adverb Clause of Purpose indicates the purpose of an action.

It is introduced by the subordinating conjunctions *that* and *lest.*

For Example:

He works hard that he may pass.

He takes exercise that he may become slim.

You study hard lest you (should) fail.

He started early lest he (should) miss the train.

5. **Adverb Clause of Condition**

An Adverb Clause of Condition indicates the condition under which an action takes place. It is introduced by the subordinating conjunctions if, whether, unless.

For Example:

We shall go to him if you accompany us.

The clause 'if you accompany us' is an Adverb Clause of Condition because it modifies the verb 'shall go'.

We will not go out if it rains.

You will not pass unless you work hard.

You must do it whether you like it or not.

I will take up the work provided you have no objection.

6. **Adverb Clause of Concession or Supposition.**

An Adverb Clause of Concession or Supposition is introduced by the subordinating conjunctions though, although, even though, even if, notwithstanding etc.

For Example:

Though he is lean, he is healthy.

The clause 'though he is lean' is an Adverb Clause of Concession because it expresses what is conceded. Against this background the verb 'is' in the main clause comes into action.

I will go out even if it rains.

I will enter the hall even if I am prevented.

Although she is strict she is just.

Although it was dark we were able to catch the thief.

7. **Adverb Clause of Result or Consequence.**

An Adverb Clause of Result or Consequence indicates the result or consequence of an action and is introduced by the subordinating conjunction *that*

For Example:

He worked hard that he passed the exam.

The subordinate clause 'that he passed the exam' is the result of his hard work and modifies the verb 'worked' in the main clause.

He is so intelligent that he can answer any question.

He behaved in such a way that all liked him.

8. **Adverb Clause of Comparison**

Adverb Clauses of Comparison are classified as

(*a*) Adverb Clauses of Comparison of Manner.

(*b*) Adverb Clauses of Comparison of Degrees.

(*i*) An adverb clause of manner indicates how or in what manner the action of the verb in the main clause takes place and is introduced by the subordinating conjunction or relative adverb 'as'.

For Example:

It ended as he predicted.

As you sow, so shall you reap.

Do as you please.

(*ii*) An Adverb clause of comparison of degree is a subordinate clause which modifies the adverb in the main clause and is introduced by subordinating conjunctions or relative adverbs as....as, so....as, than, the.

For Example:

She is as clever as she is cunning.

She is not so clever as she is cunning. (In negative sentences we usually use 'so….as' instead of 'as…..as')

He is not so diligent as they say.

'than' is used with a comparative adjective or adverb or with the word 'other'(which is usually used in negative sentences); as,

He is stronger than his brother.

There is no bigger city in India than Mumbai.

I don't know anyone here other than you.

Note: The verb of an adverb clause of comparison is often understood.

For Example:

He is more intelligent than she (is). (the verb 'is' is not often expressed)

She understands it better than I (do).

2.10 THE ADJECTIVE CLAUSE

An adjective clause qualifies or describes a noun, a pronoun or a noun equivalent in the main clause. In other words, it does the work of an adjective.

Study the following complex sentence:

The chain which is made of gold is very beautiful.

The clause 'which is made of gold' does the work of an adjective as it qualifies(describes) the noun 'chain'. It is therefore an adjective clause. A clause which qualifies or describes a noun, pronoun or noun equivalent in the main clause is called an Adjective clause or Relative clause.

Adjective clauses may be joined to their antecedents in the main clause by the relative pronouns *who, whom, whose, which, that, etc* and by the relative adverbs *where, when, why, etc.*

The joining word that joins an adjective clause to a main clause may be omitted when it is in the objective case only.

For Example:

This is the book I bought yesterday. (This is the book which I bought yesterday)

This is the man I met in the park last week. (This is the man whom I met in the park last week.)

This is the gift I got from the shop. (This is the gift that I got from the shop)

The joining words mentioned above can introduce other types of clauses than adjective clauses. In order to identify an adjective clause we cannot, therefore, go by these joining words.

What is necessary is to check whether the class defines or describes the antecedent.

There are two kinds of relative clauses:

(*a*) Defining clause

(*b*) Non-defining clause

(*a*) **Defining Clause**

A defining clause is a relative clause (an adjective clause) which defines the antecedent (the noun, pronoun or noun equivalent lying just before the relative clause in a complex sentence).This is a clause introduced by the relative pronouns like who, which, when or where. These relative pronouns are used in a restrictive sense. They restrict and define the antecedents. A defining clause is necessary in a sentence in which an antecedent is required to be defined because it explains or identifies which person or thing we are talking about.

If it is omitted, the meaning of the sentence will not be complete.

Note. No comma is put in front of a defining clause

For Example:

This is the man who came to see you yesterday.

In the above complex sentence the antecedent of the relative pronoun 'who' is 'man'. 'This is the man' is the main clause and 'who came to see you yesterday' the subordinate clause.

The main clause 'This is the man' needs something more to make the sense clear. The question 'which man?' does arise in our mind. The relative clause (adjective clause) 'who came to see you yesterday' gives the answer. It is therefore a defining clause which defines the antecedent 'man' so as to make the sense of the sentence clear and complete.

Note. No commas are put before and after a defining clause.

(*b*) **Non-defining clause**

A non-defining clause is a relative clause (not an adjective clause) which gives us more information about the antecedent in a sentence. But it does not define or identify the antecedent. It is used in a continuative sense. A non-defining clause does not restrict or define the antecedent. The main clause in a complex sentence is complete in itself. Even if the non-defining clause is omitted the sense will be clear and complete.

A non-defining clause is therefore considered a co-ordinate clause (independent clause), and not an adjective clause.

The non-defining clause is always separated by a comma in front of it and a comma after it. If the clause is at the end of a sentence we put a full stop instead of a comma.

For Example:

I went to his office, which is housed in a multi-storey building.

Examine the following sentence:

The Chief Minister, who is a doctor, visited the hospital.

Here the main clause is 'The Chief Minister visited the hospital.' which is complete in itself. 'Who is a doctor' is a non-defining clause which gives more information about the

Chief Minister. It does not define or identify the noun 'Chief Minister'. Even if this clause is omitted the clarity of the main clause is not affected. This is a co-ordinate clause, and not an adjective clause. 'Who' (=and he) is its subject.

Non-defining relative clauses are formal and used in writing rather than in speech.

Note: If the commas separating the non-defining clause are omitted the meaning of the sentence will change. The following examples will illustrate this point:

The guides who know the city well will take you to all places worth visiting.

The guides, who know the city well, will take you to all places worth seeing.

The first sentence means that only those guides who know the city well can take you to all places worth visiting. Others cannot. Here the subordinate class 'who know the city well' is a defining clause with guides as its antecedent. It describes or defines or identifies the antecedent and is used in a restrictive sense. It is therefore an adjective clause. If this defining clause was omitted the sentence would mean that all guides would take you to all places worth visiting, which is not the actual meaning of the sentence.

The second sentence assumes that all the guides know the city well and that they can take you to all places worth visiting. The relative clause 'who know the city well' is used in a continuative sense and gives additional information about the guides. Here 'who' means 'and they'. It is a non-defining independent clause. The example sentence is therefore a compound sentence. Even if this non-defining clause is omitted the clarity of the sentence will not be affected.

More examples of the adjective clause are given below:

The pen that is filled with red ink is missing. (The clause 'that is filled with red ink' is an adjective clause because it qualifies the noun 'pen'.)

This is the man whom I saw yesterday. (The clause 'whom I saw yesterday' is an adjective clause as it describes the noun 'man' .)

Note: The word 'as' may be used as a relative pronoun with the words 'same' and 'such' to introduce adjective clauses.

For Example:

He is the same person as we saw yesterday. (Here as=that)

(He is the same person that we saw yesterday.)

It is such a place as we have never visited before.

(It is such a place that we have never visited before.)

Note: The word 'but' is sometimes used to introduce adjective clauses.

For Example:

There was not a politician but was corrupt. (Here but= a relative pronoun+ not)

The above sentence means ' There was not a politician who was not corrupt'.

There is no student but took part in the agitation.

(There is no student who did not take part in the agitation.)

Note: Sometimes relative pronouns introduce co-ordinate clauses instead of adjective clauses.

For Example:

1. He is my relative, who lives in Mumbai.

   Here the clause 'who lives in Mumbai' is not an adjective clause because it does not qualify, identify or describe the antecedent 'relative' , but it gives additional information about it. In other words it is not a relative clause, but is only a non-defining co-ordinate clause and means:

   'He is my relative and (he) lives in Mumbai.' (Here 'and he' stands for 'who'.)

2. He gave me a pen, which is this.

   (He gave me a pen, and it is this.)(which= and it)

3. He was bitten by a snake, which was killed on the spot.

   (He was bitten by a snake, and it was killed on the spot.

2.11 THE NOUN CLAUSE

A noun clause does the work of a noun, pronoun or noun phrase in a complex sentence. A noun clause usually begins with the word 'that' or 'what' and answers the question ' who? ' or ' what? '. They can also be introduced by the Conjunction 'if or whether', the (Interrogative) Pronouns *who, whom, which* and *whose* and by the (Interrogative) Adverbs *where, when, why, whence* and *how.*

For Example:

She said *that* he would come. (Here 'that' is a conjunction.)

The noun clause 'that he would come' is the object of the verb 'said'.

She knew he would come. (Sometimes the conjunction 'that' is omitted)

I don't know *what* he has said.

She doesn't know *if* (whether) he has come.

The Interrogative Pronouns *who, whom, which, whose* and *what* do not take antecedents when they are used to introduce noun clauses.

For Example:

The police did not disclose *who* the culprit was.

I do not know *which* of the three books I have to take.

I know *whom* you have met.

Do you know *whose* book is this?

The Interrogative adverbs *where, when, why, how* and *whence* do not take antecedents when they are used to introduce noun clauses.

For Example:

He told me *where* he was going.

I don't know *when* she will come.

He has explained to me *how* a computer works.

I don't know *why* he quarrelled with me.

Nobody knows *whence* he came. (whence= from where)

Note: Examine the following sentences:

I know where he is waiting.

I know the place where he is waiting.

In the first sentence 'where he is waiting' is a noun clause being the object of the verb 'know'. But in the second sentence 'where he is waiting' is an adjective clause qualifying the antecedent 'place'.

What follows from the examples given above is that the Interrogative pronouns (who, whom, which, whose and what) and the Interrogative adverbs (where, when, why, how and whence) will become Relative pronouns and Relative adverbs respectively if antecedents are present in which case the clauses coming after the antecedents will be adjective clauses.

For Example:

I know the house *where he is living.*

The clause 'where he is living' qualifies the antecedent 'house' and is therefore an adjective clause. Compare this complex sentence with the following complex sentence:

I know where he is living. (Here there is no antecedent before the Relative adverb 'where'). The clause 'where he is living' is the object of the verb 'know'. It is therefore a noun clause.

Note: *When, where* and *why* are Relative Adverbs used in place of a proposition+ the Relative Pronoun *which.*

when = in which/on which/at which etc used for time;

where = in which/at which etc used for place;

why = for which used for reason.

In general, a relative adverb = a preposition + a relative pronoun.

For Example:

I know *when he will come* = I know *the time at which he will come.*

I know the year *when he left this place* = I know the year *in which he left this place.*

She knows *where he is living* = She knows *the house in which he is living.*

There is no reason *why he should refuse the gift* = There is no reason *for which he should refuse the gift.*

A noun clause may take any one of the following positions in a_complex sentence:

(*a*) **The subject of the verb in the main clause**

Study the complex sentence given below:

What happened to him yesterday is a mystery. (The clause 'What happened to him yesterday' is equivalent to a noun or pronoun. It acts as the subject to the verb 'is' and is therefore a noun clause. If we substitute the letter X for this clause the example sentence will read thus:

X is a mystery. (Here X stands for the noun clause 'What happened to him yesterday' which is the subject of the sentence.)

More examples:

That he is a criminal is a fact.

He *who loves* lives.

Who the thief was is still a secret.

How he became rich is an interesting story.

Why he denied the statement can be explained only by him.

(*b*) **The object of the verb in the main clause**

Examine the following sentence:

He means what he says.(Here the clause 'what he says' is the object of the verb 'means'. It answers the question 'He means what?' and hence is a noun clause.

More examples:

Universal literacy is *what we want.*

He didn't tell me *what he wanted.*

I cannot say *when he will come.*

Nobody knows *where he went.*

I asked him *why he didn't come for the meeting.*

(*c*) **The complement of the verb in the main clause**

Study the following sentence:

He is what he is.

Here 'what he is' is the complement of the verb 'is' because it completes the sentence. Complement means 'that which completes'. A complement is used after linking verbs such as 'be' (am, is, was, are, were, has been, have been, had been, etc.) and 'become'. It describes the subject.

More examples:

He became *what his father wanted him to be.*

The news is *that he was killed in an accident.*

(*d*) **The object of a preposition**

Examine the following sentence:

He insisted *upon* what he had said.

Here the clause 'what he had said' is the object of the preposition 'upon' . He insisted upon what? The answer is 'what he had said'.

This clause is therefore a noun clause.

More examples:

She has full faith *in* what he says.

The old man depends *upon* what he gets by way of pension.

The boy pays great attention *to* what his parents say.

There is no point in what you say.

(*e*) **In apposition to the subject of the main clause.**

The claim that he is a doctor is false.

Here the clause 'that he is a doctor' explains the noun 'claim' that comes before it. It is therefore a noun clause in apposition to the noun 'claim', the subject of the main clause.

For Example:

(*i*) It is a fact that he is a thief. (Here the noun clause 'that he is a thief' in apposition to 'It' which is the provisional subject of the sentence.) The sentence may be recast as follows:

That he is a thief is a fact.

(*ii*) He took it as an insult that he was not invited to the party. (Here the noun clause 'that he was not invited to the party' is in apposition to 'it' which is the provisional object of the verb 'took'.)

(*iii*) It is clear that he is innocent.

(*iv*) You should not forget the proverb, that all that glitters is not gold.

Here the noun clause 'all that glitters is not gold' is in apposition to the noun 'proverb' which is the object of the verb 'forget'.

Chapter 3 THE NOUN

A word used for naming a person, place, thing (both abstract and concrete) or an animal is called a noun.

For Example:

Ram, father, husband, President, Minister, speaker, etc. (person)

Kochi, Chennai, Beach, Parliament, Museum, London, etc. (place)

Table, book, pen, mountain, tree, stone, etc. (thing-concrete)

Cleverness, intelligence, innocence, kindness, communism (an idea) socialism(an idea), catholicism, etc. (abstract)

Elephant, cow, rat, fish, bull, tiger, cat, etc. (animal)

There are five different kinds of nouns in the English Language. They are:

(1) Proper noun
(2) Common noun
(3) Collective noun
(4) Mass noun
(5) Material noun
(6) Abstract noun

3.1 PROPER NOUN

A proper noun is a word that is the name of a particular person, thing, place, or an event and is usually capitalized. (*i.e.*, using a capital letter at the beginning)

For Example:

Raju, India, Chennai, Taj Mahal, Onam, etc.

Raju went to Chennai. (Raju-person)

India is my country. (India-place)

The French Revolution began in 1789. (The French Revolution-event)

Onam is our national festival. (Onam-event)

Egg is good for health. (egg-thing)

3.2 COMMON NOUN

A common noun (or class noun) does not indicate a particular person, place, thing or an event but it is the general name common to all persons, places, things or events of the same kind or class. It is sometimes called the Class noun.

For Example:

Student, chair, book, cat, dog, flower, teacher, school, etc.

Mary is a *teacher*. (Mary belongs to the class namely 'teacher')

John is also a teacher. (John also belongs to the class 'teacher)

The noun 'teacher' represents the entire class of teachers and it does not tell us about a particular teacher. It is a common name shared by all teachers. Hence the name Common noun or Class noun.

John is a *boy*. (Here John is a proper noun while 'boy' is a common noun (class noun). John belongs to this class)

India is my *country*. (Here India is a proper noun while 'country' is a common noun (class noun). India belongs to this class).

Common nouns like *stationery, furniture, machinery, crockery, footwear, cutlery and clothing* are considered singular (uncountable) and take only singular verb.

For Example:

He bought some stationery. (not: stationeries)

Some stationery *is* to be bought.

Some more furniture *is* required. (not: furnitures)

Agricultural machinery *is* sold here. (not: machineries)

Food *is* a basic necessity.

Most footwear *is* made of leather. (not: footwears)

Warm clothing (clothes) *is* necessary in cold countries.

Cutlery (knives, forks and spoons) *is* used for eating food.

Crockery (plates, cups, bowls etc) *is* used for serving food.

3.3 COLLECTIVE NOUN OR GROUP NOUN

A collective noun is the name of a group or collection of persons, animals or things taken together as one thing.

For Example:

Army, class, crowd, flock, fleet, parliament, staff, company, jury, group, board, congregation, government, the Cabinet, the public, the clergy, the laity, the aristocracy, the bourgeoisie, etc. an army of soldiers , a crowd of people, a crew of sailors, a flock of sheep, a fleet of ships, a herd of cattle, etc.

('Army' stands for a group of soldiers taken together to form one body. Similarly, the word 'crowd' denotes a collection of people. 'People' is not normally a group noun, but it is the plural of the noun 'person'). A collective noun takes only a singular verb.

The Indian army *has* its headquarters in Delhi.

A flock of sheep *was* grazing in the field.

The crowd *was* dispersed by the police.

Some collective nouns or group nouns stand for a group of people having common identity. They are considered either singular or plural depending on whether the group is taken as one unit or as individuals forming the group. Committee, government, family, audience, team, council, etc. are examples of such collective nouns.

For Example:

The committee *has* unanimously passed the resolution.

(singular— 'committee' taken as one unit because the resolution was passed unanimously. In other words, the members of the committee stood united in passing the resolution. Hence singular verb).

The committee *were* divided in *their* opinion.

(plural- 'committee' taken as individuals. Here the members of the committee did not stand united in expressing their opinion. Hence plural verb)

The government *has* decided to order a probe into the allegations of corruption.

(government taken as one unit-singular)

The government *have* decided to grant bonus to the coir workers.

Meaning 'the ministry concerned has decided...

(Here, 'government' is used in the plural and considered to be consisting of a number of ministries.)

3.4 MASS NOUNS OR NON-COUNT NOUNS

These nouns refer to substances both liquid and solid. They are always singular barring a few exceptions.

For Example:

Water (waters), butter, oil, wood (woods), glass (sheets of glass), milk, furniture (pieces of furniture), grass (blades of grass), hair (strands of hair), land, anger, courage, advice, news, poetry, behaviour, conduct, safety, work, etc.

He drank some milk.

Butter is good for health.

This table is made of wood.

We bought some furniture or pieces of furniture.

Grass is given to horses.

His hair is thick.

He sold a piece of land.

I gave him a piece of advice.

This news is stale.

He wrote a number of poems. (not: poetries)

Note: Mass nouns can be subdivided by using nouns like piece, bit, part, slice, block, pint, etc.

For Example:

A piece of paper (a sheet of paper), a piece of bread (a slice of bread), a piece of land (an acre of land), a part of butter, a block of ice, a bundle of hay, a speck of dust, a metre of cloth, a litre of water (a bottle of water), a litre of paint, a kg of butter, a pint of liquor, etc.

She took *a sheet of paper* to write on.

I gave the beggar *a slice of bread.*

He bought *a piece of land.*

She ate *a part of the butter.*

He bought *a block of ice.*

A bundle of hay costs rupees ten.

There is not even *a speck of dust* on the glass.

Mass nouns can also be divided into species or types by the use of nouns like kind, species, class, variety, sort, type, etc.

For Example:

There are different *kinds* of paper.

He likes this *type* of cloth.

There are different *classes* of jail.

This hotel serves different *varieties* of food.

They eat all *sorts* of meat.

The cow is a *species* of mammal.

Note: After a species noun we can use either the singular or plural of a count noun.

For Example:

I like all *kinds* of dogs or dog.

Sometimes, a singular species noun is used even if the determiner and the verb are plural.

For Example:

These kind of *questions* are difficult to answer. (These- determiner)

This kind of question(s) is difficult to answer. (better construction)

Exceptions: Waters: 'waters' (plural) means water in a particular lake, river, sea or ocean.

For Example:

The *waters* of the Ganges are believed sacred.

Woods: *'woods'* (plural) means a small area of trees or a small forest.

For Example:

The children went into the *woods* in search of birds.

Note: There are some mass (non-count) nouns_which can be treated as count nouns when used in classificatory senses.

For Example:

He drank two coffees. (meaning two cups of coffee)

She asked for two sugars. (meaning two lumps of sugar)

Quite a few food nouns can be used as both count nouns and mass nouns.

For Example:

I bought a few *eggs*. (Refers to the article of food.)

Egg is one of the ingredients. (Refers to the content.)

He took a big potato.

Potato is good for health.

He bought a cake.

I like eating cake.

He ate a piece of cheese.

There are different kinds of cheeses.

Many mass nouns can be used either as mass nouns or as count nouns. Trouble, experience, difficulty, work, etc.

For Example:

His financial *troubles* are not over yet.

He is suffering from knee *trouble.*

He has enough *experience* as doctor. (used as mass noun)

It was *an* unforgettable *experience.* (used as count noun)

She got into *difficulties* while crossing the busy road.

He had no *difficulty* in tackling the problem.

We had some *work* to do urgently.

The complete *works* of Shakespeare are available in the library.

There are many automobile *works* in the city. (works=workshops)

But: He has got *a* good *knowledge* in history.

('knowledge' – mass noun used as count noun by using the indefinite article 'a'. It can be used as a count noun only when the reference is to a particular person.)

His aim was to give his son *a* good *education.*

('education' – a mass noun used as a count noun. It can be used as a count noun only when the reference is to a particular person.)

3.5 MATERIAL NOUN

A material noun is a name that indicates the material of which a thing is made.

For Example:

This table is made of *steel*. (Steel is a material noun)

That ring is made of *gold*. (Gold is a material noun)

Rice, wheat, water, wood, stone, etc. are material nouns.

Note the difference between 'gold ring' and 'golden ring'

Gold ring- Ring made of gold.

Golden ring- bright yellow in colour like gold; need not necessarily be made of gold.

3.6 ABSTRACT NOUN

An abstract noun usually denotes a quality, state or an action. While thinking of quality we do not consider the persons or things that possess them.

The four kinds of nouns already described denote objects that can be seen, touched, heard, smelt or tasted. But an abstract noun denotes a quality, state or an action which cannot be seen, touched, smelt, heard or tasted.

For Example:

Quality – Cleverness, kindness, honesty, beauty.

State – Childhood, manhood, poverty, truth.

Action – laughter, movement, judgment, fight, theft, hatred.

The word abstract means *'drawn off.'*

Note: We can speak of a clever boy, a faithful slave, a dead man, a beautiful girl. We can also speak of cleverness, slavery, death, beauty, childhood, faithfulness, etc without relating them to any person or thing.

She is a clever girl.

Cleverness is different from *intelligence*.

She is beautiful.

Beauty is skin deep.

Nouns of Multitude

A collective noun denotes a group of similar individuals taken as one and it takes only a singular verb. *committee, jury, army,etc.* are examples of collective nouns.

For Example:

The *committee* consists of six members.

(Here all the members on the committee are thought of as a single body and hence 'committee' is a collective noun.)

The jury is unanimous in its decision.

A noun of multitude on the contrary denotes the individual members of a group and so it takes a plural verb.

For Example:

The *committee* are divided in their decision.

(Here 'committee' is thought of as consisting of individual members.)

The *jury* were divided in their decision.

3.7 THE NOUN-GENDER

Gender: The difference in sex in grammar is referred to as the difference in gender.

There are four different kinds of genders.

(*a*) **Masculine gender:** Nouns denoting male animals (including human beings) are said to be of the masculine gender.

For Example:

Man, boy, father, tiger ,bull etc.

Note: The following nouns although neuter (without life) are personified and considered masculine in the English language. Such personified nouns are written with a capital letter. Those things which are remarkable for superiority, strength, etc are considered males. This use is mainly confined to poetry now.

The Sun, Summer, Death, Time, Winter, Thunder, etc.

For Example:

The sun shines with all *his* splendor.

Summer is here with all *his* fury.

(*b*) **Feminine gender:** Nouns denoting female animals (including human beings) are said to be of the feminine gender.

The following nouns though neuter are personified and considered feminine in English. They are written with a capital letter. Those things which are supposed to possess grace, beauty, virtue and which are regarded as inferior are considered feminine. This use is mainly confined to poetry now.

The Earth, the Moon, Spring, Autumn, Nature, Justice, Mercy, Peace, Hope, Charity, Virtue, Ship, Countries etc.

For Example:

The earth with all *her* resources makes our life easy.

The ship lost *her* direction.

Nature is here with all *her* beauty. (**Not:** the Nature)

The moon shines at *her* best.

Virtue smiles on all who love *her*.

India is proud of *her* rich heritage.

For Example:

Woman, girl, mother, tigress, cow etc.

(*c*) **Neuter gender:** Nouns denoting neither males nor females are said to be of the neuter gender.

For Example:

Book, pencil, mountain, etc.

(*d*) **Common gender:** Nouns denoting either males or females are said to be of the common gender.

For Example:

Child, parent, student, friend, etc.

(*e*) A list of personal masculine/feminine nouns is given below:

Masculine	**Feminine**
Father	Mother
Brother	Sister
King	Queen
Uncle	Aunt
Man	Woman
Gentleman	Lady
Monk	Nun
Bachelor	Spinster
Hero	Heroine
Bridegroom	Bride
Emperor	Empress
God	Goddess
Host	Hostess
Widower	Widow
Waiter	Waitress
Steward	Stewardess
Bull	Cow
Dog	Bitch
Drake	Duck
Drone	Bee
Horse	Mare
Husband	Wife
Hen	Cock
Administrator	Administratrix

Executor	Executrix
Prosecutor	Procecutrix
Lord	Lady
Master	Mistress
Nephew	Niece
Dancer	Danseuse

(*f*) The following personal nouns are in the common gender: artist, chairman (chairperson), cook, criminal, statesman, doctor, enemy, fool, friend, musician, servant, teacher, guest, professor, lecturer, writer, novelist, speaker, foreigner, librarian, student, neighbour, nurse, servant, doctor, etc.

For Example:

He/She is an artist.

He/She is a doctor.

But, we add the word *male (man)* or *female(woman)* before these nouns of common gender to indicate whether they are masculine or feminine gender; as, male (man) artist, female (woman) artist, chairman, chairwoman, statesman, stateswoman, female teacher, male teacher, boy friend (gentleman friend or man friend), girl friend (lady friend or woman friend), female novelist, male novelist, male nurse (nurse generally stands for female nurse), boy or girl student, man servant, woman servant(maid-servant or servant girl), male doctor, lady doctor or woman doctor, etc.

For Example:

There are three male (man) and five female (woman) artists in the troupe.

He was elected chairman of the company.

She was made chairwoman (chairperson) of the corporation.

Note: The words 'lover' and 'master' are common to both genders when used predicatively.

For Example:

She/He is master of the ceremony.

She/He is a lover of nature.

Note: 'He' and 'she' also may be used to indicate difference in gender.

For Example:

He-goat, she-goat, he-rabbit, she-rabbit, etc.

(*g*) A list of the names of living beings each having three separate words, one each for each of the three genders is given below:

Common	**Masculine**	**Feminine**
Child	Boy	Girl
Child	Son	Daughter
Sheep	Ram	Ewe
Deer	Stag	Hind

Horse	Stallion	Mare
Ox	Bull	Cow
Swine	Boar	Sow
Parent	Father	Mother
Chicken	Cock	Hen
Monarch	King	Queen
Elephant	Bull elephant	Cow elephant

3.8 THE NOUN-CASE

The form of a noun, pronoun or an adjective that shows its relationship with another word or the change of form that indicates this relationship is called the Case.

There are Five Cases in the English language:

(*a*) The Nominative Case

(*b*) The Vocative Case or The Nominative Case Of Address

(*c*) The Genitive Case or The Possessive Case

(*d*) The Accusative Case or The Objective Case

(*e*) The Dative Case

(*a*) **Nominative Case.** When a noun is used as the subject of a verb it is in the Nominative Case.

For Example:

Raju gave me a pen.
(Who gave me a pen ? The answer is Raju who is the subject of the verb 'gave' and hence ' Raju' is in the nominative case.)
The *boy* took a book from the shelf.
The noun 'boy' is in the Nominative Case.

(*b*) **The Vocative Case or Nominative Case of Address.** A noun used to address a person or thing is in the Vocative or the Nominative Case of Address.

For Example:

Father, where are you going? (Father- Vocative case)
Friends, let us have some fun.
John, please give me your pen.

(*c*) **Genitive Case or Possessive Case:**

(*i*) It shows ownership, relationship or possession.

For Example:

This is Seeta's book.

In order to show ownership, relationship or possession the noun Seeta is changed to Seeta's. (by adding 's to the noun)

Seeta's therefore is in the possessive or genitive Case.

To find out whether a noun is in the possessive case, ask the question: Whose?

In the given example Seeta's is the possessive case of the noun 'Seeta'.

The possessive case is not always indicative of possession. It is also used to show relationship, authorship , origin, kind, etc.

For Example:

Nature's law – Law of nature.

Court's decree – decree passed by a court of law.

Ramu's book – book owned by Ramu.

Shakespeare's plays – plays written by Shakespeare.

Sun's rays – rays from the Sun

God's own country – favourite country of God.

Note: Genitive case is rarely used with names of inanimate objects.

We do not say, ' the house's address or sugar's price or the bus's door.'

In such cases we use 'of' to indicate the relation; as,

the address of the house.

the price of sugar.

the door of the bus.

(*ii*) The possessive case of a singular noun is formed by adding 's (apostrophe's) at the end of the noun.

For Example:

The *girl's* umbrella.

The *student's* book.

Note: 's is omitted if the singular noun ends in 's' or 'ce' sound. Only the apostrophe is placed after such words.

For Example:

For *goodness'* sake (not goodness's sake)

for *Jesus'* sake (not Jeus's sake)

for *Justice'* sake (not justice's sake)

Exception: James's book, Venus's beauty, Keats's poetry, etc.)

(*iii*) When two nouns are in apposition (*i e,* when the second noun describes the first) the possessive sign *'s* is placed at the end of the second noun.

For Example:

Ramu is her uncle Ravi's son. (Uncle and Ravi are in apposition)

This book is my teacher Krishnan's first novel.

(*iv*) When a plural noun ends in s, its possessive is formed by adding only an apostrophe ('); as, girls' school, merchants' union , dogs' show ,etc.

(*v*) When a plural noun does not end in 's', the possessive is formed by adding 's.

For Example:

Men's hostel, *children's* park, etc.

(*vi*) When a possessive qualifies another, then both the possessives will have the 's.

For Example:

Rama's brother's wife.

(*vii*) Personified nouns (written with a capital letter) are put in the possessive case as shown below: China's sorrow, India's concern, etc..

(*viii*) The nouns denoting time, space, weight and value can be put in the possessive case.

Examples of time: a day's wages, a month's salary,

two weeks' holiday, in three hours' time, a year's tour, etc.

Examples of space: a stone's throw, a hair's breadth, etc.

Examples of value: a rupee's worth, five lakh's worth, etc.

Examples of weight: a kilo's weight, two tonne's weight, etc.

(*ix*) We use the Possessive case with some familiar phrases for the sake of brevity (shortness).

For Example:

At one's wit's end – at the end of one's wit.

At one's fingers' end – at the end of one's fingers.

The ship's crew – the crew of the ship.

To one's heart's content – to the content of one's heart.

(*x*) The possessive case is formed by adding 's to the last element of a compound consisting of a noun followed by a prepositional phrase; as,

his father- in- law's house.

the Government of India's ordinance.

the President of Pakistan's orders.

Note: A novel of Tolstoy – meaning a novel possessed by Tolstoy.

A novel of Tolstoy's – meaning a novel written by Tolstoy.

A photograph of Ramu – meaning a photograph owned by Ramu.

A photograph of Ramu's – meaning his own photograph.

(*xi*) The possessive sign 's is added to the last noun to show joint possession when two or more different nouns are joined; as, Sam and John's room – shows joint possession of the room.

(Note the singular form of the noun after the possessive.)

Menon and Krishnan's college – joint possession-one and the same college.

Note: If individual possession is meant, the possessive sign 's is added to each person; as, Sam's and John's rooms. (Note the plural form of the noun after the possessive.)

Raju's and Krishnan's colleges.

(*xii*) A noun denoting certain kind of place or building is sometimes omitted after a noun in the possessive case.

For Example:

We shall meet at the Saritha's. (Saritha theatre)

Raju had his dinner at the Plaza's. (Hotel Plaza)

He was educated at St. Paul's. (St.Paul's college)

Ravi bought bread from the baker's. (bake shop)

(*xiii*) A noun-adverb compound derived from a combination of a verb and an adverb is made plural by adding 's to the noun:

For Example:

Lookers-on, runners-up, goings-on, passers-by.

They are made genitive by adding 's to the last element:

For Example:

Lookers-on's, runners-up's, etc.

(*d*) **Accusative or Objective Case.** When a noun is used as the object of a verb it is said to be in the Accusative or Objective case. It is a case of the direct object.

For Example:

Ramu took a pen.

(What did Ramu take? Answer–a pen.)

The noun 'pen' is therefore the object of the verb 'took' and hence it is in the Objective or Accusative Case.

Seeta sang a song.

Here 'song' is in the Objective Case because it answers the question 'what'.

Note: Nouns have the same forms for the Nominative and the Accusative.

The former generally comes before the verb and the latter after the verb.

For Example:

Ramu gave *John* a pen. (Ramu-Nominative; John- Accusative)

(*e*) **Dative Case:**

This is the Case of the indirect object.

For Example:

Ramu gave John a pen.

There are two objects in the sentence namely 'pen' and 'John'.

'John' was the person to whom Ramu gave a pen.

The noun 'pen' is called the direct object and is said to be in the Accusative case.

The noun 'John' is called the indirect object and is said to be in the Dative case.

The indirect object usually comes immediately after the verb and before the direct object.

For Example:

Raju gave the child a doll. Here, 'child' is the indirect object and therefore is in the Dative Case.

The indirect object of the verb stands for the person *to* whom something is given or *for* whom something is done.

For Example:

Raju gave *me* a book.

Without altering the meaning we can write this sentence as follows:

Raju gave a book to me. (Here the Direct and Indirect objects are interchanged.)

She bought Raju a book.

She bought a book for Raju. (Here the Direct and Indirect objects are interchanged.)

In the above examples it may be seen that after the interchange the indirect object has taken the preposition 'to' or 'for' before it.

This peculiarity in construction must be borne in mind whenever the Dative Case (Indirect object) is used.

Other Examples:

She bought her child a doll.

She bought a doll *for* her child.

Shall I give you this book?

Shall I give this book *to* you?

Bring the guest a cup of tea.

Bring a cup of tea *for* the guest.

Note: Nouns in apposition. (Placing near)

Two nouns or noun phrases are said to be in apposition when one follows immediately after the other to refer to the same person or thing.

For Example:

(*i*) 'Othello' was written by Shakespeare, *the* great English dramatist.

Here, *the great English dramatist* is in apposition to *Shakespeare.*

(*ii*) John, our neighbour, died yesterday.

'Our neighbour' is in apposition to John.

(*iii*) We met Ramu, our family doctor, at his clinic.

'Our family doctor' is in apposition to doctor Ramu.

(*iv*) Delhi, *the* capital of our country, is a clean city.

'The capital of our country' is in apposition to Delhi.

(*v*) Mulk Raj Anand, *an* Indian writer in English, passed away recently.

Note: There is a growing tendency among journalists to omit the definite or indefinite article before a noun or noun phrase in apposition to a name. It is preferable not to omit these articles.

3.9 THE NOUN-NUMBER

There are two groups of nouns in the English language.

(*i*) The Nouns that can be counted – count nouns, countable nouns or countables. A countable has a plural form and it can be used after 'a or an' when it is singular. It is indicated by [C] in any standard English dictionary.

(*ii*) The nouns that cannot be counted – uncount nouns, uncountable nouns or uncountables. An uncountable has no plural form and is indicated by [U] in any standard dictionary.

Countables can be classified into:

(*i*) Singular number or simply singular

(*ii*) Plural number or simply plural.

(*i*) Singular Number: The form of a noun that denotes one person or thing is said to be in the singular number.

For Example:

Man, boy, girl, book, mango etc.

(*ii*) Plural Number: The form of a noun that denotes more than one person or thing is said to be in the plural number.

For Example:

Men, boys, girls, books, mangoes etc.

Note: Proper, material and abstract nouns normally have no plural forms. They are usually uncountable nouns. But if they are used as common nouns they become countable nouns.

For Example:

(*i*) Raj is a Keats. (a great poet like Keats – ' Keats' used as a common noun)

(*ii*) There are many Wordsworths in our state. (poets like Wordsworth)

(*iii*) He did many kindnesses. (Here, *kindnesses* means acts of kindness)

Formation of Plurals:

(*i*) Singular nouns are generally made plurals by adding 's'.

Ball – balls, boy – boys, picture – pictures, girl – girls etc.

(*ii*) But if the nouns end in s, sh, ch or x the plurals are formed by adding - es.

Glass – glasses, brush – brushes, batch – batches, box – boxes.

(*iii*) Nouns ending in 'y' but preceded by a consonant form their plurals by changing the 'y' into 'ies'.

City – cities, army – armies, lady – ladies, story – stories.

(*iv*) If nouns end in 'o' and if there is a consonant just before that ('o') the plural is formed by adding –es to the singular form.

Mango –mangoes, cargo – cargoes, hero – heroes, Negro –negroes, potato – potatoes.

But, the following nouns ending in 'o' take 's' in the plural.

Radio – radios, dynamo – dynamos, piano – pianos, photo – photos, solo – solos, memento – mementos, quarto – quartos, stereo – stereos.

(*v*) Nouns ending in 'f' and 'fe' become plural by changing 'f' and 'fe' into 'v' and adding *-es*.

Calf – calves, knife – knives, wife – wives, leaf – leaves, life – lives.

But, the following nouns form their plurals, by adding 's'; as,

Belief – beliefs, chief – chiefs, roof – roofs, dwarf – dwarfs, hoof – hoofs, proof – proofs, serf – serfs, gulf – gulfs, still life- still lifes.

A few nouns take two forms in the plural; as,

Staff – staffs or staves, scarf – scarfs or scarves.

(*vi*) Certain nouns form their plural by changing the inside vowel/ vowels in the singular form.

Man – men, woman – women, goose – geese, mouse – mice, foot – feet, louse – lice, tooth – teeth.

(*vii*) The following singular nouns form their plural by adding *-en*.

Ox – oxen, child – children, brother–brothren (old use)

(*viii*) The following nouns are used both in the singular and in the plural without any change.

Sheep, deer, pair, dozen, score, hundred, thousand.

For Example:

A sheep, ten sheep; a deer , hundred deer, etc.

Note: Hundred, thousand, pair, dozen, score, gross and couple take the same form both in the singular and in the plural only when they are used after numerals or after 'several' or 'a few'.

Three hundred (not hundreds), five thousand (not thousands) two pair, three couple, five dozen etc.

For Example:

He gave me a sum of *three hundred* rupees.

Six thousand candidates attended the interview.

He bought *two pair* of shoes.

There are *five dozen* mangoes in the basket.

Two couple were killed in the accident.

There are *several dozen* eggs in the basket.

He walked a *few score* metres.

Note: In modern English 'pairs' and 'couples' are more usual.

For Example:

He bought *two pairs* of shoes.

Five couples were present at the meeting.

But, when the nouns of numbers are followed immediately by 'of', their plural forms (hundreds, thousands, pairs, dozens, scores, etc.) are used.

For Example:

Hundreds of people, hundreds of thousands of people, tens of hundreds of mangoes.

He bought *ten dozen* mangoes. (not: 'ten dozens')

But: He bought dozens of mangoes.

I have two *pair* of dresses.

But: I have a number of pairs of dresses.

His age is two *score* and five.

(Here, 'score' means twenty and in this sense its plural is 'score' itself)

But: *Scores* of people attended the meeting. (Here, 'scores' means very many)

Raju bought ten *gross* of writing paper.

But: Raju bought a few *grosses* of writing paper.

Hundreds of people were killed in the war.

Note: The nouns 'brace' (two) and 'gross' which denote fixed number do not take plural ending.

For Example:

Three *brace* of rabbits were killed.

Ten *gross* of paper were bought.

(*ix*)(*a*) The following nouns relating to tools and articles of dress consisting of two equal parts joined together always occur in the plural.

Scissors, tongs, spectacles, trousers, pants, binoculars, pliers, pyjamas, shorts, scales (balance), bellows, shears, knickers, etc. They can be made count-nouns by using 'a pair of', 'two pair(s) of', etc.(e.g. a pair of tongs, five pair(s) of scissors, three pair(s) of pants, etc.). The word 'pair' used in this manner is called Numerative.

Note: The numerative 'head' used before collective names of animals particularly 'cattle' does not take the plural form ' heads'

For Example:

There are five *head* of cattle (cows, sheep, bulls etc)(not heads)

We can also say: a kitchen tongs, a garden shears.

There is a tendency in modern English to use the plural form of certain nouns mentioned above as singular; as, a scissors, a kitchen tongs, a garden shears.

For Example:

He bought a pair of *scissors.*

(Or He bought a scissors.)

She keeps a pair of *tongs* in the kitchen.

(She keeps a tongs in the kitchen.)

He has two pairs of *spectacles.*

(He has two spectacles.)

Note: 'A pair of', 'this pair of' and 'that pair of' are singular if it is followed by any of the nouns mentioned above.

For Example:

A pair of scissors *is* required for this work.

This pair of trousers *is* enough for him.

But we can use the plural verb if we omit the phrase 'a pair of' etc.

For Example:

These scissors are required for this work.

These trousers are enough for him.

(*b*) The following nouns occur only in the plural:

Annals, ashes, arrears, bowels, earnings, fireworks, lodgings, manners, outskirts, savings, surroundings, thanks, valuables, wages, tidings, assets, sale proceeds, shears, braces, news, outskirts, riches, etc.

For Example:

Gandhiji's struggle for freedom went down in the *annals* of Indian history.

The *annals* of Greek history are full of heroic deeds.

The building was reduced to *ashes* in the recent fire.

His *ashes* were immersed in the Ganga.

Names of the following diseases are plural in form, but take only singular verb.

Measles, mumps, rickets, diabetes, etc

For Example:

Measles causes fever and small red spots on the body.

Mumps causes painful swellings in the face.

(*x*) The following plural forms are generally used in the singular.

Alms, mathematics, physics, politics, statistics, classics, phonetics, innings, barracks, headquarters, means, shambles, gallows, etc.

For Example:

Mathematics is an important branch of science.

Politics is an interesting subject.

Statistics is a branch of mathematics.

After the earthquake the building was/is in a shambles.

(not: in a shamble)

The *Internet* is a modern means of communication.

The *headquarters* of the Army *is* in Delhi.

A *gallows* was erected to hang criminals.

But: My *mathematics* (calculations) *are* not always correct.(plural)

Internal *politics* (struggle for power in a group) *are* really bad.(plural)

His *politics* (political views) *are* very strange.(plural)

The latest *statistics* (information collected in numbers) about the birth and death rates *are* not very clear. (plural)

The *statistics* (number) is that Kerala has achieved 100 per cent literacy.

His *means are* not enough to meet both ends. (Plural -The money that he gets)

Headquarters of several banks are in Mumbai. (plural)

(*xi*) The following words are always used in the plural.

Poultry, cattle, vermin, people, gentry, police, youth, clergy (used also in the singular), folk, etc.

For Example:

Our *poultry* give us enough meat and eggs. (not: 'gives')

These *cattle* belong to us. (not: 'belongs')

Vermin – wild animals or birds that destroy plants, food, etc.

Vermin destroy cultivation in the high ranges.

The *people* of Kerala are very clever.

All the *clergy* in the area were present at the meeting. (plural)

(He is a clergy of the local church) (singular)

The *police* are closely watching the developments.

(*xii*) Both 'people' and 'peoples' are plural. 'People' refers to the people of a nation or a country while 'peoples' refers to nations; as,

The *people* of India are highly patriotic.

The *peoples* (nations) of Europe have different cultural background.

Similarly, both 'youth' and 'youths' are plural. 'Youth' refers to young people while 'youths' refers to young men.

(*xiii*) Animal names like fish, herring, reindeer, antelope, etc., have two plurals, the zero plural(plural without any plural suffix) and the regular plural (with plural suffix).While the zero plural is usually used in connection with hunting/fishing, the regular plural is used to indicate different individual fish.

For Example:

They went fishing and caught a few fish.

There are *fishes* in the sea.(different kinds)

The fishermen caught quite a few herring.

The herrings in the Arabian sea are quite good.

A singular compound word is made plural by either adding –s to the principal word or making it plural. But, if the principal word is a verb the compound word is made plural by adding –s at the end of it; as,

post-*man*	post-men
post- *woman*	post- women
passer-by	passers-by
son-in-law	sons-in-law
governor-general	governors-general
step-*son*	step-sons
maid-*servant*	maid-servants
court-martial	courts-martial
drawback	drawbacks
good-for-*nothing*	good-for-nothings
go-between	go-betweens (go-verb)
lock-out	lock-outs (lock-verb)
hold-up	hold-ups (hold-verb)
hold-all	hold-alls

The words *in italics* are the principal words

Note: There are some singular compound words which take double-plural in the plural; as,

woman-servant	women-servants	(sometimes woman-servants)
man-servant	men-servants	
gentleman councillor	gentlemen councillors	
woman advocate	women advocates (sometimes woman advocates)	

But:	lady doctor	lady doctors
	boy scout	boy scouts
	girl guide	girl guides

Note the following plurals:

spoonful	spoonfuls
handful	handfuls
mouthful	mouthfuls
basketful	basketfuls
boy friend	boy friends
breakdown	breakdowns
grown-up	grown-ups
sit-in	sit-ins
stand-by	stand-bys
assistant manager	assistant managers
take-off	take-offs

(*xiv*) The following nouns have different meanings in the singular and the plural:

Abuse .... offensive remarks
Abuses .... wrong use of powers
Advice .... Counsel
Advices............. information regarding dispatch of goods
Air .... atmosphere
Airs .... unnatural behaviour
Content .... satisfaction
Contents .... things inside
Damage .... physical harm done to something
Damages .... money paid for loss or injury
Force .... strength
Forces .... soldiers
Good .... nice
Goods .... merchandise
Iron .... metal
Irons .... fetters
Manner .... method
Manners .... behaviour
Minute .... time (1/60 th of an hour)
Minutes .... the proceedings of a meeting)
Physic .... medicine
Physics .... physical science

Quarter 1/4

Quarters .... Dwelling place

Work .... job

Works .... factory or workplace

(*xv*) Plurals of letters, figures, and other symbols are made by

Adding 's (apostrophe s); as, Count the p's and r's on this page.

Add all 5's and 4's

Note: In modern English the apostrophe is often omitted.

For Example:

ps and rs

5s and 4s

(*xvi*) The names of countries and books are treated as singular; as,

The United States of America is the most powerful country in the world.

Gulliver's Travels is a famous book.

(*xvii*) 'More than one' is treated as singular.

For Example:

More than one person was present in the room.

(*xviii*) 'A number of ' is plural and 'the number of ' is singular.

For Example:

A number of people were present in the hall.

The number of people present at the meeting was small.

(*xix*) Belongings (moveable things), savings, hangings (curtains) and earnings are always used in the plural.

For Example:

His *belongings* were destroyed in the fire.

(Don't say: His belonging was destroyed)

He put his *savings* in the post office.

(Don't say: He put his saving in the post office.)

Ramu's *earnings* are quite sufficient to meet his expenses.

(Don't say: Ramu's earning is..............)

(*xx*) 'Craft' (a boat, ship, spacecraft or an aircraft) is used in a collective sense and takes plural verb.

For Example:

Five *aircraft* (aeroplanes) were shot down by the enemy.

Many *craft* were seen fishing in the sea.

(*xxi*) Some nouns take the singular forms as attributive (qualifying) nouns to other nouns.

For Example:

A *stamp* collector, a *tooth*-brush, a *flower* show, a *vegetable* oil.

Note the following compound nouns:

	billiards	a billiard-table (not: billiards-table)
	holidays	a holiday trip (trip conducted during holidays)
	barracks	a barrack unit
	sights	sight-seeing
	spectacles	a spectacle frame
	ashes	an ash tray
	customs	the custom house
	two-thirds	a two-thirds majority
But:	arms	arms depot
	savings	savings bank
	goods	a goods train
	trades	trades union or Trade union
	sales	sales Tax or sale tax
	customs	customs duty

Compound Nouns

There are a number of compound words that are made up of two or more words belonging to different parts of speech.

A few compound words that are in common use are given below:

Food-craft, silversmith, sunrise, housekeeping, housekeeper, bloodthirsty, self-respect, self-command, night club, headache, handwriting, dinning room, inkpot, inkstand, goldfish, bull-elephant, cow-elephant, he-goat, she-goat, cow-dung, newspaper, steel ware, rainbow, lawsuit, motor-cycle, arm-chair, blackboard highbrow, cut-throat, blockhead, potbelly, hunchback, playground, grindstone, drawing-room, looking-glass, flashpoint, washing-machine, sparking-plug, hearsay, make-believe, hush-hush (secret), shilly-shally, (vacillate), goody-goody, wishy-washy, dilly-dally(in two minds), see-saw, zig-zag, hanky-panky (dishonest behaviour), helter-skelter (in a disordered hurry), hocus-pocus (meaningless words to deceive people), hotch-potch (a mixture of things without any order), hurly-burly (a noisy and busy situation), namby-pamby (emotional), pell-mell (quick and uncontrolled way), razzle-dazzle, walkie-talkie (a small portable radio set to send and receive messages), sabre-rattling (military action), down-bridge, outpost, looker-on, passer-by, bread and butter, bedroom-cum-study, chairman-cum-managing director, child's play, bird's nest, good-for-nothing, free-for-all (fight), smash-and-grab (attack), cease-fire(stop fighting), fly-over, make-up, pick-up, go-between, forget-me-not, cut-throat (stop fighting), pick-pocket, foot-bridge, after-thought, green-room, easy-chair, free-trade, son-in-law, father-in-law, leftovers, look-out, make-up, forget-me-not, never-do-well, know-how, cut-throat, hold-all, make-shift, turn-coat, downpour, up-to-date, happy-go-lucky, well-to-do, red-hot, overcome, hand-made, dark-blue, over-anxious, over-sensitive, Anglo-Saxon, Franco-German, red-hot, Roman-Catholic, over-ripe, under-ripe, all-important, hit-and-run (attack and escape), etc.

(*xxii*) Nouns like *fruit, hair, coal,* may be used as collectives.

They may be used either in the singular or in the plural with plural suffix 's'.

When used in the singular:

Coal is used as a fuel.

Her *hair* is black.

Fruit is good for health.

When used in the plural:

He has put a few coals on the fire.(a few pieces of coal)

She has a few gray hairs. (meaning: individual strands of hair)

The basket contains fruits.(different kinds of fruit)

Correct Use of Some Nouns

Poetry: (Always singular – meaning - collection of poems)

Shelly's poetry is famous.

Don't say: Shelly's poetries are famous.

We can say: Shelly's poems are famous.

Summons: (Always singular though it appears plural)

(plural - summonses)

A summons was issued by the court.

Hair: She has thick hair.

Don't say: she has thick hairs.

We can say: She has a few gray hairs on her head.

Here, 'hairs' means individual strands of hair.

Equipment: This word is used when only one kind of equipment is meant.

For Example:

Raju bought drawing equipment.

Don't say: Raju bought drawing equipments.

'Equipments' means different kinds of equipments.

Our shop deals in different kinds of equipments.

Fruit: This word is uncountable. (Plural- fruit or fruits)

I bought some fruit from the market.

Don't say: I bought some fruits from the market even if you mean different kinds of fruit.

Fruits: (plural)- The good results of an action or situation.

For Example:

He could not enjoy the fruits/fruit of his labour.

Sky: The word *'sky'* is uncountable in the normal sense.

For Example:

The sky is clear today.

But, 'skies' means the great expanse of the sky; as,

It is a land of blue skies.

Rain: This word is uncountable.

For Example:

He went out in the rain. (not: He went out in rains)

But, the word *'rains'* means the season of heavy continuous rain; as,

The rains come in June in our state.

Sand: This word is an uncountable material noun in the ordinary sense.

Sand is one of the building materials.

But, *'sands'* means a large area of sand; as,

Children play on the sands.

Return: An uncountable noun meaning 'coming back'.

For Example:

His return from Delhi is uncertain.

But, *'returns'* means written official statements; as,

He filed his returns before the sales tax officer.

Wood: An uncountable noun meaning 'timber'.

This table is made of wood.

But, *woods (plural)* means a small area of trees or a small forest.

They went into the woods.

Pain: means 'ache'.

He has pain in his chest.

But, *'pains'* means trouble or effort; as,

Ramu took pains to explain the matter to the police.

Water: An uncountable noun.

We drink water when we feel thirsty.

But, *'waters' (plural)* means the water in a particular lake, river, sea or ocean; as,

The ship entered the waters of the Indian Ocean.

Premise: A statement or an idea based on reasonable argument.

For Example:

They arrived at the conclusion on a false premise.

But, *premises* means a house or building with a compound; as,

Smoking is prohibited on the college premises.

Odds: (Usually *the odds*). This word is generally used in the plural.

It means the extent to which something is likely to happen.

For Example:

The odds are in our favour.

The odds are that he will be selected for the post.

Amends: This word means 'to do something to compensate for a past mistake'. It is generally used in the plural in modern English.

For Example:

He made amends for his rude behaviour towards his teacher.

Eaves: This word is always used in the plural. It means the lower edges of a roof projecting over the walls.

For Example:

The eaves of our building are touching the compound wall.

Note: The verb 'eavesdrop' means ' to listen to other people's conversation secretly ' .

For Example:

He eavesdropped sitting in the adjacent room.

Note: the plurals of the following abbreviations.

Singular	Plural
l (line)	ll (lines)
p (pages)	pp (pages)
para	paras
MS (manuscript)	MSS (manuscripts)

Note: The plural form of 'Miss Nair' is either 'the Miss Nairs' or 'the Misses Nair'.

The plural form of 'Mr' is 'Messrs'.

Nouns taken from foreign languages.

Singular	Plural
Agendum	Agenda

Note: In modern English the word 'agendum' is not used and the word 'agenda' is treated as singular .

For Example:

What does the agenda contain?

He has prepared an agenda for the meeting.

Memorandum	Memoranda or memorandums
Basis	Bases (The last syllable rhymes with 'seas')
Crisis	Crises (")
Formula	Formulae or Formulas
Radius	Radii
Series	Series
Apparatus	Apparatuses
Terminus	Termini or Terminuses
Datum	Data

Note: The singular noun 'datum' is not normally used. The plural noun 'data' is uncountable and is treated as both singular and plural in the English language.

For Example:

The data collected by the scientist is quite inadequate. These data are quite adequate.

(Don't say: These datas are.....)

Don't use *'datas'* as the plural of data. The plural of data is 'data' itself in English. It always takes a singular verb except in technical/scientific English where it can be followed by a plural verb, in which case the singular is 'datum'.

Index	Indices (in mathematics) or Indexes
Stratum	Strata
Analysis	Analyses (the last syllable rhymes with 'seas')
Hypothesis	Hypotheses (")
Oasis	Oases (")
Thesis	Theses (")
Axis	Axes (")
Parenthesis	Parentheses (")
Gymnasium	Gymnasiums
Criterion	Criteria
Phenomenon	Phenomena
Adieu	Adieux or adieus
Bureau	Bureaus or Bureaux
Tableau	Tableaux or tableaus
Graffiti	Graffiti (drawings or writing on a wall in a public place)
Cherub (angel)	Cherubim

Chassis (last 's' is not pronounced)	Chassis (last 's' is pronounced)
Corps (Rhymes with 'core')	Corps ('s' is pronounced 'z')
Faux pas	Faux pas ('s' in the second word is pronounced 'z')

('x' in the first word and 's' in the second word are not pronounced)
(Meaning: socially incorrect action or remark that causes embarrassment)

Nouns Derived from Verbs

Payee	—The postman paid the money order to the payee. (to pay-verb)
Addressee	—The postman gave the letter to the addressee. (to address-verb)
Trainee	—He is working as a trainee in a factory. (to train-verb)
Employee	—The employees of the bank went on strike. (to employ-verb)
Lessee	—The agreement was signed by the lessee. (to lease-verb)
Lessor	—The lessor handed over the agreement to the lessee. (to lease-verb)
Vendee	—The street vendor sells things to the vendee. (to vend-verb)
Painter	—He is a painter of repute. (to paint-verb)
Worker	—He is a worker of the nearby factory. (to work-verb)
Writer	—She is a well-known writer. (to write-verb)
Giver	—He is a liberal alms giver. (to give-verb)
Drinker	—The police rounded up the unruly drinkers. (to drink-verb)
Organizer	—She is a good organizer. (to organize-verb)
Lawn-mower	— The worker used a lawn-mower to cut the grass. (to mow- to cut grass)
Eye-opener	—The incident was an eye-opener for him. (to open-verb)

Errors in the Use of Nouns

1. My sister lives in a boarding. (wrong)
   My sister lives in a *boarding house.* (say always: boarding house)
2. We had a visitor today morning .
   We had a visitor *this* morning. (say: this morning, this evening, this afternoon)
   We shall go to the cinema today night. (wrong)
   We shall go to the cinema *tonight.*
   We went to the picture yesterday night. (wrong)
   We went to the picture *last* night.
3. We cook vegetable every day. (wrong)
   We cook *vegetables* everyday.

4. We are living in my brother's quarter. (wrong)

We are living in my brother's *quarters.* (say always: quarters in this sense)

5. My house is under repairs. (wrong)

My house is *under repair.* (The phrase is 'under repair' meaning 'being repaired'.)

This house is built of bricks and mortar. (wrong)

This house is built of *brick* and mortar.

Note: Brick here means the material and not the number of bricks.

6. I got my hairs cut. (wrong)

I got my *hair* cut. (Hairs means individual stands of hair)

For Example:

A number of hairs were found in the food.

7. I have received all the informations about the matter. (wrong)

The noun 'information' is uncountable and hence has no plural form. (Only countable nouns have plural forms.) It is made plural by adding either 'pieces of' or 'items of' before it.

For Example:

I have received *many pieces/items of information* about the matter.

8. I am very particular about keeping my words. (wrong)

The phrase is: to keep one's word.

For Example:

I am very particular about keeping my *word.*

9. He died without issues. (wrong)

'Issue' in the sense 'children' will not take the form 'issues'.

He died without *issue.*

He died leaving behind two *issue.* (two children)

10. Two- third of the cake was eaten. (wrong)

Two-thirds of the *cake* was eaten. (Single cake and hence singular verb)

Two-thirds of the boys were absent.

(Boys plural or countable and hence plural verb)

11. I have a hundred-rupees note. (wrong)

I have a hundred-rupee note (or)

I have *hundred rupees* with me.

In 'hundred–rupee note' *hundred rupee is* functioning as an adjective qualifying.

Note: Use always 'hundred–rupee note', 'two hundred – rupee note', etc.

So also, seventy-foot road, hundred-foot tower, three thousand–foot mountain etc.

(Not seventy-feet road, hundred-feet tower etc.)

12. Kerala is full of beautiful sceneries. (wrong)

'Scenery' is an uncountable noun (meaning that it has no plural form).

The correction therefore is:

Kerala is full of *scenery*. (or) Kerala is full of *scenes*.

13. He has to do many works. (wrong)

Work in the sense of job is uncountable and hence has no plural form.

He has to do many *jobs*. or

Say: He has to do many *items of work*. (or) He has to do *much work*.

Note: 'Works' means factory or place of work.

14. Our cat has three offsprings. (wrong)

Offspring means children. It does not have a plural form.

Same word is used in both the singular and the plural.

So the correction is:

Our cat has three *offspring*.

15. It is a beautiful poetry. (wrong)

It is a beautiful *poem*.

'Poetry' means a collection of poems. It may also mean poems in general. We can say: It is a beautiful piece of poetry.

16. There are twenty six alphabets in English. (wrong)

There are twenty six letters in the English *alphabet*.

'Alphabet' is a set of letters in a specific order used in a language.

For Example:

He has learnt the *alphabets* of English, French and Spanish.

Note: Alphabet of one language but alphabets of many languages.

17. He went for higher study. (wrong)

He went for higher *studies*.

'Study' means the activity of acquiring knowledge through books etc.

'Studies' means the activity of acquiring knowledge by a person at a college or university.

18. His father died last week. Under the *circumstance* he could not go to work. (wrong)

His father died last week. In/ under the *circumstances* he could not go to work.

(Use always 'circumstances' in such contexts. Here this plural form means 'conditions'.)

19. He paid Rs 500 for boarding and lodging. (wrong)

He paid Rs 500 for *board* and lodging.

'Board' means the cost of daily meals in a lodge.

We can say: There is a boarding house or boarding school.

Errors in the use of Cases

1. My wife's neighbour's son is an intelligent boy. (wrong)

   The son of my *wife's neighbour* is an intelligent boy.

   Note: Use of double possessive should be avoided.

2. He reached the mountain's top. (wrong)

   He reached the *top of the mountain*.

   Normally /usually possessive forms of inanimate things are not used.

   Use, instead, the 'of' form.

3. Between you and I there is no dispute. (wrong)

   Between you and *me* there is no dispute.

   Use only the objective case of a personal pronoun after a preposition.

   (The objective case of 'I' is 'me')

Chapter 4 The Pronoun

A word used instead of a noun or a noun equivalent is called a pronoun.

A pronoun avoids repetition of a noun thus making a sentence or text more readable and better expressed.

Pronouns are generally of eight kinds:

1. Personal pronoun
2. Reflexive pronoun
3. Relative pronoun
4. Reciprocal pronoun
5. Distributive pronoun
6. Demonstrative pronoun
7. Indefinite pronoun
8. Compound pronoun
9. Interrogative pronoun
10. Exclamatory pronoun

4.1 PERSONAL PRONOUNS

The Personal pronouns stand for the three persons namely the first person, the second person and the third person.

I, we, thou, you, he, she, it, they are the personal pronouns in the English language.

(*a*) The first person denotes the person speaking - I, we.

For Example:

I am going to do this work.

(*b*) The second person denotes the person spoken to - you, thou.

For Example:

You will get the job.

(*c*) The third person denotes the person speaking of (about)-he, she, it, they .

For Example:

He is the chairman of the company.

(*i*) Personal pronouns when used as subjects (in the Nominative case)

	Singular	plural
First person	I	we
Second person	thou	you
Third person	he, she, it	they

(*ii*) Personal pronouns when used as objects (in the Accusative (objective) or Dative case)

	Singular	Plural
First person	me	us
Second person	thee	you
Third person	him, her, it	them

(*iii*) Personal pronouns when used as possessives (in the genitive case)

	Singular	Plural
First person	mine	ours
Second person	thy (thine)	yours
Third person	his, her, its	his, hers, theirs

Note: *Me, him, her, his, us, them* are the objective or accusative forms of the personal pronouns. The personal pronouns must be used in the following cases.

(*a*) When 'the personal pronoun' in its place is the object of a preposition:

For Example:

It is between him and her. (not 'he and she')

It is between you and me. (not 'you and I')

(After the preposition 'between', only the objective form should be used)

Note (*i*) Don't write: our's, your's, her's, their's.

Always write: ours, yours, hers, theirs.

Note (*ii*) The order of the first, second and third persons to be used in a sentence which conveys a favourable idea and which contains different kinds of pronouns must be as follows:

Second person + third person + first person

For Example:

You, he, and I are going to attend the meeting.

If the sentence conveys an unfavourable idea the order must be:

First person + second person + third person

For Example:

I, you and he are at fault.

(*b*) The possessive forms - *my, thy, his, her, its, our* and *your* are used as adjectives. They are then called possessive adjectives.

For Example:

It is my book. ('my' qualifies book)

That is her pen. ('her' qualifies pen)

Its colour, his hat, our house, your map, thy God etc.

(*c*) The possessive forms *mine, hers, ours, yours* and *theirs* are called possessive pronouns. They are used:

1. When separated from the noun by a verb coming in between
2. When the noun is not expressed
3. When preceded by the preposition 'of'; as,

(*a*) This pen is mine. (see (1) above)

(*b*) That cat is theirs. (see (1) above)

(*c*) My pen and yours are of the same brand. (yours = your pen- see (2) above)

(*d*) That pen of yours is not good. (preceded by 'of', see (3) above)

(*e*) These books are ours.

Note I: The possessive adjective comes before the noun while the possessive pronoun comes after the noun.

For Example:

This is *my* pen. (my-possessive adjective)

The pen is *mine.* (mine-possessive pronoun)

Note II: There is no difference in the meaning between a possessive adjective and a possessive pronoun. But there is difference in their positions in sentences.

'His' is used both as a possessive adjective and as a possessive pronoun.

For Example:

That is his pen. (possessive adjective)

That pen is his. (possessive pronoun)

Further examples in the use of the possessive adjective:

This is *my* dress. These are *my* books.

That is *her* picture. That is *his* box.

Further examples in the use of the possessive pronoun:

This umbrella is *mine.* That book is *yours.*

A book of *mine* was stolen. This book is *ours.*

Uses of 'its'

'Its' is the possessive form of 'it'.

For Example:

I know its value.

Note: Don't use *it's* in place of *its;*

it's is the short form of *it is.*

(*i*) The personal pronoun must be of the same number, person and gender as the noun for which it stands.

For Example:

Radha has done very well in the examination. *She* is likely to get a first class.

Ramu is a clever boy. *He* cannot be easily cheated.

There are forty students in the class. *They* are well disciplined.

(*ii*) When a pronoun denotes a collective noun it must be in the singular if the collective noun is considered a single entity.

For Example:

The committee *has* viewed the lapse seriously. *It* has decided to take action against the official concerned.

(This means that all the members of the committee are unanimous in their decision. In such contexts the collective noun 'committee' is considered singular. Hence the use of singular verb 'has' and the pronoun 'It'.)

Use of the word 'it':

The third person pronoun has three genders:

Masculine - he

Feminine - she

Neuter - it

(*i*) ' it' is used when the sex is not clearly known or when it is uncertain.

For Example:

The child is playing. *It* will ask for milk soon.

There is a dog in the next house. *It* is a good breed.

(*ii*) 'it' is used to denote things without life.

For Example:

I do not want that chair. Please remove it form here.

This is my book. Please give it to her.

(*iii*) 'it' is used to denote a child or baby.

For Example:

The child is crying. Give it milk.

The baby wants milk. Please take it to its mother.

(*iv*) 'it' is used as an introductory subject which is provisional and temporary. It is sometimes called the 'introductory it'.

For Example:

It is easy to understand the idea behind the statement.

(*i.e.*, To understand the idea behind the statement is easy.)

It is fortunate that he escaped unhurt.

(*i.e.*, That he escaped unhurt is fortunate.)

(*v*) 'it' is used to emphasize the noun or pronoun following it.

For Example:

It was *he* who came first.

It is *you* who have said it.

It is *I* who have done it.

(*vi*) 'it' is used as an impersonal pronoun.

For Example:

It snows; it rains; it thunders.

In the sentence 'it snows'- 'it' stands for the subject 'the snow' and therefore the sentence means 'The snow snows'.

The verb 'snows' is called an Impersonal verb.

(*vii*) 'it' is used when we speak of the weather, distance or time; as,

For Example:

It is spring.

It is raining today.

It is 12 O'clock.

It is walking distance to the city.

(*viii*) 'it' is normally used to refer to inanimate things.

For Example:

Is it your book? Yes, it is mine.

Death, nature, names of nations, etc. are often treated as inanimate things.

For Example:

Death is inevitable. *It* comes unnoticed.

India is an independent country. *It* is the largest democracy in the world.

Nature is bountiful. *It* has unending resources.

(*ix*) 'it' is used to refer to some statement or a part of it already made.

For Example

He has his own views on all matters. I appreciate *it*.

('it' stands for the statement ' He has his own.......'.)

He tried to cross the river, but *it* was not easy.

('it' stands for the word-group ' to cross the river')

4.2 REFLEXIVE PRONOUNS OR COMPOUND PERSONAL PRONOUNS

Reflexive pronouns or Compound personal pronouns are formed by adding 'self' to my, your, him, her, it, one (myself, yourself, himself, herself, itself, and oneself) and 'selves' to our, your, them (ourselves, yourselves, themselves).

1. They are used to show that a person or thing does something to himself or itself. In other words, they are used reflexively (*i.e.* used as direct objects) to indicate the identity between the subject and the object.

   (*a*) They may be used as direct objects.

   For Example:

I enjoyed myself. He enjoyed himself.	singular
She enjoyed herself. You enjoyed yourself.	subjects
We enjoyed ourselves. They enjoyed themselves.	plural
You enjoyed yourselves.	subjects

   The crow bathed itself.

   The computer will turn itself off if it is kept idle for a specific period.

   (*b*) They may be used as indirect objects:

   For Example:

   She made herself an object of ridicule.

   He gave himself the entire credit.

   (*c*) They may be used after a preposition:

   For Example:

   He said to himself that his actions were incorrect.

2. They are sometimes used for emphasis.

   For Example:

   I myself did it. (= I did it without anybody's help)

   He himself did it.

   He is the leader himself.

   They themselves did the work.

   We will do it ourselves.

   The room itself is congested.

   They caught the thief themselves.

   The house itself is very clean, but its surroundings are dirty.

   He will not do the work himself, but will send someone to do it.

3. They are sometimes used as subject complements.

   He is not himself today. (*i.e.* He does not behave normally)

   She is not quite herself nowadays. (*i.e.* slightly abnormal)

4. They are used after preposition.

He did the work *by himself.* (alone)

He was *beside himself* with joy. (uncontrollable joy)

You should verify the facts *for yourself.* (personally)

5. They are sometimes used after the words *but, like, than.*

My father is a lawyer like myself.

She is younger than myself. (younger than I am) younger to (wrong)

No one but himself (or he) is at fault. (not like 'elder to')

Note: A reflexive pronoun should not be used as a subject or an object in place of a personal pronoun in a sentence.

For Example:

He and myself went to the market. (wrong)

He and I went to the market.

She taught himself and me. (wrong)

She taught him and me.

Note: Some verbs can be used both as transitive and intransitive.

He used to wash before going out. (wash- used as intransitive verb)

He washed himself and went out. (wash-used as transitive verb)

He dressed neatly and went out. (dress-used as intransitive verb)

He dressed himself neatly and went out. (dress-used as transitive verb)

6. The verbs *to avail, to pride, to perjure* always take a reflexive pronoun as a direct object.

For Example:

He availed himself of the opportunity. (to avail oneself of something)

He availed of the opportunity. (wrong)

I prided myself on my creditable performance. (to pride oneself on something)

I prided on my creditable performance. (wrong)

He perjured himself. (to tell a lie in a court of law after taking the prescribed oath.)

The court found that he had perjured. (wrong).

But: The court found that he had committed perjury. (perjury-noun)

7. They are sometimes used after the prepositions 'among' and 'between'.

For Example:

The five friends distributed the sweets among (or between) themselves. (In such sentences the use of 'among' or 'between' is very common in modern English although traditional grammar permits only the use of 'among' ; 'between' is used only when there are two persons or things).

For Example:

The *two* brothers shared the sweets *between* them.

4.3 RELATIVE PRONOUNS

A relative pronoun serves two purposes. It refers to some noun going before it and at the same time joins two sentences together. Hence it is sometimes called a *conjunctive pronoun.*

Examine the following example sentences:

This is the pen. John bought it (the pen) yesterday.

The following two sentences convey exactly the same idea:

This is the pen and John bought it yesterday. ...(*i*)

This is the pen which John bought yesterday. ...(*ii*)

Here 'which' in sentence (*ii*) is a relative pronoun. It stands for the conjunction 'and' and the pronoun 'it (the pen)' in sentence (*i*) above. It relates/refers to the word 'pen' and at the same time joins the two sentences: This is the pen. I bought it (the pen) yesterday.

The noun to which the relative pronoun refers is called the 'Antecedent' which goes before the noun. In the given example the noun 'pen' goes before the relative pronoun 'which' and therefore 'pen' is the *antecedent* of the relative pronoun 'which'.

The following are the different forms of the relative pronouns:

Which, what, that, who, whose and whom. Sometimes 'but' and 'as' are also used as relative pronouns. They have the same form for singular, plural, masculine and feminine.

Which: Used to refer to animals and inanimate things; has the same form for the nominative and accusative cases.

What: Used to refer to things; used only in the singular; has the same form for the nominative and accusative cases.

That: Used to refer to persons, animals and things; has the same form for the singular and plural, and for the nominative and accusative; has no possessive or genitive case.

Who: Nominative (subjective) case used for persons only; has different forms for accusative and possessive cases.

Whose: Possessive or genitive form of 'who'; used for persons only.

Whom: Accusative or objective form of 'who'; used for persons only.

For Example:

He is one of the boys who were arrested yesterday.

Here, boys - antecedent; who - relative pronoun.

This is the book which (that) I bought yesterday.

I have lost the pen that I bought from Delhi.

He did not give me what I had asked for.

What he said I did not understand.

She went to the hotel where he was staying.

The boy whose father died yesterday is my neighbour.

Study the following sentence:

She is our teacher and she teaches very well.

She is our teacher who (=and she) teaches very well.

Both the above sentences convey exactly the same idea. The word 'who' in the second sentence is a relative pronoun and stands for both the conjunction 'and' and the pronoun 'she'. It joins the two sentences 'She is our teacher. She teaches very well' and is in the nominative(subjective) case because 'she' is the subject of the sentence.

Examine the following sentences:

(*a*) He is a cruel man. Everyone hates him.

(*b*) He is a cruel man *and* everyone hates *him*.

(*c*) He is a cruel man whom (= and...him) everyone hates.

All the above sentences convey exactly the same idea. The word 'whom' in the last sentence (*c*) is a relative pronoun and stands for 'and' and 'him' in the second sentence (*b*). Here it does the functions of a conjunction and a pronoun. It is in the accusative case because it is the object of the verb 'hates'.

Study the following sentence:

This is the boy whose (= and his) father died yesterday.

Here the word 'whose' is a relative pronoun and stands for the conjunction 'and' and the pronoun 'his'. It is in the possessive form because it represents the possessive 'his' besides the conjunction 'and'.

'whose' and 'whom' are the possessive and accusative forms respectively of the relative pronoun 'who'. Only does 'who' have this change of forms.

Note: When the antecedent is non-personal the 'of-phrase' is used instead of the genitive 'whose'.

For Example:

He has bought a dining table the top of which is made of marble. (not: whose top was made of marble.)

But: In modern English the use of 'whose' for non-personal antecedent is very common.

Note: The relative pronouns 'which', 'what' and 'that' do not have different forms for the accusative and possessive cases as 'who' does.

For Example:

He will resign his chairmanship *which* he has been holding for the last ten years.

(nominative case- 'which' stands for 'chairmanship')

This is the picture *which* he has bought from Delhi.

(objective case- 'which' stands for 'picture')

This is the picture, the frame of which is to be changed.

(possessive case- 'the frame of which' stands for 'its frame')

The following rules must be kept in mind when relative pronouns are used:

(*i*) The relative pronoun and the antecedent must be placed as near as possible.

For Example:

(*a*) It is *they who* made me angry.

(*b*) There was a man in the *market who* was very quarrelsome.

(Wrong because, as the sentence stands, the relative pronoun '*who*' stands for the noun market, which is absurd. The real antecedent is 'man'.)

Correct the sentence as follows:

In the market there was a man who was very quarrelsome. (correct)

(*c*) I met his brother in the *theatre* who was very handsome. (wrong)

In the theatre I met his brother who was very handsome. (correct)

(*d*) The answer in the *book* which I was searching for was finally found out. (wrong)

The answer which I was searching for in the book was finally found out. (correct)

(*ii*) A relative pronoun must always agree with its antecedent in number, gender and person.

For Example:

It is *you* who *are* responsible .

It is *I* who *am* to blame.

It is *she* or he who *is* negligent.

This is the *purse* that *was* lost.

Tolstoy was one of the *greatest novelists* that *have* ever lived.

It is they who were present.

But: This is *the only one* of the paintings that *is* worth seeing. (Right)

(Note that in the above sentence the real antecedent is not *paintings* but *one* before 'of'; 'that' is therefore singular.)

For Example:

A sentence is a *group* of words which *makes* complete sense.

(Here, the real antecedent is not 'words' but 'group' which comes before 'of'. Hence the relative pronoun 'which' is singular.)

The relative pronoun 'who' and its possessives 'whom' and 'whose' are used for persons only; 'which' is used for inanimate things, animals and infants; 'which' is also used for persons when a selection from among a number of persons is to be made.

For Example:

The girl *whose* father died last year is in the hostel.

The man *whom* you met in the office is a broker.

This is the pen *which* I bought yesterday.

This is the monkey *which* came to our house last Monday.

Tell me *which* is your box. (which among these boxes)

Uses of 'that'

(*a*) 'That' is used for persons, animals and inanimate things. It may refer to singular or plural and has no possessive or genitive case.

It is never used with a preceding preposition and is used only in defining clauses.

It is often used for *who, whom* or *which* but never for *whose.*

For Example:

This is the girl that (whom) I met in the hostel yesterday.

The elephant that (which) you saw at the temple is owned by our neighbour.

This is the book that (which) I took from the library.

The man that (who) came here in the morning is a poet.

(*b*) 'That' is used with the interrogative pronouns who, which and what.

For Example:

What is it that makes you happy ?

Who is there that is perfect?

Which is the one among these birds that lives in the forest?

(*c*) 'That' is used after the words - all, none, nothing.

For Example:

It was all that I had.

There is nothing that I can do for you.

(*d*) 'That' is used instead of who, whom or which after the superlative degree of adjectives and the word 'none'.

For Example:

There is none that is infallible.

He is the richest man that I have ever seen.

This is the best novel that I have ever read.

Uses of 'what'

'What', when used as a relative pronoun, is used only to denote things. It then means 'that which'.

For Example:

The officer listened to what the clerk said.

I said what I meant.

This is what I have.

Note down what I am going to say.

This is what is available in the shop.

Note: The antecedent is sometimes omitted; as,

Whom the officer likes are retained. (*Those* whom ....)

Note: The relative pronoun is sometimes omitted; as,

This is the pen I bought yesterday. (This is the pen *that* I.......)

The man I met yesterday is a thief. (The man *whom* I met ......)

Note: The relative pronoun should not be omitted if it is the subject of the relative clause; as,

The man who is working in the field is my uncle.(Here 'who' is the subject of the relative clause 'who is working'. If we omit 'who' the sentence will become meaningless.)

Use of who and whom:

'Who' must be used if the relative pronoun is the subject of a clause and whom if it is the object.

Don't say: This is the man *whom* I think is my best friend.

As the sentence stands the subordinate clause is 'whom is my friend' which is incorrect because 'whom' cannot be the subject of a clause.

Say: This is the man who (I think) is my best friend.

Don't say: This is the man who I saw in the market.

In this case the subordinate clause is ' who I saw in the market' which is incorrect because 'who' cannot be the object of a clause.

Say: This is the man whom I saw in the market.

Don't say: The man whom the police were searching for was arrested.

Say: The man *who* the police were searching for *was arrested.*

('who' is the subject of the clause ' who was arrested')

Uses of 'who', 'and who', 'which' 'and which'.

A relative pronoun does the functions of a conjunction.

No conjunction like 'and', 'but', etc should therefore be used before a relative pronoun if there is only one relative clause.

We use 'and who' or 'and which' only if there is a previous clause beginning with 'who' or 'which'.

For Example:

My friend is a man of dignity and self respect, and who always fights for justice. (wrong)

My friend is a man of dignity and self-respect, who always fights for justice.

But: My friend is a man of dignity and self-respect, who always fights for justice, *and who* is respected by one and all.

The above sentence is correct because there is already a relative clause beginning with 'who' in the above sentence.

But: 'but' is sometimes used as a relative pronoun after a negative.

It then means 'who…not' or 'which…not' and is used only in the nominative case. It is sometimes called *negative relative pronoun.*

For Example:

There is not a politician but hopes to become a minister.

(*i.e.* There is not a politician who does not hope to become a minister.) (but hopes = who does not hope. Here 'but' is used as a negative relative pronoun. In the example sentence 'but' stands for the antecedent 'politician' which is the subject of the subordinate clause.)

There is no child but likes ice cream.

(*i.e.* There is no child that does not like ice cream.)

As: 'as' is sometimes used as relative pronoun after 'the same' and 'such', and more often after 'as'.

For Example:

He has bought such things as are necessary. (as=which or that)

Nehru was such a leader as is remembered by all Indians at all times. (as = who)

This is not the same boy as I met last week. (as= that or whom)

This is not the same flower as we saw yesterday. (as=that or which)

It was such a film as I have never seen before.

Tell me as many stories as you can (tell).

Compound Relative Pronouns

Pronouns formed by adding 'ever', 'soever' to *who, which,* and *what* come under this category. They are:

whoever, whosoever, whoso, whichever, whichsoever, whatever, whatsoever. They do not have the antecedent expressed.

Of the five forms only three namely *whoever, whichever* and *whatever* are normally used.

For Example:

Whoever comes to me will be given a gift. (whoever= any person who).

Whosoever does this work will be recommended for promotion.

(whosoever= any person who; used where more emphasis is required.)

Use *whichever* colour you prefer. (whichever = any which)

You may go with *whomsoever* you like. (any one whom)

He took *whatever/whatsoever* action was necessary in the case. (anything which)

Have you any grievances? None *whatsoever.*

Restrictive Relative Pronouns and Continuative or Non-restrictive Relative Pronouns

Relative clauses

There are two kinds of relative clauses:

(*a*) Defining clause (*b*) Non-defining clause

(*a*) **Defining Clause.** A defining clause is a relative clause (an adjective clause) which defines the antecedent(the noun, pronoun or noun equivalent lying just before the relative clause in a complex sentence).This is a clause introduced by the relative pronouns like who, which, when or where. These relative pronouns are used in a restrictive sense. They restrict and define the antecedents. A defining clause is necessary in a sentence in which an antecedent is required to be defined because it explains or identifies which person or thing we are talking about. If it is omitted, the meaning of the sentence will not be complete.

Note: No comma is put in front of a defining clause.

For Example:

This is the man who came to see you yesterday.

In the above complex sentence the antecedent of the relative pronoun 'who' is 'man'. 'This is the man' is the main clause and 'who came to see you yesterday' the subordinate clause.

The main clause 'This is the man' needs something more to make the sense clear. The question 'which man?' does arise in our mind. The relative clause (adjective clause) 'who came to see you yesterday' gives the answer.

It is therefore the defining clause which defines the antecedent 'man' so as to make the sense of the sentence clear and complete.

Note: No commas are put before and after a defining clause.

(*b*) **Non-defining clause.** A non-defining clause is a relative clause (not an adjective clause) which gives us more information about the antecedent in a sentence. But it does not define or identify the antecedent. It is used in a continuative sense.

A non-defining clause does not restrict or define the antecedent. The main clause in the complex sentence is complete in itself. Even if the non-defining clause is omitted the sense will be clear and complete. A non-defining clause is therefore considered a co-ordinate clause (independent clause), and not an adjective clause.

A non-defining clause is always separated by a comma in front of it and a comma after it. If the clause is at the end of a sentence a full stop is put instead of a comma.

For Example:

I went to his office, which is housed in a rented building.

Examine the following sentence:

The Chief Minister, who is a doctor, visited the hospital.

Here the main clause is 'The Chief Minister visited the hospital' which is complete in itself. 'Who is a doctor' is a non-defining clause which gives more information about the Chief Minister. It does not define or identify the noun 'Chief Minister'. Even if this clause is omitted the clarity of the main clause is not affected. This is a co-ordinate clause, and not an adjective clause. 'who' (=and he) is its subject.

Non-Defining relative clauses are formal and used in writing rather than in speech.

Note: If the commas separating the non-defining clause are omitted the meaning of the sentence will be changed. The following examples will illustrate this point:

The guides who know the city well will take you to all places worth visiting.

The guides, who know the city well, will take you to all places worth seeing.

The first sentence means that only those guides who know the city well can take you to all places worth visiting. Others cannot.

Here the subordinate class 'who know the city well' is a defining clause with guides as its antecedent. It describes or defines or identifies the antecedent and is used in a restrictive sense.

It is therefore an adjective clause. *If this defining clause was omitted the sentence would mean that all guides would take you to all places worth visiting, which is not the actual meaning of the sentence.*

The second sentence assumes that all the guides know the city well and that they can take you to all places worth visiting.

The relative clause 'who know the city well' is used in a continuative sense and gives additional information about the guides. Here 'who' means 'and they'.

It is a non-defining independent clause. The example sentence is therefore a compound sentence. Even if this non-defining clause is omitted the clarity of the sentence will not be affected.

The Relative pronouns 'who', 'which' and 'that' are sometimes used to introduce an adjective clause that restricts or defines the antecedent.

Such clauses are then called Relative clauses and 'who', 'which' and 'that' Restrictive Relative Pronouns.

For Example:

This is the man who came here yesterday.

In the above sentence the relative clause 'who came here yesterday' defines or restricts the antecedent 'man'. This defining clause gives necessary information to make the antecedent specific or definite.

'This is the man' is not complete. 'who *the man* is' remains unanswered.

The relative clause 'who came here yesterday' defines the antecedent 'man'. If this clause is excluded the example sentence will remain incomplete. This relative clause is therefore essential for the completion of the sentence.

Examples using the restrictive relative pronouns 'which' and 'that':

The dictionary that he bought yesterday is quite useful.

The park which is in the heart of the city is visited by many people.

Note: 'Who' may be used both as restrictive and as continuative. 'That' is always used as restrictive.

Note: Since both 'which' and 'that' refer to animals and inanimate things 'which' is normally reserved for continuative relative and 'that' for restrictive relative.

To distinguish between the continuative and restrictive relatives the following test may be applied:

In a sentence containing a relative clause if the relative pronoun can be replaced with 'and it', 'and this', 'and they' or the appropriate form of this without altering the meaning of the sentence, the relative pronoun is continuative or non-defining and 'which' should be used.

If the relative pronoun cannot be replaced with any one of the above phrases ('and it' etc) the relative pronoun is restrictive and 'that' should be used.

He told her a story, which (and this) he had read long ago.

(Here 'which' is non-restrictive)

The book which he bought yesterday is a novel.

(Here 'which' is a restrictive relative pronoun because it defines the antecedent 'book'- 'the book he bought yesterday'.)

Similarly, in a sentence containing a relative clause if the relative pronoun can be replaced with 'and he, and she and they (personal)' or the appropriate form of this without altering the meaning of the sentence the relative pronoun is continuative and 'who' should be used; as,

My sister is a nurse, who is working in Mumbai.

(My sister is a nurse, and she is working in Mumbai.)

Note: When the relative pronoun is preceded by a preposition use always 'which'.(not 'that')

For Example:

The state *from* which we come is Andhra Pradesh.(not: from that)

The house *in* which we live is in a remote village.

Note: When the relative clause contains a parenthesis use only 'which'.

For Example:

The doctor advised him to take rest which, in his opinion, will make him all right.

('in his opinion' is a parenthesis)

Note: When the demonstrative pronoun 'that' is used in the main clause, we use the relative pronoun 'which' in the relative clause to avoid repetition.

For Example:

That is the book *which* he bought yesterday. (to avoid repetition)

Relative Adverbs

Study the following sentence:

This is the school where he studied.

Here the word 'where' is an adverb modifying the verb 'studied'.

Besides, it refers back or relates to the antecedent 'school' and also connects two clauses together as a relative pronoun does.

'where' is therefore called a relative adverb.

In other words, the relative adverbs relate or refer back to some antecedent, expressed or not expressed, and they are formed from relative pronouns. 'where', 'when', 'why' and 'how' are the relative adverbs. They are used in both restrictive (defining) and non-restrictive (non-defining) clauses. 'when' and 'where' may be replaced by a preposition + the relative pronoun 'which'.

For Example:

The house *where* he lives is very convenient.

(The house *in which* he lives is very convenient.)

The day *when* he came here was a Sunday.

(The day *on which* he came here was a Sunday.)

For Example:

I know the *house* where he lives. (antecedent expressed)

She knows the time when the meeting will begin. (")

I know where he lives. (antecedent not expressed)

She knows when the meeting will begin. (")

That is the reason why he refused to accept the offer. (antecedent expressed)

That is why he refused to accept the offer. (antecedent not expressed)

This is how he behaved. (*With 'how' no antecedent should be used* because 'how' means 'what way or manner')

Don't say: This is the way how he behaved.

4.4 RECIPROCAL PRONOUNS

' Each other' and 'one another' are the reciprocal pronouns.

Each other is used when we speak of two persons or things.

'One another' is used when we speak of three or more persons or things.

For Example:

The two guests introduced themselves to each other.

The five guests introduced themselves to one another.

In Modern English the above rule is not always observed.

For Example:

The two guests introduced themselves to one another.

The five guests introduced themselves to each other.

4.5 DISTRIBUTIVE PRONOUNS

Each, every, either and *neither* are the Distributive pronouns.

Each is used to refer to *every one* of two or more people or things of a group when we are thinking of them. *It is used when the group* (number) is definite and small.

For Example:

Each question carries ten marks.(Here we are thinking of every question individually.)

Identity cards will be given to each member of a family.

Every is used with singular nouns to refer to all the members of a group of things or people collectively.

For Example:

Every one in the locality attended the meeting.

(Here, we are thinking of all the people of the locality.)

I enjoyed every minute of our stay in Delhi.

Remember: When the number in a group is definite and small we use 'each' to refer to every member of the group.

When the number is indefinite we use 'every' to refer to all the members of the group collectively.

Note: The phrase 'each and every' is used for emphasis. and takes singular verb.

For Example:

Each and every member of the family has cast his/her (their) vote.

Either:This means one or the other of two people or things.

(Only singular verb is used)

For Example:

Either of the two men is a rogue. (not 'were rouges')

Either of the two girls was present. (not 'were present')

Neither: This means *not* the one *nor* the other of two people or things.

(Only singular verb is used)

For Example:

Neither of the boys was present. (not 'were present')

4.6 DEMONSTRATIVE PRONOUNS

These pronouns are used to identify the persons or things that are referred to.

This, these, that, those, such, so, one, ones, same, some, one, etc. are the Demonstrative pronouns in English.

When used independently they are Demonstrative Pronouns (DP); when used with nouns they are Demonstrative Adjectives (DA).

For Example:

This is my book. ('This' refers to the book and hence DP.)

This pen is useful. ('This' qualifies the noun pen and hence DA.)

He was a rogue. Such was her opinion before meeting him. (DP)

(Here 'such' means 'that')

He is a clever boy. I like such boys. (DA)

I bought some oranges. (DP)

Those oranges were very good. (DA)

My friend gave me a novel. That was a very good one.

(Here 'one' stands for the noun 'novel' and hence is a DP.)

There were so many shirts in the shop. I bought three cotton ones.

Note: The pronoun 'one' can be substituted for a noun or a noun Phrase. The plural of 'one' is 'ones'.

For Example:

Have you got pencils ? I need one. (one= a pencil)

Do you sell mangoes? Give me a few ripe ones. (ones=mangoes)

'One' cannot be substituted for mass nouns. Instead, they are omitted. We can omit both count and mass nouns. But, count nouns cannot be omitted after the indefinite article 'a' or 'an'.

I like the white shirt more than the black (one). Here 'one' is optional.

I like a white shirt more than a black one. Here 'one' cannot be omitted because of the presence of 'a'.

For Example:

A: Give me some water.

B: Do you want cold or hot. (Don't say: cold one or hot one.)

The population of Delhi is more than that (the population) of Bangalore.

('That' stands for the population of Bangalore.)

Do not say: The population of Delhi is more than Bangalore.

(This sentence means that the population of Delhi is more than (the city of) Bangalore, which is absurd.)

He is a good cricket player and will be so for years to come.

(Here 'so' means a good cricket player.)

He is a well-wisher of mine and will always be so.

Note: When 'so' is used after the verbs *to think, to tell, to hope, to suppose, to believe, to say, to be afraid, etc,* it refers to the whole preceding sentence or clause.

For Example:

Will he pass the exam? - I think so. (so = he will pass)

He is straightforward and honest as I guessed- I told you so.

His injury seems fatal - I am afraid so.

She will survive this difficult situation - I hope so.

Study the following sentences:

She has called me a communist. So I am. (I am a communist- confirmation of the statement made in the first sentence.)

I read the novel. So did she.

(not a confirmation of the statement made in the first sentence)

In the first example the second sentence takes the form so + pronoun + Verb ('so' in front position + pronoun + 'verb' in end position). Here, the emphasis is on the end position verb 'am'. In this case, the second sentence confirms the statement made in the first.

In the second example the second sentence takes the form so + verb + pronoun. Here, the emphasis is on the end position pronoun 'she'. In this case, the subjects are different and hence the predicate of the first sentence applies only to the subject of the second sentence which is not used to confirm the statement made in the first.

This difference must be clearly understood.

4.7 INDEFINITE PRONOUNS

These pronouns are used indefinitely in the sense that they refer to persons or things in a general way but do not refer to any definite person or thing.

They are: None, any, all, some, they, few, many, anybody, everybody, everyone, others, enough.

For Example:

None of the boys were present. (plural)

None but the brave deserves the fair. (singular)

Is there any message for me?

There is none./There are none.

They say he is a rogue

Note: When 'one' is the subject it should always be followed by the possessive one's and not by his or her; as,

One should not forget *one's* duty to the nation.

One should obey *one's* parents.

In the case of Indefinite pronouns like anybody, everybody, everyone, anyone and each, the pronoun he or she is used according to the context. But when the sex is not clearly expressed the pronoun of the masculine gender is used. *In modern English this rule is not always observed.* Instead, the pronoun of the third person plural is used.

For Example:

Each must do *their* duty.

Everybody has *their* own opinion on the matter.

Every one has done *their* best.

4.8 COMPOUND PRONOUNS

These are pronouns formed by adding ever, so, soever to the relative pronouns who, which and what. This addition of ever, so, soever (whoever, whosoever, whichever, whatever, whatsoever) gives the meaning of totality.

The antecedents of these compound pronouns are not expressed.

For Example:

(*i*) Whoever comes can attend the meeting . (*i .e.,* Any person who comes can attend the meeting 'Any person' is the antecedent.)

(*ii*) Whosoever comes may join us. (*i e, Any and every* person (antecedent) who comes may join us.)

(*iii*) Whichever you find feasible you may accept. (any which)

(*iv*) Whatever you say I shall obey. (anything)

(*v*) 'Whatsoever' and 'whatever' are interchangeable. (not at all, anything)

Whatsoever you do I do not mind. (anything)

Have you any doubt about your success? None whatsoever. (not at all)

4.9 INTERROGATIVE PRONOUNS

A pronoun which asks a question is called an interrogative pronoun.

Who, whose, whom, which and what are the Interrogative pronouns.

1. **Who:** 'Who' is used to introduce independent as well as dependent questions.

For Example:

Who is coming to see you ? (independent question)

Do you know *who* took the book? (dependent question)

2. **Whose:** 'Whose' is usually used as an attributive (adjective). But, it can also be used as an independent possessive.

   For Example:

   Whose book is this? (attributive)

   Whose is this book? (independent possessive)

3. **What:** 'What' has no other form than itself. It is used both as subject and as adjective. As a subject it takes only a singular verb, but with a plural nominal predicate it is followed by 'are, or 'were'. It may also be used with a personal subject when more information is required.

   For Example:

   What are you writing?

   He wanted to know what she was doing.

   What are the points to be noted?

   What is the problem?

   What do you want me to do?

   What were you taking this medicine for?

   What are you? (What is your occupation?)

   What is he?

   'What' is sometimes used attributively with nouns indicating persons or things.

   For Example:

   What *man* in your place wouldn't have told so?

   He wanted to know what *books* I brought.

'What' is used with ' sort of, kind of, manner of ' to indicate a group or type of people or things that are similar in a particular way.

What sort of mangoes are these?

What kind of woman is she?

What manner of woman could face such a situation?

(manner of=kind of)

'What' is used attributively in exclamatory sentences.

For Example:

What a sight it is!

What a pity!

What a beautiful scenery!

'What' is used in the idioms ' and what not' and 'what have you' both meaning 'and other things of the same kind' .

For Example:

This packet contains sweets, biscuits, snacks and what not.

We need, sweets snacks and what have you for the party.

What is usually used for something other than a person only; as,

What have you got?

What did you say?

What was the matter?

What are the differences between these two things?

Note: Please note the differences in meanings of the following sentences.

Who is your father? (name)

What is your father? (occupation)

Which is your father? (selection from among a group of people)

'What' is not used in a selective sense. Only 'which' is used in that sense.

For Example:

Which building is that? (wrong)

What building is that? (right)

Whom

While 'who' is used as the subject of a verb, 'whom' is used as the object of a verb or preposition.

For Example:

Who took it?

Whom did you tell? (object of the verb 'tell')

Of whom are you speaking? (object of the preposition 'of')

Modern English prefers 'who' instead of 'whom' although it is ungrammatical.

For Example:

Who are you speaking of?

Who did you tell?

In the case of indirect object whom (who) is accompanied by the preposition 'to'.

To whom did you give the pen?

Who (whom) did you give the pen to?

(*a*) Who, whom, whose are used for persons only.

Who is your teacher? (name)

Whom do you want to see?

Whose book is this?

(*b*) **Which**

Which is used for persons and things. It implies selection from among more than one person or thing of a limited number and has only one form. It has no genitive form either. When a selection not possible use 'what' instead of 'which'.

Which among the visitors is your father? (from among a limited number)

Which of these books you have read?

Which shirt will you wear today?

Which of you has been to Chennai?

Will you tell me *what* books are to be bought? (if there is collection of books)

4.10 EXCLAMATORY PRONOUNS

Pronouns used in the exclamatory sense are called the Exclamatory pronouns. 'What' may be used in an exclamatory sense.

For Example:

What a wonderful thing it is !

What a pleasant surprise!

Usually exclamations are shortened to a noun phrase or adjective phrase; as,

What a sight!

How stupid!

EXERCISE

Correct the following sentences:

1. I availed a day's leave.
2. Raju and me were walking together.
3. This is for Raju and I.
4. Between you and I, there is no secret.
5. He is as old as me.
6. It is me who is to blame.
7. She can talk as well as him.
8. It is good for you and I.
9. They arranged a party for my friend and I.
10. They offered presents to Raju and I.
11. No one can act like he.
12. Let you and I be present at the court.
13. You who is the owner is responsible for the safety.
14. I who is only a clerk is helpless in the matter.
15. I am the agent who is dealing in this item.
16. Neither of the two books are good.
17. Either of the books are available.
18. He is more intelligent than either of his three classmates.
19. I gave him two scores of rupees.
20. I bought two grosses of pencils.
21. A lakh rupees was spent on the project.
22. The man who you saw yesterday had been for a long time.
23. This is the man who you met yesterday.

Chapter **5** # The Verb

A word used to express an action, an event, or a state is called a verb.

For Example:

Ramu ate his food. (The word 'ate' expresses an action.)

Ramu happened to meet his friend. (The word 'happened' expresses an event.)

Water exists in three forms. (The word 'exists' expresses a state.)

A few verbs sometimes denote suffering by the subject:

For Example:

He underwent a series of mishaps.

She died of Cholera.

He received bullet injuries.

Some verbs can denote an action in some context and in others a suffering by the subject:

For Example:

He cut a knot. (action)

He cut a sorry figure. (suffering)

A few verbs can be used in two different ways with the same meaning.

For Example:

The house abounds with rats.

Rats abound in the house.

Children swarm in the park.

The park swarms with children.

Tears were streaming down her face.

Her face was streaming with tears.

The park is crawling with snakes.

Snakes are crawling in the park.

Some verbs are used with or without a preposition.

For Example:

He put a stone into the well.

He *put on* his new dress. (wore)

She took a book.

She *took to* begging. (take to=to begin something as a habit)

Note: Examine the following sentence:

The problem is easy to solve. (to solve what? the problem)

Here the subject 'problem' is the object of the infinitive 'to solve'. (The given sentence can be rewritten as 'It is easy to solve the problem.')

Another example: Some people are difficult to deal with.

5.1 FINITE AND NON-FINITE FORMS OF VERBS

A finite verb is limited by the number (singular or plural) and the person(first, second or third) of its subject. It also indicates the tense (present, past or future).

For Example:

Ramu goes to school. (singular subject-present tense-third person).

They go to school. (plural subject- present tense-third person).

I like sweets. (singular subject-present tense-first person).

Ramu went to school. (past tense)

A verb that is limited by the number and the person of its subject is called a finite verb.

The infinitive (present and perfect, with or without 'to'), the gerund, and the present and past participles are the non-finite forms of verbs. Those forms other than the non-finite forms are their finite forms.

A verb that is not limited by the number and the person of the subject in a sentence is called a non-finite verb.

For Example:

The non-finite forms of the verb 'be' are:

(to) be – present infinitive (with or without 'to')

(to) have been – Perfect infinitive (with or without 'to')

being – gerund (verbal noun) and present participle (both having the same form)

been – past participle

Its finite forms are: am, is, are, was, were.

The non-finite forms of the verb 'write' are:

(to) write, (to) have written, writing and written.

Its finite forms are: write, writes and wrote.

The non-finites of 'do, are: (to) do, (to) have done, doing and done. Its finites are: do, does and did.

Note: The gerund and the present participle of a verb take the same form.

For Example:

They are *playing*.(present participle)

Children like *playing*.(gerund or verbal noun)

Note: to-infinitive and bare infinitive or plain infinitive.

When an infinitive is used with 'to', it is called 'to-infinitive'. When it is used without 'to', it is called 'infinitive without to' or 'bare infinitive' or 'the dictionary form' or 'plain infinitive'.

For Example:

He came to see me. (Here 'to see' is *to-infinitive.*)

He did not see me. (Here 'see' is *bare infinitive.*)

Linking Verbs

A linking verb links or joins the subject of a sentence with its Complement (*i.e.,* with the subject complement). The subject complement can be a word or expression that describes the subject. The most common linking verbs are: the different forms of 'be' (*i.e.,* am, is, are, was, were, will be, has been, etc.), appear, become, feel, grow, look, remain, seem, smell, sound, stay, taste.

For Example:

He is *the local leader of the party.*

('He'- subject; 'the local leader of the party'- subject complement)

He appears quite confident.

She became president of our club.

He feels shy.

He grew tall.

She looks innocent.

The fruit tastes sour.

Auxiliary verbs or Auxiliaries (Helping verbs)

An auxiliary verb is one which is used with main verbs to show tense, mood, voice, etc. and to form questions and negatives. (Auxiliary =helping)

The following are the auxiliaries – be (and its finite forms: am, is, are, was, were), have (and its finite forms: has, had), do (and its finite forms: does, did), can, could, may, might, shall, should, will, would, must, ought, used (with 'to'), need and dare. Of these auxiliaries only *be, have* and *do* (when they are not used as full verbs) have both non-finite and finite forms. They are called primary auxiliaries because they change their form according to the number and the person of the subject in the present tense; as,

I am, you are, he is, they are; I do, you do, he does, they do; I have, you have, he has, they have, etc.

Note: The auxiliaries *be, have* and *do* are sometimes used as full verbs; as, Be patient. (The subject is *you* – used in commands. When be is used in statements it takes the forms am, is, was, are, were.)

For Example:

I am a college student.

He is a coward, etc.

Be attentive. (The subject is *you*)

Don't be mischievous. (The subject is *you*)

I have a pen. (possession)

I have my breakfast at 8. (take or eat - habitual)

I have severe body pain. (experience)

I do my duty sincerely.

In all the above sentences *be, have* and *do* are full verbs.

Non-finite and finite forms of the auxiliaries *be, have* and *do*

Auxiliary	**Non-finite forms**
be	(to) be (infinitive) being (present participle) been (past participle)
have	(to) have (infinitive) having (present participle) had (past participle)
do	(to) do (infinitive) doing (present participle) done (past participle)
	Finite forms
be	be, am, is, are (present tense) was, were (past tense)
have	have, has (present tense) had (past tense)
do	do, does (present tense) did (past tense)

The auxiliaries *shall, will, may* and *can* have only finite forms

Auxiliary	**Finite forms**
shall	shall (future) should (past)
will	will (future) would (past)
may	may (present) might (past)
can	can (present) could (past)

The auxiliaries *must, ought, need,* and *dare* are finite forms. They are in the present tense and they have no non-finite forms. The finite of the auxiliary *used (with to)* exists only in the past tense. It has the same form for all persons. In the negative construction both 'did he used to' and 'did he use to' are used. The former construction 'did he *used* to' (*e.g.,* Did he used to go to bed early?) is preferred to ' did he *use* to' (*e.g.,* Did he use to go to bed early?)

Auxiliary	Finite forms
must	must(present)

ought	ought(present)
need	need (present)
dare	dare (present)
used(with to)	used (past tense)

Anomalous Finites (Anomalous = different from what is normal)

Thus there are twenty four finites of auxiliary verbs. They are given below: am, is, are, was, were, have, has, had, do, does, did, shall, should, will, would, can, could, may, might, must, ought, need, dare, used(to). These twenty four finites are called *Anomalous finites* which are usually used as auxiliary verbs. Some of them are also used as principal verbs. When they are auxiliary verbs they help the principal verbs to form their tenses and moods. When they are anomalous finites they are irregular. The functions of these finites are different from those of other irregular finites and hence they are called *anomalous (different from what is normal) finites*. The distinguishing feature of these finites from others is that they can be directly combined with the contracted form *' n't '* of *'not '*.

For Example:

isn't (is+not), aren't (are+not) , wasn't, hasn't, don't, didn't, shouldn't, can't, oughtn't, usedn't (*d* is silent) (to) or didn't use (to) (used +not), etc.

Note: Certain anomalous finites become non-anomalous when they are used as ordinary verbs.

For Example:

When the verb 'have' is used in the sense possess, take or eat, 'receive or experience' or when the reference is to something habitual, general or usual, the finites are not anomalous. Thus in ' I haven't met him' 'have' is anomalous, but in ' I have my bath in the morning' 'have' is not anomalous. (Here 'have=take' is an ordinary verb.)

Its negative is ' I don't have my bath in the morning' and not 'I haven't bath in the morning'. As it does not combine with 'not' it is not anomalous. (See the definition of anomalous verbs)

Note: The anomalous finites mentioned above are not always auxiliary verbs.

For Example:

I have a computer.

(Here 'have' is *not* an auxiliary verb as it does not help any other verb. It is used as an ordinary verb.)

They are students.

(Here 'are' is *not* an auxiliary verb. It is a linking verb)

5.2 MODAL AUXILIARIES OR MODALS

The finite auxiliaries *can, could, may, might, shall, should, will, would, must, ought, used* (with 'to'), *need* and *dare* are called Modal auxiliaries or Modals because they are used to express moods like permissions, possibility, necessity, duty, obligation, etc. The modal auxiliary cannot stand alone. It is always used with a main verb. It does not have the third person singular form with 's' in the present tense. It has no infinitive (to +verb)forms, 'ing' forms or –ed participles.

Uses of the Anomalous finites

1. The anomalous finites are used to form the negative by adding 'not'/n't directly to them.

   For Example:

   He is a good boy.

   He is not (isn't) a good boy.

   We can wait.

   We cannot (can't) wait.

   They ought to go.

   They ought not (oughtn't) to go.

   She will go.

   She will not (won't) go.

Note: The non-anomalous finites are made negative by using the appropriate form of the helping verb 'to do'.

For Example:

He wants help.

He does not (doesn't) want help.

He ate rice.

He did not (didn't) eat rice.

2. The anomalous finite helps to put a sentence into the form of a question (the interrogative) by the inversion of the subject and itself (the anomalous finite).

   For Example:

   She is going.

   Is she going?

   They are working.

   Are they working?

   We can do it.

   Can we do it?

Note: If the verb is a non-anomalous finite we use the appropriate form of 'to do' to form the interrogative.

For Example:

They came.

Did they come?

She works.

Does she work?

Note: We use not (n't) after the subject to form the interrogative negative.

For Example:

Does he eat it?

Does he not eat it? (Doesn't he eat it?)

Did they come?

Did they not come? (Didn't they come)

Note: As a rule, inversion of the subject and the anomalous finite should take place when a sentence begins with a word or phrase having a negative or semi-negative meaning. This inversion is found more in literary style.

Scarcely, hardly, seldom, little and *rarely, etc.,* are semi-negatives and *not only, no sooner, by no means, in no way, on no account, at no time, nowhere, etc.,* are negatives. *They are followed by positive tag-questions or question tag.*

For Example:

I have never disobeyed my parents.

Never have I disobeyed my parents. (*have* and *I* interchanged)

(Tag-question: Have I?- positive tag.)

I don't like him, nor do I like his friends.

He little knew that they were thieves.

Little did he know that they were thieves.

They had hardly reached the station when the train left.

Hardly had they reached station when the train left.

He was at no time in Chennai.

At no time was he in Chennai.

She could not find him anywhere.

Nowhere could she find him.

Note: There are verbs with negative meaning. They take only positive form.

For Example:

He denied he had stolen the book.

Don't say: He denied he had *not* stolen the book.

3. The anomalous finites are used in brief answers to questions

For Example:

Can you go to the market? Yes, I can. Or No, I can't.

Do you want it? Yes, I do. Or No, I don't.

Did you go there? Yes, I did. Or No, I didn't.

Has she been informed? Yes, she has. Or No, she hasn't.

4. The anomalous finites are also used in co-ordinate clauses to avoid repetition of a verb.

   For Example:

   He doesn't normally get angry, but when he does (gets angry) he becomes wild.

   They don't often complain, but when they do they will go to any extent to get their complaint redressed.

5. The anomalous finites are used in question tags or tag questions when the subject in the tag question is a pronoun or the introductory 'there'.

   For Example:

   It is a mistake, isn't it?
   He made a box, didn't he?
   They can't do it, can they?
   There is a table in the room, isn't there?

6. The anomalous finites are used in the following pattern.

   For Example:

   He goes to the temple everyday and so does his father.
   (His father also goes to the temple everyday.)
   She will come to the garden and so will he.
   I can read it and so can you. (You can read it too)

7. The anomalous finite 'do' is used to lay emphasis.

   For Example:

   I do like it. ('do' lays emphasis on 'like')
   He did attend the meeting.

8. Adverbs usually follow anomalous finites and precede non-anomalous finites.

   For Example:

   You can always come to me for help. (can- anomalous finite)
   He should never go there.
   I can hardly believe it.
   You always come to me for help. (come- non-anomalous finite)
   He never goes there.
   I hardly believe it.

5.3 DEFECTIVE VERBS

Verbs that are not used in all the moods and tenses are called Defective Verbs. The auxiliaries such as *shall, will, can* and *may* have only Simple Present and Simple Past forms namely *will-would, shall- should, can- could* and *may- might*. They do not have 'infinitives' and 'participles'. The following are defective verbs.

Shall, will, may, can, must, dare, ought, used to

Use of can/ could/ be able to:

Can: This is a defective verb with only two forms: can and could. It is therefore necessary to find out another verb which can be used in tenses that cannot be formed with 'can' or 'could'. 'Be able to' is such a verb.

The Present and Past forms of 'be able to' are:

Present	*Past*	*Negative form*
am able to	was able to	(am or was)unable to
is able to	was able to	(is or was)unable to
are able to	were able to	(are or were)unable to
Future		*Negative form*
will be able to		will not be able to
shall be able to		shall not be able to
Present Perfect		
have been able to		- have not been able to
has been able to		- has not been able to
Past Perfect		
had been able to		- had not been able to

Use of 'can':

This is a transitive verb used to express

1. bodily or mental ability or inability.
2. permission

For Example:

He can walk the entire distance.	(bodily ability)
He cannot lift this weight.	(bodily inability)
You can think of evolving a new formula.	(mental ability)
I cannot think of being cruel.	(mental ability)
You can meet the officer now.	(permission)
Can I meet the officer?	(permission)

Note: To ask permission 'may' is better than 'can'.

For Example:

May I meet the officer?

'Can' is used to make questions?

For Example:

Can you do this work?

Who can do this work?

When can you do this work?

Use only 'be able to' to form the Future and Perfect tenses, and the infinitives:

For Example:

We shall be able to do this work shortly.

She has been able to meet the Minister.

We have not been able to complete the work.

3. 'Can' means 'sometimes' in general statements.

For Example:

Snakebite can be fatal. (can be= is sometimes)

Driving along a wet road can be dangerous.

Note: To express impossibility use 'cannot'.

For Example:

I cannot do this work. (It is impossible for me to do this work.)

He is so lazy that he cannot pass the exam.

Don't say: It can be possible for him to do this work.

(Both 'can' and 'possible' indicate 'possibility'.)

Say: It is possible for him to do the work.

Or

He can do this work.

Similarly, It may be possible for him to do this work. (wrong)

It is possible for him to do this work.

Or

He may be able to do this work. (Both 'may' and 'possible' indicate 'possibility')

Note: It may perhaps be possible for him to do the work. (wrong)

It is possible for him to do the work.

Perhaps it may be easy for him to the work. (wrong)

Perhaps it is easy for him to do the work.

(Both 'may' and 'perhaps' indicate 'possibility')

Use of 'Could':

1. The past tense of can is 'could'. We therefore use could in place of can in the conversion of Direct speech into Indirect (reported) speech.

For Example:

They said," We can do this work".

They said that they could do that work.

2. 'Could' is used to indicate ability in the past.

For Example:

He could swim very fast five years ago. (Not: He was able to swim very fast)

While he was young he could run a long distance.

Note: If we wish to express a past achievement (in something actually done or accomplished in the past) we should use only 'was able to' or 'were able to' in place of *could* depending upon the context.

For Example:

(*a*) I could walk the whole distance in ten minutes. (wrong, if I actually walked)

I was able to walk the whole distance in ten minutes. (a past achievement)

In other words, I actually walked the whole distance. (It is a past achievement)

(*b*) They could complete the work in a day. (wrong, if they actually completed the work)

They were able to complete the work in a day.

(It is an achievement in the past and hence ' were able to')

But, in negative sentences and questions and sentences with verbs of perception (see, hear, feel, taste, smell and understand) we can use 'could' even if we wish to express a past achievement.

For Example:

We could not / were not able to do the work.

I could not do the work yesterday.

Could you give me your pen?

Could you tell him to meet me?

I could not / was not able to understand what it was all about.

He could see what it was.

I could hear the sound.

She could understand what the teacher said.

(*c*) 'Could' is used for hypothetical possibility.

For Example:

If I were rich, I could help him. (But I am not rich)

Or

If I were rich, I might help him.

(*d*) 'Could' is used to show remote possibility.

For Example:

He could be in the office.

(It is possible that he is in the office. But the possibility is remote.)

5.4 REGULAR VERBS AND IRREGULAR VERBS

Regular verbs: Those verbs which have the suffix *'-ed'*, *'-d'* or *'-t'* for their past and past participle are called regular verbs. In some cases the past and past participle of the verbs are formed by slightly changing the verbs and then suffixing *'-ed'*, *'-d'* or *'-t'*

For Example:

walk, walked, walked

search, searched, searched

mark, marked, marked,

lend, lent, lent

feel, felt, felt,

weep, wept, wept

sell, sold, sold,

put, put, put

hut, hurt, hurt

bleed, bled, bled,

shoot, shot, shot etc.

From the base of a regular verb we can easily predict its other forms, namely present singular, present participle, past, past participle.

For Example:

walk (base), walks, walking, walked, walked.

search, searches, searching, searched, searched.

mark, marks, marking, marked, marked, etc.

Most of the verbs belong to this category.

Irregular verbs:

Although irregular verbs are like regular verbs in that both have the same singular and 'ing' forms (*e.g.* cut(base), cuts, cutting) we cannot predict the other forms from the base.

Those verbs which do not have the suffix '–ed', '-d' or '-t' for their past and past participle are called irregular verbs.

For Example:

take-took-taken

make-made-made

give-gave-given

mean-meant-meant

cut-cut-cut,

can, could (no past participle)

may, might, (no past participle)
must, must (no past participle)
shall, should (no past participle)
will, would (no past participle)
sing, sang, sung
hold, held, held, etc.

5.5 DYNAMIC VERBS AND STATIC VERBS

Verbs that admit a progressive form ('ing' form) are called dynamic verbs.

Verbs that do not admit the progressive form are called Static verbs.

For Example:

He writes his book

He is writing his book.

They do their homework.

They are doing their homework.

What follows from the above examples is that verbs like 'write', 'do' etc. are dynamic verbs because they take the progressive form.

But: He knows English.

He is knowing English. (Incorrect)

This may be corrected as follows:

He knows English.

This tablet contains Vitamin-A. (Not: This tablet is containing Vitamin-A)

This is because the verbs 'know' and 'contain' do not occur in the progressive form. Such verbs are called static verbs.

The following verbs in their normal meaning do not occur in the progressive form. In other words, they are static verbs: love, hate, posses, contain, believe, belong, deserve, know, mean, own, please, prefer, recognize, remember, resemble, satisfy, seem, sound, suffice, suit, surprise, understand, see, hear, notice, smell, recognize, want, wish, desire, feel, like, hope, prefer, refuse, suppose, think, agree, consider, remember, forget, mind, have, contain, possess, etc.

The following verbs in their usual sense do not occur in the progressive. But they can occur in the progressive in a slightly different sense:

hear, see, think, suppose, mind, forget etc.

For Example:

I see the picture clearly.

(The progressive form of 'see' is used in its usual sense to show improvement in seeing.)

He is seeing the picture more clearly now.

I am seeing my relatives off.

I hear a noise.

(The progressive form of 'hear' is used in its usual sense to show improvement in hearing.)

He is hearing you better now.

The judge is hearing the appeal.

She *thought* of writing a book.

What was she *thinking* of?

I don't *mind* your coming late.

She is *minding* (looking after) the baby.

I *forgot* to take my book.

He is *forgetting* his parents.

Most of the verbs in English are dynamic verbs.

There are three kinds of verbs.

(1) The Transitive verb

(2) The Intransitive verb

(3) The Auxiliary verb or helping verb

For Example:

He made a kite.

The child sleeps.

They have come here.

In the first sentence given above, the action of the verb 'made' does not stop with the doer 'He' but passes on to the thing 'kite' so as to make the sense complete. The verb 'made' is therefore a Transitive verb. (Transitive means *passing over*)

A verb is transitive if the action denoted by the verb does not stop with the doer (agent or subject), but passes from the doer to something else called the object of the verb.

In the second sentence, the sense is complete. The verb 'sleeps' stops with the subject (agent) and does not pass on from the agent to anything else to make the sense complete. Such a verb as 'sleep' is an Intransitive verb. Intransitive means 'not passing over'.

A verb is intransitive if the action of the verb stops with the subject (agent) and does not pass from the subject to anything else.

In the third sentence, the verb 'have' helps us to form the present perfect tense of the main verb 'come'. In that process it (have) loses its original meaning (possess) .The verb 'have' is therefore called an auxiliary verb.

5.6 CONJUGATION OF VERBS

Conjugation means the way in which a verb shows its different forms according to the tense. The Present tense, the Past tense and the Past participle are these forms. The Active and Passive forms can be formed from these three.

For Example:

take, took, taken (conjugation of the verb 'take')

see, saw, seen, etc.

Different forms of the Object

Most transitive verbs take a single object. The object to a verb can be a noun, a pronoun, an infinitive, a gerund, a phrase or a clause.

For Example:

Noun – Raju bought a pen.	Object: pen
Pronoun – He put it on the table.	Object: it
Infinitive – He wants to go to Delhi.	Object: to go
Gerund – He does not like smoking.	Object: smoking
Phrase – I do not know what to do.	Object: what to do
Clause – I could not guess who he was.	Object: who he was

Position of the Object

The object to a verb is usually placed after the verb to which it belongs.

For Example:

He bought *a book.*

She drew *a beautiful picture.*

Note: (Exception)

If the object is a Relative Pronoun (RP) or an Interrogative Pronoun(IP) it is used before the verb.

For Example:

(*i*) The picture that I saw in the exhibition was very beautiful. ('that' is RP)

(*ii*) The woman whom I met at the railway station was deaf. ('whom' is RP)

(*iii*) What is the matter? ('what' is IP)

(*iv*) Whom are you searching for? ('whom' is IP)

Direct and Indirect Objects

Some verbs take two objects: The Direct Object (DO) and the Indirect Object (IO). The indirect object is usually placed first followed by the direct object. The direct object answers the question 'what' or 'whom' while the indirect object answers the question 'to whom' or 'for whom'.

For Example:

I gave him a pen. ('him' is IO and 'pen' is DO)

Or

I gave a pen *to him.* (This construction is preferred when the IO is to be emphasized.)

Ramu bought me a shirt. ('me' is IO and 'shirt' is DO)

Will you give me the book?

He paid the doctor a sum of three hundred rupees.

Could you tell me his address?

Note: If the IO is placed after the DO it must be preceded by the preposition 'to' or 'for'. This construction is used to emphasize the IO.

I gave *him* a pen. (IO first)

I gave *a pen* to him. (DO first)

Raju bought *me* an umbrella. (IO first)

Raju bought *an umbrella* for me. (DO first)

Verbs of Incomplete Predication

There are verbs that cannot form a complete predicate by themselves. They always need the addition of some adjective, noun, or pronoun (or noun equivalent) referring to the subject or object. Such verbs are called Verbs of Incomplete Predication. The adjectives, nouns or pronouns (or noun equivalents) that are used to complete the predicate of a verb are called predicative adjectives, predicative nouns or predicative pronouns respectively. They are often referred to as 'complements'.

For Example:

She is a doctor. (noun complement)

She seems sad. (adjective complement)

He became president. (noun complement)

She looks beautiful. (adjective complement)

It is he. (pronoun complement)

Distinction Between Predicative Noun(or Subject Complement) and Object

Examine the following sentences:

He is a student.

She became an actress.

In the first sentence the noun 'student' stands for the subject 'He' and in the second the noun 'actress' stands for the subject 'She'. These nouns are called predicative nouns or 'subjective (or subject) complements'. They stand for the subject as in the above example sentences and are required to complete the sense of the sentence. They are used after intransitive verbs like 'to be' with all its forms (*e.g.* am, is, are, was, were, will be, shall be, etc.,), become, seem, etc.

Now examine the following sentence:

They elected the president.

In the above sentence the noun 'president' does not represent the subject 'They'. It is different from the subject and is the object of the transitive verb 'elected'. Such a noun or noun equivalent is an object.

Transitive verb of incomplete predication

Some transitive verbs take one object only but they still require some word or words to make the predication complete.

The additional word or words that are necessary to make the predication complete are called *the objective complement or Object complement.*

For Example:

They bought him clothes.

Here the verb 'bought' is a transitive verb with 'him' as its object. But the sense of the sentence 'They bought him' is not complete without the noun 'clothes' which is the object complement. The verb 'bought' is therefore a transitive verb of incomplete predication.

For Example:

They made him king. (king-complement)
(s) (v) (o) (c)

Here, 'made' is a transitive verb of incomplete predication.

The complement may be a noun, an adjective, a participle, a preposition with its object, an infinitive verb, an adverb or a noun clause.

For Example:

(*i*) The people made him (the) *President.* (noun)
(See the Note below)

(*ii*) They made him *angry.* (adjective)

(*iii*) They found him *bathing.* (participle)

(*iv*) The magic show filled us *with surprise.* (preposition with object)

(*v*) My mother asked the servant *to go.* (infinitive)

(*vi*) They saw him shout *loudly.* (adverb)

(*vii*) They bought him what he wanted. (noun clause)

Objective (or object) complement / Subjective (or subject) complement

Examine the following sentences:

(*i*) They made him king.

(*ii*) He was made king by them.

These sentences convey the same meaning. The first sentence is in the active voice and the second one in the passive voice.

As we have already seen 'king' is the *objective complement (or object complement)* of the first sentence as it refers to the object 'him'. In the second sentence the verb is in the passive voice. The word 'king' refers to the subject 'He'. It is called the *subjective complement (or subject complement)*.

Note: *The* and *a* are often omitted with noun-objective complement.

For Example:

He was elected president. *Or* He was elected the president.

(Assuming that there is only one president)

The government made him secretary. (if there is only one secretary.)

Or

The government made him a secretary. (if there is more than one secretary.)

5.7 TRANSITIVE VERBS USED AS INTRANSITIVE

A transitive verb usually has an object, and an intransitive verb does not have one. But, some verbs are often used both transitively and intransitively, when the meaning of the object is clear from the context in which they are used intransitively.

(*i*) We eat to live. (Here the transitive verb 'eat' is used as intransitive – no object, but the meaning of the object is clear from the context - we eat food etc.)

(*ii*) He cannot see; he is blind (Here the transitive verb 'see' is used as intransitive- no object)

(iii) I drew near him. ('drew' is a transitive verb. This sentence actually means ' I drew myself near him')

(*iv*) He moved forward.('moved' is a transitive verb. This sentence actually means ' He moved himself forward')

(*v*) He plays well. (The verb 'play' is transitive. But, it is used here as intransitive - no object)

(*vi*) She *left* in the morning. ('leave' transitive-used here as intransitive)

(*vii*) He *smokes* occasionally. ('smoke' transitive -used here as intransitive.)

(*viii*) The moral of the story is: Crime doesn't *pay*.

(*ix*) *It pays* to fence the compound to keep out cattle. (to result in some advantage)

(*x*) *That will do*, boys- you are getting tired. (stop doing something.)

(*xi*) He doesn't *take after* his father. (He doesn't look like his father.)

(*xii*) It is a wet cloth. Fire won't *catch* easily.

(*xiii*) They *put* to sea from Mumbai. (They left Mumbai port by ship or boat.)

(*xiv*) The door will not shut.

(*xv*) The door opened, and the guests entered.

(*xvi*) The hall filled in no time. *Or* Her eyes filled with tears.

(*xvii*) Wet clothes dry in the sun.

(*xviii*) The fishermen pulled towards the shore. (Pull= row)

(*xix*) The terrorists were ready to strike. (strike=attack)

(*xx*) The fire caught rapidly.

The verbs of motion and change are frequently used as both transitive and intransitive although they are originally considered transitive.

For Example:

Transitive	**Intransitive**
Change the rule.	Rule *changes.*
Roll the drum.	Drum *rolls.*
Begin the match.	The Match *begins* at 3 p.m.
Move the stone.	The stone *moves.*
Pass the train.	The train *passed.*

Intransitive Verbs of Complete Predication

These are verbs which do not require any additional word or words to be added to them to make complete sense. Such verbs are called Intransitive verbs of complete predication

For Example:

Birds *fly.* (This makes complete sense without any additional word/words.)

Rivers *flow.*

Rabbits *run.*

They *sleep.*

Intransitive Verb of Incomplete Predication

Some Intransitive verbs do not make complete sense by themselves. They require a complement to complete the sense. Such verbs are called Intransitive verbs of incomplete predication.

For Example:

(*i*) The cow *is a domestic animal.*

('is'- intransitive verb; 'a domestic animal'-noun complement)

(*ii*) He *is blind.* (blind-adjective complement)

(*iii*) He *seems to be satisfied.* (participle complement)

(*iv*) He *goes running.* (participle complement)

(*v*) This *is of no use.* (phrase complement)

(*vi*) They *are ready to go.* (infinitive complement)

(*vii*) The man *seems to be worried.* (infinitive complement) (*viii*) The boy *fell asleep*. (adverb complement)

(*ix*) This *is what he told me*. (clause complement)

Note: The complement that comes after an Intransitive verb is called the subjective (or subject) complement because it refers to the subject.

5.8 INTRANSITIVE VERBS USED AS TRANSITIVE

Verbs like *March, fly, grow, float, etc.*, are normally considered Intransitive verbs. They can also be used as Transitive verbs.

For Example:

The volunteers *marched* along the road . (intransitive)

They *marched* the soldiers along the road. (transitive)

(here, the object is 'soldiers'.)

The bird *flew* out of the cage. (intransitive)

He *flew* the bird. (transitive with object 'bird')

Children *grow* at home.

He *grows* his children.

The log *floated*.

They *floated* the log.

Intransitive verbs like *fall, rise,* and *lie* can be made transitive by changing some vowel; as,

The tree *falls*. (intransitive)

The woodcutter *fells* the tree. (transitive -'fells the tree' means 'causes the tree to fall')

The sun *rises* in the morning. (intransitive)

It is very difficult to *rouse* him. (transitive-'rouse him' means 'cause him to rise')

They *lie* on the floor. (intransitive.)

The hen *lays* eggs. (transitive-'lays eggs' means 'causes eggs to lie')

Intransitive verbs like *stand, work, ring* and *dine* are often used as transitive verbs. When they are used as transitive verbs, they are called causative verbs.

For Example:

The child *stood* on the table. (intransitive)

She stood the child on the table. (transitive)

(*i.e.,* She caused the child to stand on the table.-causative)

He worked in a factory. (intransitive)

He worked his employees twelve hours a day. (transitive)

The bell rings. (intransitive)

He rings the bell. (transitive)

I dined at a restaurant. (intransitive)

I dined my family at a restaurant. (transitive)

Note: Intransitive verbs *lie* and *sit* have separate transitive forms namely, *lay* and *set* respectively. (lie, lay, lain; sit, sat, sat and *lay, laid, laid; set, set, set.*)

Although *set* is the transitive form of the verb *sit,* sit itself is used as its transitive form in a causative sense (See examples 1 and 2 above) because 'set' generally means *put* or *place.*

Note: The special use of some transitive verbs as intransitive ones may be noted carefully. Only in certain *special combinations* are they used.

For Example:

This novel won't sell- special use. Here the sentence conveys a passive meaning. In other words, the novel is considered here to be active to some extent and does the function of a bookseller. (But, we cannot say: His car sold yesterday. This is a single act of selling where 'sell' cannot be used intransitively. Hence, we should say: His car was sold yesterday. In other words, only the passive form should be used in such cases.) Further examples are given under:

This play won't act.

They photographed well.

This shirt washes well.

His shoes won't wear out easily.

The meat cuts tender.

His essay reads like a short story.

These numbers will add up to the required sum.

The door will not shut.

Note: Some intransitive verbs become transitive when a proposition is added to them. Such verbs are treated as real transitive verbs if only they can be used in the passive voice.

For Example:

(*i*) He spoke *of* the incident. ('spoke' – intransitive; 'spoke of' – transitive. He spoke of what? – the incident) The incident was *spoken of* by him. (used in the passive voice)

(*ii*) They laughed *at* him.

He was laughed at by them.

(*iii*) The officer looked *into* the matter carefully.

The matter was carefully looked into by the officer.

Note: When a verb contains in itself the meaning of a following preposition the preposition may be omitted. The verb is then treated as transitive.

He climbed the tree. ('He climbed up the tree.' is also correct.)

Jump, flee, pass are examples of this kind of verbs.

He jumped over the fence. *Or* He jumped the fence.

They were forced to flee from the country. *Or* They were forced to flee the country.

She passed by my house this morning. *Or* She passed my house this morning.

Note: In some cases the preposition is put before the verb.

The army *overcame* the enemy. (over+came = succeeded in dealing with)

The minister *withstood* the pressure from his party. (with+stood= stood against)

The river *overflows* its banks. (over+flows =flows out of the blanks)

The area is *overgrown* with plants. (over+grown= covered.)

5.9 STRONG AND WEAK VERBS

Verbs are classified as: *Strong* and *Weak.*

This classification is made according to the manner in which they form the past tense and the past participle.

Weak Verbs

All verbs the past tense of which ends in 'd' or 't' are weak verbs.

For Example:

Ask, asked; pass, passed; beg, begged; lend, lent; keep, kept; bring, brought.

All verbs the past tense of which is formed by shortening the vowel of the present tense are weak.

Shoot, shot; bleed, bled; feed, fed; lead, led; meet, met; shoot, shot.

All verbs the past tense of which is the same as the present tense are weak.

Hit, hit; cast, cast; hurt, hurt; cut, cut; shut, shut; spread, spread.

Strong Verbs

All verbs which form their past tense by changing the inside vowel and which do not suffix 'd' or 't' in their past tense are strong verbs.

For Example:

To be ; am, is, are ; was, were; break, broke; choose, chose; do, did; fall, fell; hold, held; sit, sat; find, found; drive, drove etc.

All verbs which form their past participle by adding 'en' or 'n' at the end are strong verbs.

For Example:

Take, took, taken

Draw, drew, drawn

See, saw, seen.

Shake, shook, shaken.

Throw, threw, thrown

Write, wrote, written etc.

Note: The following verbs have no 'to-infinitive' form. They exist only in two tense forms – present and past. They have no past participle.

Present	Past
can	could
shall	should
may	might
will	would
must	must

Note: Some verbs have two past participial forms of which one is used as the participial adjective and the other the past participle. The following participles are used only as participial adjectives (the ones within brackets as past participles.)

bounden (bound)	– bounden duty
drunken (drunk)	– drunken brawl
molten (melted)	– molten lead
sunken (sunk)	– sunken ship
rotten (rotted)	– rotten egg
shorn (sheared)	– shorn lamb
graven (graved)	– graven image
shaven (shaved)	– clean shaven face
cleft (cloven)	– a cleft chin
lighted (lit)	– a lighted candle
roast (roasted)	– roast chicken

The cognate object:

An Intransitive verb may sometimes be followed by an object (noun) related (some way and therefore similar) to the verb. Such an object is called the cognate object.

For Example:

He lived a long life.

Here, the noun 'life' is related in meaning to the verb 'lived'. The noun 'life' is therefore called the cognate object of the verb 'live'.

Cognate Objects may be formed in four different ways.

Directly from the verb:

For Example:

Ramu laughed a funny *laugh.*

He died a tragic *death.*

The patient slept a sound *sleep.*

The Army fought a brave *fight.*

My guest sang a melodious *song.*

He dreamed a horror *dream.*

He ran a long *race.*

When he escaped from the accident he sighed a deep *sigh.*

From a noun of similar meaning

They travelled a long *way.*

The army fought a brave *battle.*

He struck a deadly *blow.*

They ran their own *course.*

From a noun which is equivalent in meaning to the cognate object

She played the heroine. (She played the part of the heroine)

She shouted joy. (She shouted the shout of joy)

He ran a great risk. (He ran a course of great risk)

From an adjective quantifying a cognate noun that is understood.

The poet wrote his *best.* (poem)

The soldier fought his *best.* (fight)

He tried his *best.* (trial)

He played his *best.* (play)

5.10 MOOD

Mood is the form of a verb showing the mode or manner in which something is said by it.

In the English Language there are four moods, three finite moods and one infinitive. They are:

(*i*) The Indicative mood

(*ii*) The Imperative mood

(*iii*) The Subjunctive mood

(*i*) **The Indicative mood**

A verb is said to be in the Indicative mood if it makes or indicates a statement of facts or asks a question or expresses a supposition which is assumed as a fact.

(*a*) Statements of facts:

For Example:

The earth moves round the sun.

Raju studies well.

Leela does not like him.

(*b*) Questions:

For Example:

Have you finished your work ?

Does he do his work?

Is she a lazy girl?

(*c*) A supposition which is assumed as a fact:

For Example:

If he comes, we shall go to the cinema. (Assuming as a fact that he will come)

If he is a gentleman, he will honour his word.

(Assuming as a fact that he is a gentleman)

If he is a foreigner, he will not be permitted to enter our country.

(Assuming as a fact that he is a foreigner.)

(*ii*) **The Imperative mood**

A verb which expresses a command, an exhortation (advice), an entreaty (request) or a prayer is said to be in the imperative mood.

For Example:

Don't move. (command)

Please help me; I am in distress. (entreaty)

O God! Have mercy upon us. (entreaty or prayer)

Respect your elders. (exhortation or advice)

In all the above examples the subject is 'you' which is understood.

The verb 'let' is also used to express the imperative mood.

For Example:

Let me do it. (Allow me to do it)

Let him study his lessons.

Let them study now.

Let us go. ('You' is the subject in all the above examples.)

We use 'Let's go' dropping the vowel 'u' if it is an advice (exhortation) given to all including both the person(s) spoken to and the speaker. If that is not the case, 'let' assumes its original meaning (allow) and we use 'Let us' instead of ' Let's' 'Let us go' now takes the meaning 'Allow us to go' and its subject is 'you'. (*i.e.*, You let us go)

Meaning of *let alone*: 'Let alone' is used in the sense ' not to mention'. It is used after a statement to emphasize that if the first thing in it is not true or possible, the next thing cannot be true or is not possible.

For Example:

There is not enough food for us, let alone your friends.

We cannot walk even a kilometre, let alone ten kilometres.

Note: If the imperative mood is negative, the auxiliary 'do' is used with the verb.

For Example:

Don't go out. (do not go out)

Don't (do not) make him sad.

(*iii*) **The Subjunctive mood:** A verb is said to be in the subjective mood if it expresses *a purpose, a wish, a condition(unfulfilled* or *unreal) or a supposition.*

The auxiliaries may, might, should and would are used to form this mood. The subjunctive mood is

(*a*) **used to express a purpose:** To express a purpose the word 'that' or 'lest' is placed before the verb in the subjunctive mood. If the reference is to a present or future purpose we use the auxiliary verbs 'may' and if the reference is to the past we use 'might'. After 'lest' we use 'should' or 'the bare form of the verb' in both the tenses.

For Example:

I shall send you abroad that you may acquire advanced knowledge in many things. (Future)

I shall keep your purse lest you should loose it. (or lest you loose it)

I give you another opportunity that you may do it better. (Present)

I gave you another opportunity that you might do it better. (Past)

I kept your wallet lest you should lose it. (Past)

Or

I kept your wallet lest you lose it. (past)

(*b*) **used to express a wish, desire or a prayer and is used in certain set expressions:** God save the king! (May God save the king)

God be with you!

Bless you!

Come what may... (Despite any problems or difficulties that may happen)

For Example:

She has decided to go with him come what may.

Or

Come what may she has decided to go with him.

Suffice it to say...(Used for saying that whatever the speaker has said contains his/her idea)

For Example:

Suffice it to say that living with her was horrible.

Be that as it may....(Used for saying that even if something is true it does not affect your opinion)

For Example:

Be that as it may, I still believe that I am right.

There are two forms of the subjunctive mood:

(*i*) The present subjunctive mood

(*ii*) The past subjunctive mood

(*i*) **The Present subjunctive mood:**

This mood is used to express a desire, a resolution, an order, etc. It is used in the 'that clauses' after expressions like suggest, insist, demand, require, desire, order, resolve, be necessary, obligatory, etc. The verb form used in such clauses is the base or bare form of the above verbs for both singular and plural subjects, and present and past tenses.

For Example:

He suggests that Mr. Nair *inaugurate* the function. (Not: inaugurates)

He desired that Mr. Nair be appointed president. (Not: was appointed)

Or

He suggested that Mr Nair *should inaugurate* the function.

(Modern English prefers this form.)

The Minister ordered that the officer *be* suspended. (order)

She desires that he *inform* her of the latest development. (Not: informs)

The meeting resolved that the secretary be removed.

It is necessary for us to remember our duties to society. (be necessary+to-infinitive)

It is obligatory for us to respect our elders.

Note: The verb 'be' is the same in both the present and past tenses.

(*ii*) **The Past subjunctive mood.**

1. If the reference is to the present time,

(*a*) simple past tense is used in all kinds of verb except 'to be' and the past subjunctive '*were*' is used if the verb is 'to be' to indicate a <u>wish</u> ; as,

I wish I *knew* the secret. (Actually, I do not know.)- note the past tense of the verb to indicate the wish.

I wish I *were* a king. (Actually I am not a king)

He wishes he *lived* in England.

Note: If the reference is to the past time (*a*) becomes:

I wish I had known the secret. (The wish is indicated in the past perfect tense) (Actually I did not know the secret)

I wish I had been a king.

He wishes he had lived in England.

Note: If the reference is to the future time (*a*) becomes:

I wish I would know the secret.

I wish I would be a king.

He wishes he would live in England.

(*b*) to express a supposition, or a less probable/unlikely situation, or imaginary situation after 'if'.

For this purpose the past subjunctive *were* is used in the conditional clause if the verb is 'to be' and the past indicative (ordinary past tense) if it is any other verb. The *'future in the past'* is used in the main clause.

(A past event which was future when viewed from a particular point of time in the past is said to be in the *'future in the past'* tense.)

Examine the following examples:

If I pass the exam I'll get a job.

If I passed the exam I'd get a job.

'If I pass' and 'If I passed' in the above examples do not indicate a difference of time. Both the forms can indicate the present or the future.

But, the past subjunctive form (If I passed) suggests that the situation is imaginary, or less probable, or impossible. More examples are given below:

If I were you I would attend the meeting. (Actually I am not you)

If she taught me I would pass the exam.

If the train started now it would reach Delhi in time.

I could go to the cinema if it were a holiday.

If I had a novel I would read it.

If I were not ill I would attend the meeting.

Note: In the above sentences 'if' can be omitted and *should, were*, or *had* can be placed in its place before the subject.

For Example:

Were I you I would attend the meeting.

Should she teach me I would pass the exam.

Had I a novel I would read it.

Should the train start now I would reach Delhi in time.

Were I not ill I would attend the meeting.

2. If the reference is to the past time, (*a*) and (*b*) take the following forms to indicate an impossible or a hypothetical condition:

If I had been you I would have attended the meeting.

(but, I was not you so I did not attend the meeting–two past events which cannot be fulfilled now – impossible conditions.) = 39 + 35.5

If she had taught me I would have passed the exam.

If the train had started then I would have reached Delhi in time.

I could have gone to the cinema if it had been a holiday.

If I had had a novel I would have read it.

If I had not been ill I would have attended the meeting.

Note: In modern English 'was' is more common than 'were'.

But, only *were* is used in the phrase 'as it were' (=so to speak or in a sense) and *were* is preferred in 'If I were'.

For Example:

She is, as it were, responsible for his failure in the exam. (Not: as it was)

(*c*) after 'it is time' to indicate delay; as,

It is time you *ate* your food. (It is already late for you to eat your food)

It is time he *went* to bed. (It is already late for him to go to bed)

Note: In this type of construction the verb in the clause after ' It is time' is always *in the past tense.*

(*d*) after 'as if/ as though' to indicate an unreal or imaginary condition; as,

He spoke to me as if I were his servant. (Actually I am not)

He moved about as though he were all in all.

He lay as if he were dead.

(*e*) after 'would rather' to indicate priority or preference.

I would rather you accepted the post. (I should prefer you to accept the post)

They would rather you went by train. (They would prefer you to go by train)

Note the use of the past tense after 'would rather'

5.11 NON-FINITE VERBS

Non-finite verbs can be classified into three categories:

(1) The Infinitive

(2) The Participle

(3) The Gerund or Verbal Noun

5.12 THE INFINITIVE

I drink water.

I wish to drink water.

In the first sentence 'drink' is a finite verb.

In the second sentence 'drink' is a non-finite verb.

This non-finite verb is called the Infinitive.

It takes the ' to + bear form of the verb'.

For Example:

to eat, to sleep, to speak, etc., are examples of present infinitives. to have read, to have eaten, to have shouted, to have written etc. are examples of perfect infinitives. The perfect infinitive takes the form to + have + past participle of the verb.

To-infinitive and bare infinitive or plain infinitive:

For Example:

She wants *to buy* a book.

They want *to buy* some books.

He ought *to have* bought the book.

She can *buy* a book.

She could *have* bought a book.

They could *have* bought the books.

In the first three examples given above the verbs 'buy' and 'have' are used with 'to'. They are known as 'to–infinitive'. In the last three these verbs are used without 'to'. They are then known as 'infinitive without to', or 'bare infinitive' or 'plain infinitive'. In other words, the infinitive may occur either with or without 'to'.

The infinitive may, therefore, be defined as a form of the verb which has no independent subject and which is unaffected by the number and the person of the subject unlike a finite verb. (A finite verb has its own subject and is affected by the number and the person of the subject.)

While the *plain infinitive* is used *only* in a verbal function, the 'to-infinitive' can be used as the subject, object, or complement to a verb of a sentence.

For Example:

To praise him is to please him.

(Here, 'to praise' is the subject and 'to please' is the nominal predicate or complement to the verb.)

I like to play. (Here, 'to play' is the object of the transitive verb 'like'.)

The infinitive denotes an action without referring to the agent or the doer (subject).

Note: The infinitive has no future form.

Different kinds of infinitives:

There are two kinds of Infinitives:

(1) The Noun Infinitive or Simple Infinitive

(2) The Gerundial or Qualifying Infinitive.

The Noun Infinitive:

It may be used as

(*a*) a subject to a verb.

For Example:

To drink water is good for health. (*i.e.*, Drinking water is good for health)

(*b*) an object to a verb

For Example:

He likes *to sleep.* (He likes sleeping – object to the verb 'likes')

(*c*) a complement to a verb

For Example:

He is to sing tonight. (complement to 'is')

I am to go. (complement to 'am')

He seems to be dreaming. (complement to 'seems')

The Gerundial or Qualifying Infinitive:

It may be used

(*a*) to qualify a verb; as,

They came *to assess* the damage caused by the recent earthquake.

(Shows purpose – qualifies the verb 'came')

They were frightened *to see* the death scene.

(Shows cause – qualifies the verb 'frightened')

(*b*) to qualify a noun; as,

It was a day *to enjoy.* (shows purpose – qualifies the noun 'day')

He bought a house *to live in.* (qualifies the noun 'house')

I bought a chair *to sit on.* (qualifies the noun 'chair')

This is not a thing *to play* with. (qualifies the noun 'thing')

(*c*) to qualify an adjective; as,

He was happy *to see* me. (qualifies the adjective 'happy')

They were eager *to hear* the news. (qualifies the adjective 'eager')

Note: When intransitive verbs like *live, sit* and *play* are used they must be followed by the appropriate preposition.

See examples 2 to 4 under (b) above.

(*d*) To introduce a *parenthesis* or *'not to'*; as,

I am, *to be frank,* not an expert in this field. ('to be frank' – Parenthesis)

He has a huge deposit in the bank, *not to mention his landed property.*

The infinitive without 'to' or the bare infinitive/plane infinitive.

'To' is generally considered to be the sign of the Infinitive.

For Example:

English grammar is easy *to learn.*

Children like *to play.*

But, there are infinitives which are used without 'to'.

The infinitive without 'to' is used after the auxiliary and defective verbs.

Defective verbs:

can, could, may, might, shall, should, will, would, must and *ought* are called *Defective verbs* because they are not used in all tenses and moods. They do not have the to-infinitive, 'ing' or the third person singular with 's' (such as goes, sees, plays etc.) forms.

For Example:

I shall sing = I am willing to sing.

We will go = We are determined to go.

She can read = She is able to read.

I could write = I was able to write.

You must do it = You are forced or compelled to do it.

I need not go there. (It is not necessary for me to go there)

He dare not do it = He hasn't the courage to do it.

Note: If the verbs *do, need* and *dare* are used as main or principal verbs 'to' is not used before them; as,

I do part of the work to help him. ('do' used as a main verb.)

He dares to question my authority. ('dare' used as a main verb)

He needs to go there. (' need' used as a main verb).

The plain infinitive or the infinitive without 'to' is often used after the following principal or main verbs:

(*a*) *see, hear, feel, watch, notice, observe* and the phrasal verbs *listen to, look at* denoting physical perception

(*b*) *let, make* to mean 'to cause'

(*c*) *have* to mean 'to experience', 'to permit', 'to get'

(*d*) *need, dare, let, bid, know, behold.*

For Example:

I saw him cross the river.

I heard him speak at the seminar.

He felt his head throb violently.

She watched the children play in the park.

They noticed the plane disappear in the sky.

She observed a thief enter the house.

The children listened to the teacher explain the theory.

We looked at the magician vanish into the air.

They need not go to school today.

I dared not do it in his presence.

They made him cry.

He could feel his heart throb.

They let him do the work.

She would not let him go. (She would not like him to go.)

He had a strange thing happen to him. (He had a strange experience.)

The teacher would not have students do it.

(The teacher would not permit the students to do it.)

The people would have the government control prices.

(The people would like the government to control prices.)

We watched the waves rise.

My father bade him go.

Note: The present participle may be used after the verbs 'to see', 'to hear', 'to watch', 'to feel', and 'to observe' with subtle difference in meaning.

For Example:

I saw him crossing the river.

I heard him speaking at the seminar.

He felt his head throbbing violently.

She watched the children playing in the park.

They noticed the plane disappearing in the sky.

She observed a thief entering the house.

The children listened to the teacher explaining the theory.

We looked at the magician vanishing in the air.

The difference in meaning between is given below:

'I saw him cross the river.' and 'I saw him crossing the river.'

The first sentence implies that he crossed the river and I saw him do so. In other words, I saw the action from beginning till end (I saw the complete action). The second sentence means that I saw him while he was crossing the river, but it does not mean that I saw him do so from beginning till end. (I saw only a part of the action.) In modern English this difference in meaning is often ignored and the present participle form is usual unless it is necessary to state clearly that the action has been performed.

If the verbs make, see, watch, hear, feel, observe, bid and behold are used in the passive voice, the word 'to' must be used after them; as,

He was seen to go to school.

He was heard to speak at the seminar.

He was made to do the work.

They were watched to enact the play.

She was beheld to attend the meeting.

He was seen to bid farewell.

His heart was felt to throb.

Raju was bidden to keep quiet.

The National flag was held to flutter.

The man was observed to create trouble.

The infinitive without 'to' is used after the verbs 'find', 'know' and 'help'.

For Example:

He finds it pay.

She has never known him drink.

(mostly used in the perfect tense to mean 'experience')

He helped him (to)do the work. (to-infinitive is also common)

The infinitive 'without to' can be used

(*a*) without subject:

All I suggested was (to) make him president.

(*b*) With subject:

Rather than he do it, I would like to do it myself.

The bare or plain infinitive is used after the conjunction 'than'.

For Example:

It is better to resign this job than *suffer* humiliation. (not: 'to suffer')

He would rather die than *surrender.* (not: 'to surrender')

After *better, had better, had rather, would rather, sooner than, rather than* bare infinitive is used; as,

Better *bend* than *break.*

You had better do the work. (It would be better for you to do the work)

You had rather study than play. (It would be better for you to study than play)

I had sooner start than wait. (better for me to start)

The bare infinitive is used after the prepositions 'but' and 'except' when they are preceded by the verb 'do'; as,

We did nothing but *wait.*

I did not do anything except *view T.V.*

The plane infinitive may be used with 'why' or 'why not'.

For Example:

Why *waste* your time?

Why not *spend* some time on reading newspapers.

The plain infinitives drop, fall, fly, go, pass and slip may be combined with 'to let' to form inseparable units; as,

The quiz-master *let fall* a clue.

He let drop a few drops of medicine into her eyes.

The hunter let fly the bird.

He let go the parrot.

The teacher let pass the book to the student.

He let slip a golden chance.

The plain infinitive is used after the phrases *do nothing but, do no more than, etc.*

For Example:

He is doing nothing but find fault with others.

He did no more than accompany her.

The plain infinitives 'believe' and 'do' are combined with 'to make' to form the phrases 'to make believe' meaning ' to pretend' and 'to make do' with something meaning 'manage with something that is not satisfactory'.

For Example:

He made believe that he was poor.

He succeeded in making believe that he was poor. (Not: make believing)

She had to make do with a low income.

She succeeded in making do with a low income. (Not: make doing)

Note: The noun form of 'make-believe' is 'make-believe' itself, and not 'make-belief'.

'To-infinitive' is used absolutely in exclamations and questions

Oh! To believe that he has done such a cruel thing! ('To believe' is used absolutely or independently)

Where to go now?

How to reply?

Why not go to the park?

Why not spend this night with us?

Note: When a to-infinitive is the subject of a sentence the sentence can be rewritten by using 'it' without altering the sense; as,

To sit always is not good for health.

It is not good for health to sit always.

To use offensive language is against decency.

It is against decency to use offensive language.

The to-infinitive 'to come' is used to mean ' in the future' or 'forthcoming'.

For Example:

The prices will come down in days *to come.* (in the future)

These are the shapes of things *to come.* (in the future)

He has received a list of books to come. (forthcoming)

The 'to infinitive' is used after 'the first, the second etc.' and 'the last' and after the adverb 'about'.

He was the first to attend the interview.

He is the second person to get this award.

She was the last to speak.

He is about to come.

The thief was about to enter the house.

The 'to-infinitive' when preceded by an interrogative pronoun like 'what', 'where' etc., or a relative pronoun like 'which', 'whom', etc., is often equivalent to a subordinate clause.

For Example:

She did not know what to say. (She did not know what she was to say.)

I do not know where to go. (I do not know where I am to go.)

She doesn't know how to go about it. (She doesn't know how she is to go about it.)

I do not know which to buy.

I do not know whom to ask.

The 'to-infinitive' of *let, blame* and *seek* may be used predicatively.

For Example:

The room is to let. *Or* (The room is to be let.)

He was not to blame for the fault. *Or* (He was not to be blamed for the fault.)

The reason for the accident is not far to seek.

Note: 'to be blamed' and 'to be let' are sometimes used in place of 'to blame' and 'to let' respectively.

The 'to-infinitive' followed by 'how' is used after 'to know', 'to learn' 'to-forget and 'to teach' to indicate manner or way.

For Example:

I know how to explain it.

He has leaned how to use it.

She has forgotten how to do it.

He taught them how to play the game.

I know how to arrange my books.

Note: The use of 'how' is dispensed with after 'to learn', 'to forget', and 'to teach' if the manner or way is not required to be indicated.

For Example:

She has forgotten to do it.

He has learned to use it.

He taught them to play the game.

When the 'to-infinitive' depends on a noun or an adjective 'for' is used before it.

For Example:

It is for *him* to decide.

It is high time for John to react.

It is too heavy for us to carry it.

It is difficult for anyone to do this work.

Note: In the above examples the noun or pronoun after 'for' may be treated as the subject of the following 'to-infinitive'.

When 'noun or pronoun + to infinitive' is the subject of a sentence for is used before it.

For Example:

For us *to do this work* is very difficult.

The 'to-infinitive' after the verbs 'to want', 'to like', 'to wish', 'to prefer' does the function of an object, the subject being the doer.

He does not want to work.

I prefer to meet the Minister.

I like to play Tennis.

She wishes to go home.

Note: If the action of the subject in the above examples is to be shifted to a personal subject of the infinitive the structure changes as follows:

He does not want *John* to work.

I prefer *him* to meet the Minister.

I like *them* to play Tennis.

She wished *her husband* to go home.

Note: A 'that' subordinate clause may be used after 'to prefer'.

I prefer that he should meet the Minister.

Note: If the second subject does not denote a person, the 'to-infinitive' is not considered the object of the verb in the case of the verbs 'to allow' and 'to permit'.

For Example:

The Principal allowed *enough time* to write the exam.

The traffic authorities permitted *vehicles* to ply.

The 'to-infinitive' is used after verbs like 'to allow', 'to advise' 'to command', 'to ask', 'to permit', 'to enable', 'to encourage', 'to force', 'to persuade', 'to invite', 'to order', 'to request', 'to tell', 'to urge', 'to lead', etc., to express an action one wants to impose on another person.

For Example:

I advised him to behave properly.

He allowed me to think over the matter.

She asked me to quit the place.

The officer commanded his men to attack the enemy.

She enabled me to go abroad.

The audience encouraged the actors to perform better.

The police forced him to surrender.

The committee decided to invite the President.

His advice led me think twice.

A noun or pronoun with a 'to-infinitive' is used after the verb 'expect'. A dependent clause may as well follow it. It may also take a plain infinitive (*i.e.*, to- infinitive) immediately after it.

For Example:

She expects him to accompany her.

The officer expects all his subordinates to do their work properly.

He expects that he will be promoted soon.

We expect to meet him shortly.

'to be' is optional after the verbs 'to nominate', 'to appoint', 'to promote'. Avoid the use of 'as' after these verbs.

For Example:

The government nominated him to be chairman of the committee.

Or The government nominated him chairman of the committee.

He was appointed to be Principal.

Or He was appointed Principal.

But not: He was appointed as Principal.

The 'to-infinitive' is used in the passive constructions with 'to make', 'to know', 'to see', 'to hear', to find', 'to say' etc., with the exception of 'to let'.

For Example:

He was seen to wait at the bus stop.

She was heard to recite the poem.

He was made to suffer.

They were never found to waste time.

He is said to have done it.

He has been known to adhere to principles.

The 'to-infinitive' is sometimes used in the passive.

The criminal was sentenced to be hanged.

He is believed to have been beaten to death.

The prisoner was ordered to be released.

The Split Infinitive:

This is the form in which an adverb is inserted between 'to' and the 'verb'; as,

The CBI has to thoroughly investigate the case.

I failed to really understand the problem.

To split an infinitive (split infinitive) as in the above two examples is considered bad style. But in Modern English especially in informal style 'split infinitive' is quite common as it sometimes helps the sentence convey the meaning as it should.

For Example:

I failed to really understand the problem.

It is not possible for us to shift the adverb 'really' to any other position in the sentence without affecting the meaning. In the normal course the sentence should have been:

I failed to understand the problem really.

This does not really mean the same as:

I failed to really understand the problem.

The latter (underlined) is evidently a better construction although it is against the accepted style. However, it is advised to avoid the use of 'split infinitive' if it is not absolutely necessary.

5.13 THE PARTICIPLE OR VERBAL ADJECTIVE

A word which serves the purpose of both a verb and an adjective is called a Participle or Verbal Adjective.

For Example:

Crossing the road Ramu met with an accident. (Ramu while crossing the road ...)

Here, the word crossing is the 'ing' form of the verb 'cross'. This word qualifies the noun Ramu. Hence it has duel functions: It acts both as a verb and as an Adjective. Such a word (as 'crossing') is called a *participle.* It is sometimes referred to as a *'Verbal Adjective'.*

For Example:

Hearing the news about the earthquake many people came out of their houses.

Reading the novel he fell asleep.

Playing football he enjoyed himself.

Different forms of the participle:

(*a*) The Present Participle

(*b*) The Past Participle

(*c*) The Perfect Participle

The Present Participle

The present participle is used to express an action which is continuing and which is incomplete. Present participles are formed by adding 'ing' to the root (original) form of the verb.

For Example:

I am reading .

I was reading.

I shall be reading. (read+ing)

The Past Participle

Past participles are used to express a completed action. They usually end in -en, -ed, -d, -t, -n or –ne.

For Example:

Insulted by his colleagues he committed suicide.

It is a forgone conclusion.

He is a retired officer.

She is a burnt child.

He is a man with a broken heart.

It is a faded flower.

The Perfect Participle

Perfect participles are used to denote an action which was completed sometime in the past before another action in the past. They are formed by using 'having' before the past participle of the verb (*i.e.*, having + past participle) in the Active voice and by using 'having been' before the past participle of the verb (having + been+ past participle) in the Passive voice.

For Example:

Having finished reading he went to bed.

(After he had finished reading he went to bed)

(Having finished reading – First action; he went to bed- Second action)

Having been dismissed from service he left the country.

(After he had been dismissed.....

Use of the past participles of transitive verbs: The past participle of a transitive verb should not be used in the active voice. It should be used only in the passive voice.

For Example:

His politically *inspired* speech had a telling effect on the audience.

(the verb 'inspire' is transitive) When expanded, the sentence will take the following form:

His speech *which was politically inspired* had a telling effect on the audience.

I ate a candy *made* of sugar.(I ate a candy *that was made of sugar*)

Note: The sentence ' The officer, arrived from Trivandrum yesterday, is staying here' is wrong because the verb 'arrive' is an intransitive verb. When expanded this sentence will take the form ' The officer who *was* arrived from Trivandrum yesterday is staying here ' which is absurd. The sentence should therefore be ' The officer who arrived from Trivandrum yesterday is staying here'. Here 'arrived' is used as the past tense of the finite verb 'arrive', and not as its past participle. In such cases, the relative pronoun must be used after the noun so as to make the verb a finite one.

Use of the participles of intransitive verbs:

(*i*) The Past participle of intransitive verbs is not normally used.
If at all it is used, it must be placed before a noun.

For Example:

He is a *retired* person. (retire- intransitive)

It is a *faded* flower. (fade-intransitive)

We paid homage to the *departed* leader. (depart-intransitive)

Satan is a *fallen* angel. (fall-intransitive)

(*ii*) The past participle is sometimes used to show certain 'state' or 'character' ;as,

He has a well-shaven face.

Raju is a well-dressed boy.

Ram is a well-behaved man.

He is an outspoken man.

Seeta is a hard-hearted woman.

He is a thick-skinned man.

Bat is a warm-blooded animal.

(*iii*) The Participle may be used attributively to qualify a noun or pronoun; as,

For Example:

It was a *thrilling* experience.

I saw a *boring* picture.

He is an *outspoken* politician.

5.14 THE GERUND (VERBAL NOUN)

A gerund is a form of the verb ending in 'ing' and does the functions of a noun and a verb. It can be used as a subject, predicate or object and as the object of a proposition.

For Example:

Seeing is believing.

Here the word 'seeing' is formed by adding 'ing' to the verb 'see'.

It is used in the above sentence as the subject of the verb 'is'. It therefore does the function of a noun.

In other words , the word 'seeing' has in it the power of a verb and that of a noun. *It is therefore a verbal noun and is called a gerund.*

In short, a gerund is a verbal noun. A gerund is sometimes called a participial noun because both the gerund and the present participle are formed by adding 'ing' to the verb.

Note: The difference between the gerund and the present participle should be well understood.

For Example:

Running is a good exercise.

(gerund- Here 'running' is treated as a noun and is the subject of the verb 'is')

I saw him *running* along the road. (present participle – qualifies the pronoun 'him')

While the gerund is a verbal noun the present participle is a verbal adjective. They are same in form but different in their uses.

Examine the following sentence:

I do not like you meeting her.

In the above sentence, 'you' is the object of the verb 'like'.

It is qualified by the present participle 'meeting'. But, what ' I do not like' is not *you*, but 'your *meeting* her' which is the real object of the verb *like*. The given sentence does not therefore convey the real meaning. The sentence should therefore be recast as follows:

I do not like your meeting her. (Here, *meeting* is a gerund or verbal noun which is qualified by the possessive adjective *your*.)

Relation between the Gerund and the Infinitive

Since both the Gerund and the Infinitive have the same nature as that of the Verbal Noun they are interchangeable. The sentence, "Seeing is believing" is equivalent in all respects to the sentence "To see is to believe".

He taught me to read.

He taught me reading.

Both the sentences convey the same meaning.

Difference in the use of the Verbal Noun and the Gerund

Although Verbal nouns and Gerunds are considered to be one and the same there is a subtle difference between them in their uses.

For Example:

(*i*) Teaching English is interesting. (Here, 'teaching' is used as a Gerund)

(*ii*) The teaching of English is interesting. (Here, 'teaching' is Verbal Noun)

In the second example the definite article 'the' is used before and the proposition 'of' after the word 'teaching'. It is used like an ordinary noun.

This distinction is not strictly observed in Modern English.

But, remember whenever 'of' is used after a gerund, 'the' must be used before it or leave out both as in the examples given below.

For Example:

The writing of the novel is over. *Or* Writing the novel is over.

The making of the table is not complete. *Or* Making the table is not complete.

Compound Gerund forms

Compound gerund forms are made by using a past participle a verb after 'having' or 'being'.

For Example:

I heard of his having come to Delhi.

We have come to know of his having been arrested.

The thief is afraid of being caught by the police.

Gerund is used in the following compound nouns.

Writing table - a table for writing

Walking stick - a stick for walking

Looking glass - a glass for looking

Cooking vessel - a vessel for cooking

Cleaning brush - a brush for cleaning

Note: Some compounds in 'ing' may appear gerund compounds, but they are actually participle compounds.

For Example:

a barking dog – a dog that is barking.

a crying child – a child that is crying.

a flying bird – a bird that is flying.

The possessive (or genitive) of nouns and pronouns are used before gerunds; as ,

(*a*) The teacher insisted on my doing homework. ('my' is the subject of the gerund 'doing')

(*b*) Every thing depends on *his* getting admission to a professional course.

('his' is the subject of the gerund 'getting')

(*c*) We are happy about *his* getting appointed chairman.

(*d*) The judge insisted on *Raju's* coming to the court.

(The genitive *Raju's* is the subject of the gerund 'coming')

Exception: (1) The name of an object should not be in the possessive (or genitive) if an inanimate object is followed by a gerund.

For Example:

There is no danger of the house collapsing. (not: ....the house's collapsing.)

There is a chance of the train coming early. (not:......the train's coming)

Note: In modern English the use of the genitive (or possessive) personal names/pronouns before a gerund is not insisted upon. This is because some words have no genitive (or possessive) at all. The pronouns 'this', 'that', 'each', etc., come under this category. According to strict grammatical rules the possessive adjectives my, his, her, our, your, their, its of pronouns are to be used with gerunds (formal), but it is very common now to use the objective (accusative) personal pronouns *me, him, her, us, you, them, it* instead (informal).

For Example:

I don't like your following me. (formal)

Or

I don't like you following me. (informal)

I don't mind John's talking to her.

Or

I don't mind John talking to her.

He doesn't like his brother's meeting her.

Or

He doesn't like his brother meeting her.

Study the following sentence:

There is no possibility of that being false.

In the above sentence it is not possible to use the possessive or genitive of 'that' (the subject of the gerund 'being') because it does not have either. Although 'being' is a participle qualifying 'that', the preposition 'of' is treated as governing the whole phrase 'that being false', thus making it a gerund. It may be called a 'participle-gerund or half gerund'. In other words, the object of the preposition 'of' is not 'that' but it is the whole phrase 'that being false'. The same is true in the case of some word-groups which cannot be put in the genitive.

For Example:

He cannot remember his neighbours ever being hostile to him.

I like my friends and well- wishers coming to my house.

I cannot permit anyone going out.

In spite of my parents and sisters being poor, they don't go to anyone for help.

They objected to John and me attending the meeting.

There is no need of both of us going there.

Impersonal Gerunds

These are gerunds without the subject.

Examine the following sentence:

Walking is good for the health.

In this sentence no subject is explicitly mentioned for the gerund 'walking'.

As it is a general statement we may rewrite the sentence as follows:

(One's) walking is good for the health.

Similarly, ' Smoking is injurious to health' means (One's) smoking is injurious to health.

In the two examples given above the gerunds 'walking' and 'smoking' are impersonal.

Omission of the subject of a gerund

When the subject of a gerund and that of the sentence in which it is used are the same the subject of the gerund is omitted.

For Example:

She does not like eating fish. (Don't say: She does not like her eating fish.)

I don't mind going there. (Don't say: I don't like my going there)

Uses of the Gerund:

(*i*) Being a verbal noun a gerund does all the functions of a noun.

It may therefore be used as

(*a*) subject of a verb.

For Example:

Smoking is injurious to health.

Walking is a good exercise.

(*b*) object of a transitive verb.

For Example:

I enjoy reading novels.

They like playing cards.

(*c*) complement of a verb.

For Example:

Seeing is *believing*. ('believing' is the complement of the verb 'is'.)

His hobby is *reading* novels.

(*d*) object of a preposition.

For Example:

He is accustomed *to* having bath in the morning.

He is fond *of* drinking milk.

(*ii*) The gerund is sometimes used absolutely; as,

Reading books being his hobby, we bought him some latest books.

Coming late to the office being his habit, the officer does not like him.

(*iii*) The gerund is used after the verbs excuse, enjoy, avoid, dislike, deny, intend, like, remember, mind, stop, admit, resent, defer, dread, fancy, forgive, anticipate, regret etc.

For Example:

The teacher excused my coming late.

He enjoys cooking.

He avoided meeting his enemy.

He dislikes drinking wine.

He denied having taken the book.

I intend going to Chennai.

He likes eating banana.

He remembered *meeting* her.(Here 'meeting' is the first action and 'remembering' is the second. In other words, he recalled (brought back to his mind) his meeting her sometime in the past.)

Note: He remembered *to meet* her.(Here 'remembering' is the first action and 'meeting her' is the second one. In other words, he did not forget to meet her.)

Important: This distinction must be borne in mind when the verb 'remember' is used with a gerund or an infinitive.

Examine the following sentences:

I don't mind meeting him.

The verb 'mind' is usually followed by a gerund. It can also be followed by an 'if clause'. It is mainly used in negative and interrogative sentences.

For Example:

Would you mind giving your pen? (A request meaning ' please give me your pen'.)

I don't mind helping him.

Do you mind if I smoke? (This is equivalent to ' Would you mind my smoking?')

Would you mind not using slippers in the room?

(It is a request meaning 'Please don't use slippers in the room'.)

He stopped working. (meaning ' He ceased to work')

On the way he stopped to buy a book. (stop meaning 'halt')

He admitted having accepted bribe.

They resented his becoming the president.

The officer deferred taking a decision on the matter.

I dread facing the police.

He fancied becoming an actor.

They forgave his behaving rudely.

He imagined acting the role of Gandhiji.

He did not anticipate meeting his uncle in the bar.

The teacher pardoned his making a noise in the class.

I regretted *meeting* him.

(Here 'meeting' is the first event and 'regretting' is the second. In other words, I am sorry that I have met him)

Note: I regret *to convey* this sad news. (Here 'regretting' is the first action and 'conveying' is the second. In other words, I regret that I have to convey this sad news.)

Causative Verbs

A causative verb expresses a cause. In a sentence using a causative verb the subject himself does not carry out the act, but it is carried out by someone for him. The causative verb helps cause the actual action. *Make, help, have, get etc*. are causative verbs.

For Example:

He repaired his TV. (meaning 'He himself repaired it')

He got his TV repaired (meaning ' Somebody repaired his TV for him.)-causative.

He cried.

They made him cry. (causative)

He has done it.

He has got it done. (causative)

He felt sad.

I made him feel sad. (causative)

She understood the meaning.

They made her understand the meaning. (causative)

Post the letter.

Get the letter posted. (causative)

He stood on the bench.

They made him stand on the bench. (causative)

Note: If a sentence is in the active voice the 'to-infinitive' is not used after the causative verbs 'make' and 'help'.

For Example:

I made him feel. (right)

I made him to feel. (wrong)

He helped her do the work. (right)

He helped her to do the work. (wrong)

But, if the sentence is in the passive voice the 'to-infinitive' should be used.

For Example:

He was made *to do* the work.

He was helped by his mother *to do* his homework.

Auxiliary Verbs (contd.):

An auxiliary verb is one that helps another verb (called the principal or ordinary verb) to form the tense, voice , mood and other forms.

The following are the auxiliaries:

be, have, do, can, could, may, might, shall, should, will, would, must, ought, used, need and dare.

Note: The auxiliaries can, could, may, might, shall, should, will, would, must, ought, used, need and dare are known as Modal auxiliaries or Modals.

These auxiliaries are sometimes called Anomalous or Special verbs because these verbs invariably come before the subject in the formation of Interrogative sentences. They also combine with 'n't' in the formation of negatives.

For Example:

Have you a brother ?

Can I help you ?

Should I do it ?

I can't go there.

You haven't given the book.

We shouldn't go there.

The following auxiliaries have different forms (Inflections). They change their forms according to the number and the person of the subject:

be, have and do.

The different forms of 'be' are: *am, is, are, been* and *being*.

'Has' is the only inflection of 'have' and 'does' is the only inflection of 'do'.

The auxiliaries *can, shall, will, may, must, need, ought, dare and used have the same form in all persons and numbers; as,*

He can do it. They can do it.

('Can' does not change even though the subjects are different in number.)

The auxiliaries given below are followed by either 'to–infinitive' or infinitive 'without to' (bare infinitive):

(*a*) The auxiliaries *be(its different forms), have, ought, and used (to)* take ' to-infinitive' after them; as,

I am to do this work.

He has to go to school.

He ought to observe the rules.

I used to get up early in the morning.

(*b*) The auxiliaries do, can, may, must, will and shall, take 'infinitive without to' (bare infinitive) after them; as,

I can do it.

He does the work.

They may come.

We must do it.

I shall meet you.

You will get the money.

The auxiliary 'have':

(*a*) 'Have' (including 'has' and 'had') is used with the past participle of a verb to form perfect tense.

For Example:

They have gone.

They had gone.

They will have gone.

They should have gone.

It has been done.

(*b*) When 'have' is followed by a 'to-infinitive' it indicates obligation

For Example:

I have to help him. (meaning 'I must help him'.)

I had to go. (meaning 'I was obliged to go' – past obligation)

(*c*) **Use of 'have got' instead of the auxiliary 'have'**

These are interchangeable without any difference in meaning when used in the affirmative, negative and interrogative sentences provided *they do not* begin with the word 'do'.

(*i*) Affirmative.

For Example:

I have got to do it.

I have to do it.

(*ii*) Negative.

I haven't got to do it.

I haven't to do it.

(*iii*) Interrogative.

Have I got to do it?

Have I to do it?

(*iv*) Examine the following sentence:

I employed someone to wash my shirt.

This sentence may also be written in the following form:

I had my shirt washed. ('Who washed my shirt' is not at all important here and therefore this is a better construction.)

More examples of this type of construction are given below:

I had my pants stitched. (instead of saying ' I employed a tailor to stitch my pants.)

I am having my hair cut.

I was having my hair cut.

Do you have your hair cut regularly?

I don't have my clothes washed. I wash them myself.

Important: The order of words in the above construction may carefully be noted as any change in the order will alter the meaning.

The order of words is ' have/had (having) + object + past participle of the verb'.

Use of 'have' as an ordinary verb

When 'have' is used as an ordinary verb it means 'possess'

For Example:

She has brown hair.

I have a dozen novels.

'Have' and 'have got' forms can be used in this case in both the present and past tenses without any change in the meaning.

For Example:

He has/had a blue shirt.

He has/had got a blue shirt.

With 'do' and 'does' we use 'have' for habitual action.

For Example:

Does he have egg every day?

He doesn't have egg every day.

They don't have liquor with dinner.

Do you have bath every day?

'Have' can also be used to mean *receive (guest), take (a meal), give (a party) , experience (difficulty), encounter (trouble), enjoy* etc.

In this case

(*i*) 'got' is not used after it.

(*ii*) it can be used in the continuous tenses.

(*iii*) the do-construction is used in the negative and interrogative sentences.

For Example:

I usually *have* my breakfast at eight.	(eat)
We *have* a party tonight.	(give)
When he came to see me I was having my lunch.	(taking)
Does he have any trouble with his neighbour?	(experience)
I have a guest from Germany.	(receive)
He didn't have supper yesterday.	
They are having a get-together tomorrow.	(future)
Did you have a nice time at the exhibition?	(enjoy)

'Have' is not followed by 'got' when parts of the human body are referred to.

For Example:

Human beings have only two hands.	(Don't say: ….have got only two hands)
He has only one eye.	(Don't say: He has got only one eye)

'Have' is sometimes used to mean 'to experience', 'to permit' 'to wish', 'to get' (usually with 'would', and 'would have')

For Example:

We won't have you do such things. (We do not want you to do such things.)

We would have the UN control all the nations.

(We would like the UN to control all the nations.)

He had a very unusual thing happen to him last night.

(He had a very unusual experience last night.)

We have our servant do all work.

(We have all our work done by our servant.)

I like to have my parents stay with me. (I wish my parents to stay with me.)

The auxiliaries 'need' and 'dare':

(*a*) Need – (necessity or obligation). When used without 'do' it has no inflected forms (*For Example:* Needs and needed) and it takes infinitive without 'to' after it in negative and interrogative sentences and also in sentences containing the words 'scarcely' and 'hardly' which are semi-negative.

For Example:

He need not do it (negative)

Need I help him? (question)

They need hardly take his advice.

She need scarcely believe it.

When 'need' is used as an ordinary verb it changes according to the person and the number of the subject (*i.e.*, it takes inflected forms like 'needs' and 'needed') and it takes the 'to-infinitive' form of the verb after it. It is used with 'do' in negative sentences and questions. It is sometimes used without 'do' in affirmative sentences too; as,

For Example:

He does not need to do it.

Do I need to attend the meeting?

He needs to be alert. (affirmative)

She needs my help.

They need food and shelter.

Note: affirmative X negative.

(*b*) Dare - (To be brave enough to do something)

The auxiliary verb 'dare' (to be brave enough to do something) is different from the ordinary verb 'dare' (challenge). The former does not take's' in the third person singular present tense. It is usually used in negative and interrogative (questions) sentences. When used without 'do' it takes an infinitive without 'to'. When used with 'do' it is followed by an infinitive with or without 'to'.

For Example:

How dare you speak to me?

She dare not go to him.

She dare not face her husband.

They dared not go to the police station.

She does not dare (to) do such a thing.

He dares me to find out the truth about the murder.

Note: Can, could, may, might are usually used to indicate different levels of possibility.

1. 'Can' is used to indicate theoretical possibility while 'may' is used to indicate practical possibility.

   For Example:

   He can do the job.

   (He has got the capacity to do the job. But, it is not sure whether he will do it.)

   He may do the job. (He is likely to do the job.)

   They can win the trophy.

   They may win the trophy.

   He can improve his performance.

   (Meaning: His performance is not up to the mark. He is to improve it.)

   He may improve his performance.

   (He has got some idea to improve his performance.)

2. 'Can' is used to mean 'sometimes'

   For Example:

   Snake bite can be fatal. (Snake bite is sometimes fatal.)

   Liquor can be injurious to health.

3. To indicate impossibility we always use 'can't'.

   For Example:

   He can't do this work. (It is impossible for him to do this work.)

   He may not do the work. (It is possible that he will not do this work.)

   Can he do this work? (Is it possible for him to do this work?)

4. May + perfect tense will indicate the present possibility of something happened in the past.

   For Example:

   He may have missed the train. (He has possibly missed the train.)

   My parents have not yet come. They may have cancelled the programme.

5. For past possibility we use 'could'.

For Example:

In those days they could send him to England.

In my younger days I could run a long distance.

6. 'Could' and 'might' are sometimes used to express hypothetical/theoretical and uncertain possibility.

For Example:

If the plan were to be approved, the drawing could /might be altered.

(Hypothetical possibility)

She could/might be giving wrong information. (Uncertain or tentative possibility).

(It is possible that she is giving wrong information.)

Could you have forgotten to take your book?

(Is it possible that you have forgotten to take the book?)

7. To express weaker possibility we can use 'should' and 'ought to'.

For Example:

He should be in the office by now. (He is likely to be in the office by now.)

Or

He ought to be in the office by now. (He is likely to be in the office by now.)

Compare: He must be in the office. (He is *certainly* in the office.)

8. Improbability is indicated by 'shouldn't' and 'oughtn't.

For Example:

There shouldn't be any objection. (It is improbable that there will be any objection.)

There oughtn't to be any problem. (It is improbable that there will be any problem.)

Errors in the use of verbs ;

1. I am twenty years old and she sixteen. (wrong)

   I am twenty years old and she is sixteen. (right)

   Here, the verb 'am' is made to serve two subjects namely 'I' and "she'.

   This is wrong. Hence the correction.

2. I have never and I will never call him fool. (wrong)

   I have never called and I will never call him a fool.

   Here, two auxiliaries are made to agree with the verb "call". This is wrong because the correct form of call after 'have' is called and not call. Hence the correction. This wrong sentence can be corrected as follows.

   I have never called him a fool and I will never.

3. Ten M.L.As have attended the meeting and one boycotted it. (wrong)

   Ten M.L.As have attended the meeting and one has boycotted it.

   Here plural and singular nouns are made to agree with same Auxiliary verb 'have'. Hence the correction.

4. These points were discussed in the meeting and a decision taken . (wrong)

   Here 'were' is made to agree with both 'points' (plural) and 'decision' (singular). It may be corrected as follows:

   These points were discussed in the meeting and a decision was taken. (or)

   These points were discussed in the meeting and decisions taken.

Errors in the use of Gerunds and Infinitive

1. Raju is interested to read novels. (say: Raju is interested in reading novels.) The phrase is 'interested in'. After the preposition use only either noun or a gerund.
2. Would you mind to come with me. (say: Would you mind coming with me. Gerund should be used after the following verbs : enjoy, prevent, avoid, deny, stop, forgive, finish, consider, keep, delay, resist, postpone, resent, understand.
3. We have heard of him winning the award. (say ... of his winning.)
4. I was delighted to see him. (say: I was ... at seeing him.)
5. He was ashamed to come to me. (say: ... ashamed of coming to me)
6. We enjoyed to play the game. (Say: We enjoyed playing the game.)
7. His hobby is to sing. (say: His ... is singing)
8. He aims to get a first class. (say: He aims at getting a first class)
9. I insisted to see the officer. (say: I insisted on seeing the officer)
10. He worked hard with a view to get a rank. (say: He ... with a view to getting a rank. In Modern English 'with a view to get' is considered correct.)
11. I am capable to do that job. (say: I am capable of doing that job)
12. I am used to eat rice. (say: ... used to eating rice)
13. He was busy to prepare for his exam. (say: He is busy preparing for his exam.)
14. The exhibition is worth to see. (say: The exhibition is worth seeing)
15. We should avoid to smoke. (say: We should avoid smoking.)
16. I can't help to criticize. (say: I can't help criticizing.)

    Note: Verbs like enjoy, remember, avoid, stop, finish, hate and intend will take gerunds after them.

    The verbs begin, like and dislike can take either 'to–infinitive' or 'gerund' without change in meaning; as,

    He began to read. He began reading.

    He likes to read. He likes reading.

    He dislikes to read. He dislikes reading.

17. I have great pleasure to invite you to the party . (say: ....pleasure in inviting.......)
18. He was desirous to go to Madras. (say: He ....desirous of going ....)
19. It is no use to cry over spilt milk. (say; ......use crying over....)

    Note: Phrases like look forward to; to take pride in, bent upon, passion for, to charge with and persist in are always followed by gerunds.)

20. There is possibility of Ramu's being questioned. (say: There....... of Ramu being questioned.)

    Note: If a noun is used in the passive sense possessive form of the noun should not be used before the gerund.

21. The danger of a war's breaking out is remote. (say: The danger of a war breaking out is remote.)

    Note: If the name of an inanimate thing comes before the gerund, the possessive form of the name (noun) should not be used.

22. I don't remember to have seen you. (say: I don't remember seeing you.)

    Note: When you remember a past event use only the gerund form. If you want to draw the attention of a person what he has to do in the future, use 'to-infinitive' of the verb after remember, as;

Remember to do your homework.

Similar is the case with the following verbs; attempt, continue, forget, hate, intend, bear, love, prefer, regret, try, see, watch, allow, advise, forbid, start, stop, propose.

The following adjectives also follow the same rule; sorry, certain, interested, afraid, sure, used, accustomed.

For Example:

(1) Sorry to interrupt you. (When we are apologetic about doing something).

When we say " we are sorry for wounding your feelings."

Or

When we say; " we are sorry for having wounded your feelings" we mean we are apologetic about what we have already done.

(2) "I like playing cricket" means I really enjoy playing cricket.

" I like to play cricket" means I prefer or choose to play cricket.

(3) I advise you to take a season ticket.

I advise taking a season ticket.

In the first sentence there is a personal object. If there is a personal object we use the to-infinitive form of the verb 'advise'.

In the second sentence there is no personal object. If there is no personal object we use the 'ing' form of the verb.

The verbs *permit, allow,* and *forbid* follow the same rule.

(4) When I entered the hall I heard him speaking.

Note: When we hear only part of an event we use 'ing' form with 'hear'.

I heard him speak. (Meaning: I heard him from beginning till end)

The verbs 'see' and 'watch' follow the same rule.

Verbs used as nouns and vice versa

Verbs used as nouns:

Go (*v*)- He goes to school.

Go (*n*) singular – He ate the whole cake at/in one go. (in one attempt)

Goes (*n*)- plural – (more than one attempt)- It took many goes for him to get his grievances redressed.

Read (*v*)- He reads a novel.

Read (*n*)- He likes to have a quite read at home.

Cry (*v*)- He cried aloud.

Cry (*n*)- She had a good cry.

Boil (*v*)- Water boils at 100 degree centigrade.

Boil (*n*)- The milk is on the boil.

Make (*v*)- He made a kite.

Make(*n*)- This is new make of TV.

Divide (*v*)- He has divided the cake into three equal parts.

Divide (*n*)- Watershed- The highlands stand as a divide between the two river systems. (highlands- an area of land at a high level consisting of hills and mountains)

Have (*v*)- We have a good system of water supply.

Haves (*n*)- The haves should help the have-nots.

(Rich people should help poor people or The rich should help the poor)

Repeat (*v*)- The teacher asked the student to repeat the lines.

Repeat (*n*)- This serial on TV is a repeat. (of an old one)

Must (auxiliary verb)-You must obey your parents.

Must (*n*) This book is a must for every student.

Wash out (*v*)- The mark on your shirt won't wash out.

Wash out (*n*)- The open-air programme was a wash out. (a complete failure)

Field (*v*)- Kerala fielded a strong team for the match.

Field (*n*)- There is a field in front of the house.

Elbow (*v*)- He elbowed his way through the crowd.

Elbow (*n*)- When he fell down his elbow got fractured.

Nouns used as verbs

Back (*n*)- He lay on the back.

Back (*v*)- This political party backed us in the recent election.

Better (*n*)- Always listen to your elders and betters.

(betters- people having higher status in society)

Better (*v*)- Forget the past and try to better your future.

Close (*n*)- The journey came to a close.

Close (*v*)- He closed the door.

Down (*n*)- There are ups and down in life.

Down (*v*)- The shop downed its shutters.

Fast (*n*)- Observing fast once a month is good for health.

Fast (*v*)- The trade union leaders fasted for a day as a protest against certain government policies.

Last (*n*)- We have come to the last of the meeting.

Last (*v*)- The rain lasted for a few days.

Like (*n*)- The question of likes and dislikes does not arise.

Like (*v*)- He likes eating sweets.

Need (*n*)- Our needs are limited.

Need (*v*)- We need food and water for survival.

Right (*n*)- Freedom of speech is our fundamental right.

Right (*v*)- She righted the wrong.

Round (*n*)- The Police officer was on his routine rounds.

Round (*v*)- He rounded the corner of the glass.

Still (*n*)- The stills taken by the photographer were lost.

Still (*v*)- He stilled the crying child.

Wrong (*n*)- Two wrongs don't make a right.

Wrong (*v*)- He wronged his friends.

Motor (*n*)- The motor of the engine went faulty.

Motor (*v*)- He motored along the highway.

Mother (*n*)- She is a mother of two children.

Mother (*v*)- She mothered the orphans.

Dog (*n*)- When a dog bites a man it is not news.
When a man bites a dog it is news.

Dog (*v*)- The police dogged the suspected criminal. (followed)

Adjectives used as verbs

Black (*a*)- He has black hair.

Black (*v*)- He has blackened his hair.

Back (*a*)- The news appeared on the back page.

Back (*v*)- Our party backed him in the recent election.

Better (*a*)- It is a better proposal.

Better (*v*)- He is trying to better his future.

Close (*a*)- My house is in close proximity to the market.

Close (*v*)- He closed his business.

Down (*a*)- The system was down yesterday.

Down (*v*)- He downed the shutters of his shop.

Like (*a*)- They are people of like mind.

Like (*v*)- He likes his teacher very much.

Right (*a*)- His right hand was wounded.

Right (*v*)- He righted his wrong.

Verbs derived from verbs and other parts of speech.

To Antedate (predate)- He Antedated his letter. (date-noun)

To belittle – He belittled his friend. (made his friend unimportant)(little-adjective)

To bemoan- She bemoaned her father's death. (moan-verb)

To besmear- He besmeared his body with oil. (smear-verb)

To blacken- She blackened her hair. (black-adjective)

To deepen- The crisis deepened. (deep-adjective)

To roughen- Anger roughened his voice. (rough-adjective)

To shorten- She shortened her hair.(rough-adjective)

To co-operate- We should co-operate with our friends. (operate-verb)

To counteract- The medicine counteracted the effect of poison. (act-verb)

To counterbalance- The weight counterbalanced the load. (balance- verb)

To counter-attack- The army counter-attacked the enemy. (attack-verb/noun)

To de-code- The police de-coded the secret message. (opposite of the verb code-verb)

To de-train- The troop de-trained. (the train-verb from the noun train)

To de-frost- She defrosted the fridge. (frost-noun)

To de-mobilize- The army chief de-mobilized some soldiers. (mobilize-Verb)

To de-nationalize- Government of India de-nationalized certain banks. (nationalize-verb)

To de-humanize- The witch de-humanized the captive. (nationalize-verb)

To de-hydrate- The machine de-hydrated the fruit. (hydrate-verb)

To destabilize- There was agitation to destabilize the government. (stabilize-verb)

To discourage- (dis- This makes the verb negative.)

She discouraged him from taking liquors. (opposite of encourage)

To disagree- He agreed to disagree with him.

To disbelieve- She disbelieved him.

To dishonour- He tried to dishonour her.

To empower- (em- used only before the nouns beginning with the letters 'b' and 'p'.)

The government took initiative to empower women. (to give power)

To embed- Diamonds were embedded in a gold locket.

To empanel- He was empanelled in the list of jury.

To endanger- She endangered his chances of becoming a minister.

To sub-edit- The article was sub-edited. (editor-noun)

To transplant- The surgeon has successfully transplanted donor's kidney into another man. (plant- verb)

To undress- She undressed and went into the bathroom. (dress-verb)

To unbutton- He unbuttoned his shirt. (button-verb)

Unearth- The police unearthed the secret. (earth-verb)

Chapter **6**

AGREEMENT OF THE VERB WITH THE SUBJECT

A thorough knowledge of the agreement of the verb with the subject is quite necessary to write correct English. The following guidelines should be carefully noted:

(*a*) A finite verb must agree with its subject in number and person.

For Example:

Raju likes to play.	(Subject : Third person singular. Verb: singular)
Raju and Rama like to play.	(Plural subject – third person; plural verb)
She goes to school.	(Singular subject – Third person; singular verb)
They go to school.	(Plural subject – third person; plural verb)
I want to play.	(Singular subject – first person; plural verb)
We are friends.	(Plural subject – first person; plural verb)

(*b*) Two or more singular subjects joined by 'and' (called compound subjects) take a verb in the plural; as,

Raju and Ramu are friends.

He and his friend are coming here.

They go to the temple every day.

Raju, Ramu and Seeta are classmates.

(*c*) If two singular nouns joined by 'and' refer to the same person or thing the verb must be in the singular.

The proprietor and manager is present.

(Proprietor and manager are one and the same person.)

The secretary and manager is a good orator.

Note: The definite article 'the' is used only once in both the examples.

Note: If two singular nouns joined by 'and' refer to different persons or things, the article should be used before each noun, and the verb should be plural.

The editor and the publisher *are* present. (two different persons)

A red and a blue sarees *are* on display. (two sarees)

A red and blue saree *is* on display. (only one saree)

(*d*) If two subjects or nouns joined by 'and' express one idea, the verb should be in the singular.

Bread and butter is our food. (Here both bread and butter represent food)

Slow and steady wins the race.

The long and the short of the matter is this.

(*or*)

The long and short of the matter is this. (The second 'the' is optional)

Truth and honesty pays always.

Rice and curry is our daily food. (Here food consists of rice and curry.)

(*e*) If singular subjects joined by 'and' are preceded by each or every, the verb should be in the singular.

Each boy and girl is responsible for this.

Every man and woman is to be considered.

Every teacher, boy and girl was present.

Each boy and each girl is to blame.

Each and every book is readable.

(*f*) When two singular subjects are joined by 'not only ... but also' the verb should be singular. But, if the subjects differ in number, person or both, the verb should agree with the nearer subject.

Not only Raju but also Ramu is responsible for this loss.

Not only you but also I am interested in it.

(*g*) When subjects differing in number, person or both are connected by 'and' the verb should be in the plural.

For Example:

Raju and I are friends.

Raju and his sisters are present.

My sisters and Geetha are in the same class.

You and I are responsible for this confusion.

(*h*) (*i*) When two or more singular subjects of the same person are joined by 'or', 'nor' 'either....or' or 'neither...nor' the verb should be in the singular; as,

Raju or his brother is going to attend the meeting.

Neither he nor his brother is innocent.

Either John or Jack is to blame.

Either Leela, Seeta or their father is at fault.

(*ii*) When two or more singular subjects connected by or, nor, either ....or, neither....nor are of different person *the verb* agrees with the nearer/the nearest subject.

Either he or you are expected to be present.

Neither you nor I *was* present.

Either you or his friend *is* to blame.

Either I or she *is* at fault.

Either he or you *are* to come.

Either Ram, Gopi or I *am* to attend the meeting.

(*i*) When one of the subjects connected by or, nor, either....or, etc. is singular and the other plural, *the plural subject must be placed immediately before the verb so as to make the verb plural.*

For Example:

No Minister or MLAs have come. (Not: No MLAs or Minister has come)

Neither the boy nor the girls were to blame.

Either John or his parents were aware of it.

Neither Ram nor his friends were present.

Note: Neither Ram was present nor were his friends.

(This type of construction is preferred in all the above examples in this category.)

(*j*) When two singular subjects are joined by 'as well as' the verb should be in the singular.

Ramu as well as his father has gone to Bombay.

He as well as she is employed.

Note: When the subjects joined by 'as well as' differ in number, person or both the verb should agree with the first subject ; as,

She as well as her friends *has done* it.

They as well as he *are* responsible for this.

He as well as you *is* my friend.

Note: Singular subjects joined by words 'with', 'together with', 'in addition to', 'along with' etc. take singular verb; as,

He, together with his parents, is capable of doing it.

Raju, in addition to his sisters, has done it.

Raju, along with his brothers, is traveling by train.

(*k*) When the subject of a verb is a Relative Pronoun the verb should agree in number and person with the antecedent of the relative pronoun.

You, who *are* a reporter, should report news correctly. ('you' is the antecedent of 'who'.)

I, who *am* your neighbour, want your help.

He who *is* my benefactor came yesterday.

Raju is one of the boys who *study* well.

He who *loves* lives.

(*l*) Collective nouns generally take a singular verb. But they take plural verb when the individual members constituting the group are thought of; as,

The committee has agreed to the proposal.

(Here the committee is thought of as a whole –all the members of the committee have agreed to the proposal – unanimous proposal.)

The committee were divided on the matter.

(Here all the members constituting the committee did not agree on the matter ; some disagreed.)

The Government has decided to grant subsidy.

(The government is considered a single body.)

The Government have decided to give relief to fisherman.

(Here 'the Government' stands for the ministry concerned.

It is considered to be consisting of a number of ministries.)

The parliament was adjourned sine die.

The Parliament were divided in their opinion.

The majority stands united.

The majority are divided on the matter.

(*m*) Words like 'news', 'wages', 'politics' and 'mathematics' which are plural in form but singular in number take singular verbs; as,

The news *is* good.

The wages of sin *is* death. (When 'wages' is used to mean punishment for doing something bad it is considered singular. When it is used to mean the amount of money received for working, it is considered plural.)

Wages are paid on Saturdays.

Mathematics *is* a difficult subject. (as a science)

Politics is an interesting subject. (When the word is used to mean 'activities involved in getting power' or to mean 'political science'.)

(*n*) Words like people, cattle and sheep are singular in form but plural in number; as,

The people of India are peace loving.

The cattle are brought from North India.

Sheep are domestic animals.

(*o*) Some plural nouns denoting some quantity or amount thought of as a whole generally take a singular verb.

For Example:

Fifty rupees *is* a small amount.

Five kilometers *is* not a long distance.

Ten litres of oil *is* sufficient for a day.

Two and a half kilograms of rice *is* not sufficient.

Two hundred and fifty rupees *is* not a big amount.

But: There are five rupees in my pocket. (If I mean five individual rupees.)

(*p*) A verb must agree with its real subject instead of with the noun close to it; as,

The *behaviour* of one of the boys *is* far from satisfactory. ('behaviour' is the real subject, not 'boys'.)

The *fate* of the children *is* quite tragic.

His knowledge in all these subjects *is* commendable.

One of his brothers *is* very intelligent.

(*q*) 'Many a' has a plural meaning but is singular and takes only a singular verb.

For Example:

Many a patient comes to this hospital.

Many a student *was* absent.

(*r*) *One of', each of', every one of , none of + uncountable noun etc.* always take singular verb; as,

For Example:

One of the boys who were present *was* a good speaker.

Each of the girls *was* given a prize.

Every one of the pictures *is* good.

None of the water *is* good. (water – uncountable noun)

But: *None of* the speakers *were* present. (speakers – countable noun)

(*s*) Half of, some of, one-third, two-thirds, etc. take a plural verb if the nouns following them are countable (*i.e.,* that can be counted) but they take a singular verb if the nouns following them are mass nouns or non-count nouns (*i.e.,* that cannot be counted).

For Example:

Half of the bread *was* eaten. (Here 'bread' is uncountable)

Half of the mangoes *are* ripe. (Here 'mangoes' is countable)

Some of the boys *are* absent.

Some of the milk *is* left.

One-third of the bread *was* used.

One-third of the mangoes *are* bad.

Two-thirds of the sugar *was* not used.

Two-thirds of the apples *were* sold.

If two nouns joined by 'and' stand for a single idea a singular verb is used; as,

Bread and butter is his breakfast. (Breakfast consisting of bread and butter)

Rice and curry is the favourite food of Malayalees.

Truth and honesty is the best policy.

(*t*) Titles of books, names of countries etc. which are plural in form but singular in meaning take a singular verb; as,

The United States is a big country.

'Gulliver's Travels' is an interesting book.

(*u*) The phrase 'more than one' is singular.

For Example:

More than one person *was* present at the site.

(*v*) The phrase 'a number of ' is plural, but 'the number of ' is singular.

For Example:

A number of boys *were* absent.

The number of students in a class *is* limited to thirty.

(*w*) Nouns following the distributive adjectives 'either' and 'neither' are always singular and therefore the verbs following them should be singular.

For Example:

Either novel is worth reading.

Neither novel is good.

Either of the boys was absent.

(Either means ' the one or the other of two persons or things'.)

Neither of the pens is good.

(Neither means 'not the one nor the other of two persons or things'.)

Neither has come. (Don't say: Both have not come.)

(*x*) Agreement in inverted sentences.

The subject of an inverted sentence always comes after the verb. In other words, in an inverted sentence the subject follows the verb.

Interrogative sentences are usually inverted.

For Example:

Are you ready?

Is he ready?

Does he like pudding?

Do they sing well?

From the crowd *emerges* the leader.(after a prepositional phrase- singular subject – singular verb- verb used before the subject.)

From the crowd *emerge* the leaders. (after a prepositional phrase- plural subject- plural verb- verb used before the subject)

There *is* a table in the room. (Inversion is usual after 'there' or 'here')

There are three chairs in the room.

Here comes John.

Here come the guests.

But: Here she comes. (Subject-verb inversion is not done if the subject is a pronoun)

Chapter 7

THE ADJECTIVE

An adjective is a word that describes a person, thing or quality. To be precise, it is a word used to qualify/describe a noun or pronoun.

For Example:

A small boy, a beautiful flower, a blue ribbon, a big tree, a blue sky, a black car, bad smell etc.

In the above examples the words *small, beautiful, big, blue, black* and *bad* are adjectives because they describe or qualify the associated nouns.

7.1 KINDS OF ADJECTIVES

Adjectives may be classified into:

Proper adjectives — Descriptive or Qualitative adjectives
Quantitative adjectives — Numeral adjectives
Demonstrative adjectives — Distributive adjectives
Interrogative adjectives — Possessive adjectives.
Emphasizing adjectives — Exclamatory adjectives.

1. **Proper Adjectives:** These adjectives are formed from Proper nouns; as,

   Indian citizens (the adjective 'Indian' from the proper noun India)
   British Islands (British from Britain)
   Chinese toys (Chinese from China)

2. **Descriptive Adjectives:** (Qualitative adjectives)

   These adjectives show the quality or the kind of persons or things; as,

   She is a *beautiful* girl. — India is a *big* country.
   Ramu is a *clever* boy. — The dog is a *domestic* animal.

3. **Quantitative Adjectives:** These adjectives show how much of a thing is meant.

   The following adjectives are mainly used as Quantitative adjectives:

   some, any, no, none, enough, sufficient, all, whole, half and much, etc.

   For Example:

   I bought *some* sugar.

   I have *no* licence to drive a car.

   None of my friends attended the party.

   He has *enough* money with him.

   He gave me *sufficient* amount.

   They gave me *all* the books.

   I experienced *much* difficulty in getting a passport.

   Ramu ate the *whole* ice cream.

   Half knowledge is no knowledge.

4. **Numeral Adjectives:** These adjectives show the number of persons or things or in what order a person or thing stands.

   These can be further classified into three sub classes.

   (*i*) **Definite numeral adjectives:** These show the exact number or serial order of persons or things.

   For Example:

   Five years, ten days, six mangoes, second prize, fifth division etc.

   He lived in Chennai for *five years.*

   He won *second prize* in the competition.

   She stood *first* in the class.

   There are *six* oranges in the packet.

   (*ii*) **Indefinite Numeral Adjectives:** All, many, few, some, any, certain, several etc. are Indefinite numeral adjectives.

   For Example:

   He ate all the rice.

   Many people did not attend the meeting.

   Few people attended the meeting.

   Some mangoes were rotten.

   You take any book from the shelf.

   Merchants are to maintain certain registers.

   Several people witnessed the accident.

   All (the) members of the club were present. ('the' optional)

5. **Distributive Adjectives:** These show persons or things taken one by one. Each, every, either, neither are the four Distributive numeral adjectives.

   Each:

Each can be used to talk about one of two things or persons or one of more than two *when we think of them one at a time and not as a group.* Each refers to a limited number.

For Example:

Each student has his/her (their) own place in the class.(A class has a limited number of students and the word *each* considers these students singly.)

Every:

Every is *not* used for one of two things or persons. It is used to talk about three or more things or persons. It is always used to refer to *all* things or persons in general. (We never say 'every two students' which means 'both students'.) In other words, *every* has the same meaning as *all*. But, there is a difference in their usage. *Every* is used only with singular words while *all* can be used both with a plural noun and with a plural verb.

For Example:

Every Indian is proud of his/her (their) country.

(Every Indian=all Indians. The word *every* does consider them (all Indians) as a whole and not singly as the word *each* does.) The example given above may be replaced with the sentence given below without any change in meaning.

All Indians are proud of their country.

Note: In modern English the difference between *each* and *every* is seldom observed and 'their' is used in place of the pronoun 'his/her'.

Either: Either is usually used to mean 'one or the other'.

Sometimes it means 'both' especially with words 'end' and 'side'.

For Example:

You can park on either side of the road.	(one side or the other meaning 'both sides')
You can take either book.	(one of two books)
There are big trees on either side of the river.	(both sides)
You can enter the park from either end.	(both ends)

Neither: Neither is the negative of either. It means 'not one nor the other of two things or persons'.

For Example:

Neither question was answered. (means ' None of the two questions was answered.)

Note: The numeral adjectives which show the number of persons or things are called *Cardinals.*

For Example:

one, two, three, four, etc.

Those numeral adjectives which show the serial order of persons or things are called *Ordinals.*

For Example:

first, second, third, etc.

Note: The words *some, enough, any, no, all* may be used as Numeral Adjectives or as Quantitative Adjectives.

If the noun qualified is Material or Abstract, the Qualitative Adjective (QA) is used. But, if the noun is Common the Numeral Adjective (NA) is used; as,

He ate *much* rice.	(Material Noun- 'rice' QA)
He had *little* rice.	(Material Noun- 'rice' QA)
He had *enough* rice.	(Material Noun- 'rice' QA)
He had *some* rice.	(Material Noun- 'rice' QA)
He had *no* rice.	(Material Noun- 'rice' QA)

He had *all* the rice.	(Material Noun- 'rice' QA)
Had he *any* rice?	(Material Noun- 'rice' QA)
He had *many bowls* of rice.	(N.A –'bowls' Common Noun)
He had *a few bowls* of rice.	(N.A –'bowls' Common Noun)
He had enough *bowls* of rice.	(N.A –'bowls' Common Noun)
He had *some* bowls of rice.	(N.A –'bowls' Common Noun)
He had *no* bowls of rice.	(N.A –'bowls' Common Noun)
He had *all* the bowls of rice.	(N.A –'bowls' Common Noun)
Had he *any* bowls of rice?	(N.A –'bowls' Common Noun)

Note: The adjectives 'aplenty' and 'galore' are used after the nouns they modify.

For Example:

There are apples *aplenty* in the market.(more than enough)

There are festivals *galore* in India.(large quantity or amount)

6. **Demonstrative Adjectives:** These adjectives point out person(s), place(s) or thing(s); as,

This book, that book, these books, those books, such books, same books, some books, any books, certain books, this place, that place, etc.

There are two classes of Demonstrative adjectives.

(1) Definite. (2) Indefinite.

When we want to point out an exact person or thing we use the *Definite* Demonstrative Adjective. For this purpose we use *this, that, these, those, such, same etc.*

For Example:

This book is mine. These books are mine. That book is mine. Those books are mine.

Such a book as the Ramayana is to be read. I got the same answers from him.

When we do not want to point out exactly a person or thing we use Indefinite Demonstrative Adjectives. In such cases we use *some, any, certain, any other, other;* etc; as,

Certain members of the club did not attend the meeting.

You may meet *some* officer to get the required information.

You may take *any* other book than this.

7. **Possessive Adjectives**

The words *my, his, her, its, your, their* and *our* when used before a noun attributively (*i.e.* used before a noun to describe it) are called Possessive Adjectives.

For Example:

This is *my* book. That is his pencil.

She is lying on her bed. They are holding their bags.

Our school is near the post office. I took your pen.

Its colour is blue etc.

8. **Emphasizing Adjectives:** 'Own' and 'very' are Emphasizing Adjectives.

   For Example:

   I heard it with my *own* ears. ('ears' emphasized by 'own' meaning 'I myself heard it'.)

   He is my *own* brother. ('brother' emphasized by 'own')

   This is the *very* table I supplied. ('table' emphasized by 'very' (Meaning 'no other table than this one'))

9. **Interrogative Adjectives:** *What, which* and *whose* are the Interrogative Adjectives.

   These adjectives are used with nouns to ask questions; as,

   1. What book do you like to read? ('what' does not imply any selection or choice.)
   2. Which book do you like to read? Fiction or poetry. (which implies a selection or choice.)
   3. Whose book is this?

10. **Exclamatory adjectives:** The word 'what' is used in an exclamatory sense; as,

    What a wonderful idea! What a piece of work is man!

    What a tragedy it is! What a fool he is!

7.2 USES OF ADJECTIVES

1. Attributive use 2. Predicative use

1. **Attributive use:** In this case the adjective qualifies its noun directly; as,

   It is a *beautiful* flower. It was a *wonderful* show.

   (The adjectives 'beautiful' and 'wonderful' qualify directly the nouns 'flower' and 'show' respectively.)

2. **Predicative use:** In this case the adjective qualifies its noun or pronoun indirectly and it comes after the verb; as,

   The flower is beautiful. (The adjective 'beautiful' is a part of the predicate and qualifies indirectly the noun 'flower'.)

   The show is wonderful.

Note: The following adjectives are used only attributively:

Former, olden, live, little, main, sheer,

For Example:

He is the *former* Chairman of the bank. ('former' qualifies 'Chairman')

People used to travel on foot in the *olden* days.

Some channels broadcast *live* coverage of the match.

I saw a *little* boy in the garden.

Mathematics is her *main* subject.

It is *sheer* negligence on his part.

Note: Some adjectives which are used attributively change their meaning depending upon their position:

Proper, present, live, old, poor, early, late are examples.

Follow the proper procedure? (proper=right)

Do you live in Ernakulam proper? (proper=strictly in Ernakulam)

The member present in the meeting did not offer his comments. (the member who was present)

The present member did not attend the meeting. (current member)

We saw the programme live on TV. (not recorded)

It is a live fish. (living)

He is an old man.

He is an old friend of mine. (friend for a long time)

The poor man has lost his money. (Here, 'poor man' does not mean a man having little or no money but means a man deserving sympathy.)

He is very poor, but his friend is very rich.

The early bird gets the worm.

It is too early to comment on his remarks.

He is late.

The flight is late.

He is in his late teens. (near the end of teens. 'Teens' means the years of a person's life when he is between 13 and 19.)

Note: Some adjectives ending in "able' or 'ible' are sometimes used after the noun.

These are the only books *available* in the market.

This is the only solution possible.

He is the person *responsible* for the accident.

Note: An adjective may become part of a phrase or an expression.

For Example:

Here is a boy good at English.

(Here is a boy who is good at English. The adjective 'good' forms part of the phrase 'good at English'.)

This is my friend going to the USA shortly. (... who is going...)

Note: Sometimes the noun may be inserted in a phrase or an expression.

For Example:

This is a better *novel* than that. (This novel is better than that.)

It was an easy *question* to answer. (It was a question easy to answer.)

He is the best *man* to judge.

It is an impossible *job* to do.

Note: The following adjectives are used only predicatively (used only after verbs):

Afraid, asleep, alive, ill, well, awake, content, aloof, alike, ashamed, afraid, afloat, alive, ill, well, content and aware.

For Example:

I am *afraid* of my boss. He is *asleep*.

She kept me *aloof.* I was *awake* the whole night.

He is still *alive.* The sisters look *alike.*

He is not *ashamed* of his failure in the exam. They were *aware* of the consequences.

He is *content* with what he has. He is *ill.*

He kept himself *aloof* from his friends.

Note: The definite article 'the' and the indefinite article 'a or an' are adjectives.

For Example:

He is *the* man whom I met yesterday. ('the' qualifies the noun 'man')

She gave me *an* apple. ('an' qualifies 'apple')

Note: 'an' is used before a vowel or a silent 'h'.

I spent *an* hour at the park. (silent or unaspirated 'h' in hour)

I bought *a* pen. ('a' is used before a consonant , before 'u' with a 'yoo' sound and before 'o' with an 'wu' sound.)

For Example:

He is flying a *kite.* ('k' is a consonant)

She is a *university* student. ('u' with 'yoo' sound)

This is a *one* year course. ('o' with 'wu' sound)

Sometimes participles (both present and past) are used as adjectives.

For Example:

The *injured* man was admitted to hospital.

The man *injured* in the accident was admitted to hospital.

He is a *visiting* Professor.

This is the only remedy *left.* (used only after the noun)

The matter *discussed* was of a secret nature. (used only after the noun)

This is the student *taking part* in the seminar. (used only after the noun)

The witness *examined* turned hostile. (used only after the noun)

The participles *concerned* and *adopted* have one meaning when they are placed before the noun and another when placed after it.

For Example:

The party concerned may meet the secretary. (the interested party)

The *concerned* party may meet the secretary. (worried or aggrieved)

The method *adopted* was time consuming. (selected)

He is an *adopted* child.

The participle *involved* has two different meanings according to its position with respect to the noun.

For Example:

It is an *involved* issue. (complicated and difficult to understand)

The issues *involved* in the agitation were discussed in detail. (connected with the agitation)

Some adjectives like transitive verbs can take objects.

For Example:

This place is not *worth* seeing. (worth what? seeing)

He looks *like* a fool.

They study in a college *near* the railway station.

I will not be here the *next* six months.

7.3 POSITION OF ADJECTIVES

1. Attributive adjectives (acting as pre-modifiers of nouns) usually precede the nouns they qualify.

   For Example:

   It is a *beautiful* flower.

   She is an *intelligent* girl.

2. When there are two or more adjectives preceding a noun, the ones referring to inherent qualities like colour, physical state, material, nationality, purpose, origin, etc. *usually* come last.

   These guidelines are not always observed.

   For Example:

   She has got long *black* hair. (colour)

   It is a narrow *zigzag* road. (physical state)

   He bought an exquisite *gold* ring. (material)

   She is a beautiful *American* girl. (nationality)

   He bought a new *folding* umbrella. (purpose)

   She gave me a cheap *Chinese* doll. (origin)

   Adjectives of purpose or function come just before a noun.

   For Example:

   He bought a *shaving* stick.

   It is a *dwelling* house.

   He had a deeply *moving* experience.

Adjectives for shape, age, size, quality, etc. come first.

For Example:

He bought a *round* dining table. (shape)

He is an *old* sickly person. (age)

I saw a *big* African elephant. (size)

I ate a *sweet* Kashmiri apple. (quality)

Adjectives indicating the material of which a thing is made come first.

For Example:

I bought an *wooden* rocking chair. (material)

This *porcelain* tea set was bought last year.

Numbers, if used, come first.

For Example:

There were *three* uniformed police men.

He bought *two* stainless steel frying pan.

7.4 COMPARISON OF ADJECTIVES

Degrees of comparison:

There are three degrees of comparison.

1. Positive degree
2. Comparative degree
3. Superlative degree.

1. The positive degree of adjective shows absolute or simple quality.

For Example:

Ramu is a *clever* boy. Radha is a *beautiful* girl.

2. The comparative degree of adjective shows a higher degree of quality than the positive degree does.

For Example:

Ramu is *cleverer* than Mohan. Radha is *more beautiful* than Meera.

Note: The Comparative degree is used when two persons or things are compared. It is usually followed by 'than'.

3. The superlative degree of the adjective shows the highest quality.

For Example:

Ram is the *cleverest* boy in the class.

Radha is the *most beautiful* girl in the college.

Note: The Superlative degree is used when more than two things or persons are compared. It is usually preceded by the definite article 'the'.

Note: When we compare two qualities in two different persons or things we use the 'er' form.

For Example:

Ramu is *cleverer* than Mohan.

But, when we compare two different qualities in one person/ thing, we do not use the 'er' form. Instead, we use the positive degree with the word 'more' placed before it.

For Example:

Ramu is *more clever* than *cunning*. (right)(both Ramu's qualities.)

Ramu is cleverer than cunning. (wrong)

Note: When two things or persons are compared with each other the word 'other' should be used to exclude the first person or thing from the other.

For Example:

Ramu is cleverer than *any other* boy in the class.

Gold is more precious than *any other* metal.

Here, the comparison is between gold and all other metals taken as one set.

If we say, 'Gold is more precious than any metal.' gold is also included in the expression "any metal". So, to exclude gold from the other group of metals we should use 'other' which means 'any other metal than gold'.

The following comparatives borrowed from Latin have no positive, comparative or superlative degree. They all end in 'or':

Interior, exterior, major, minor.

They are used as adjectives in the positive degree or nouns.

For Example:

Interior walls, exterior paints, major issue, minor issue, etc.

For Example:

The interior walls of the building were painted dark. (Adjective)

The interior of the theatre can be seen from outside. (Noun)

The following Latin adjectives are used in comparison. They are followed by 'to' and not 'than'.

Senior, junior, superior, inferior, prior, anterior, posterior.

For Example:

John is senior to me in age. (not senior than)

Janu is junior to me in age.

Tea is superior to coffee. (not superior than)

He reached home prior to my arrival.

This is an anterior (coming before) room to the operation theatre.

This is a posterior (coming after) room to the operation theatre.

The police reached the place prior to the attack.

These Latin comparatives can be used in the positive form:

For Example:

Superior quality, inferior stuff, senior officer, junior assistant, prior knowledge, etc.

This bag is of superior quality.

This shirt is made of inferior stuff.

He is a senior officer.

She is working as a junior assistant.

I didn't have any prior knowledge of his arrival.

Note: Avoid using double comparatives or double superlatives.

For Example:

This question is more easier than that. (wrong)

This question is easier than that.

She is the most cleverest of their five children. (wrong)

She is the cleverest of their five children.

This question is more simpler than that. (wrong)

This question is simpler than that.

Radha is more cleverer than Meera. (wrong)

Radha is cleverer than Meera.

The following adjectives do not have positive degrees

Comparative	Superlative	
Inner	innermost	('in' is not the positive degree)
Upper	uppermost	('up' is not " " ")
Farther	farthest	('far' in not " " ")— shows distance
Further	furthest	('far' is not' " " ") — shows time

The following adjectives do not have Comparative degrees.

Positive	Superlative
Eastern	Easternmost
Southern	Southernmost
Northern	Northernmost
Western	Westernmost
Top	Topmost

In Modern English the comparatives *inner, former, latter, upper* and *elder* are used as absolute or positive adjectives.

For Example:

The inner walls of the room are painted white.

He is the former Principal of our college.

Rama and Krishna are classmates. The former is older than the latter.

The following adjectives cannot be compared as they themselves express the ultimate.

perfect, unique, universal, ideal, excellent, extreme, eternal, complete, square, round, supreme, chief, dead, empty, right, wrong etc.

In the strict sense we cannot use 'more unique' or 'more perfect' etc.

But, this rule is not always observed in Modern English.

For Example:

He has got a unique opportunity. (correct)

But in Modern English 'more', 'very', 'quite' etc. often used with 'unique'.

For Example:

He has a *very* unique position in his company. (right)

The achievement *of hundred percent literacy* is *quite* unique to Kerala.

Similarly,

This is the most *perfect* work of art he has ever produced. (right)

If something or somebody is unique to some person or thing, this 'unique quality' does not take any modifier.

For Example:

This is a perfect square. (wrong)

Omit perfect, as a square is a square (unique in itself). It cannot be perfect or imperfect.

The sentence may be corrected as shown below:

This is a square. (right)

That is more or less complete. (wrong)

Omit 'more or less', as 'complete' is ultimate and it cannot be 'more or less'.

The sentence may be corrected as follows:

That is *almost* complete.(or) That is incomplete. (right)

The words *late* and *old* in the positive degree have the following forms in the comparative and superlative degrees.

Positive	**Comparative**	**Superlative**
Late	later }	latest
	latter }	—
Old	older	oldest
	elder	eldest

The following adjectives are used differently:

1. Later, latter

 Later refers to time.

 Latter refers to position.

 For Example:

 Ramu came by a later train.

 Latest refers to time and is the superlative degree of late.

 For Example:

 All of us are interested in reading the *latest* news.

 Latter is used to refer to the second of two people, things or groups that have just been mentioned.

 For Example:

 John and *Martin* are my friends. The latter is an orphan.

2. Elder and eldest

 These adjectives are used to qualify persons, not animals or things. Their use is now confined to members of the same family or parents. 'Elder' is not followed by than, but it is sometimes followed by 'to'.

 For Example:

 Sheela is her elder sister. Ramu is her eldest brother.

 Ramu is elder to Sheela.

3. Older, oldest

 Older is the comparative of old.

 For Example:

 Raju is older than Rema. (Raju is senior in age to Rema.)

 Oldest is the superlative of old.

 For Example:

 Leela is the oldest of his three children.

7.5 ADJECTIVES USED AS NOUNS

(*i*) The following adjectives act as *plural nouns* when the definite article 'the' is placed before them. They take plural verbs; as,

the brave (brave people) the rich (rich people)

the poor (poor people) the insulted (insulted people)

the injured (injured people)

For Example:

The brave fight their enemy.

The rich are supposed to help the poor.

The poor deserve our sympathy.

The insulted feel that they are helpless.

The injured were admitted to hospital.

(*ii*) Some adjectives become abstract nouns when the definite article 'the' is placed before them. They take singular verbs.

For Example:

The future is quite uncertain. (future time)

He is an admirer of *the beautiful*. ('the beautiful' means 'beauty' in a general sense)

The latest is that she is going to get married. (The latest- the latest news/thing)

The very best is awaited. (The very best- the very best part/thing)

4. The following words are nouns derived from adjectives.

Singular		Plural
Indian	–	Indians
American	–	Americans
Russian	–	Russians
junior	–	juniors
senior	–	seniors
minor	–	minors
elder	–	elders
secret	–	secrets
total	–	totals

Note: Arabian - Arabs (Arabian is used to describe places; as, the Arabian countries, the Arabian sea, etc. The people of Arabia are Arabs and the adjective to describe the Arabs is Arab; as, Arab women, Arab travelers, etc., but their language is 'Arabic'. (the Arabic Language)

5. The following adjectives–turned nouns are used only in the plural: eatables and valuables.

For Example:

You should not buy eatables from outside. (Not: 'eatable')

He bought valuables from the shop. (Not: 'valuable')

Some adjectives are used as nouns in certain phrases.

in short, in general, before long, for good, at best, in black and white, the long and(the) short etc.

For Example:

In short, he is a gentleman.

In general, his performance was very good.

Following his illness he was admitted to hospital. He died *before long*.

He left us *for good.* (forever)

He is not a judge; he is a lawyer *at best.* (the best thing that can happen)

He submitted his grievances in *black and white.* (in writing)

The long and(the) short of the book is that it is worth reading.

(in essence). ('the' may be omitted)

6. Use of Nouns as Adjectives.

In English the use of nouns as adjectives is very common; as,

He is a *business* man. ('business' qualifies 'man')

She is a *college* girl. ('college' qualifies 'girl')

There is a *passenger* train in the evening.

There is a *letterbox* near our house.

The *Ooty* climate is very good.

He won the *gold* cup.

The *Delhi* correspondent is a woman.

7. In some expressions consisting of noun and adjective the adjective is placed after the noun; as,

Notary *Public* – an official witness when somebody signs a legal document.

Time *immemorial* - ancient

Heir *apparent* – an heir with legal right which cannot be changed.

Heir *presumptive*- an heir without legal right.

God *Almighty* - All powerful God.

Body *politic* - the State regarded as an organized group of citizens.

Note:

1. If the comparison is between positive forms of the adjective, use as……..as in affirmative sentences and as…..as or so …….as in negative sentences.

For Example:

Raju is as good as his brother.

Ram is not *so* good *as* Raju.

or

Ram is not *as* good *as* Raju.

2. When two persons or things are compared only the positive and comparative degrees are possible. The word 'the' is placed before the comparative.

He is not *so good as* his brother.

His brother is *the better* of the two.

3. When a superlative is used we usually place 'the' before and 'of' after it; as,

Raju is the cleverest of all boys in the class.

4. But when the superlative is preceded by a possessive adjective the construction of the sentence is as follows:

Rama is *my best* friend. ('my' is possessive adjective)

Don't say: Rama is my the best friend.

Some adjectives and their uses:

1. Farther and further:

Farther is the comparative of far and means at a greater distance in space or time.

For Example:

Trivandrum is *farther* from Kochi than Kottayam.

Further means additional.

For Example:

He has no *further* plans.

You may contact him for *further* details.

2. Nearest and next:

Nearest refers to distance and *next* refers to position.

For Example:

The Nedumbassery International Airport is the *nearest* Airport to Cochin.

My brother sat *next* to me.

Classification of the adjective 'some':

(*a*) It is used to indicate quantity.

I have some water.

(*b*) It is used to indicate number.

I have some mangoes.

(*c*) It is used as a demonstrative adjective.

You must take some person to do that work.

(Here 'some' does not indicate quality or quantity, but it acts as a Demonstrative adjective.)

EXERCISE

Errors in the use of Adjectives:

1. He is taller than any person. (wrong)

He is taller than any other person. (right)

(The first sentence means that he is taller than any person including himself. This is absurd and hence the correction.)

Use 'other' after positive and comparative when two things of the same kind are compared.

2. Milk is superior than water.

(superior *to* water- always superior to, not superior than).

3. Rich should help poor.
(The rich ... *the* poor. The poor means poor people)

4. Rice is preferable than wheat.
(preferable *to* wheat)

5. I drank little milk I had.
(the little milk I had)

6. He is the most wise man of all other men.
(wise man of all men- 'other' should not be used after superlatives in comparison)

7. I did not bring some money.
(Say: any money)

8. Please give me any food to eat.
(Say: some food)

9. He gave me few books to read.
(Say : a few books)

10. Give me little water to drink.
(Say : a little)

11. He has a little time to waste. (Say : little)

12. Give me few mangoes. (Say: a few)

13. The three brothers quarrelled with each other. (Say: one another)

14. Ramu is the cleverest of the two brothers.
(Say : the cleverer of the two brothers)

15. Rani is cleverest of all other girls.
(Say: the cleverest of all girls)

16. He is my the greatest friend.
(Say: my greatest friend).

When possessives like my, his and our are used before a superlative, do not use the definite article 'the' before them. When a superlative is used to indicate 'majority' do not use 'the' before it; as,

Most of the boys were present.

(*Do not say:* The most of the boys were present. (Say: Most of the.........)

The most of the ice melted.
(Say: Most of the ice melted)

17. He is the cleverest boy.
(Say: He is a very clever boy. There is no comparison involved)

18. She is one of the best and beautiful actresses.
(wrong)

She is one of the best and the most beautiful actresses.

(If the first of the two or more adjectives is a superlative, the others should also be superlative.)

19. He occupies the most unique position.
(Say ; a unique position)

Adjectives like unique, perfect, complete, extreme, chief, ideal do not admit of any comparison because they stand for the ultimate or absolute.

20. He is my older brother. (Say: elder.)

When members of the same family are referred to 'elder' and 'eldest' are used and they are applied only to persons . Do not use 'than' after 'elder'. 'Older' and 'oldest' are used when 'age' is referred to. They are applied to both things and persons.

21. We should help poor.
(Say: the poor = poor people)

22. He left India for the good. (Say: for good or for good and all. This means forever – never to return.) 'for good and all' and 'for good' are interchangeable.

Chapter 8 THE ADVERB

An adverb is a word that adds more information about place, time, manner, cause or degree to a verb, an adjective, another adverb, a phrase or a clause, a conjunction, a preposition and a whole sentence sometimes. In other words, an adverb modifies all parts of speech except noun and pronoun.

For Example:

1. He reads *quickly.* ('quickly' modifies the verb *reads*)
2. He reads very *quickly.* ('very' modifies the adverb *quickly*)
3. He is *very* sensitive. ('very' modifies the adjective *sensitive*)
4. He is *very* gloomy. (*'very'* shows to what degree or extent he is gloomy)
5. He completed the construction *long* before the monsoon. (modifies the preposition 'before')
6. They had finished the work *well* before the rain started. (modifies the conjunction 'before')
7. He parked his car *right* in front of the gate. (modifies the phrase 'in front of')
8. Luckily, I got this job. ('luckily' modifies the entire sentence)
9. Probably, he will marry her. ('probably' modifies the entire sentence)
10. Unfortunately, he did not get a first class. ('unfortunately' modifies the entire sentence)
11. Eventually, he died. ('eventually' modifies the entire sentence)
12. Finally, I succeeded in my attempt. ('finally' modifies the entire sentence)

Note: Although we have stated that adverbs do not modify nouns and pronouns the use of adverbs in the following sentences may be noted carefully.

The above facts throw light on the matter.

Here the adverb 'above' appears to modify the noun 'facts'.

In good English this use of 'above' is not considered correct although modern English has accepted it. The sentence may be corrected as follows:

For Example:

The *above-mentioned* facts throw light on the matter.

(The compound word 'above-mentioned' is adjective.)

Or

The facts mentioned *above* throw light on the matter. (above-adverb)

Note: The following words usually used as adverbs can be used as adjectives, nouns or pronouns: above, then, down, far, downstairs and upstairs.

1. **Then:** The *then* President of India declined to sign the ordinance.

Here, 'then' is used as an adjective. It is used to describe some person or persons who had some title at the time in the past, which is being discussed now.

2. **Above:** This word is used as an adjective, a noun or a preposition.

No one is *above* rules. (preposition)

You may write to me at the *above* address. (adjective)

Please inform me if the *above* is required. (noun-singular)

All the *above* were present in the meeting.

(noun-plural meaning all the people mentioned above.)

3. **Down:** This word is used as an adjective, a preposition, a verb or a noun.

For Example:

Tears ran *down* her cheeks. (preposition-it connects the noun phrase 'her cheeks')

The shops *downed* their shutters. (verb)

He is very much *down* today. (adjective)

My system was *down* yesterday. (adjective)

The *down* time of the computer system was too much. (adjective)

The *duck down* is very soft. (fine soft feathers of a duck- noun)

4. **Far:** This word is used as an adjective besides an adverb.

For Example:

He went *far.* (adverb)

He was standing at the *far* end of the hall. (adjective qualifying the noun 'end')

5. **Downstairs**

They stayed *downstairs.* (adverb)

There are two *downstairs* bedrooms. (adjective)

They cleaned the *downstairs.* (noun)

6. **Upstairs**

He went *upstairs.* (adverb)

There are two *upstairs* rooms. (adjective)

The upstairs of the *building* is a hall. (noun)

There are three kinds of adverbs:

(*i*) Simple adverbs

(*ii*) Interrogative adverbs

(*iii*) Relative adverbs.

8.1 SIMPLE ADVERBS

A simple Adverb merely modifies a word.

For Example:

He is *very* intelligent. (modifies the word (adjective)intelligent)

He does his work *diligently.* (modifies the verb does)

Simple adverbs are further classified according to their meaning:

(*a*) Adverb of time

(*b*) Adverb of place

(*c*) Adverb of number (frequency)

(*d*) Adverb of manner

(*e*) Adverb of degree or extent or quantity

(*f*) Adverbs of affirmation and negation

(*g*) Adverb of reason

(*h*) Conjunctive Adverb

(*a*) **Adverb of Time:** This indicates the time of an action. (when)

For Example:

I have seen him *before.*

I met him *before;* I have not seen him *since.*

He came here ten years *ago.*

He will come *soon.*

I have *already* told him about the matter.

The following is a list of some adverbs of this class: Ago, since, before, already, early, immediately, now, then, soon, presently, instantly, today, yesterday, yet, early, late, recently, formerly, afterwards, shortly, daily, tomorrow, etc.

(*b*) **Adverb of Place:** This indicates the place of an action. (where)

For Example:

I went *there;* he came *here.*

He came *in;* I went *out.*

The following is a list of main adverbs of this class: here, there, in, out, hence, thence, inside, outside, hither, thither, within, above, below, down, for, near, everywhere, anywhere, elsewhere, backward, forward, etc.

(*c*) **Adverb of Number (frequency):** This indicates the frequency (how often) of an action.

For Example:

He came here *twice.*

She *often* comes here.

She *seldom* comes here.

He *always* comes here.

She *frequently* commits mistakes.

The main adverbs of this class are: once, twice, often, seldom, always, never, again, frequently, sometimes, firstly, secondly, thirdly, etc., usually, normally, generally, regularly, occasionally, rarely, hardly ever, scarcely ever, etc.

Everyday, every night, every two days, etc., hourly, daily, weekly, monthly, yearly, once a day, twice a day, thrice a day, four times a day, once a month, twice a year, once everyday, thrice weekly, twice monthly, every other week (every two weeks), every other month, etc these indicate exact or definite frequency.

'Always' indicates the maximum frequency or occasion and 'never' zero frequency (no occasion). All the other frequencies will come between these two.

hourly, daily, weekly, etc can be used both as adverb and as adjective.

For Example:

He comes *daily.* (adverb)

He gets *daily* allowance. (adjective)

He is paid *hourly.* (adverb)

He gets *daily* wages. (adjective)

What is the *weekly* consumption of patrol? (adjective)

They are paid *weekly.* (adverb)

(*d*) **Adverb of Manner:** This indicates the manner in which an action is performed.

For Example:

She understands everything *clearly.*

He works *hard.*

The soldiers fought *courageously.*

I was asked to do *so.*

The main adverbs of this class are: clearly, merely, badly, fluently, soundly, sadly, slowly, agreeably, bravely, courageously, steadily, hard, fast, probably, so, well, ill, certainly, conveniently, etc.

(*e*) **Adverb of Quantity, Degree or Extent:** This indicates the quantity, degree or extent of an action.

For Example:

He is *very* intelligent.

She is *too* arrogant.

This is *much* better than that.

The arrangement is *somewhat* satisfactory.

The following is the list of main adverbs in this class: enough, too, much, quite, entirely, wholly, more, most, less, half, partly, so etc.

(*f*) **Adverb of Affirmation and Negation:** This indicates affirmation or negation of an action.

He did his homework. (an example of affirmation)

He did not do his homework. (an example of negation)

Did he do his homework? *No*, he didn't. (adverb of negation)

Did he do his homework? *Yes*, he did. (adverb of affirmation)

The following is the list of main adverbs of this type:

Yes, no, not, certainly, indeed, not at all, by all means, etc.

Note: In the examples ' Did he do his homework?' 'Yes' stands for an affirmative sentence namely: ' He did his homework' and in

'Did he do his homework?' 'No' stands for the negative sentence

'He did not do his homework.'

(*g*) **Adverb of Reason:** This indicates the reason for an action.

He had misbehaved towards his colleague, and *hence* he was suspended from service.

He is a very old man and *therefore* he cannot run fast.

He is only a minor and *hence* he is not eligible to vote.

The words 'hence', 'therefore', etc are adverbs of reason.

(*h*) **Conjunctive Adverbs:** Conjunctive Adverbs are somewhat like coordinating conjunctions. They are often used in place of the latter with a view to making the relationship between two clauses clearer.

For Example:

She is very intelligent, *but* she is lazy. ('but'–coordinating conjunction.)

She is very intelligent; *nevertheless* she is lazy. ('nevertheless'-conjunctive adverb)

He fell unconscious *and* was admitted to hospital.

He fell unconscious; *consequently* he was admitted to hospital.

Some of the commonly used conjunctive adverbs are given below:

besides, also, moreover, furthermore – used to replace 'and'.

however, nevertheless, still – used to replace 'but'.

so, thus, therefore, consequently – used to state a result.

Similarly, equally, likewise – used to indicate equality.

8.2 INTERROGATIVE ADVERBS

These are adverbs which are used in asking questions.

For Example:

What is your name?
Why are you sad?
When did they go?
How did they manage it?
How many people attended it?
How big is your building?

The following is the list of main adverbs in this class: what, where, why, when, how, whence, how often, how many, how far etc.

8.3 RELATIVE ADVERBS

These are adverbs which act both as adverbs and as relative pronouns.

where, why, when, how, etc, are relative adverbs.

For Example:

This is the college *where* I studied.
That is the reason *why* I quit the job.
He knows the time *when* the train will come.

But, the relative adverb 'how' does not take an antecedent.

For Example:

This is how we do it.

Here, in example (1) above the adverb 'where' modifies the verb 'studied'. At the same time it relates to its antecedent 'college' like a Relative pronoun. Similarly in example (2) the adverb 'why' is a Relative adverb.

The above examples can be written without the antecedents being expressed; as,

This is where I studied.
That is why I quit the job.
He knows when the train will come.

Adverbs used as Adjectives : Some adverbs have the same form as their respective adjectives. Such adverbs are used as adjectives sometimes.

For Example:

He is *quick* to react.	(adj.)
Go *quick.*	(adv.)
I heard a *loud* noise.	(adj.)
He spoke so *loud.*	(adv.)
An *early* bird gets the worm.	(adj.)
His *early* days were spent in the village.	(adj.)
He woke up *early* this morning.	(adv.)
This is the *only* solution.	(adj.)

You can *only* criticize him. (adv.)

There was *much* noise in the room. (adj.)

It is *much* better to follow what he says. (adv.)

Note: We can tell whether a word is used as an adverb or adjective only by a careful observation of how the word is used.

Some adverbs have two forms with the same meaning.

For Example:

loud, loudly.

He spoke *loud*. He spoke *loudly*.

Some adverbs have two forms with different meanings.

For Example:

He has studied *hard*. (studied well)

He has *hardly* studied. (studied very little)

Come *near*.

The cost is *nearly* one rupee.

The words close, closely, late, lately, pretty, prettily belong to this category.

Adverbs used as nouns after prepositions.

For Example:

He lives in a village. He daily comes from *there*.

(meaning from that place; from-preposition)

The stone came from *above*. (from a place above)

Bombay is far from *here*. (from this place)

The play starts from *now*.

By *then* the situation has gone out of control. (by that time)

Use of 'the' as Relative and Demonstrative Adverbs:

For Example:

The more you get, the more you spend.

Here, the first 'the' is a Relative Adverb of quantity and the second 'the' is a Demonstrative Adverb of quantity.

The sentence means 'to what extent you have money to that extent you spend.'

More Examples:

The sooner you go, the better for you.

The more you write, the more mistakes you commit.

Note: The definite article 'the' is used as an adverb only with an adjective or adverb in the comparative degree.

It may be noticed that the Relative Adverb 'the' and its antecedent Demonstrative Adverb 'the' are used in pair. The Relative Adverb is not used alone. But, the antecedent Demonstrative Adverb 'the' may be used alone; as,

For Example:

He drove the sooner as he was to reach his office in time.

Adverbial Adjectives: Nouns indicating adverbial relations of place, distance, time, weight, measurement, value, etc are often used as adverbs.

For Example:

I went home. (home - adverb. It indicates adverbial relation of place.)

He came last week. (week - adverbial relation of time)

He walked a few yards. (yards - adverbial relation of measurement.)

The well is fifty feet deep. (fifty feet - adverbial relation of Measurement.)

It costs five hundred rupees. (five hundred rupees - adverbial relation of value.)

It weighs ten kilograms. (ten kilograms-adverbial relation of weight.)

Use of 'there' as Adverb: When the word 'there' is used to begin a sentence, it is used as an adverb, sometimes called 'Introductory Adverb'; as,

There was none in the house. (*i.e.*, no one was in the house)

There lived a great king. (a great king lived)

There are many books in the shelf. (many books are in the shelf)

Note: The introductory 'there' has no reference to place.

8.4 SENTENCE ADVERBIALS

An adverbial is a word or group of words used as an adverb. A sentence can have more than one adverbial. There are two kinds of adverbials, the regular adverbials and the sentence adverbials. While the regular adverbial is integrated in the sentence, the sentence adverbial exists separately in it.

For Example:

Obviously, it was a mistake. (sentence adverbial)

It was *obviously* a mistake. (adverb)

Verbless clauses, noun phrases, noun phrases preceding, 'ago', 'long', 'before' etc. come under adverbials.

The sentence adverbials are generally used at the beginning of a sentence. They help us understand one's idea both in speech and in writing by giving some hint how the idea expressed in a sentence leads us to a new thought. In other words, they are used to give us some additional information about the action, happening or state described by a sentence. Besides, they often give us the speaker's remark on the idea contained in what he is saying. Hence, they are called the *sentence adverbials*.

Well, now, surely, indeed, certainly, admittedly; officially, superficially, technically, theoretically; luckily, naturally, preferably, surprisingly, 'in other words', etc. are examples of sentence adverbials.

For Example:

I have already mentioned about the evils of the dowry system.

Well, the government is now seriously thinking of banning this evil system.

('well'- adverbial used in speech)

Press Correspondent: How are you going to solve the drinking water problem?

Minister: *Well,* we will see that the ongoing project is completed within three months. *Now,* tell me what you wanted me to do in the matter of laying pipes along the new road. ('now' – adverbial used to go back to an earlier subject)

Introducing change of subject in the course of conversation:

We use *'by the by'*, 'incidentally' etc to change the subject in the course of a conversation.

For Example:

We will buy the medicine from this shop.

By the by, have you taken the prescription.

Or

Incidentally, have you taken the prescription.

Miscellaneous Examples:

The office functioned *yesterday.* (yesterday-adverb) indicating the time of action)

He is working *in the office.*

('in the office'- prepositional adverbial indicating place of action.)

He is running quickly. ('quickly'- adverbial indicating the manner of action)

He worked hard although he failed.

('although he failed'-a finite clause used as an adverbial.)

We eat to live. ('to live' an infinitive used as an adverbial)

Being a student, he is eligible for certain travel concessions.

(Being- Non-finite adverbial- 'ing' or present participle form.)

When questioned by the police, he admitted his role in the crime.

('questioned' – Non-finite adverbial – past participle form.)

She stood before me, not knowing what to do.

('not knowing what to do' – verbless non-finite clause as an adverbial.)

He came here last Friday. ('last Friday'- Noun phrase as an adverbial.)

He met her two months ago.

('two months ago' – 'ago' preceded by the noun phrase 'two months')

I met her two years back.

He is not a stranger. *In fact,* he is my cousin. (speaker's comment)

Indeed, it was quite unfortunate. (speaker's comment)

Sentence adverbials used for explanation

The following sentence adverbials are used for giving further explanation/clarification of the meaning of a point in a sentence.

(Latin abbreviation *i.e.,*- read as 'that is', 'that is to say'- We can explain a point further by expanding and clarifying its meaning by using 'that is', 'that is to say'),

(Latin abbreviation e.g.,- read as 'for example', 'for instance' – We can explain a point further by giving an illustration using this).

(Latin abbreviation viz.- read as 'namely'. Using this we can further describe a point.)

For Example:

The main units of the computer *i.e.,* the CPU, the Monitor and Key Board are easy to assemble and dismantle.

Eating plenty of vegetables is good for health. For example, leafy green vegetables are rich in vitamins.

One of the states viz. Kerala has attained hundred percent literacy.

He is no longer a student of this college. In other words, he has been dismissed from this college.

Formation of Adverbs: A good number of adverbs are formed from adjectives by adding 'ly' (a short form of 'like'.)

For Example:

Adjective	Adverb
Clever	cleverly
Wise	wisely
Kind	kindly
Glad	gladly
Quick	quickly
Beautiful	beautifully
Skilful	skilfully
Past participle: devoted	devotedly
Present participle: knowing	knowingly
Present participle: surprising	surprisingly

Some adverbs are formed by combining a noun and a qualifying adjective; as meantime, sometime, meanwhile, otherwise, yesterday, midway etc.

Some adverbs are formed by compounding the preposition 'on' and a noun; as asleep, afoot, ahead, abroad, away, abed etc.

Here, asleep = on sleep, afoot = on foot, where 'a' is the weekend form of 'on'.

Some adverbs are formed by combining a preposition and a noun; as,

Besides, indeed, overboard, today, tomorrow etc.

Here, besides = by + sides

Overboard = over + board etc., where 'be' is the old form of 'by'.

Some adverbs are compounds of a preposition and an adjective, as;

Along, abroad, aloud, across, below, behind, anew etc.

Here, along = on + long

Behind = by + hind

Some adverbs are by combining a preposition and an adverb; as,

Before, within, without, beneath, forever etc.

Here, Within = with + in

Before = by + fore.

Pronominal Adverbs: The adverbs derived from the pronouns *the, he* and *who* are called Pronominal Adverbs.

The.........there (place)

Thither (meaning 'to there'- indicates motion to that place)

For Example:

He migrated thither from England.

Thence (motion 'form that place')

For Example:

He went to Chennai first and thence to Mumbai.

Then (time)

Thus (manner)

He ... here (place)

Hither (meaning 'to here'- indicates motion to this place)

For Example:

Hither he brought his family from Calicut.

Hence (motion 'from now')

Who ... where (place)

Whither (meaning 'to where'- indicates motion to which place)

For Example:

I do not know whither I am going.

Whence (meaning 'from there')

For Example:

I returned the defective pen whence I had bought it.

When (time)

How (manner)

We can compound many of the above adverbs with prepositions or other adverbs to form adverbs;

(*i*) *there*: therein, thereto, therefore, therefrom, therewith, thereon or thereupon, thereof, thereby.

(*ii*) *here:* hereto, herein, heretofore (before this time), herewith, hereof, hereby, hereafter

(*iii*) *where:* wherein, whereto, whereon.

(*iv*) *thence:* thenceforth, thenceforward.

(*v*) *hence:* henceforth, henceforward.

Note: The word 'from' should not be used with 'thence', 'hence', and 'whence' for the following reason,

'thence = from + that place, whence = from + where.

'hence = from there.

For Example:

He joined the firm as Manager and *thence* he was promoted. (from that place)

He went to Trivandrum and *whence* to Kochi. (from where to Kochi).

I shall go to Chennai and send your books *hence.* (from there)

Adverbial Phrases: These phrases do the functions of Adverbs.

of course, in fact, at random, in general, in short, in particular, at large, at last, in future, at best, at present, by all means, by the by, inside out, upside down, to be sure, by the way etc.

For Example:

He passed the exam with flying colours. Of course he was very happy.

I thought that he was a gentleman. In fact, he is not.

They took samples of the soft drink at random for testing.

The following adverbs go together in pairs joined by 'and'.

by and by, up and down, far and wide, far and away, out and out, over and above, to and fro, first and foremost, far and near, now and then, off and on, here and there, backwards and forwards, hither and thither.

For Example:

By and by he found out the reason for her quarrel.(before long)

He walked up and down the street.

Delegates from far and wide attended the meeting.

Position of adverbs: The following rules are generally observed in the use of adverbs.

Rule 1 : Adverbs of manner

fast, well, quickly, carefully, calmly etc. – which answer the question 'how ?'

- are generally placed after the verb or after the objects if there is one.

For Example:

He ran *fast.*

She walked *quickly.*

He plays tennis *well.*

The boy is *calmly* sitting in the corner.

Rule 2: Adverbs of place.

They are placed after the verb or after the object.

For Example:

She went there.

He was not seen anywhere.

He went to Delhi on foot.

Rule 3: Adverbs of time

They are placed after the verb or after the object, usually at the end of a clause or sentence. Then, now, yesterday, next Monday, yet, still, always, never, regularly, often, sometimes, occasionally, rarely, hardly, nearly, etc. are adverbs of time.

He came *yesterday.*

They will come *next week.*

He will play tennis *next month.*

He is playing *now.*

The fashion was different *then.*

They were *then* in London.

Note on *yet* and *still*: The word *yet* means_'up to the time of speaking' and is used usually in negative and interrogative sentences. It is normally placed at the end of a sentence; as,

He hasn't come yet. (' He hasn't yet come' is also correct.)

Have you not read the book yet?

"Are you ready to go?" "Not yet".

'He has yet to complete the work' means 'He has not completed the work at the time of speaking.'

'As yet' means *until now* or *until a specific time in the past.* It is an idiom that is used only in negative sentences.

For Example:

The work is in progress, but as yet nothing can be said about its completion.

As yet nothing was known about the motive behind the murder.

'Still' tells us that the action continues

He is still in the office.

She still suffers from fever.

Rule 4: When two or more adverbs are to be used after a verb the following is the normal order.

Adverb of manner (which answers the question 'How?')

+

Adverb of place (there, here etc)

+

Adverb of time (yesterday, today etc)

For Example:

He spoke *well in the meeting.*

I went *there yesterday.*

The meeting ended *well* at *the Town Hall yesterday.*

Rule 5: Adverbs of frequency:

They are placed between the subject and the verb if the verb consists of only one word. If the verb consists of more than one word, they are placed after the first word.

Adverbs of frequency are: often, always, usually, never, rarely, generally, etc.

They answer the question 'How often?'

For Example:

He *never* tells lies.

She has *never* misguided anyone. (verb placed after the first word 'has'.)

He has *often* disobeyed his father.

He *always* comes late.

You must *always* obey your parents.

I *usually* drink tea.

He *rarely* tells the truth.

Officers *generally* come at 10.

Rule 6: Adverbs like almost, already, nearly, quite, hardly, just, etc are placed between the subject and the verb;

For Example:

He has already completed the work.

He hardly makes mistakes.

His boss quite agreed with him.

Note: If the verb is am, is, are, was or were the adverbs mentioned under rules 5 & 6 are used after the verb.

For Example:

He is always late.

He is never attentive in the class.

Rule 7: When an adverb modifies an adjective or another adverb it is usually placed before it; as,

For Example:

He was quite *correct*. (correct- adjective)

He walked very *fast*. (fast- adjective)

It was a very *interesting* picture. (interesting- adjective)

He did it very *nicely*. (nicely-adverb)

Note: The adverb 'enough' is always placed after the word which it modifies.

For Example:

He was rude *enough* in his behaviour. (enough modifies the adj. 'rude')

He was intelligent *enough* to score high marks. (modifies 'intelligent')

She was beautiful *enough* to be selected for the beauty contest. (modifies 'beautiful').

Note: When 'enough' is used as a determiner (a word such as *the, my, some, his, her, etc.),* it is placed before a noun; as,

I gave him enough money.

I ate enough bread.

Note: In ' Enough is enough', it is used as an independent pronoun. (subject).

Note: 'Enough' is used before nouns. If it is used before a determiner, the form 'enough of' must be used, but 'of' is not used with it if there is no determiner ; as,

We have enough of *the* cake.('Enough' is used before the article 'the' which is a determiner.)

We have enough cake. (There is no determiner between 'enough' and the noun 'cake')

Note: 'Enough' can be used in the sense 'sufficient'.

'Enough' can be used to qualify an adjective as in – good enough, cold enough. It can be used to modify an adverb as in 'carefully enough' , 'soon enough'.

For Example:

I would like to sing a song but my voice is not good enough.

You are not teaching carefully enough.

'Enough' can be used with nouns as in:

We have got enough rice.

I had enough of this nonsense.

I have enough money to spend.

'Enough' is used as a complement of 'to be' as in;

It is not enough. (Here the subject is a pronoun)

But when the subject is a noun it takes a different structure as in:

There is not enough money.

The money is not enough. (wrong)

Rule: Enough + noun / adjective + enough

For Example:

The car has *enough petrol* to run a hundred kilometers. ('petrol' - noun.)

He is *strong enough* to carry the box. ('strong' - adjective.)

Rule 8: The word 'only' should be placed immediately before the word which it modifies because the meaning of the sentence changes according to its position in the sentence. This is the same case with the words never, often, not and merely.

For Example:

They gave me only a certificate. (only = nothing but)

They gave only me a certificate (only = no one except me)

They gave me a certificate only. (only = simply or merely)

Only they gave me a certificate. (no one other than they)

Rule 9: The following adverbs and adverb phrases can be placed at the beginning of a sentence for emphasis. They are then followed by the inversion of the subject and verb . This is sometimes called subject–verb inversion; if the verb contains an auxiliary (operator), the subject and the operator are inverted. It is called subject-operator inversion.

Inversion is usually used in literary style.

Hardly…when, scarcely…when, rarely, never, seldom, ever, no sooner…than, nowhere, only by, only then, only after, only when, either, nor, on no account, in no circumstances, not only, little (in contrast to the positive 'a little') , few (in contrast to the positive 'a few'), etc.

For Example:

Hardly had I reached the station when the train left. (Subject-operator inversion. The sentence means: The train left soon after I (had) reached the station.)

No sooner had I left home than his sister reached.

Only by memorizing the poem was he able to recite it.

Rarely is she seen with her husband.

(Or) She is rarely seen with her husband.

Nowhere have I met him.

(Or) I have not met him anywhere.

Little did he know about my parents.

Note: These inversions are followed by negative tag-questions or question-tags.

For Example:

He rarely does his homework, does he?

They seldom do any work, do they?

Note: When the adverbs down, in, out, up, over, etc are used at the beginning of a sentence inversion of the verb is necessary if the subject is not a pronoun.

For Example:

Down flows the river.

Up flew the bird.

In came Rani.

If the subject is a pronoun, inversion is not used.

In she came. (Not: In came she.)

Note: When a negative word is used at the beginning of a sentence, subject–operator inversion is necessary unless the negative word is part of the subject.

For Example:

Never have I met him.

Not a candidate did turn up for the interview.

No one told me about the accident. (Here, the negative word 'No' is part of the subject. Hence no inversion)

8.5 COMPARISON OF ADVERBS

Adverbs of manner, degree and time have three degrees of comparison. Other forms of adverbs do not admit of comparison.

Case 1: *Monosyllable adverbs:*

They have one syllable which is the smallest unit of a word containing a vowel sound and usually one or more consonants. They form their comparatives by adding '-er' and the superlative by adding '-est' to the positive form; as,

Soon - sooner - soonest

Late - later - latest.

Fast - faster - fastest

Loud - louder - loudest

For Example:

He spoke loud. (positive)

He spoke louder than Raju. (comparative)

He spoke the loudest of all. (superlative)

Case 2: *Those adverbs which end in '-ly' form their comparatives by adding 'more' and their superlatives by adding 'most', as;*

Carefully - more carefully - most carefully
Clearly - more clearly - most clearly
Skillfully - more skillfully - most skillfully

For Example:

He wrote carefully.

He wrote more carefully than his friend.

He wrote most carefully of all students in the class.

Note: The word 'early' takes the following forms

Early - earlier - earliest.

For Example:

I got up early in the morning.

He completed the work earlier.

He completed the work the earliest of all the workers.

Case 3: Some adverbs form their comparative and superlative degrees irregularly; as,

Little - less - least
Well - better - best
Bad - worse - worst
Much - more - most
Far - farther - farthest

For Example:

Raju plays well.

Seetha plays better than Raju.

Rama plays the best of all.

Adverbs used as adjectives

For Example:

The *above* sentence is a good example. (above- adverb. Used here as adjective.)

He got into the *up* train. (up-adverb. Used here as adjective)

I took the *down* train. (down used here as adjective)

It was an *up-hill* task. (up-hill used here as adjective)

Errors in the use of Adverbs

I have money enough to buy the book. (say: I have *enough* money…adjective.)

I am enough strong to face the enemy. (say: I am strong *enough* to face the enemy - adverb)

He is fluently speaking. (say: He is speaking fluently.)

(When the verb is intransitive the adverb is placed after the verb.)

He fluently spoke English. (say: He spoke English fluently.)

(When the verb is transitive the adverb is placed after the object.)

He fortunately escaped unhurt. (say: Fortunately, he escaped unhurt.)

(When the adverb modifies the whole sentence place it at the beginning.)

He goes to church seldom. (say; He seldom goes to church)

(When the adverb of time like always, often, never, rarely, sometimes, seldom, ever and frequently are used in a sentence they are placed before the verb.)

For Example:

He often makes mistakes. He frequently goes to Madras.

I am mistaken very often for my brother.

I am very often mistaken for my brother. (When adverbs are used in sentences containing auxiliary verbs they are placed immediately after the auxiliary.)

He swiftly ran. (say: He ran swiftly)

(When adverbs of manner such as swiftly, slowly, gently, softly and fluently are used they are placed after the verb they modify.)

For Example:

He walked slowly.

He went soon there. (say: He went there soon.)

(When adverbs of time and place are used in a sentence, the time should be used only after the place.)

For Example:

He reached there quickly.

You are kindly requested to attend the function. (say: You are requested to attend the function. Both 'request' and 'kindly' are not required as both convey a sense of 'politeness'.)

The court united the couples together. (say: Omit 'together' since 'united' means brought together.)

He is considered as an expert. (say: He is considered an expert) **or**

He is considered to be an expert. (When we think of somebody or something in a special way we should not use 'as' after the verb 'consider')

Ramu was appointed as Managing Director. (say: ... appointed Managing Director)

She is both intelligent as well as hardworking. (say: She is both intelligent and hardworking. (or) She is intelligent as well as hardworking.

(The word 'both' is always followed by 'and' and not 'as well as'.)

This machine is rather unique. (say: This ... is unique. (The word 'unique' is absolute and does not admit of comparison.)

He is too angry. (say: He is very angry.)

Do not use 'too' to mean 'very'. It is used with adjectives and adverbs to indicate a higher degree or in the sense 'more than is desirable or allowed'. In other words, 'too' is used when there is some limit or certain standard implied.

For Example:

We are too happy to help you.

As this sentence stands it means ' We are so happy that we cannot help you' which is absurd. Here 'too' is wrongly used to mean 'very'. Correct the sentence as follows:

We are very happy to help you.

He is too cruel to show any mercy. (correct)

His negligence cost him dearly. (say: His negligence cost him dear. The idiom is ' cost somebody dear' meaning to make somebody suffer)

I am too happy to welcome you. (say: I am very happy to welcome you. The given sentence means, ' I am so happy that I cannot welcome you' which is meaningless)

He went directly to his office. (say: He went direct to his office)

Directly means straight (in a line or manner). Direct means without any interruption or without any one in between.

I will deal with him direct. (without any body in between or personally)

The two buildings are directly opposite.

Ration was distributed freely to flood victims.

(say: Ration was distributed free among the flood victims; 'freely' means liberally and 'free' means without cost. In American English 'for free' is used instead of 'free' ; as, Rice was distributed for free among the flood victims.)

When he was attacked he behaved cowardly.

(say; ... he behaved like a coward (or) in a cowardly manner; cowardly-adjective, not adverb)

He is presently the Chairman of the Company.

(say: He is currently the Chairman of the company)

'Presently' in British English means 'shortly'. In modern English, it is used to mean 'currently'.

This is comparatively a better choice. (say: This is a better choice.)

'Comparatively' and 'better' mean the same. Hence, 'Comparatively' is redundant. (repetition)

He not only was intelligent but also clever.

(say: He was not only intelligent but also clever.) (or) He not only was intelligent but also was clever.

Note: 'Not only........but also' construction should always be balanced.

In the given sentence 'was intelligent' comes after 'not only'.

So the construction after 'but also' should be similar to the one after 'not only'. So the sentence should be either " He was not only intelligent but also clever". Here the adjective 'intelligent' comes after 'not only' and the adjective 'clever' comes after 'but also', thus balancing the construction with the same part of speech after each part of the correlative conjunction. (or) He not only *was intelligent* but also *was clever.*

The teacher wants to know as to why he had been absent.

(say: The teacher wants to know why he was absent.)

"As to" means with regard to something or concerning something; as,

(*a*) As *to* the examination , his performance was very poor.

(*b*) Nothing is known *as to* his accident.

Chapter 9 PREPOSITIONS

A preposition is a word that is placed before a noun (or a noun equivalent) or pronoun or a noun clause to show its relation to some other word in a sentence so as to make the sentence meaningful.

Alternatively, prepositions are words that show the relationship between things, people or events.

'Preposition' means *'that which is placed before'*.

The words *on, in, at, between, from, out of, on behalf of, by, for, of, after, till, over, under, into, with, from within, according to, because of, by means of,* etc. are examples of prepositions.

Every preposition has generally an object with it. The object can be a noun, pronoun or a noun clause. *The object comes after the preposition.*

Noun: The boy is in the *room*. (object to the preposition 'in')

Pronoun: I talked to *him*. (object to the preposition 'to')

Noun Clause: You must be satisfied with *what you have.*

(The noun clause 'what you have' is the object to the preposition 'with')

There is no point in *what you said.*

(The noun clause 'what you said' is the object to the preposition 'in')

More Examples:

1. There is a pen *on* the table.

Here the preposition 'on' shows the relationship between the nouns *pen* and *table.*

(The preposition 'on' is used before the noun 'table' which is its *object.*)

2. I prefer tea to coffee. The preposition 'to' joins a noun to another noun.
3. He came *with* his sister.The preposition 'with' joins it object (sister) to a verb (came).
4. Rema is angry *at* what he said.

Here the noun clause 'what he said' is the object of the preposition 'at' (*i.e.,* angry at what?)

9.1 POSITIONS OF PREPOSITIONS

1. Normally prepositions are placed before nouns and pronouns.

   There is a man *in* the house.

2. Sometimes prepositions are put at the end of a sentence.

   (*i*) When the object is 'that' (a relative pronoun)

   For Example:

   This is the song *that* you were listening *to*. (You were listening to this song)

   That was the book *that* I was looking *for*. (I was looking for that book)

   Here is the thing *that* you asked *for*.

   Note: Sometimes the object 'that' is not stated, but understood.

   For Example:

   That was the man I was referring *to*. (That was the man *that* I was referring to)

   This is the photograph I was speaking *of*. (This is the photograph *that* I was speaking of.)

   (*ii*) When the object is an interrogative pronoun.

   What are you dreaming *of*? (You are dreaming *of* what)

   Whom are you talking *to*? (You are talking *to* whom)

3. Sometimes the object is placed first for emphasis.

   He is famous all the world *over*.

   (He is famous all *over* the world. Here the object is 'the world')

   This I was thinking of. (I was thinking of this.)

9.2 KINDS OF PREPOSITIONS

1. Simple Prepositions.
2. Double Prepositions.
3. Compound Prepositions.
4. Participial Prepositions.
5. Phrase Prepositions.
6. Prepositional Adverbs or Disguised Prepositions.

1. **Simple Prepositions:** These are prepositions that are not formed by any method. The following are the simple prepositions in the English Language: at, on, in, to, by, for, with, from, off, of, through, up, till.

   For Example:

   When he came we were *at* home.

   The book is *on* the table.

Ramu went *to* Delhi.

He is living *at* the end of the street.

I usually go *by* bus.

I bought a pen *for* him.

He came *with* his father.

She came *from* Mumbai.

We are still five kilometres *off* Kochi.

He is a member *of* our team.

He went *through* the crowd.

He went *up* the hill.

The shop is open *till* twenty hours.

2. **Double Prepositions:** These are prepositions containing two simple prepositions. They are used to make the sense clearer. They include: into, from among, from within, from under, out of, etc.

For Example:

He went *into* the room. (Indicates motion to inside the room)

The committee has selected the best actor *from among* a number of actors.

He came out *from within* the room.

I got the book *from under* the table.

He came *out of* the shop.

3. **Compound Prepositions:** These are prepositions which are formed by prefixing *a, be, in, out* or *with* with a noun, an adjective or an adverb. They are: *a*mong, *a*cross, *a*round, *a*midst, *be*fore, *be*low, *be*neath, *be*side, *be*hind, *in*side, *out*side, *within,* etc.

For Example:

He is one *among* the three brothers.

She went *across* the field.

The earth goes *around* the sun.

He started speaking *amidst* applause.

She came *before* me.

His performance in the class is *below* average.

He kept the book *beneath* the table. (under)

She was standing *beside* me. (by my side)

He stood *behind* me.

She was standing *inside* the room.

He was standing *outside* the room.

You should report to me *within* two days.

4. **Participial Prepositions:** These are present participles that are used as prepositions without any noun or pronoun attached to them. They are *absolute* and are prepositions for all practical purposes.

For Example:

considering, notwithstanding, barring, concerning, regarding, pending, touching , etc.

Considering (taking into account) his age, the judge let him off with a warning.

Notwithstanding (in spite of) his inexperience he was able to do the work successfully.

Or

His inexperience *notwithstanding*, he was able to do the work successfully.

Regarding (about) the press report on the charges of corruption, I believe that it is far from true.

Pending disposal of the case against him, the officer was allowed to continue in office.

Concerning (about) breach of discipline, the Principal will deal with all cases.

Touching (with regard to) your suggestion, I shall take a decision soon.

5. **Phrase Prepositions:** These are groups of words (two or more) which are used together as prepositions. A Phrase preposition has the force of a single preposition.

in front of, in spite of, according to, by means of, on behalf of, with regard to, instead of, on account of, in lieu of, for the sake of, in favour of , etc. are Phrase prepositions.

For Example:

There is a garden *in front* of their house.

In spite of his hard work he could not get a first class.

According to the register he was absent yesterday.

He came out of the well *by means* of a rope.

He spoke to the striking employees *on behalf of* the manager. (as a representative)

The library introduced certain new rules *with regard to* the lending of books. (concerning)

He gave me a pen *instead of* a pencil.

He did not attend the office yesterday *on account of* illness.

He was given a day off *in lieu of* his having worked on a holiday. (meaning 'instead of')

He gave up drinking *for the sake of* health.

He argued *in favour* of his friend.

6. **Prepositional Adverbs or Disguised Prepositions:** A word is a preposition when it has a noun or pronoun or a noun clause as its object. It is an adverb when it does not have a noun or pronoun as its object. Such a word is called a Prepositional adverb (PA) or Disguised preposition.

For Example:

They stood *outside* the hall.	('outside' is a preposition)
They stood *outside*.	(PA)
She climbed *up* the stairs.	(preposition)
He climbed up.	(PA)
He went *aboard* the ship.	(preposition)
He went aboard.	(PA)

The following is a list of some of the prepositional adverbs:

about, above, after, along, aboard, before, below, between, by, behind, beneath, besides, beyond, down, in, inside, outside, near, notwithstanding, off, on, opposite, over, past, round, since, through, under, up, within, without, throughout etc.

One word prepositions: The most common prepositions in English are simple one-word prepositions.

For Example:

about, above, abroad, at, in, on, by, off, down, over, past, under, concerning, barring, considering, regarding, pending etc.

Two word prepositions:

For Example:

ahead of, alongside of, because of, apropos of (with reference to), instead of, short of, according to, along with, as for, away from, owing to, except for, out of, up to, up till, from above, from among, from below, as against, in between, etc.

Three/four word prepositions:

For Example:

by means of, by virtue of, by dint of, by way of, at the cost of, in front of, in respect of, on behalf of, with the exception of, with an eye to, with a view to, for the benefit of, for the sake of, at the hands of etc.

9.3 RELATIONS DENOTED BY PREPOSITIONS

The most common relations expressed by prepositions are given below:

1. **Place:** on, under, at, near, behind, against, about, near, beside, between, round, over, across, along, through, into, to, up, within, without, down, upon, from, below, towards, by, before, among etc.

   For Example:

   He put the book *on* the table.

   She put the luggage *under* the table.

   He arrived late *at* the railway station.

2. **Time:** after, at, before, behind, by, during, for, from, in, into, under, on, since, through, throughout, till, towards, until, with, within etc.

   For Example:

   He reached the station *after* an hour.

   The exam begins *at* 10 O' clock.

   He left home *before* daybreak.

3. **Instrument, agency and manner:** With, by, through.

   For Example:

   He killed him *with* a knife. (instrument)

   They sent the message *by* post. (agency)

   The company got the orders *through* its representatives. (agency)

   The soldiers fought *with* courage. (manner)

   He was dying *by* inches. (manner)

4. **Possession:** of, with

   For Example:

   A book *of* mine was lost yesterday

   He is a man *of* principles.

   The man *with* gray beard came here yesterday.

5. **Cause:** for, of

   Gandhiji fought *for* India's freedom.

   He bought medicine *for* his ailment.

   The boy died *of* cholera.

6. **Reason:** from, through, with

   He died *from* fatigue.

   He lost his money *through* sheer negligence.

   Many people are afflicted *with* the disease.

7. **Measure, rate:** by, at

   Petrol is sold *by* the litre.

   We bought cement *by* the lorry load.

   The car was running *at* 60 km per hour.

   He borrowed money *at* an exorbitant interest.

8. **Contrast:** for

   For every action there is a reaction.

   For all his wealth he behaves like a miser.

9. **Concession:** with

   With all his drawbacks I like him.

   With all his criminal background he was appointed caretaker.

10. **Inference:** from

From what I have been told about him he does seem to be trustworthy.

From the information I have gathered about him he seems to be mad.

11. **Source or origin:** from

The quotation is *from* Milton's Paradise Lost.

We get ice *from* water.

The Ganga originates *from* the Himalayas.

12. **Motive:** from

He helped Ramu *from* (= out of) gratitude

He killed him *from* (= out of) revenge.

13. **Movement:** from, into, onto

Ravi was travelling *from* Kochi to Trivandrum.

He jumped *into* the well.

The cat jumped *upon* the table.

14. **Direction:** up, down, along, towards

He climbed *up* the stairs.

He walked *down* the hill.

She went *along* the road.

Raju walked *towards* the hospital.

Note: Prepositions of 'time when' (on, in, at) are omitted from the following words: next, last, this, that, some, every, yesterday, today, and tomorrow.

For Example:

I came here last Monday. (Not: *on* last Monday)

I shall come next Friday.

Rainfall is comparatively less this year. (Not: *in* this year)

There was none at home that day.

I visit Delhi every year. (Not: *in* every year)

He came here yesterday (Not: *on* yesterday)

He will come today/tomorrow.

Note: Prepositions may be used or omitted (optional) with the following phrases referring to past time more than once removed and those which indicate a time before or after a specified time in the past or future. However, Modern English prefers the sentence without preposition.

For Example:

He visited his relatives (in) the year *before last.*

She came here (on) the day *before yesterday.*

I shall go there (on) Tuesday week/this day week.

(meaning: seven days after Tuesday/this day)

We went to Mumbai (in) the previous summer.

I met him (on) the next day.

I have told him that I shall meet him (at) the following weekend.

9.4 USE OF SOME IMPORTANT PREPOSITIONS

At:

(*i*) Used with the names of small localities. (towns and villages)

They are generally treated as points without dimensions.

I met him at Thekkady. (a small town)

He was born at Edappally. (a village)

(*ii*) Used before nouns denoting definite point of time.

We went there at *Christmas.*

I woke up at *dawn.*

I shall come at 3p .m. on *Monday next.* (use either 'on Monday next' or 'next Monday')

(*iii*) Used with phrases : (at work, at play, at mid-day, at the station, at home, at an address, at the door etc.)

I met him at work. (at work- at the place where one works)

He is at home.

There is someone at the door. (at the door- at the front door of a house)

(*iv*) 'at' means 'in front of' meaning 'not in contact'.

He is *at the dining* table. (In front of the dining table)

(*v*) With expressions of *condition/state.*

The two major forces are *at war.*

When lightning occurs it is better to be *at rest.*

I met him *at leisure.*

(*vi*) With price/cost.

I bought oranges *at* five rupees a dozen.

(*vii*) Manner/method.

We walked *at* slow speed.

(*viii*) Used in speaking of things at rest.

He is standing *at* the top of the mountain.

(*ix*) Used with places of entertainment, restaurant, place of work, club, etc.

He will be at Ramavarma club now.

Yesterday we were at the theatre. (place of entertainment)

I ate at the woodlands. (restaurant)

I have been at school for the last ten years. (working as a teacher)

John was at doctor's. (at doctor's clinic)

Raj is at breakfast/lunch/dinner etc. (having breakfast/lunch/dinner etc)

Note: 'at' normally indicates a small *distant* place of less importance, 'in' is used when we refer to a place where we are at the time of speaking.

For Example:

He is now at Kottayam.

The train stops at Farok.

I am now in Kochi. (Not 'at' Kochi. See note above)

He is in Bombay/Delhi/Calcutta /Chennai/Bangalore etc.

They are now in America.

He is employed at Kochi in Kerala.

Note: The expression 'at the end' means the final part of a period of time, the final part of an event or a story, the end of a street or line etc.

For Example:

We are going to Chennai *at the end* of this week/month/year.

(Not: in the end. *For the difference between 'at the end' and 'in the end' see 'in' below.*)

At the end of the story the hero dies. (Not, in the end)

There is a shop at the end of the street.

He put a knot at the end of the thread.

You draw an arrow at the end of the line.

(*x*) 'at' is used to express intended targets or goals.

The hunter aimed his gun at the tiger.

The fish snapped at the bait.

There is a difference in the use of 'at' in the above two sentences. In the first, 'at' is used with the word 'aim' whereas in the second, 'at' is used before the object 'the bait'.

(*xi*) 'at' is used to indicate a relation between emotion and the agent that creates it.

He was shocked at his indifference.

They were surprised at the turn of events.

(*xii*) Miscellaneous:

at somebody's best/worst, etc, at all, at breakfast/lunch/dinner etc, at a party/meeting/concert etc, be at it, at that, etc.

For Example:

He was at his best/worst etc. (He was as good as he could be)

He did not understand anything at all. (not even a little)

We discussed the matter at breakfast/lunch/dinner etc.

We were at a party/meeting etc. yesterday.

I bought an umbrella, and a nice one at that. (used to give additional information)

She is at it again, borrowing money from all her friends and neighbours.

(doing something without anybody's approval)

A meeting was arranged at his request. (as requested by him)

I met the collector at the mayor's suggestion. (as suggested by the Mayor.)

I attended the seminar at their invitation.

The soldier shot at the intruder. (Shows direction)

In:

(*i*) Used with the names of very big cities, provinces, states, countries, etc. (They are generally treated as areas)

I live in India.

His brother is in Canada.

But: He lives at Kochi in Kerala.

(*ii*) Used before the names of months and years.

Raju was born in May in 1956.

Or Raju was born in May, 1956.

(*iii*) Used with phrases. in the morning, in the evening, in summer, in winter.

He started his journey in the morning.

It is very hot in (the) summer.

I met him in the evening.

(*iv*) Used to denote a place inside anything.

He travelled in a packed bus.

The blade is in the box.

(*v*) Used before a noun to denote a period of time or a time well before a particular time. (at the end of that period or beginning of the next in the future)

I shall return the book in a week. (at the end of the week and not before)

I reached the station in time. (well before the schedule)

Onam is celebrated in August.

Gandhiji lived in the twentieth century.

The budget was passed in March. Prices of commodities started rising in the following month.

Note: For time measurement referring to a point of time in the future we use 'in + period of time' or ' in + genitive of period of time 'or'in its place time' or 'period of time + from now'.

For Example:

He will come back in six months.

He will come back six months' time.

He will come back six months from now.

(*vi*) Used to denote a place (position), condition or state, motion, relation between adjective and noun, verb and object.

We met him in Delhi.

He was found in a building.

I talked to him in the morning.

India got freedom in 1947.

The boys are in uniform. (state)

She came dressed in her best clothes. (state)

My car is in good condition.

He is not in a position to help you. (state)

He is deaf in one ear and lame in one leg. (relation between adjective and noun)

David is in the Navy.

She put the coin in the box. (in = into showing motion)

She believes in God. (relation between verb and object)

He is sitting in a chair. (a chair with arms)

(He is sitting *on* a chair.- a chair without arms.)

He is in troubles.

We come across demons in folklores.

(*vii*) Used in speaking of things at rest.

For Example:

He is in bed.

(*viii*) Used to denote a particular period of time in negative sentences or after ordinal numbers like first, second, etc.

For Example:

He hasn't gone to school in days

It is the first time he has met him in two months.

(*ix*) Used to indicate physical surroundings.

For Example:

He went in the car. (if the car is owned by him)

('He went *by* car' shows the mode of conveyance).

She stood in the sun.

It is difficult to walk in the cold.

(*x*) Used to show involvement

For Example:

He took part in the discussion.

She has acted in the latest movie.

(*xi*) Used to show a ratio

For Example:

The mason was asked to provide a slop of one in eight.

(*xii*) Used to show arrangement, form, a quantity of people or thing, etc.

For Example:

The construction was completed in three stages.

They were ten in number.

They sat in a circle.

(*xiii*) Used to show material, mode, etc

For Example:

He wrote a poem in ink.

He put his complaint in writing.

She made the payment in cash.

(*xiv*) Used to show the quality of a person.

For Example:

We have lost a very good organizer in John.

(*xv*) Used in the sense of 'buy and sell':

He deals in school books. (Not: *deal with* in this sense)

Note: It is wrong to say –'He has told me that he will come back after a month'. Instead, we should say – 'He has told me that he will come back *in* a month'. ('in' means at the end of a period in the future while 'after' means at the end of a period in the past *e.g.*, He came back *after* a month.)

In modern English 'in' is often used for 'within'.

Note: The expression 'in the end' means finally, after a long time or after a long struggle.

In the end, he got a reward for his hard work. (Not: at the end)

In the end, he got a suitable job. (Not: at the end)

Don't say: In the end of the novel, the hero dies.

Say: At the end of the novel, the hero dies.

Or

In the end, the hero dies.

Remember: ' in the end of *something*' is wrong

'at the end of *something*' is right

(*xvi*) Used in metaphorical expressions.

He is in deep waters. (in trouble or difficulty)

My friend is in difficulty.

(*xvii*) Used to indicate manner.

The discussion took place in a cordial atmosphere.

Within:

(*i*) Used to denote 'before the end of a period'.

I shall return the book within a week. (before the end of a week or during the week.)

(*ii*) Used in the sense of 'inside the range or limits of something:

That topic will not come within the purview of this discussion.

She finds it difficult to meet both ends within her meagre income.

His camera captured everything within range.

(*iii*) Used to indicate distance from something

Her house is within *walking* distance from the school. (Don't say: walkable distance)

The office is within a stone's throw of his house.

The railway station is within a stone's throw from here.

Into:

Used to denote *motion towards the inside* of anything or change from one medium to another (change of condition or a point of time during a period of time).

He went into the room. (motion)

Water is converted into water vapour. (change of condition)

Translate it into Hindi. (change of condition)

He sat awake late into the night. (to a point during a period of time)

Note: The phrase *in to* (two words) should not be confused with the preposition *into* (one word). The former is made up of the adverb *in* and the preposition *to*.

For Example:

As soon as he reached home, he went into his old mother.

To:

(*i*) Denotes *motion from one place to another.*

He goes to school daily.

(*ii*) Denotes *time, direction, ratio, action and effect.*

It is ten minutes to 12. (time)

He is going to Kottayam. (place)

Delhi is to the north of India. (direction)

You may go straight and turn to the left at the junction. (")

Baby is to man as cub is to lion. (ratio)

The man came to the beggar's help. (action)

To my knowledge he is a gentleman. (effect)

To my surprise he came to my help. (")

(*iii*) Used with 'prefer'

I prefer coffee to tea. (always 'prefer to' and not 'prefer than')

(*iv*) Used with certain nouns

He is blind to reality.

He is deaf to advice.

(*v*) Used to indicate the recipient of something:

I gave the book to my friend.

(*vi*) Used with verbs like devote, accustom, etc

He devotes himself to studies.

Accustom yourself to eating vegetables.

(*vii*) Used to show relationship:

She is married to a businessman.

There is no easy solution to this problem.

He has lost the key to the door.

(*viii*) Used to show the extent of accuracy:

The amount is correct to a rupee/a paisa etc.

(*ix*) Used to show a particular state:

She put her baby to sleep.

(*x*) Used to indicate a rate or relationship between two numbers:

The latest cars will do 80 km to the gallon.

There are 100 centimetres to a metre.

(*xi*) Used to indicate time:

It is quarter to ten.

(*xii*) Used to show official relationships:

She was appointed stenographer to the managing director.

He is attached to the audit wing.

(*xiii*) Used to mean 'attached or fastened':

The boat was tied to a pole.

The compartment was attached to the engine.

(*xiv*) Used to mean 'movement with certain intention':

He managed to take the child involved in the accident to safety.

(*xv*) Used to show the reaction to something:

To his surprise, he won the first prize.

To his dismay, his request for a job was rejected.

On:

(*i*) Used to denote position of things at rest and when in contact.

The pen is on the table.

The picture is on the wall.

The book is on the floor.

(*ii*) Used with dates and names of dates.

I left for Delhi on the 15th of May. (or on 15th May)

He is getting married on Monday next. (or next Monday)

She met me on a Sunday. I requested him to meet me on the following day.

(*iii*) Used to refer to a general *point* of time.

He was born on July 1st, 1968.

The train arrived on time. (at the scheduled time)

(*iv*) Used in speaking of things at rest.

The book is on the table.

(*v*) Used to show concern, dependence, state, reason and time.

The meeting is on the first of June/ on New Year's Day. (time)

He gave a discourse on the topic for half an hour. (concern)

Children depend on parents for their needs. (dependence)

The house is on fire. (state)

We are going on a tour to Bangalore. (action)

The officer is on tour. Hence, he will not attend the meeting. (reason)

(*vi*) Used to indicate direction

There is shop on your left/on your right.

(*vii*) Used with diet or medicine

He is on a fat-free diet. (to lose weight)

(*viii*) Used to show financial support

I cannot feed them on Rs 500 a month.

He is living on a pension of Rs 600 a month.

(*ix*) Used in the sense 'about'

His book on Gandhiji is famous.

(*x*) Used to show the effect of something:

The High Court has decreed a ban on smoking.

(*xi*) Used to show how we can get something or somebody:

We get news on TV. (Not: on the TV)

We get a lot of entertainments on the Radio. (Not: on/in Radio)

You can get me on the phone.

(*xii*) Used to indicate a state:

They are on tour/vacation/business etc.

(*xiii*) Used with diet or medicine.

He is on a fat-free diet. (to lose weight)

He has been on Ayurvedic treatment for a long time.

(*xiv*) Used to show financial support:

I cannot feed them on Rs 500 a month.

He is living on a pension of Rs 600 a month.

(*xv*) Used in the sense of in or into a vehicle.

He got on the bus.

He is traveling on the train/bus.

I am now on the plane.

(*xvi*) Used to indicate the subject or topic of discussion or communication.

They had a discussion on the latest political developments.

She congratulated her brother on his success.

He wrote a book on Gandhiji.

Note: The following verbs and nouns take 'on' or 'about'.

argue, write, speak, lecture, book, discussion.

For Example:

He argued with me about/on the matter.

He wrote a book about/on the subject.

She spoke about/on the need for discipline.

He lectured about/on the educational policy of the government.

Upon:

(*i*) Used in speaking of things in motion.

For Example:

The cat jumped upon the table.

(*ii*) Used to mean 'on':

His success depends upon his luck.

From:

(*i*) Used before a noun or phrase to denote a point of time. (But, not used with perfect and perfect continuous tenses for this purpose)

I started my journey from 4 o' clock in the morning.

He was absent from Monday to Thursday.

Regular classes will be conducted from 10th June to 25th July.

(*ii*) Used to denote places of origin, cause/reason, difference, motive, inference, etc.

Ram started from Madras at 6 o' clock. (place of origin)

A Mango fell down from the tree. (place of origin)

He is from Kerala. (place of origin)

The Ganges starts from the Himalayas. (place of origin)

They are suffering from Jaundice. (cause)

This book differs from that. (difference)

All this occurred from misunderstanding. (reason)

From all what he said, I understood that he was innocent. (inference)

(*iii*) Used to show the material that something is made of:

This juice is made from oranges. (not made of oranges)

Paper is made from pulpwood. (not made of pulpwood)

Note: While changing one substance into another, if a new substance is produced we use 'from' but if the original substance is formed into some objects we use 'of'

For Example:

This table is made of wood.(Here the material used for making the table also is wood)

(*iv*) Used for stating the place from where something comes:

This is imported from China.

We get enquiries from all over the world.

(*v*) Used to show that something starts at a particular time and goes on:

The office functions from 9.00 to 5.00 during the week.

From now on I am going to be a different person.

(*vi*) Used to show distance:

He lives a few kilometers from his office.

The factory is twenty kilometers from the city.

(*vii*) Used with the verbs 'prevent' and 'protect':

He was prevented from entering the office.

The umbrella protects us from rain.

(*viii*) Used to show change of state:

It has gone from bad to worse.

I want to be free from all worries.

He translated the novel from the Malayalam. (Not: from Malayalam)

(from the Malayalam = from the Malayalam version)

(*ix*) Used to indicate place of origin.

He is from Germany.

She is from America.

(*x*) 'From' is the opposite of 'to'.

John borrowed money from him. He lent money to John.

Over:

(*i*) Used to mean 'above'– (Not in contact/ without contact)

The fan is over my head.

(*ii*) Resting on the surface of something/somebody.

The sheet was spread over the table.

(*iii*) Used to mean 'beyond'

You have to get over your laziness.

(*iv*) Denotes superiority

He overpowered me.

(*v*) Denotes conclusion

It is all over.

(*vi*) Used to mean space, time, across, more etc.

The sun shines over the earth. (space)

She didn't attend the class for over eight days. (time)

We spent over five lakh for the building. (more)

There is a narrow bridge over the river. (across)

With:

(*i*) Denotes the instrument with which something is done.

He cut the mango with a knife.

He paints nicely with a brush.

(*ii*) Also means: against, manner, cause/reason, in spite of, possession, separate.

They quarrelled with the ladies. (against)

The teacher looked at him with anger. (manner)

They received him with courtesy.

She was down with fever. (cause)

With all the success in life, he was unhappy. (in spite of)

I left the hostel with all the belongings. (possession)

I can't part with my Parker pen. (separate)

With his father away on tour, he is to manage the business alone.
(reason for doing something))

With all his drawbacks, he is a successful politician. (in spite of)

(*iii*) Used in some expressions showing human sensations or feelings.

For Example:

red with anger, blue with cold, trembling with rage, green with envy, white with fear, shivering with fever etc.

When he saw his enemy he became *red with anger.*

When he saw a snake he became *white with fear.*

My neighbour was *trembling with rage* when he saw his naughty son.

(*iv*) Used to show one's behaviour to others. e.g. pleased with, angry with, cross with, patient with etc.

I am very much *pleased with* his work. (happy)

My neighbour is *cross with* me. (Not: on speaking terms)

I am patient with my customers. (without becoming angry)

What is wrong with you? (strange behaviour)

(*v*) Used with verbs like 'make', 'build', 'construct', etc. (verbs of making) to indicate one of the items with which something is made.

The soup is made with tomato.

The house was built with brick.

The wall was constructed with stone.

(*vi*) Used to mean 'together with' or 'in company with'.

My father came with me.

John with his relatives went to Chennai.

(*vii*) Used in the sense of 'support'.

He went with the majority opinion.

(*viii*) Used to mean 'possessing'.

He is a man with a weak heart.

(*ix*) Used with 'all' to mean 'despite'

With all his drawback, he is well-behaved.

Without: 'Without' expresses the negative of 'with'.

For Example:

I took out the screw without a screwdriver.

I went out without money.

She is a woman without children.

This house is without a garden.

By:

(*i*) Refers to the future – to show the latest time ('not later than') at which an action will be completed. Used before a point of time.

My exams will be over by next Tuesday. (not later than Tuesday)

We shall reach there by 10 o'clock. (not later than 10 o'clock)

I shall wait for you by 8 p.m. (up to 8 p.m., not more than that or shorter than that)

(*ii*) Denotes an agent or a doer or the way something is done.

A snake was killed *by Rama.*

He was knocked by a bus.

She was shocked by the news.

He paid the dues by cheque.

They sent the book by post.

(*iii*) It also denotes nearness, some method or time. Also means 'on account of', 'by means of' etc.

It is safe to travel by day/by night.	(day time/night time)
He has travelled by air/by road.	(method)
Get up by sunrise.	(time)
Finish the work by next week.	(not later than)
He swears by God.	(in the name of God)
I am a citizen of India by birth.	(by= on account of)
Please stand by me.	(nearness)
They travelled by bus/car/train/plane.	(by=by mean of)

Note: The rats were killed by fire. (here, by = 'by means of' or making use of an instrument or a secondary agent) (not: with fire).

The house was completely gutted by fire. (not: in fire)

(*iv*) Near somebody or something.

He placed the table by the window.

He sat by the patient.

Between:

(*i*) In or into the space separating two or more people, objects, points, days, etc.

I shall be there between 1p.m. and 4 p.m.

Sunday comes between Saturday and Monday.

There was a quarrel between Rema and Hari.

Choose between two dresses.

(*ii*) Used when three or more people or countries are involved provided they are mentioned by name.

Switzerland lies *between* France, Germany, Austria and Italy. (separating points)

This sentence is to be interpreted as follows:

Switzerland lies between France and Germany.

Switzerland lies between Germany and Austria.

Switzerland lies between Austria and Italy.

Note: If the names are not mentioned after 'between', either *between* or *among* can be used.

Switzerland lies between four countries.

or

Switzerland lies among four countries.

(*iii*) Used while referring to the speaker himself and a group of people.

Friends, we shall divide the money between ourselves. (between *my friends* and *me*).

I distributed the oranges between me and my friends.

Note: It is wrong to say:

The meeting will be held between 1p.m. to 4 p.m.

Say: The meeting will be held between 1p.m. and 4 p.m.

Use always *'between ....and'* (*not 'to'*)

Between you and I, he is a cheat. (wrong)

Between you and me, he is a cheat.

(A preposition should always be followed by a noun or pronoun in the objective case. The objective case of the pronoun, noun 'you' is you itself and that of 'I' is me.)

Note: 'Between' is used as an adverb to mean *in the period of time separating two dates or two or more points, objects, etc. or two events , etc.*

We meet each other on Sundays and not *in between.*

Our temple is near the church but there is a road *in between.*

Among:

(*i*) Used to represent more than two persons, things, ideas etc.

The kings quarreled among themselves.

She distributed the sweets among the three children.

He is one among the corporation councillors.

(*ii*) Used to mention one or more things out of a large number:

They discussed, among other things, the impact of globalization.

(*iii*) Used to mean 'in the midst of' people or things:

He was standing among the demonstrators.

The minister was seen among a crowd of workers.

Before:

(*i*) Used to denote an earlier point of time, presence.

He reached my house before 7 o'clock.

The culprit appeared before the judge. (presence)

(*ii*) Used to refer to a place in a list:

His name comes before mine.

(*iii*) Used in expressions like 'right before my (very) eyes' and 'before long' (soon)

The accident happened right before my (very) eyes.

The motive behind the murder will be known before long.

(*iv*) Used to mean 'in front of':

She stood before the mirror.

There is car before the gate.

(*v*) Used in expressions like 'before doing something'

You should inform the police before burying the dead body.

You should consult your doctor before taking any medicine.

(*vi*) Used to mean 'something prevents someone from doing what he wants'.

Before he could contact her she left the place.

(*vii*) Used in commands, orders or warnings:

Go to your class before the teacher comes.

Complete your work before 5 o' clock.

(*viii*) Used to show what is in the future:

The challenges before us are really daunting.

The tasks before us are challenging.

After:

(*i*) Used to denote the close of a period in the past.

He reached Baroda after nine days.

We had sweets after lunch.

(*ii*) Used to mean *taking care of, in pursuit of, following* etc.

We ran after the thief. (pursuit)

Parents look after their children. (taking care)

The officer entered the room after the meeting. (following).

(*iii*) Used to show 'later than something'

He had his breakfast after 8.

We shall meet the day after tomorrow.

He reached the railway station after the train had left.

(*iv*) Used in expressions like 'day after day', 'time after time' etc.

I dislike seeing the TV serial day after day.(meaning 'repeatedly')

I reminded him time after time of the meeting.

(*v*) Used in the sense of 'finding out/catching somebody or something'

The police are after the thief.

He is after a furnished accommodation.

(*vi*) Used to mean 'about':

He asked after my father. (meaning 'enquired about my father')

(*vii*) Used to mean 'in the style of '

She named her son 'Midun' after her uncle. (Midun)

Behind:

(*i*) Refers to a place (at the back of), time (late with respect to time), inferiority, etc.

He is standing behind me. (at the back)

He locked the door behind him. (when he left)

John ran fast leaving the rest behind. (at the back)

You always come to work behind time. (late)

The train is running behind the schedule.

He has rich experience behind him.

He is behind others in studies. (inferior)

He is the man behind this achievement.

(*ii*) Used for giving support:

They stood solidly behind him.

Below: Used to mean something lower in position, dignity, expectation, less than, inferior to.

He is below my rank. (lower in position)

The book costs below twenty rupees. (less than)

His writings are below standard. (inferior)

It is below your dignity to make friends with him. (dignity)

Beneath:

(*i*) Used to mean 'under'

He waited for the girl beneath the tree.

She found her pen lying beneath the newspaper.

(*ii*) Used to mean ' not good enough/below his dignity':

What he did was beneath him.

His unruly behaviour at the meeting was beneath him.

Beside:

(*i*) Used to mean 'at the side of or next to'

She sat beside her father.

(*ii*) Used for comparison:

My knowledge is negligible beside yours.

(*iii*) Used to mean ' extremely':

He was beside himself with anger. (meaning 'extremely angry')

(Idiom: beside oneself with anger, rage, grief, sorrow, etc.)

Besides: Used to mean 'in addition to'

Besides Rahim, Ramu was also present at the meeting.

Besides being a businessman, he is a writer of repute.

I am not going to attend the cocktail party. Besides, I am a teetotaller.

(One who does not drink alcohol)

Since:

(*i*) Used before a noun or phrase to denote a *point of time* but not a period of time in the past. (Used only with the perfect tenses of the preceding verb)

I have known him since my *marriage.*

We have been doing it since *morning.*

They have not come here since *Monday last.(or since last Monday)*

I have been waiting here since *2 o'clock.*

(*ii*) Used to mean 'at or after a particular time'

I was a journalist for three years, but I have changed my profession since then.

Exception: It *is* long since we met. (The perfect tense is not used if the sentence begins with 'It is long etc. Here 'since' is used as a conjunction)

For:

(*i*) Used to denote *a period* of time, but not a *point of time.* (Used with all tenses)

I have been absent from the class for a long time. (period of time)

He has been working there for more than two years.

(*ii*) Used to show support, purpose, reason, wish, contrast (in spite of), time, cost, etc.

He is always taken for a fool. (comparison)

I bought this book for Rs 20/- (cost)

I am for what he has said. (support)

We are not for war. (support)

The patients are asked to go for a walk. (purpose)

He was convicted for stealing. (reason)

I hope for a distinction. (wish)

For the one rupee he spent he got thousands. (contrast)

For all his wealth he lives a miserly life. (in spite of)

'C' stands for character. (representation)

We were out for a long time. (time)

This message is for him. (in favour of)

He translated the book word for word. (exactly equivalent)

(*iii*) Often omitted in phrases of duration.

The programme lasted (for) the whole day.

We played (for) a lot of time.

She studied all day.

(Not used with phrases beginning with 'all' such as *all day, all (the) week/ month/year* etc.)

He lived there all (the) week/month/year etc.

Note: If the action of the verb is not continuous with the period of time the preposition 'for' should not be omitted.

For Example:

He lived there *for* three years. (He did not live there continuously for three years)

He lived there three years. (He lived there continuously for three years.)

I studied there *for* five years.

Note: If a sentence begins with a period of time, the preposition 'for' should not be omitted.

For Example:

For one year, he was ill.

Till:

Up to the point in time or the event mentioned.

I shall be here till 2.15 p.m. (not earlier or later)

He works from morning till night.

Until:

'Till' is the short form of 'until'. ('Till' is less formal and not used at the beginning of a sentence. 'Until' is used instead.)

Let us wait until he comes.

Until now I have not told a lie.

Until they tell the truth they will not be let off.

Of:

Used to mean cause, source, possession, space in time, separation, quality, apposition, opinion, possibility, material, content, identity, etc.

He died of small pox. (cause)

The table is made of wood. (source)

We live in the house of our uncle. (possession)

He returned within an hour of the appointed time. (space in time)

She is deprived of her relatives. (separation)

Gandhiji was a man of great character. (quality)

Kochi, the Queen of the Arabian Sea , is in Kerala. (apposition)

It was kind of him to have remembered my request. (opinion)

I got three of my books. (something from a group)

I took leave of him. (separation)

I asked a favour of him. (from)

This matter is of importance to me. (quality)

The law does not admit of any concession. (possibility)

This is the costliest of all items. (grading)

He was robbed of all his valuables. (deprived of)

The city of Trivandrum is the capital of Kerala. (identity).

He drank a bottle of milk. (content)

Valmiki is the author of the Ramayana. (authorship)

He is accused of murder. (offence)

OFF:

It means (away from a place, away from duty or work, take away or remove , cancelled, reduction from price, at a distance, away from something) etc.

The bus is off the road.	(away from a place)
He is off duty.	(away from duty)
Take the cap off your head.	(remove)
He was a kilometer off me.	(at a distance)
Switch the fan off.	(not functioning)
My house is off the M.G.Road.	(away from)
They put off the festival.	(cancelled)
The worker is off today.	(away from duty)
All computer books have 10% off.	(reduction in price)
He goes to the temple on and off.	(or off and on = occasionally)

Than:

('Than' is usually a conjunction but it is sometimes used as a preposition.) 'Than' follows a comparative.

Rema is fatter than Meera.

He will not give more than five rupees.

But:

(It is used more as a conjunction than as a preposition). In certain cases 'but' is used to denote exceptions.

All but him had failed.	(except him)
I passed all the subjects but Maths.	(except Maths)

About:

Used to show concern, nearness, something scattered.

I know nothing about him.	(concerning)
The books were strewn about the room.	(scattered)
Rahim is about my age.	(nearness)
He has written a book *about* the birds of Kerala.	(a general study)

Note: He has written a book *on* the birds of Kerala. (a serious study; this difference may be noted)

The following verbs and nouns take only 'about':

Read, quarrel, teach, story, ignorance, know, think.

For Example:

She quarrelled about a silly matter.

The teacher taught about the need for hygiene.

He told me a story about witches.

She pretended ignorance about the matter.

She knew about his second wife.

He thought about her sad plight.

Note: 'of' is sometimes used in place of 'about'. But, there is a slight difference in meaning.

For Example:

He thought of his dead wife. (He just remembered)

He thought about his dead wife. (He remembered many things about her.)

Above:

Used to mean higher than, at the top of, unapproachable, over, etc.

The fan is above my head. (over)

He is above all boys in his behaviour. (at the top)

Health is valued above wealth. (higher than)

A Professor is above a lecturer. (")

God is above all. (unapproachable)

Against:

Used to mean opposing/disagreeing, contrast, touching or hitting something or somebody/in contact with, etc.

She acted against my decision. (shows opposition)

The orange dress looks bright against the black background. (shows contrast)

Fishermen are warned against bad weather. (disagreeable weather)

The bird flew against the plane. (opposite)

You are not supposed to lean against the wall. (touching)

He is for banning smoking in public places rather than against it. (for x against)

Through:

Used to mean 'from one end of something to the other'.

We looked through the keyhole.

We walked through the tunnel.

The leader was cheated through foul play.

Note: Don't say, "I walked through the road."

Say, "I walked along or across the road."

Towards:

Used to denote direction, nearness of time or behaviour.

I walked towards the table. (direction)

We sailed towards the North. (")

It is getting towards evening. (nearness of time)

His attitude towards me was good. (behaviour)

Under:

Used to mean 'below', lower in position, less or cover of.

The ball is under the table. (below)

He is a worker under me. (lower in position)

The king walked about *under* the guise of a beggar. (cover of)

My brother is *under* seven years of age. (less than)

Except:

When 'except' is used as a preposition it is always followed by an object.

For Example:

Everyone except him was present.

All boys except Ramu have attended the meeting.

Don't say: All *other* boys except Ramu have attended the meeting.

Except for:

When we make a statement we use 'except for' before the only thing or person about which the statement is not true:

He got all his books except for the Bible.

He invited all his relatives except for his uncle who was away on tour.

Excepting:

Excepting is a preposition when *not, without* or *always* is placed before it.

For Example:

All were punished *not* excepting the girls.

All were punished without *excepting* the girls.

All the members of the club are *always* invited excepting the one under suspension.

9.5 PREPOSITIONS USED WITH TRANSITIVE AND INTRANSITIVE VERBS

Examine the following sentence:

He turned down the invitation.

In the above sentence the word 'down' is an adverb.

The sentence can be written in the following form without any change in meaning:

He turned the invitation down.

Now examine the sentence given under:

The river flows down the valley.

Here, the word 'down' is a preposition and the phrase 'down the valley' is an adverb phrase. Hence, the order of the words in this sentence cannot be changed. In other words, we cannot rewrite the sentence as follows:

The river flows the valley down. (wrong)

The general rule in this regard may be laid down as follows:

If the verb is transitive, any word added to it is an adverb and the position of the added word can be changed without change of meaning; if the verb is intransitive, any word added to it is a preposition and the position of the added word cannot be changed.

Thus, in the sentence ' He turned down the invitation' turned is a transitive verb with 'invitation' as its object. Hence 'down' is an adverb. But, in the sentence 'The river flows down the valley' 'flows' is an intransitive verb. 'Down' therefore is a preposition.

It, therefore, follows that in phrases like *to deal with, to look after, to look at, to look for, to frown at, to run after* which are made up of intransitive verbs followed by prepositions have the force of transitive verbs. In such phrases the two words must stand together and they should not be separated.

For Example:

He looked after his children very well.

He looked his children after very well. (wrong)

9.6 OMISSION OF PREPOSITIONS

1. Prepositions are not used after the following verbs:

   Describe, discuss, to lack, to marry.

   He described her features. (Not: describe about)

   But: He gave a description about her features. (When the noun form is used)

   They discussed the matter in detail. (Not: discussed about)

   But: They had a *discussion on/about* the matter. (When the noun form is used)

   He has decided to *marry* her. (Not: marry with)

   But: He was *married to* her. (When used in the passive voice)

   He *lacks* common sense. (Not: lacks in)

   But: He is *lacking in* common sense. (When used in the present continuous tense)

   A lack of common sense is a disadvantage. (When used as a noun)

2. The prepositions *on, at,* and *in* are not used before the following words when they are used with time expressions:

   this, every, each, any, next, last, some, all, one.

   He will not come this Monday. (Not, on this Monday)

   Hereafter you will have classes every Saturday. (Not, on every Saturday)

   You will have mathematics each day of the week. (Not, on each day)

   Come any day you like. (Not, on any day)

   He will come next Monday. (Not, on next Monday)

   But we can say: He will come on Monday next.

   He came last Monday. (Not, on last Monday.)

   But we can say: He came on Monday last.

   He will meet you some day. (Not, on some day)

   He was working all day. (Not, on all day or during all day.)

He appeared one morning. (Not, He appeared in one morning)

Don't say: Wait for a minute

Say: Wait a minute

She made him do. (Not, She made him to do)

She bid him do. (Not, She bid him to do)

9.7 PREPOSITIONS AND PREPOSITIONAL PHRASES

A prepositional phrase is of the form: preposition + a prepositional complement consisting of a noun phrase, a 'wh' clause or an 'ing' expression.

For Example:

He was standing *at the railway station.* (prepositional phrase-preposition + complement consisting of a noun phrase)

I understood this *from what he had said.* (Preposition + 'wh' clause)

The trade union has called off the strike *after entering into an agreement with the government. (Preposition + 'ing' expression)*

The following verbs and adjectives take either a prepositional complement or a that clause.

surprise, decide, inform, insist, afraid, aware, sorry, sure.

For Example:

He was surprised at *the turn of events.* (prepositional complement.)

She was surprised at his telling a lie.

He was surprised at what he had done.

He has decided on his future plans.

He has decided on what his future plans are.

He has decided that he will study well.

She informed me of her sad plight.

She informed me that she had passed the exam.

He insists on her presence in the meeting.

He insisted that she should be present in the meeting.

She is afraid of her husband.

He is afraid that he will be thrown out of employment.

I am aware of the danger.

He is aware that he should not take chances.

She was sorry about the whole confusion.

He is sorry for him.

He is sorry that they have not been taken care of.

She is sure of her success.

She is sure that she will come out successful in the exam.

Note: Sometimes an adverb or adjective may be used as prepositional complement.

For Example:

Since when, until now, before long, at least, at worst, in brief, at once, from under, etc.

Since when has he been working here?

He has not given the money until now.

He will come here before long.

It costs at least five hundred rupees.

At worst he is a rogue.

In brief, it is a story about village life.

He has at once given his consent.

He emerged from under the cot.

EXERCISE

Errors in the use of prepositions:

1. The clerk availed leave for two days. (wrong)

   The clerk availed himself of leave for two days. (right)

   (The phrase is 'avail oneself of' something . It means make use of something.)

2. We enjoyed in the party. (wrong)

   We enjoyed ourselves in the party. (right)

   'To enjoy' is a transitive verb requiring an object.

   For Example:

   We enjoyed the music. (or) We enjoyed ourselves.

3. The population of India is greater than Pakistan. (wrong)

   The population of India is greater than that of Pakistan. (right)

   In the first sentence population is compared with the country 'Pakistan'. The writer means that the population of India is greater than the population of Pakistan and not Pakistan itself.

   For Example:

   The climate of Delhi is hotter than Kochi. (wrong)

   The climate of Delhi is hotter than that of Kochi. (right)

4. Raju absented from the class. (wrong)

   Raju absented himself from the class. (right)

   'To absent' is a transitive verb and hence, it requires an object to complete the meaning.

5. Ramu prided on his achievement. (wrong)

   Ramu prided himself on his achievement. (right)

   'To pride oneself on something' is the phrase.

   or

   Ramu took pride in his achievement.

   'To take pride in something' is the phrase.

Fill in the blanks with appropriate prepositions:

1. They will arrive ......Kochi tomorrow.
2. He will reach Mumbai ....Sunday.

3. I was born...... a village ....May......
4. The incident took place ...... Palarivattom.....Kochi.
5. He reached howl......seven .....the evening.
6. The train starts.......Delhi .
7. I have been waiting......him .....this morning.
8. The cat jumped ....the table.
9. We buy bricks..... the lorry load.
10. She is older than her sister......three years.
11. All her friends are known .... him.
12. He left ......Chennai.
13. Raju was wounded .....his enemy .....knife.
14. It is now quarter ......twelve.
15. She distributed the sweets .....ten boys.
16. He was leaning ......wall.
17. He spent his holidays......Chennai.
18. He shouted ......the top of his voice.
19. The festival begins.....Friday.
20. He has been working......morning.
21. You must come.....the office .....10 O'clock.
22. She has been absent......three days.
23. He worked in the office .....10 O'clock.
24. The quality of the soap is not ....mark.
25. He was killed ......a knife.
26. He was beaten ....a rod.
27. They are sitting ....the tree.
28. She has no access ......her boss.
29. Coffee is preferable .....tea.
30. He preferred pen.....pencil.
31. My friend congratulated ....my success.
32. I agree to disagree......you.
33. My friend differed .....me.

Chapter 10 CONJUNCTIONS

A conjunction is a word that *merely* joins words, phrases or clauses. It is mainly used to join clauses together and to show the relationship between the ideas contained in them. It does not perform the functions of an adverb or a preposition.

e.g., and, but, or, although, because, etc. are conjunctions.

Ram and Rehim are friends. (The conjunction 'and' joins the words (here two names) 'Ram' and 'Rehim').

On behalf of the association and on his behalf he thanked the audience.

(The conjunction 'and' joins two phrases)

I asked him to go, but he refused. (The conjunction 'but' joins two clauses)

Although he is short, he is strong.

Or

He is strong although he is short. (Note the use of the comma in the first example.)

If a sentence begins with 'although', comma is used after the clause beginning with it.

He could not go out because it was raining.

Or

Because it was raining, he could not go out. (Note the use of the comma.)

The same word can be an adverb, a preposition or a conjunction depending upon where it is used.

For Example:

1. He left the place soon *after*. ('after'–adverb)

   He left the place soon *after* the accident. ('after'-preposition)

   He left the place of accident *after* the police had reached.

   ('after'-conjunction connecting two clauses)

2. He went there *before*. ('before'-adverb)

He left the place *before* Independence. ('before'-preposition)

She (had) slept *before* I reached home. ('before'-conjunction)

Some of the commonly used conjunctions are: and, but, if, only, when, till, until, while, because, as, since, both.....and, either....or, neither...nor, as if, not only....but also, no sooner...than, hardly ....when, even if, lest, so, so...that, etc.

Note: Only one conjunction is enough to join two clauses. The use of double conjunction should be avoided.

For Example:

Although he is rich, *but* he is kind. (wrong)

Although he is rich, he is kind. (right)

(Both ' although' and 'but' are conjunctions.)

I want to know that how he managed to escape. (wrong)

I want to know how he managed to escape. (right)

(Both 'that' and 'how' are conjunctions.)

Conjunctions are of Four Types

1. Coordinating (Co-ordinating) Conjunctions
2. Subordinating Conjunctions
3. Correlative Conjunctions
4. Compound Conjunctions

10.1 COORDINATING (CO-ORDINATING) CONJUNCTIONS

These conjunctions join together clauses of equal rank (coordinate).

And, but, for, or, also, either...or, neither...nor are some of these conjunctions.

Coordinating conjunctions are of four types:

1. Cumulative or Copulative Conjunction
2. Alternative or Disjunctive Conjunction
3. Adversative Conjunction
4. Illative Conjunction

1. **Cumulative Conjunctions.** They simply add one fact or statement to another.

   Both...and, also, not only...but also, too, as well as, and, etc. belong to this category.

   For Example:

   I as well as you *am* to blame. (The verb agrees with the first subject.)

   Ram will win the match and you also.

He went to the shop and bought a dozen mangoes. (See *Note* below)

He is not only rich but also kind.

She is intelligent and beautiful too.

He knows both English and Malayalam.

He is not only hardworking but also intelligent.

Note: If the subjects of the clauses joined together are the same the subject need not be repeated in the clause after the conjunction.

Another example:

He met the Minister and submitted a memorandum to him. (The subject *he* is omitted after the conjunction 'and'.)

2. **Alternative Conjunctions.** They are used to express a choice between two alternatives.

Either…or, neither…nor, nor, or else, whether…or etc are alternative conjunctions.

For Example:

I am not sure whether I will get the book or not.

You must study well or else you will fail.

(Don't say: You must study well, else you will fail. We can say: You must study well, or you will fail. Reason: 'else' is adverb)

Either he or his parents are to attend the meeting.

Neither she nor her husband was present.

Eat whatever you like, only do not spoil your health. (only=but, except that)

3. **Adversative Conjunctions.** They express a contrast between two statements. Yet, but, only, still, whereas, nevertheless, etc. are examples.

For Example:

He failed in the exam many times nevertheless he did not lose hope.

Some students study very well whereas others do not.

She is dark, but beautiful.

It is a small house, yet it is spacious.

He has got a good job, yet he is not satisfied.

It is a small room, still it is convenient.

4. **Illative Conjunctions.** They express an inference or a reason.

For, since, consequently, etc. come under this category.

For Example:

He failed in the exam thrice, *consequently* gave up his studies.

Since he was ill, he could not attend the interview.

He is taking rest, for he is tired.

10.2 SUBORDINATING CONJUNCTIONS

They are used to join clauses of unequal rank. They include words like till, until, before, since, because, if, that, after, although, unless, as, when, where, while, and than.

Note: By definition, these conjunctions are used to join clauses of unequal rank. 'Subordinate' means that which depends on another.

The role, therefore, of a Subordinating Conjunction is to connect a sub-ordinate clause to a main clause. In English grammar, there are three kinds of subordinate (or dependent) clauses namely the Noun clause, the Adjective clause and the Adverb clause. A subordinate clause is one that is connected to the main (principal) clause by a Subordinating Conjunction.

For Example:

I shall go to Chennai if my friend comes today.

Let us examine this sentence:

I shall go to Chennai – Main (*principal*) clause.

my friend comes today – Subordinate clause

If – the conjunction used to connect the subordinate clause with the principal clause.

Classification of the Subordinating Conjunctions according to their meaning is as follows:

1. **Time:** before, after, till, until, since, when, while, as, as soon as, as long as.

   For Example:

   He had left *before* we came.

   He left *after* we had reached.

   Do not move *till* I come back.

   Do not move *until* I come back. ('till' and 'until' have the same meaning)

   I have not seen him *since* he left this place.

   I could not attend the class as I was ill.

   When you are in doubt about anything, leave it out.

   He used to come to my house *while* I was in Delhi.

   He started as soon as the rain stopped.

   We will play as long as the weather is fine.

   I will sit here so long as you are with me. (condition)

2. **Purpose:** lest, that, so that, in order that.

   For Example:

   Work hard *lest* you should fail. ('Work hard lest you fail' is also correct)

   He works hard *so that* he may earn a livelihood.

   She studied computer science in order that she might get a job.

   He said that he was going to Mumbai.

3. **Place:** whence, where, wherever.

For Example:

This is where I differ with you.

I shall buy a book *whence* you have bought yours.

You may go *wherever* you want.

4. **Concession.** although, however, though, as, not withstanding that.

For Example:

I respect him *though* (or although) he is a rebel.

A teacher is a teacher *although* she is bad in teaching.

We lost the match, notwithstanding that we were confident of success.

Note: The special constructions to express the meaning 'even though' may be noted.

For Example:

Much as he would like to support the proposal, he did not do so. (meaning 'even though he would like to support the proposal very much, he did not do so'.)

Strange as it may seem (or strange though it may seem).

I escaped unhurt in the accident. (meaning ' even though it may seem strange I escaped unhurt in the accident')

5. **Comparison.** as.....as, as much as, than, no less than, so ...as.

For Example:

Ramu is cleverer *than* Raju.

She is as tall as you.

I have helped her as much as you. (have helped her)

He is taller than she (is).

She is no less important than you.

He is not so tall as she.

6. **Extent or manner.** as, as if, so far as, according as.

For Example:

You will reap as you sow.

Do as you please.

He behaved as if he were (or was) mad.

So far as I know, you have done your duty satisfactorily.

7. **Result or Consequence.** so...that, such...that.

For Example:

He is such a rude fellow that all hate him.

He works so hard that he gets enough money.

8. **Cause or Reason.** because, since, as.

For Example:

I go to the temple because I believe in god.

Since it was raining, I reached home late.

As he came late, he missed the train.

Note: It is better to use the clause introduced by 'as' before the principal clause.

9. **Condition.** If, provided (that), unless, etc.

For Example:

I shall go there if you permit.

He will attend the meeting provided you have no objection.

You should not enter the class unless you apologize.

10.3 CORRELATIVE CONJUNCTIONS

Correlative Conjunctions or correlatives are used in pairs. Most of them are coordinating conjunctions. The difference between the two is that correlative conjunctions can lay more emphasis on and make clearer the relationship between words or group of words than coordinating conjunctions.

Care should be taken while using Correlative Conjunctions. Usually, the part of speech that comes after the first member of the conjunction should come after the second member too. That is, there should be balancing between the pairs forming the conjunctions.

Either.....or, neither....nor, not only...but also, though...yet, both...and, not...but, hardly/scarcely...when, so...that, whether...or, such...that, no sooner...than, such...as, so...as, etc. are Correlative Conjunctions.

For Example:

1. Either Ram or Rahim has come.

(Here, the correlative conjunction is 'either...or' of which ' either' is the first member and 'or' is the second member. It connects the *two nouns* 'Ram' and 'Rahim'. There is therefore perfect balancing between the pairs forming the conjunction.)

You must either fight the enemy or retreat.

He is neither a friend nor an enemy.

My friend is not Ramu but Rama.

Both India and Pakistan will play today.

Though he is a graduate, he cannot speak English fluently.

Hardly had I reached the stadium when the match began.

He was so angry that he shouted at me.

(Indicates great degree of something (anger) and its result.)

He gave her such advice as is necessary.

(The advice given was sufficient; implies comparison.)

I will meet him whether he likes me or not. (or he does not like me.)

No sooner had I reached the station than the train left.

Such was her beauty that she stood first in the beauty competition.

2. He was not only *a poet* but also *a great singer.* (Here, a noun(poet) comes after 'not only'and another (singer) after 'but also'. The two parts therefore of the conjunction are fully balanced.

Note: It is wrong to say: He *not only* was a poet *but also* a singer. (Here, the two parts of the conjunction are not balanced because after the first part of the conjunction the verb 'was' and after its second part the noun 'singer' are used.)

The sentence may be corrected as follows:

He not only *was* a poet but also *was* a singer.

He not only was a poet but was also a singer. (better)

Or

Not only *was* he a poet but was also a singer. (When 'not only' is used at the beginning of a sentence, subject-verb inversion is required.)

Note: When two independent clauses are joined 'also' may be omitted.

For Example:

He gave money to the poor. He also lived with them.

Not only did he give money to the poor but he lived with them.

Note: When units other than independent clauses are joined 'also' is not omitted.

For Example:

He has the right to speak and to be heard.

He has the right not only to speak but also to be heard.

10.4 COMPOUND CONJUNCTIONS

A conjunction consisting of a combination of words is called a Compound Conjunction. (It is a compound expression.)

So that, provided (that), in order that, in case of, as well as, as soon as, as long as, as if, as though, even if, on condition that, etc. belong to this category.

For Example:

1. His father promised him a car provided that he passed his exams in the first class.
2. As soon as we finished the work it began to rain.
3. He works hard in order that he can look after his family well.
4. She as well as her friends has decided to have a picnic.
5. He will leave for Chennai as soon as his friend comes.
6. I will be loyal to the party as along as I am in it.
7. He behaved as if he were a stranger.
8. Attend the seminar even if you come late.
9. In case of accident, call the police. (In case of something= if something happens)

10.5 CORRECT USE OF SOME IMPORTANT CONJUNCTIONS

Conjunctions are ***mainly*** *used to join together sentences* to make them more compact. The correct use of some of them is given below:

After: meaning 'at a time later than something'. 'After' is not followed by a future tense. Instead, we use a present or present perfect tense to indicate a future meaning.

For Example:

I shall go to Chennai after my wife has come from Delhi.

Or

I shall go to Chennai after my wife comes from Delhi.

But not: I shall go to Chennai after my wife will come from Delhi.

Although/though: meaning 'in spite of the fact', 'however'.

(*i*) It is used at the beginning of a sentence.

(*ii*) It is used along with the first action, when there are two actions or things.

Note: still, yet, but – are not used with although.

For Example:

He is rich. He is not happy.

Although he is rich, he is not happy.

(Do not say: Although he is rich, *still/yet/but* he is not happy)

Although I asked her to come to school, she remained at home.

As well as: meaning 'and also', 'in addition to'.

While joining two sentences the following points should be carefully noted:

(*i*) The important matter + as well as + the less important matter.

('as well as' gives importance to the first part it joins.)

(*ii*) If the subjects of the given two sentences are the same, write the important sentence + as well as + unimportant sentence.

(*iii*) If the subjects of the given two sentences are different, the verb depends on (agrees with) the subject of the main sentence.

(*iv*) If the subject used before as well as is singular and the subject used after as well is plural, the verb always agrees with the number of the subject used before 'as well as'. In this case the verb agrees with the singular subject.

(*v*) If the subject used before 'as well as' is plural and the subject used after 'as well as' is singular, the verb agrees with the plural subject.

(*vi*) Omit *also, too.*

For Example:

(*a*) Elephants are found in India. Elephants are also found in Africa.

(or Elephants are found in Africa too.)

Elephants are found in India as well as in Africa.

(*b*) Meera as well as her friends was playing.

(*c*) The boys as well as the girl were playing.

(*d*) The cow as well as the goat gives us milk.

As: meaning 'because', 'since', 'while', 'for'.

(*i*) While joining sentences 'as' can be used at the beginning of a sentence or in between two sentences.

(*ii*) As + first sentence + second sentence.

(*iii*) Second sentence + as + first sentence.

(*iv*) Omit – *so, then* and *because* that occur in the second sentence.

(*v*) As is also used to show comparison. (Avoid using 'like' as a conjunction)

For Example:

He was suffering from fever. He did not go to school.

As he was suffering from fever, he didn't go to school.

Or

He didn't go to school as he was suffering from fever.

As soon as: meaning 'simultaneously'.

(*i*) While joining two sentences, *as soon as* can be used at the beginning of a sentence or in between two sentences.

(*ii*) It should be strictly seen that 'as soon as' is *followed* by the first action, wherever it is used.

(*iii*) As soon as + first action + second action.

Second action + as soon as + first action.

For Example:

I saw my teacher. (first action). I stopped talking. (second action)

As soon as *I saw my teacher* I stopped talking.

I stopped talking as soon as *I saw my teacher.*

I reached the station. (first action). The train started. (second action)

The train started as soon as *I reached the station.*

As if /As though: These are interchangeable.

We use past tenses after as if/as though to indicate that a comparison is unreal in the present.

For Example:

She looks at him as if/as though he is a liar.

(Real comparison because he may well be a liar. The speaker is uncertain about what he says.)

She looks at him as if/as though he were (was) a liar.

(Unreal comparison because he may not be a liar, but looks like one)

The subjunctive form 'were' is often used instead of 'was' after 'as if/as though' in unreal comparison.

He looks at me as if /as though I were a demon.(unreal comparison)

Or

He looks at me as if/as though I was a demon.(In informal style 'was' is more common instead of 'were' in unreal comparisons)

If the verb preceding 'as if/as though' is in the past tense we use the subjunctive 'were' or the past perfect after it to indicate a real or unreal comparison *in the past*.

For Example:

He looked as if/as though he were mad.(unreal)

Or

He looked as if/as though he had been mad.

Or

He looked as if/as though he was mad.

If a present tense verb follows 'as if/as though' it shows that the speaker is uncertain about what he states.

For Example:

It looks as if/as though it is going to rain.

Omit – *but, yet, still, it would seem that, it seems that* and *one might think that* from sentences containing as if/ as though.

Because : Shows the strongest cause.

***Rule*:** Never use 'because' at the beginning of a sentence.

For Example:

You failed because you had not studied at all.

I am going to Chennai because my mother is there.

But: Denotes contrast.

For Example:

He is short. He is handsome.

He is short, but handsome.

Both.......and: While joining two sentences the following rules should be observed.

Rule:

(*i*) If the subjects are the *same* in both the sentences, and if we are describing the same subject in both the sentences, then 'both' should be used in the middle-after the first sentence.

First sentence + both + second sentence.

(*ii*) If the subjects are *different*, 'both' is used at the beginning of the sentence.

Note: 'Both' should invariably be followed by 'and' and not by 'as well as'.

For Example:

1. The picture looks natural. It is beautiful.
   The picture looks both natural and beautiful.
2. Ram has gone home. Rahim has gone home.
   Both Ram and Rahim have gone home.
3. Both Ram and Rahim were present. (Not: Both Ram as well as Rahim were present.)

Note: 'Both' should not be used in the following sense.

For Example:

Both did not come. (wrong)

Neither came. (right)

Before: Used to refer to 'earlier than the time when', 'a place in a list' and to mean 'in the presence of'.

Rule:

(*i*) first action + before + second action.

He had done (did) his homework before he slept.

Or

He did his work before he slept.

(Simple past tense also is possible in the clause preceding 'before' (meaning earlier) because it is quite clear that this clause represents the first action)

(*ii*) Please do not move. The doctor will come.

Please do not move before the doctor comes.

(*iii*) His number comes before mine in the list. (a place in a list)

(*iv*) He appeared before the magistrate. (in the presence of)

Even if/Even though: though/although.

Rules for joining two sentences:

Rule:

(*i*) 'Even if' is used only at the beginning of a sentence.

(*ii*) The 'may' in the first sentence shall be changed into simple present.

(*iii*) Omit – but, still, yet.

For Example:

1. You may cry, but he won't give your book back.
   Even if you cry, he won't give your book back.
2. What you say may be true. I can't help you.
   Even if what you say is true, I can't help you.

'Either ....or' and **'neither .....nor.'**

Either (pronoun- singular)= the one or the other of two persons or things.

Neither (pronoun-singular)= not the one nor the other of two persons or things.

'Neither' is the negative counterpart of 'either'.

Rule:

(*i*) When two or more singular subjects are joined by 'either .....or' or 'neither....nor', a singular verb should be used

For Example:

Either Raju or his agent is to be present.

Either Ramu, John, or Seetha has to attend the meeting.

Neither John nor his friend is to blame.

(*ii*) When the subjects are different, 'either/neither' should be used at the beginning of the sentence.

For Example:

Ram should take charge. You should resign.

Either Ram should take charge or you should resign.

Neither Ram should take charge nor should you resign.

(*iii*) When two singular subjects connected by 'either ....or' or 'neither nor' are of different persons, the verb agrees with the nearer subject.

For Example:

He will get the benefit. She will get the benefit.

Only one of them will get the benefit.

These three sentences can be joined by using 'either...or' as shown below:

Either he or she will get the benefit.

Now consider the following three negative sentences. They can be joined by using 'neither.....nor'.

He will not get the benefit. She will not get the benefit.

None of them will get the benefit.

Neither he nor she will get the benefit.

(*iv*) When one of the subjects connected by 'either.....or' or 'neither...nor' is singular and the other plural, the plural subject must be placed just before the verb so as to make it plural.

For Example:

Either John or his parents were asked to attend the meeting.

Neither John nor his parents were asked to attend the meeting.

Hardly/Scarcely: While joining two sentences, the following rules are to be followed.

Rule:

(*i*) If the given sentences are in the simple past, change the first sentence to the past perfect.

(*ii*) Omit–soon, than, then etc. found in the second sentence.

(*iii*) When a clause begins with 'hardly' or 'scarcely', there should be subject- verb/operator inversion. The auxiliary verb should be placed before the subject as in the case of an interrogative (question) sentence. This is known as subject-operator(auxiliary) inversion.

Hardly/ Scarcely + had + subject+ past participle of the verb + when + second sentence. ('had' –auxiliary or operator)

Subject + had + hardly/scarcely + past participle of the verb + when + second sentence.

For Example:

1. He shut his book. Soon the headmaster entered the class.

   Hardly had he shut his book when the headmaster entered the room.

   (Don't use 'than' instead of 'when'. Always use 'hardly/scarcely ......when'.)

   Or He had hardly shut his book when the headmaster entered the room.

2. We got into the room. Soon the baby began to cry loudly.

   Scarcely had we got into the room when the baby began to cry.

   Or We had scarcely got into the room when the baby began to cry.

However: not mattering how.

Rules for joining two sentences:

Rule:

(*i*) Used at the beginning of a sentence and in between sentences.

(*ii*) It is followed immediately by an adverb or adjective.

(*iii*) Omit – but, yet, still.

For Example:

He is rich. Still he wants more.

However rich he is, he wants more.

However hard you work, you cannot pass.

If: Expresses a condition. To express a condition we use a conditional sentence consisting of a conditional clause (if clause) and a main clause.

(*a*) To express a probable condition (a condition which might be fulfilled) we use the present tense in the 'if' clause and auxiliaries can, shall, will, may, must or should in the main clause.

For Example:

If you pass the exam, what will you do next ? (It is probable that you will pass the exam.)

If you start now, you can reach the office in time.

If it rains, I shall postpone my journey.

If the teacher tells you to go out, you must obey.

If you should go walking, you are sure to reach the station late.

Note: The above sentences may begin with the main clause as well. In this case no comma is used after the main clause.

For Example:

What will you do next if you pass the exam.

You can reach the office in time if you start now.

Note: In the above examples the present continuous (progressive) tense or the present perfect tense or 'should' to indicate a probable situation may be used in the if clause.

If you are going on foot, you will not reach the office in time.

If you have telephoned him, he will certainly come.

If you should change your decision, please let me know.

(*b*) To express a condition that has the same effect.

For Example:

If it is very hot, we start sweating.

(*c*) To show an unlikely condition (a condition which is unlikely to be fulfilled) in the present we use the past subjective (were) in the conditional clause if the verb is 'to be' and the past indicative (ordinary past tense) if it is any other verb and could, would, might, or should in the main class.

Here, the past tense of the conditional clause (the ' if clause') does not indicate a true past. It refers to the present or future.

For Example:

If he ran fast, he would reach in time. (present conditional)
(It is unlikely that he will run fast)

If I were you I would reject the offer. (but I am not you.)

(*d*) To show an improbable or unreal condition in the future.

If I were you I should help him. (but I am not you; an impossible condition)

(*e*) To show a condition that did no happen or that was impossible in the past we use the past perfect tense in the 'if' clause and *would have, should have, might have* and *could have* in the main caluse.

For Example:

If you had informed me of the theft, I should have reported the matter to the police.
(but you didn't inform me; so I didn't report etc.)

If I had been you, I should have done it. (but I was not you; an impossible condition)

Note: We can write these conditional clauses under (*c*), (*d*) and (*e*) without using the 'if'. In this case the sentence must begin with *should, had, or were;* as,

Should he run fast, he would reach in time.

Were I you, I should reject the offer.

Had you informed me of the theft, I should have reported the matter to the police.

Had I been you, I should have done it. (*For more details see Subjunctive Mood under 'Verb'*)

(*f*) It is used to mean 'whether'.

He wants to know if you will attend the meeting.

(*g*) It is used to mean ' whenever '

If I go to Chennai I buy something.

(*h*) It is used to mean ' admitting that'

If I am rich, yet I am kind.

(*i*) 'if only ' is used to express a wish:

If only I knew her husband. (I wish I knew her husband.)

Note: Never say 'supposing if '.

In case: 'In case' is not a substitute for 'if'. It is used to speak of precautions to be taken beforehand.

For Example:

1. Go early in case you miss the train.

   (Here the meaning is: You start early to avoid the possibility of missing the train.)

2. Insure your luggage in case it may be stolen.

Note: 'In case of' has the same meaning as 'if'.

In case of an accident call 100. (If there is an accident call the police. Only after the accident we are expected to call 100, not before)

Unless: If not.

Rule: As 'unless' has negative meaning, don't use 'not' again.

For Example:

(*i*) Unless you don't work hard you will fail. (wrong)

Unless you work hard you will fail. (right)

(Meaning: If you don't work hard you will fail)

(*ii*) You will be dismissed unless you don't obey my orders. (wrong)

You will be dismissed unless you obey my orders. (right)

Lest: So that not. (negative in sense)(meaning: in order to prevent something from happening.)

Rule:

(*i*) Only the infinitive without 'to' should be used after 'lest'.

(*ii*) The only auxiliary verb that can be used after 'lest' is 'should'.

(*iii*) As it is already negative 'not' should not be used again.

For Example:

1. Take care lest you fall.

Or

Take care lest you should fall. (Both these constructions are permissible)

Take care lest you should *not* fall. (wrong)

2. Study well lest you should fail.

He studied well lest he should fail. (past)

Or

He studied well lest he fail. (not: he failed)

He does his work well lest he *lose* his job. (not: loses)

He does his work well lest he should lose his job.

He will have to study well lest he should fail.

Not only........but (also): Used to emphasize that although something is true, something else also is true. 'Not' and 'not only' are the units commonly used with 'but' to form correlatives. 'But' is mostly used to introduce two contrasting ideas.

For Example:

I went there *not* to harm him, *but* to help him. (not...but)

She *not only* gave him money, *but* (also) helped him get a passport.

('not only......but(also))

Rule:

(*i*) When two sentences are connected by using 'not only......but (also)', each unit forming the correlative should stand before the same parts of speech. In other words, balancing between the two parts is required. It is used to connect two positive sentences.

(*ii*) Omit – and, also.

Note: When two independent clauses are joined, 'also' may be omitted.

For Example:

1. He gave money to the poor. He also lived with them.

He not only gave money to the poor, but (also) lived with them.

Or

Not only did he give money to the poor, but he (also) lived with them.

(Literary style; note the subject-verb inversion when 'not only' is used at the beginning of the sentence.)

2. He gave me food. He also asked me to stay with him.

He not only gave me food, but (also) asked me to stay with him.

3. The moon gives us light. The stars also give us light at night.

Not only does the moon, but the stars also give us light at night.

4. He is here. His brothers are also here.
   Not only is he here, but his brothers are also here.
5. He works in her office. He loves her too.
   Not only does he work in her office, but he also loves her.
6. He is sincere and honest.
   He is not only sincere but also honest.
7. The students are here. The Principal also is here.
   Not only are the students, but the Principal (also) is here.

Note: When units other than independent clauses are joined 'also' is not omitted.

For Example:

1. He has the right to speak and to be heard.
   He has the right not only to speak but also to be heard.

No sooner.........than:

Rule:

(*i*) Use 'no sooner' at the beginning of the first event sentence with subject-verb inversion.

(*ii*) According to the tense of the verb add— do/ does/ did/ had + subject.

(*iii*) Omit soon, at once, quickly, suddenly, immediately and add *than* with the second sentence.

No sooner + do/ does + subject + present tense of the verb + than + present tense.

No sooner + did + subject + present tense of the verb + than + present tense.

No sooner + had + subject + past participle of the verb + than + past tense.

For Example:

(*a*) No sooner does she hear the bell than she stands up.
(As soon as she hears the bell she stands up. Meaning: Immediately after hearing the bell she stands up)

(*b*) No sooner did he hear the bell than he stood up.

(*c*) No sooner had he heard the bell than he stood up.

Note: When a clause begins with no sooner the auxiliary verb should be placed before the subject as we do in an interrogative sentence. (See – Hardly/ Scarcely)

Note: Don't use 'when' instead of 'than' with 'no sooner'.

Now that: (= because of, since)

Rule:

(*i*) Use 'now that' only at the beginning of a sentence.

For Example:

Now that the boy has slept, let us go.

Or, Or else, Otherwise:

Rule:

(*i*) Used only between two sentences.

For Example:

Shut your mouth. I will complain.

Shut your mouth, or I will complain.

Shut your mouth, or else I will complain.

Shut your mouth, otherwise I will complain.

Rather ...... than : (= shows preference)

(Can be used in two ways)

For Example:

I would rather go with him than stay here alone.

I would go with him rather than stay here alone.

So ...... that: (= shows result/ effect)

Subject + verb + so + adjective / adverb + that + ...

For Example:

I am so weak that I can hardly walk.

This problem is so difficult that he cannot solve it.

He was so desperate that he committed suicide.

She is so beautiful that she was selected for the beauty contest.

So that: (used to show purpose)

For Example:

I am going to Delhi by air so that I can get there early.

Such ...... that:

Subject + verb + such + a/ an + adjective /noun + object + that + second sentence.

For Example:

The teacher spoke in such a low voice that the students could not hear.

I have such respect for him that I will not do anything against him.

The medicine has such a taste that I am reluctant to take it.

Such ...... as:

I gave him such advice as was necessary to get over the crises.

The police took such actions as the situation warranted.

Such evidence as the thief left helped the police to trace him.

So: (= reason)

Rule:

(*i*) Used at the beginning of the second sentence.

For Example:

He is ill. He will not come.

He is ill, so he will not come.

Since: (= strong reason)

For Example:

(*a*) It is hot. We cannot go out now.

Since it is hot, we can't go out now.

We can't go out now, since it is hot.

Too ...... to: (used only in the negative sentence)

While joining two sentences observe the following rules

Rule: (*i*) If the subjects are the same in both sentences, write the

Subject + auxiliary+ too + adjective / adverb + to before the verb + object.

(*ii*) If the subjects are different ,

Subject of the first sentence + too + adjective / adverb + for + object form of the subject in the second sentence + to + verb + object.

(*iii*) Omit the words like very, much, many, so, but, can, will, would, shall, should, could etc.

For Example:

(*a*) He is very tall. He can't go in.

He is too tall to go in.

(*b*) The problem was very difficult. I couldn't solve it.

The problem was too difficult for me to solve it.

Where:

For Example:

This is where we lived for a year.

I don't know where I went wrong.

When : (While joining two sentences 'when' can be used at the beginning or between them.)

1. The girl saw her mother. She ran to her.

   When the girl saw her mother, she ran to her.

   (comma after the clause beginning with 'when')

   Or

   The girl ran to her mother when she saw her. (no comma after the main clause)

2. The bell rang. The school dispersed.

   The school dispersed when the bell rang.

   Or

   When the bell rang, the school dispersed.

While: (While + first action)

1. I was looking through the window. I saw the thief.

   While I was looking through the window, I saw the thief.

2. The bus is moving. Don't get off.

While the bus is moving, don't get off.

Note: When and While - The difference in usage.

'When' is used with two shorter actions or events or situations taking place at the same time as in :

When I saw her she ran to me.

'While' is used with two longer actions or events or situations taking place at the same time as in :

While I was in Delhi I used to visit the Parliament House.

Note: 'While' means 'during the time that' or 'duration'

The word 'during' is a preposition.

While he was in Chennai he used to visit us = During his stay in Chennai he used to visit us.

He came while the discussion was in progress. (He came during the discussion was going on)

Note: Used when contrasting things, people or situations; as,

While the rich become richer the poor become poorer.

While she is innocent he is guilty.

Note: When it is used as a noun it means 'a period of time'. 'for a while' means for a short time.

He attended the meeting for a while.

He came here a while ago.

She arrived a short while/a little while ago.

He has been sleeping quite a while. (for a long period)

They worked together all the while. (all the time)

We meet once a while. (occasionally)

Note: Worthwhile(single word)-Adjective meaning 'worth the time', 'worth the effort', 'worth the money', etc.

It is worthwhile to do some social work.

You do some worthwhile work/business.

Wherever, Whenever, Whoever:

1. **Wherever:** (wherever + first action)

He visited many places. He made friends with many people.

Wherever he visited, he made friends with many people.

Or

He made friends with many people, wherever he visited.

2. Whenever: (Whenever + first action)

(*a*) He speaks to me often. Still I am afraid.

Whenever he speaks to me , I am afraid.

Or

I am afraid whenever he speaks to me.

3. Whoever: (whoever + first action)

(*a*) He will do well. He is not bothered about his teacher.

Whoever teaches him, he will do well in the exam.

Or

He will do well in the exam, whoever teaches him.

Since, For: (Used as prepositions)

Since: Denotes a point of time. It is used to denote time from some specified point of time in the past to and also including the time of speaking.

I ←——←—— I *For Example:* Since 1997.

Time of speaking Past Point of time

It connects a past activity with the present. It therefore follows that 'since' must be preceded by the present perfect tense of the verb.

Ago : This denotes a period of time from the time of speaking backwards to the past.

I——→——→——I Ago

→

Time of speaking *For Example:* 3 years ago

A few examples of points of time are given below :

Since ————→ !—— 1996, 2000, 1865 etc.
! Monday, Tuesday, Thursday
! March , April, August etc.
! 8 O'clock
! Last Onam, Christmas etc.
! Morning, Evening etc.
!—— Death, marriage, birth etc.

For Example:

1. I have not seen him since Sunday.
2. They have worked here since 1985.
3. She has attended the class since 8 O'clock in the morning.
4. We have lived in this house since March.
5. We have not met him since last Onam or Christmas.

6. I have waited for him since this morning.
7. I have not spoken to him since his father's death.

If an activity or situation has been going on continuously since the time specified and is still going on at the time of speaking we must use the present perfect progressive (continuous) tense of the verb.

For Example:

1. I have been waiting for him since 8 O'clock. (waiting still continues)
2. I have been studying since morning.

When 'since' is used as a conjunction joining two clauses:

If since is used as a conjunction joining two clauses then the clause after 'since' must be in the simple past tense.

For Example:

1. We have not met each other since his father died.
2. She has lived with her father ever since her husband left her.
3. They have been feeling happy ever since they changed their residence.

If the main clause is about length of time, between the point of time in the past and the time of speaking , simple present tense is used in this clause and past tense in the other clause.

For Example:

1. It is now a week since we left Cochin. (Not: It has been ......)
2. It is a long time since we met. (Not: It has been ......)
3. How long is it since you left Cochin.

More Examples:

1. We met last Tuesday. We haven't met after that.
   We haven't met since last Tuesday.
2. He wore glasses in 1984. Still he is wearing it.
   He has been wearing glasses since 1984.
3. Mr. Raj got married. He lives in Calcutta.
   Since his marriage, Mr. Raj lives in Calcutta.
4. I like you very much. I shall give you a present.
   Since I like you very much, I shall give you a present.
5. My parents are away. I visited them a year ago.
   It is a year since I visited my parents.

For: 'For' denotes a period of time till now. (the time of speaking.)

For Example:

1. I have been teaching for a year. (Not since a year)
2. He has worked in this office for ten years. (Not since 10 years)

For Example:

a second, two seconds, five seconds, a minute, three minutes, ten minutes, two hours, three hours, one hour, a week, two weeks, three months, one month , four years, one year etc. are examples of period of time.

When 'since' is used as an adverb:

When used as an adverb the word *since* means 'from then'

(From some time in the past to now)

For Example:

1. I saw a lion three years ago and have not seen another ever *since*. (adverb)
2. I was with him in Bombay but have met him once ever *since*. (adverb)

More examples:

1. I am reading this book. Today is the 6th day.
   I have been reading this book for six days.
2. I am working in this office. It is the third year.
   I have been working in this office for the third year.
3. He is very angry. His mother scolded him.
   He is very angry for his mother scolded him.
4. I reached late. I missed the regular bus.
   I reached late for I missed the regular bus.

As and like: (Do not use 'like' as a conjunction)

For Example:

1. He did *like* he was told.
   (wrong because the word *like* is used as a conjunction joining two clauses. In such cases use the word *as*)
   He did *as* he was told. (right) (*as* used as conjunction)
2. He fought *like* a hero. (right) (*like* used as a preposition)
   (This means that he was actually not a hero, but he fought in the manner of a hero.)
   He fought *as* a hero. (right)
   (*as* used as a preposition.He was actually a hero and fought in that capacity.)

But: He fought as a tiger. (wrong) . This sentence means that when he fought he was a tiger. Correct it as follows:

He fought like a tiger. (He was actually not a tiger. He was only compared to a tiger)

He is as strong as I . (right) (as I am strong)

He is as strong as me. (wrong because *as* is used here as preposition)

He called me as a fool. (wrong)

He called me a fool. (right)

Chapter 11 TENSES

Tense indicates the time of an action or event. The tense of a verb expresses the time of an action and the degree of its completeness. It tells us whether it took place in the past (The Past tense), whether it takes place now (The Present tense) or whether it will take place some time in the future. (The Future tense). The verb shows the time of an action by changing its form.

A verb therefore has three tenses:

(*i*) The Present Tense–shows an action that takes place now.

For Example:

He plays football.

(*ii*) The Past tense–shows an action that was completed or going on in the past.

For Example:

He played football yesterday.

(*iii*) The Future tense–shows an action that will take place in the future.

For Example:

He will play football tomorrow.

Each of these tenses has four different forms.

1. The Present Tense:

(*i*) Simple Present

For Example:

He plays football.

(*ii*) Present continuous

For Example:

He is playing football.

(*iii*) Present Perfect

For Example:

He has played football.

(*iv*) Present Perfect Continuous

For Example:

He has been playing football.

2. **The Past Tense:**

(*i*) Simple past

For Example:

He played football yesterday.

(*ii*) Past continuous

He was playing football.

(*iii*) Past Perfect

For Example:

He had played football.

(*iv*) Past Perfect continuous

For Example:

He had been playing football.

3. **The Future Tense:**

(*i*) Simple Future

For Example:

He will play football.

(*ii*) Future Continuous

For Example:

He will be playing football.

(*iii*) Future Perfect

For Example:

He will have played football.

(*iv*) Future Perfect Continuous

For Example:

He will have been playing football.

Meaning of the words *Simple, Continuous, Perfect* and *Perfect continuous* in the context of tenses

Simple: This denotes the simplest form in each of the three tenses.

For Example:

I laugh. I laughed. I shall laugh.

Continuous: This denotes that an action in all the three tenses is still continuing or not yet completed.

For Example:

I am laughing. I was laughing. I shall be laughing.

Perfect: This denotes that an action in all the three tenses is in a completed state.

For Example:

I have laughed. I had laughed. I shall have laughed.

Perfect continuous: This denotes an action that has already started, is not yet complete and is still continuing in all the three tenses; as,

For Example:

I have been laughing. I had been laughing. I shall have been laughing.

11.1 THE PRESENT TENSE

(*a*) **The Simple Present tense:** The simple present tense usually expresses an action that has happened several times in the past, that is likely to happen again in the future and that may be or may not be going on at this moment. The following are the different forms of the present tense:

Assertive form:

(*i*) Subject + base form of the verb. Used with all plural subjects including I and You.
I write. You write. They write. We write.

(*ii*) Subject + singular form of the verb + s/es. Used with all singular subjects except I and you.
He writes. She writes. Ram writes. He does. She goes etc.

Negative form:

(*i*) Plural subjects + do not + base form of the verb.
I do not write. (I don't write). We do not write.(We don't write.)
They do not write. (They don't write.)

(*ii*) Singular subjects + does not + base form of the verb.
He does not write. (He doesn't write.) She does not write.
(She doesn't write.)

Note: The short form of 'do not' is 'don't'.

The short form of 'does not' is 'doesn't'.

Interrogative form:

(*i*) Do + plural subject + base form of the verb?.
Do you write? Do I write? Do we write? Do they write?

(*ii*) Does + singular subject + base form of the verb?.
Does he write? Does she write? Does Ram write?

Negative Interrogative form:

(*i*) Do not + plural subject + base form of the verb? If the subject is a noun.

Do not the boys write? (Don't the boys write? – Shortened form of 'Do you not = Don't you'.)

Do + Plural subject + not + base form of the verb?

Do they not write? (Don't they write?)

Note: *'Not' is placed after the subject if it is a pronoun.(pronoun subject)*

Do we not write? (Don't we write?) (pronoun subject)

Do they not write? (Don't they write?)

(*ii*) Does not + singular subject + base form of the verb?

Does he not write? (Doesn't he write?)

Does she not write? (Doesn't she write)

Does not Rema write? (Doesn't Rema write?) (noun subject)

Note: *'Not' is placed before the subject if it is a noun.(noun subject)*

Interrogative form with 'have /has' :

(*i*) Have they done it? Has she done it?

Negative Interrogative form with 'Have/has'

Have we not done it? (Haven't we done it?)

Has he not done it? (Hasn't he done it?)

Uses:

(*i*) To express a habitual action.

For Example:

He smokes.

My father goes for a walk in the morning (even if spoken at any time of the day).

Meera returns from school at 3.30p.m.

(*ii*) To express Universal facts.

For Example:

The sun rises in the East.

The earth goes round the sun.

Time and tide wait for no man.

Blood is thicker than water.

(*iii*) To express exclamations

For Example:

There goes the thief ! (Do not say: There is going the thief.)

Here comes the Headmaster! (Do not say: Here is coming the headmaster.)

Listen! How wonderfully he sings.

(*iv*) To show planned activities. (Usually official programmes)

For Example:

Our school reopens next Monday.

The PM visits China next year.

(*v*) To introduce quotations.

For Example:

The Minister says , "All must undergo the training."

The sign board says, " No parking."

(*vi*) Used in commentaries. (To describe actions while they happen)

For Example:

Ravi receives the ball and passes it to Mani.

(*vii*) Used in newspaper headlines.

For Example:

Police raid Surya TV. (meaning: The Police raided Surya TV.)

(**Note:** The noun *police* is always plural. Don't say: The police has arrested him. Say: The police have arrested him.)

CM announces relief measures to flood victims.

(meaning : CM announced relief measures to flood victims.)

Bush calls on President Narayanan. (meaning : Bush called on President Narayanan.)

(*viii*) Used for actions that spread over a long period of time.

For Example:

I learn swimming at the club.

She writes a novel.

(*ix*) Used to describe a future action in adverbial clauses beginning with *when, as soon as, once, before, after , if , till , until , etc.* when the verb in the main clause is in the future tense.

For Example:

I shall meet you when you come to Ernakulam.

They will start as soon as he comes.

We will do the work once you give orders.

She will reach there before they start.

If you give advance they will begin the work.

I will wait for him till the train starts.

We will not give him any money until he asks for it.

(*x*) Used to describe past events vividly. This is called Historic or Dramatic present. Often this present is combined with the past.

For Example:

He came to my office and greeted me with a smile; further he tells me he is getting married next month.

After marriage they are planning to settle in the USA.

(*b*) **The Present Continuous or Progressive tense:** The Present Continuous form is used to show that an activity is taking place at the time of speaking. It is formed with the present tense of 'to-be' + the 'ing' form of the verb. (There are verbs which do not take the progressive form in the usual sense. Such verbs are called static verbs.

A few examples of static verbs are given below:

love, hate, posses, contain, believe, belong, deserve, know, mean, own, please, prefer, recognize, remember, resemble, satisfy, seem, sound, suffice, suit, surprise, understand, see, hear, notice, smell, recognize, want, wish, desire, feel, like, hope, prefer, refuse, suppose, think, agree, consider, remember, forget, mind, have, contain, possess, etc.)

(See 'Static and Dynamic verbs' under the chapter 'Verbs' for more details.)

Assertive form:

Subject + am/is/are + verb + ing (i.e. Present participle)

For Example:

I am reading. He is reading. They are reading.

You are reading.

Negative form:

The negative form is formed by using 'not' after the auxiliary.

Subject + am/is/are + not + verb + ing

For Example:

He is not sleeping. They are not sleeping.

You are not sleeping.

I am not playing.

Interrogative form:

This form is made by the interchange of the subject and the auxiliary.

Am/ Is/are+ subject + present participle?

For Example:

Is he reading? Are you playing?

Negative Interrogative form:

For Example:

Are you *not* playing?	(Aren't you playing.)(subject-pronoun)
Is he *not* playing?	(Isn't he playing.)
Is *not* Rama playing?	(Isn't Rama Playing)(subject –noun)

Important: Note the positions of 'not' in examples 1 & 3 above.

Uses:

(*i*) To express an activity taking place at the time of speaking.

For Example:

We are reading. He is having breakfast.

He is painting.

(*ii*) To express an action that is temporary- an action that is happening now and that is continuing.

For Example:

She is doing her homework.

He is drawing a picture.

I am writing a novel.

(*iii*) To express an action that will take place some time in the future. The sentence generally contains an indication of time.

For Example:

We are visiting Agra this month.

I am getting married day after tomorrow.

The exams are starting next week.

(*iv*) 'Going to + verb' is used to show futurity.

For Example:

When are you going to sleep?

We are going to do it.

Note: The 'going-to' form is not used with the verbs 'go' and 'come'. Instead, the 'ing' form of these verbs are used to express futurity.

He is going to Chennai tomorrow. (Not: He is going to go to......)

He is coming next week. (Not: He is going to come next week.)

(*v*) Not used in statements containing generalization or simple truth.

For Example:

Water consists of Oxygen and Hydrogen

(Do not say: Water is consisting of Oxygen and Hydrogen.)

The sun rises in the east. (Not: 'The sun is rising in the east'.)

(*c*) **The Present Perfect Tense:** Used to indicate an action that has just been completed at the time of speaking. It is formed by adding the past participle of the verb to the present tense of 'to-have'.

Assertive form:

Subject + have /has+ past participle of the verb.

For Example:

I have gone. You have gone. They have gone.

We have gone. She has gone. He has gone.

Raju has gone.

Negative form:

The negative form of the present perfect tense is formed by adding 'not' to the auxiliary.

Subject + have/ has + not + past participle

For Example:

I have not seen it. You have not seen it. They have not seen it.

She has not seen it. He has not seen it. We have not seen it.

Interrogative form:

This is formed by interchanging the auxiliary and the subject.

Have/ Has+ subject + past participle?

For Example:

Have they done the work ? Has she seen it?

Negative Interrogative:

Haven't / Hasn't +subject + past participle?

For Example:

Haven't they done the work? (Have they not done the work?)

Hasn't she seen it? (Has she not seen it?)

Hasn't Ravi come? (Has not Ravi come?)(subject-noun)

Uses:

(*i*) To express an action recently completed. The Present perfect tense is the continuation of the past up to the present.

For Example:

I have read the book. We have visited Kochi. He has arrived.

(*ii*) To express a past action leading up to the present. We usually use adverbials like *already , before , ever , never , yet , so far and till now* with this tense.

For Example:

I have *never* seen her.

(I did not see her in the past nor have I seen her till the time of speaking.)

He has *already* helped me. (a recently completed action)

I have read twelve chapters *so far.* (till now)

My father has not come *yet.* (up to this time)

We have not done this type of work *before.*

(We did not do this type of work in the past ; only now are we doing /have we done this type of work.)

(*iii*) Used with an indication of some length of time to express an action or event in the past and still continuing in the present. The tense is neither past nor present. It is a mixture of the two. It is sometimes called the *Inclusive present.*

For Example:

We have not seen him since his marriage.

He has not gone home for a long time.

They have lived here for a year.

Corresponding to the Inclusive Present we have the Inclusive Past and Future.

(*iv*) To express an action the result of which is felt even now.

For Example:

I have done my work. (Now I am free.)

Raju has been the Manager many times.

(He is conversant with all that is connected with this position)

(*v*) To show a habit or past action – with 'ever' and 'never'.

For Example:

Have you ever smoked ?

I have never seen it.

(*vi*) To express a very recently completed action the Present Perfect tense is used with the word 'just' :

For Example:

I have just come from the office. (I came a short time ago.)

Note: The word 'just' is normally used between the auxiliary verb and the main verb.

For Example:

He has just come.

Note: He has come just now. (This sentence is correct. Here 'just now' means 'only a short time ago')

(*vii*) The Present Perfect can be used with an incomplete period of time; as,

I have met him today. ('Today' (the day) is not over at the time of speaking.)

I have met him this morning. (This is wrong if the time of speaking is any time other than 'this morning'. If that be the case use the simple past; as, I met him in the morning.)

Note: In the same way we can use 'this week' , 'this month', 'this year', etc. with the present perfect tense.

For Example:

I have met him this month/this year etc.

(*viii*) The present Perfect tense is used with the Prepositions 'since' and 'for'.

He has not come to the office since Monday last. (He is still absent)

He stayed in this house for a year. (He does not stay here now)

He has stayed in this house for a year. (He still stays here)

(*ix*) The present perfect tense is used with conjunctions like *after, before, when,* and *as soon as* to indicate an action to be completed in the future.

For Example:

I will come to you after I have finished my work.

He will go to Chennai as soon as he has come back from leave.

Note: The word 'since' is used both as a conjunction and as a preposition to connect an action in the past with the present.

It is always followed by a point of time and *not by a period of time.*

Note: A few examples of period of time: *Five minutes, two hours,* one day, two weeks , one month, five years, etc.

Note: A few examples of point of time: (Definite time)

6'o clock, 7.30, etc.(any time), Monday, Tuesday, etc. (any day), January , February, etc (any month), 1998, 2000, etc (any year) , any Specific event like *marriage , transfer, death, etc.*

For Example:

I have lived in this house since I was transferred from Trivandrum. (I am still living in this house). Here 'since' is used as a conjunction to connect two clauses.

I have lived in this house since 1998. (I am still living in this house)('since' used as a proposition)

He has been reading this book since last Monday.

He has stopped smoking since he got married.

The word 'for' is used to connect an action in the past with the present. It is always followed by a period of time.

Examples of period of time are given at the beginning of this *note.*

For Example:

I have lived in this house for the last (or past) two years. (I am still living)

He has been in Ernakulam for three years. (He is still in Ernakulam)

We should not use a point of time with 'for' and a period of time with 'since'.

For Example:

He has lived in this house since the last two years. (wrong)

Say: He has lived in this house for the last two years.

Now examine the following sentences:

I have lived in this house.

I have lived in this house for six years. (I am still living here.)

In the first sentence the adverb of time is not used.

It is therefore not clear whether I am still living there whereas in the second sentence the adverb of time (six years) is used and hence it is clear that I am still living there.

Look at the following sentences :

He has been in Trivandrum.

He has been in Trivandrum for a week.

The first sentence tells us that he went to Trivandrum and came back whereas the second sentence indicates that he went to Trivandrum and is still there.(because of the presence of the adverb of time – *for a week*)

This difference in the use of the Present Perfect Tense should be clearly understood.

The Present perfect tense should not be used with an adverb of time indicating the past.

For Example:

This accident has happened yesterday (Clearly , the accident took place in the past. The word *yesterday* is an adverb of time indicating the past and hence the sentence is wrong.)

Correct the sentence as shown below:

This accident happened yesterday. (Simple past tense)

The present perfect tense is used with conjunctions like *after, before, when* , and *as soon as* to indicate an action to be completed in the future.

For Example:

I will come to you after I have finished my work.

(The work is to be completed in the future)

He will go to Chennai as soon as he has come back from leave.

(*d*) **The Present Perfect Continuous Tense:** The Present Perfect Continuous tense is used to denote an activity which

(*i*) began in the past

(*ii*) continues up to the present and

(*iii*) still continues.

Although the Present Perfect tense is used to convey almost the same meaning it does not categorically tell us that the activity still continues. But the use of the Present Perfect Continuous tense ensures that the activity still continues.

Examine the following sentences:

He has studied in this school for five years.

He has been studying in this school for five years.

The first sentence conveys the meaning that he continued to study in this school up to the present time but it does not clearly convey the meaning that he is still studying in this school.

But the second sentence tells us beyond any doubt that he is still studying in this school. This clarity of meaning can be obtained only by using the Present Perfect Continuous tense.

It is therefore used to express an action that began in the past and is still continuing. It is formed by the Present Perfect tense of the verb 'to be' + the present participle of the verb. H*as been* and *have been* are the present perfect tense forms of the verb 'to be'.

Assertive form

Subject + was /have + been + past participle of the verb

For Example:

I have been reading. He has been reading. They have been reading.

You have been reading. I have been reading. It has been raining.

Negative form:

Subject +has not/ have not + been + past participle of the verb.

For Example:

I have not been speaking. They have not been speaking.

You have not been speaking. She has not been speaking.

He has not been speaking. It has not been working.

Interrogative form:

Have / Has + subject + been + present participle of the verb.

For Example:

Have you been complaining? Have I been complaining?

Has she been complaining? Has he been complaining?

Have we been complaining?

Negative Interrogative form:

Has he not been playing? (Hasn't he been playing?)

Have they not been playing? (Haven't they been playing?)

Have you not been playing? (Haven't you been playing?)

Have we not been playing? (Haven't we been playing?)

Have I not been playing? (Haven't I been playing?) (subject-pronoun)

Has not John been playing? (Hasn't John been playing?)

Uses : (subject-noun)

(*i*) To express an action which began at sometime in the past and which is still going on; as,

For Example:

We have been doing this work for five years.

She has been learning dance since last December.

11.2 THE PAST TENSE

(*a*) **The Simple past tense:** This tense is usually used to describe events completed in the past at a time indicated by such adverbs of time as *yesterday, ago, last month, last week* and *last year.*

Assertive form:

To express an action that was completed in the past.

Subject + past tense of the verb + object.

For Example:

We went home. I got it. He sat on the bench.

Negative form:

Subject + did not + base form of the verb

I did not talk. We did not see. You did not come.

Interrogative form:

Did + subject + base form of the verb.

Did she speak? Did we talk ?

Negative Interrogative form:

Did + subject + not + base of the verb.

Did she not tell you? (Didn't she tell you?)

Did I not request him? (Didn't I request you?)

Uses:

(*i*) To express an action that happened in the past.

Ram went home last week. He came the day before yesterday.

(*ii*) To express a habitual action in the past.

John went to the park every evening.

She sang at the parties regularly.

(*iii*) To express an action that happened over a long time in the past.

The poor boy struggled and became rich.

The thief grew into a big dacoit.

(*iv*) After *it is time* either the past tense or the infinitive is used.

For Example:

It is time he stopped smoking.

Or

It is time for him to stop smoking. (With 'for' the infinitive form is used.)

It is time he got married.

Or

It is time for him to get married.

(*v*) The simple past is used after conditional clauses using
If only, as if , as though , wish, etc.

For Example:

If only I were rich. (I am not rich.)

He spoke to me as if he were my boss. (He is not my boss.)

I wish I had wings. (I do not have wings.)

(*b*) **The Past Continuous Tense:** The Past Continuous tense is used to express an action that was going on for sometime in the past.

For Example:

He was sleeping.

She was sweeping the room.

Examine the following sentence:

When I reached home, she was sleeping.

There are two actions in this sentence:

When I reached home Action (1)

She was sleeping Action (2)

There are two actions in the past, one in the past tense and the other in the past continuous tense. The whole sentence tells us that the second action began before the first one and that it (second action) might continue. That is, the first action took place during the course of the second action.

Now Examine the following sentence:

When he reached home, she slept.

The two actions in the above sentence took place almost simultaneously and hence they are in the simple past tense.

Hence the rules are:

(I) If there are two actions in the past one of which began before the other, the earlier action is expressed in the past continuous tense and the later one is expressed in the simple past tense.

(II) If the two actions took place one closely followed by the other, we use the simple past tense for both the actions.

(III) If there are two events in the past that were continuing side by side, both the events are expressed in the past continuous tense; as,

He was singing while she was dancing.

Assertive form:

Subject + was/ were+ present participle of the verb.

For Example:

I was reading the book.

They were painting.

Negative form:

Subject + was not / were not + present participle.

For Example:

She was not reading the newspaper.

You were not talking over the phone.

Interrogative form:

Was/Were + Subject + present participle

For Example:

Was she cooking?

Were they coming?

Negative Interrogative form:

Wasn't/Weren't+ subject + present participle

For Example:

Wasn't he sleeping? (Was he not sleeping?)

Weren't they cooking? (Were they not cooking?)

Wasn't Ram absent? (Was not Ram absent?) (subject-noun)

Uses:

(*i*) To express an action that was continuing in the past.

For Example:

Last night I was watching a movie.

He was learning Physics yesterday.

It was getting late.

(*ii*) To express an action that was continuing, when another action (simple past) happened.

For Example:

I met him when he was entering the office.

We were driving fast when the break failed.

(*c*) **The Past Perfect tense:** When one event follows another in the past the earlier (before-past time) event is expressed in the past perfect tense.

Consider the following two events:

I reached home. (1)

My daughter slept. (2)

If (2) above is the earlier action it should be in the past perfect tense

Then the sentence should be:

When I reached home my daughter had slept.

If (1) is the earlier action then the sentence should be:

My daughter slept after I had reached home.

Note: We can also use the simple past tense for both the actions as shown below:

My daughter slept before I reached home.

Or

My daughter slept after I reached home.

Note: In the above sentences the 'time-conjunctions' after and *before* themselves indicate which event took place first.

In this tense there should be two events in the past.. The event which happened earlier is expressed in the past perfect tense and the one that happened later is expressed in the simple past tense.

Assertive form

Subject + had + past participle of the verb.

For Example:

We had finished our dinner before he came.

My father had gone to the office before I got up.

He opened the door after I had knocked for the second time.

When I reached the station the train had left.

Negative form:

Subject + had not + past participle of the verb

For Example:

The train had not left when I reached the station.

We had not finished our dinner before he came.

Interrogative form:

Had +subject + past participle of the verb.

For Example:

Had you gone to his house on Monday before I called you ?

Had I read the book?

Had they come back soon?

Negative Interrogative form:

Had + subject (pronouns/ nouns) + not + past participle

For Example:

Had the girls not completed the work? (Hadn't the girls completed the work?)

Had they not gone to the office? (Hadn't they gone to the office?)

Uses:

(*i*) To express the action that happened earlier when two actions occurred in the past

For Example:

(*i*) When they reached the airport the plane had taken off.

(*ii*) The bell had rung by the time we reached school.

In the following example are given sentences belonging to the past and the past perfect tenses.

It *was* a holiday. John *got up* late in the morning. He *had travelled* extensively the previous day. He *had come* home very late in the night and *had gone* to bed around midnight.

(*d*) **The Past Perfect Continuous tense:** This tense is usually used to provide the past form of the present perfect continuous.

Assertive form: To express an action that began before a certain point in the past and still continuing. When there are two actions, the first action should be in the Past Perfect Continuous tense and the second in the Simple Past tense.

Subject + had been + present participle

For Example:

You had been playing the whole day.

She had been watching cricket.

He had been working in the field when I met him.

Negative form:

Subject + had not been + present participle

For Example:

I had not been watching her.

We had not been listening to the radio.

Interrogative form:

Had + subject + been + present participle ?

For Example:

Had she been drawing ?

Had you been writing a letter ?

Negative interrogative form:

Had + subject +not been + present participle?

For Example:

Had you not been talking to her? (Hadn't you been talking to her)

Had they not been waiting for us? (Hadn't they been waiting for us?)

Had not the Ministers been discussing the matter?

(Hadn't the Ministers discussing the matter) (subject-noun)

Uses:

(*i*) To express an action which began in the past and was in progress before the next action started.

For Example:

When I went to Delhi in 1998 Mr. Raj had been staying there for three years.

When my father came I had been doing my homework.

Note: A good knowledge of the past perfect and past perfect continuous tenses is particularly useful in the conversion of the Direct speech into the Indirect, besides writing good English.

Important Note: We have already seen that_the Present perfect and Past perfect are formed by means of the present and past tenses of 'have' with the past participle of the verb. But, formerly the auxiliary 'be' was used with verbs of movement for this purpose.

For Example:

He was gone. (meaning 'He had gone')

They are come. (meaning 'They have come')

An idea is suddenly come into his head.

(meaning 'An Idea has suddenly come into his head.)

But in modern English the auxiliary 'be' is used with the past participle of verbs to form the Present to emphasize the idea of a state or condition rather than the idea of movement.

For Example:

They have gone. (Present Perfect indicates the idea of movement.)

They are gone. (meaning 'They have gone and are not here now'. It indicates an idea of a state or condition.)

He will be gone before you come.

(He will have gone before you come and he will not be there.)

The train is left. (The train has left and is off the station now- state.)

He is come. (He has come and is here now - state.)

She is subscribed to the magazine.

(She has subscribed to the magazine and is now a subscriber - state.)

He is determined. (He has determined and is firm in his decision- state.)

2. The imperative (command, request, etc) 'be gone' means 'go at once'. It conveys the same meaning with 'let', 'must' and some other phrases which have reference to the future.

For Example:

Let him *be gone.* (Let him go at once.)

She must be gone.

We shall be gone.

Will she be gone?

He is eager to be gone.

11.3 THE FUTURE TENSE

This tense is used to express an action that will take place in the future.

There are different methods of expressing the future time in the English Language. They are

(1) Simple future tense with *shall and will*

(2) Future time with the *simple present tense*

(3) Future time with *be going to*

(4) Future time with the *present continuous tense*

(5) Future time with *be about to, be to, be on the point of, be on the verge of, etc.*

(*a*) **Simple Future Tense**

By the simple future tense we mean the mere future time. In this sense we use *shall* with the first person, singular and plural.

Assertive form:

(I/We) and *will* with the second and third persons, both singular and plural (*you, he, they, it,* etc). It does not imply the idea of intention, command, willingness or determination.

Subject +will/shall + base form of the verb

For Example:

I shall go. He will come. We will meet tomorrow.

They will go. You will go.

Negative form:

Subject + will not/shall not + base form of the verb.

For Example:

I shall not tell her. He will not talk to me.

Interrogative form:

Shall/ Will + subject + base form of the verb.

For Example:

Shall I come in? Will he talk to you?

Will it rain today?

Negative Interrogative form:

Shall/Will + not + subject + base form of the verb if the subject is a noun.

Shall/will + subject + not + base form of the verb if the subject is a pronoun.

For Example:

Will not Ram come tomorrow? (subject-noun)

Will he not talk to me? (subject-pronoun)

Shall I not go there?

Uses:

(*i*) For future actions; as,

I shall meet you next week.

He will meet you tomorrow.

(*ii*) When there is an intention in the future, 'going to + base form of the verb' is used.

We are going to swim in the river.

She is going to see her mother.

Note: *Shall* is used with the first person singular and plural *I/We* and *will* is used with the second and third persons *you, he, they etc* to form the simple future tense.

Note: In modern English *will* is used with all persons to express the Simple future tense, but *shall* is used in this sense only with *the fist person I/We.*

Note: The contracted form of both *will* and *shall* is ' ll.

This form is usually used in spoken English.

Note: Difference between ' in future' and ' in the future '.

'In future' means 'henceforth' or 'from now on'

For Example:

You must be very careful *in future.* (warning)

'In the future' means 'the time that is coming after the present'

For Example:

See whether you can become a successful businessman *in the future.*

(*b*) **Future Continuous Tense:** This tense is used to represent an action as taking place in the future.

For Example:

I shall be eating my food by this time tomorrow.

I shall be travelling by train next week.

(*c*) **Future Perfect Tense:** This tense is used to denote the completion of some action before a certain *point of time* in the future; as,

He will have reached the Railway station before the train starts.

(Meaning: His reaching the Railway station will be completed before the starting of the train. ('before the train starts' is the point of time in the future)

They will have arrived at Chennai by the time he reaches home.

(Their arrival will be completed before his reaching home.)

He will have completed his work by tomorrow.

Note: Remember that the Future perfect tense is always followed by a time expression.

(*d*) **Future Perfect Continuous Tense**

This tense is used to indicate an action as going on over a period of time that will end in the future; as,

Today is Monday. I am travelling by Train. By Wednesday morning I will have been travelling more than twenty four hours.

Future time with *be going to;*

This form is used to speak about the future with some intention.

Form

Be going to + base form of the verb.

For Example:

We are going to the cinema this evening. (Shows our future intention)

He is going to meet the Principal.

They are going to boycott the meeting.

Note: This form is not used with the verbs 'go' and 'come'. See the Note under the present continuous tense.

Future time with the Present tense

The simple present tense is used in conditional clauses beginning with *if, unless, though, etc* and adverbial time subordinate clauses beginning with *when, after, as soon as, before etc.* The future tense is then used in the main clause.

For Example:

As soon as I come back from Delhi I shall meet you.

(In this sentence, 'As soon as I come back' is the adverbial clause in the present tense and 'I shall meet you' is the main clause in the future tense.)

If it rains I shall not come. ('If it rains' – conditional clause in the present tense)

Before I go back I shall tell you the details.

The simple present is also used to indicate some events or states which are certain in the future.

For Example:

Sunday comes after Saturday.

The meeting begins tomorrow at 10 a.m.

He leaves for London tomorrow.

Future time with Present continuous tense.

This form is used to indicate a definite future plan or arrangement indicated by a time limit which is in the near future.

For Example:

He is leaving for Chennai tomorrow.

We are inviting the Minister for the forthcoming meeting.

We are having a party next week.

Future time with be about , be to , etc.

This form is used to indicate immediate futurity.

For Example:

He is about to leave the hall.

He is to attend the Board meeting tomorrow.

They are to meet the Collector this afternoon.

Uses of *shall* and *will*

Uses of *shall*

Shall is used with the first person *I/We* to indicate simple futurity. It does not then convey the speaker's willingness or intention. (In Modern English 'will' is preferred with all persons to indicate simple futurity and the contracted form' ll is used for both 'shall and will'.

For Example:

I 'll come tomorrow.

He 'll come tomorrow.

For Example:

If time permits I shall meet you after the seminar.

We shall come to your house this week.

I shall go for the exhibition next Monday.

We shall become members of the club soon.

Shall is used with the second and third person to express *a command, promise, threat , etc*

For Example:

You shall not tell a lie. (command)

You shall be given a prize. (promise)

He shall be fined if he violates the rules. (threat)

Every member shall follow the club rules. (regulation)

You shall not question the authority of the court. (command)

Note: In modern English the following forms are preferred:

'You must not tell a lie' instead of 'You shall not tell a lie'

'I promise that you will be given a prize' instead of

'You shall be given a prize'

'Every member must follow the club rules' instead of

'Every member shall follow the club rules' etc.

Note: Commands using 'shall' are mainly confined to legal documents, rules and regulations in modern English.

For Example:

The agreement shall be in force for two years from the date of its execution.

"The proceedings shall not be published", the court ordered.

Uses of *will*

In Modern English 'will + infinitive' is generally used with all persons to indicate simple futurity despite the conventional rule that 'shall' should be used with the first person I and We for this purpose. It does not then indicate willingness or intention on the part of the speaker. 'Shall' is now optionally used with I and We in place of 'will'.

For Example:

We will/shall go to Chennai tomorrow.

You will get the book tomorrow.

She will come next week.

They will go to Delhi shortly.

(*i*) Will + infinitive (base form of the verb) used with the first person to show willingness, intention and determination without any preconceived idea or notion.

For Example:

I will help my father in his old age. (determination)

Will you please do it? Yes, I will. (willingness)

As I want to become an engineer I will study hard. (intention)

We will never do anything against him. (determination)

(*ii*) *'Will'* is sometimes used to express a command when used in the affirmative.

For Example:

"The Collector will carry out my instructions", said the Minister. (command)

"All the junior officers will attend the seminar", said the Secretary. (command)

(*iii*) 'Will' is sometimes used to express *willingness, wish* or *intention* in conditional clauses and clauses of time.

It does not then indicate simple futurity.

For Example:

If he will work as a clerk I shall ask him to come. (If he is willing...)

If you will come with me I shall take you. (If you wish to come with me...)

Important: To express simple futurity 'will' is not used in conditional and in clauses of time.

(*iv*) 'Will' is sometimes used in the sense 'like' (verb)

For Example:

Call it what you will, it is still a mystery.

Note: Uses of 'will', 'must', 'ought to' and 'should'.

We use 'will' and 'must' to predict an event which is certain to happen.

For Example:

She will have reached home *by now/evening/tomorrow, etc.*

She must have reached *by now.*

(But not: by evening/tomorrow, etc. with 'must')

This is the difference between 'will' and 'must' when they are used to predict an event which is certain to happen.

'ought to' and 'should' are used to predict an event which is not certain to happen.

For Example:

He ought to be here now. (He is likely to be here, but not certain.)

He should be here now.

Uses of *would* and *should*

Would

1. Would is the past equivalent of 'will' and is used in the past reported speech to indicate 'future in the past'.

For Example:

She said, " He will come tomorrow."

She said that he would come the next day.

The Principal said, " Monday will be a holiday."

The Principal said that Monday would be a holiday.

Note: It is usual to use 'should' in place of 'would' with 'I' and 'we' in past reported speech. This could sometimes cause misunderstanding.

For Example:

I said, "We will help him." (This indicates simple future tense)

I said that we should help him. (Past reported speech)This may be mistaken for obligation on the part of the speaker.

This mistaken idea may be avoided by using 'would' itself, as;

I said that we would help him.

2. Would is used to express a habitual or customary action in the past.

For Example:

He would go for a walk in the evening. (meaning: He was in the habit of going for a walk in the evening.)

He would take bath everyday in the morning.

3. Would is used to express willingness in the past.

For Example:

She said she would help him in his office work.

She said she would go with him to the temple.

4. Would is used to express conditions. This is called 'conditional would'.

For Example:

If she should come, I would/could go with her.

If I were to meet him, I would start early.

If you should buy a car, you would take a loan.

In this construction the past tense is used in the subordinate clause and would (or 'd) + infinitive or could + infinitive in the main clause.

For Example:

If I had a car I would/could take my friends to the park tomorrow.

Here the past tense does not indicate past time. It indicates present or future. To express past time we use the past perfect tense.

For Example:

If I had gone there I would/could have met them.('had gone' and would have met' indicate past time.) (meaning: but I did not go there)

5. Would is used to express hypothetical meaning.

If he had met them, he would have known all about their plight.

(but he did not meet them.)-past tense

Or

Had he met them he would have known all about your plight.

If I were you I would go there. (I am not you)-present tense

6. Would is used to make a request.

For Example:

Would you please come with me?

(' will' may be used in place of 'would'. But, 'would' is more polite.)

Would you help me to get a loan from the bank?

7. 'Would rather' is used to express a preference or choice.

For Example:

I would rather buy a house than stay in a rented house.

He would rather marry than remain a bachelor .

They would rather pay the tax than pay fine.

8. Would is sometimes used to express determination.

For Example:

He would choose his own partner. (He is determined to choose his own partner.)

For Example:

He would have his own way.

I would not budge an inch.

9. Would is used to express assumption about a past action.

For Example:

" Someone from Mumbai came here yesterday", they said.

"That would have been my friend, I would say", said he. (I presume)

Uses of *should*

1. Should is used as the past equivalent of 'shall' in past reported speech.

For Example:

The teacher said, " No one shall make a noise in the class".

The teacher said that no one should make a noise in the class.

The judge said, " The accused shall pay a fine of ₹ 500".

The judge ordered that the accused should pay a fine of ₹ 500.

2. Should (not as the past tense of 'shall') suggests an obligation or advice.

For Example:

You should be present in the court when the trial begins.

You should revise your lessons well in advance.

3. Should is used to express a supposition.

For Example:

If you should come, I shall send you a vehicle.

Or

Should you come, I shall send you a vehicle.

4. Should is sometimes used after *that* to express a suggestion or recommendation.

For Example:

I suggest that the minister should be invited to the function.

Or

I suggest that the minister be invited to the function. ('should' may be omitted. But in Modern English the use of 'should' is preferred.)

The doctor has recommended that she should take rest.

Or

The doctor has recommended that he take rest.

Note: Look at the following sentence:

The committee has decided that he should be appointed Manager.

We cannot omit 'should' from this sentence where it refers to a decision and not to any suggestion/recommendation.

5. Should is sometimes used to express a doubt.

   For Example:

   I can't imagine why he should do it.

   (I can't imagine what makes him do it.)

6. Should is used to express possibility, assumption, etc in conditional clauses.

   For Example:

   If you should go there, they will give you the amount.

7. It may be noted that the possibility indicated by should is less than that indicated by 'shall'.

   I shall help him if he so desires.

   I should help him if he so desires.

8. Should is sometimes used to mean mild compulsion.

   For Example:

   I can't understand why he should say so.

   I can't understand what compels him to say so.

9. Should is sometimes used to express neutral idea. This is called 'putative should'.

   For Example:

   I know that he will improve. (This is a factual statement.)

   He suggests that she should improve. (This is a neutral statement. Whether he will improve is a matter to be seen.)

   It is quite surprising that you should have to support him.

   I am surprised that you should quarrel with your friend.

   It is unimaginable that she should win the first prize.

   It is a pity that the terrorists should kill an innocent person.

The following are also neutral statements:

How should you go?

Why should he kill him?

Who should take such bold decisions but the Prime Minister himself.

Compatibility of tenses: When a sentence contains two or more events the tenses used to describe them should be compatible with the events. This is necessary to convey clear ideas of the events without any confusion or difficulty.

For Example:

The officer said that he needs some time to take a decision. (Both the events in the sentence took place in the past. But, the first event is in the past tense and the second one in the present. Here the tenses are incompatible. To make them compatible, the sentence should be recast as follows:

The officer said that he needed some time to take a decision.

Errors in the use of verbs and tenses:

1. The murderer was hung. (say: hanged)
2. I am forty and my wife thirty five. (say: my wife <u>is</u> thirty five)
3. Thirty students are present and one absent. (say: one <u>is</u> absent)
4. They never have and will never admit their lapses.

   (say: They never have admitted and never will admit...)
5. He had met with an accident. (say: He met with ...)
6. He said that he will come the next day. (say; ... that he would come the next day.)
7. Much water has flown under the bridge. (say: has flowed)
8. The canal has overflown its banks. (say; overflowed...)
9. He awaited for the train. (say; awaited the train (or) He waited for the train.)
10. He told that he would go to Bombay shortly. (say: He said that...(or) He told me that he ...)
11. Poet Vallathol has founded the Kalamandalam. (say: Poet Vallathol founded)
12. The festival has ended yesterday. (say; The festival ended)
13. I am reading this book for the last one hour. (say; I have been reading)
14. He has been punished in a criminal case two years ago. (say: He was punished)
15. Go to eat your breakfast. (say; Go and eat your breakfast.)

    In imperative sentences of this type , do not use the 'to' infinitive.
16. He addressed to the main issue. (say: Addressed the main issue)

    (or) He addressed himself to the main issue.
17. He avenged on his brother's wrongs. (say: He avenged his brother's wrongs. Meaning; "He took vengeance for the wrongs done to his brother)
18. He avenged his father's murder. (say: He avenged his father's murderer – meaning he took vengeance on his father's murderer)

    Note: Take vengeance on somebody or take vengeance for something.
19. The train left when I reached the station. (say: the train had left...)
20. Colombus had discovered America. (say: Colombus discovered America.)

21. He asked me to do next work. (say ... the next work)
22. This is not a thing to play. (say ... thing to play with.)
23. There is no chair to sit. (say; There is no chair to sit on/in.)
24. This is the house I am living. (say ... I am living in)
25. Crossing the road a car hit me. (say: While I was crossing the road ...)
26. Being a rainy day we did not go out. (say: It being a rainy day ...)
27. It is I who is responsible for this mishap. (say: It is I who am ...)
28. It is you who is to blame. (say: It is you who are ...)
29. He was to immediately come to me. (say: He was to come to me immediately)
30. He never has and never will do that. (say: He never has done and never will do that)
31. The students availed of the concessions. (say: The….availed themselves of the concessions.)
32. I want to know where is he going. (say: I want to know where he is going.)
33. Do you know who are they ? (say; Do ... who they are ?)
34. How you know he is innocent ? (say: How do you know he is innocent ?)
35. A large number of people is attending the meeting. (say ... are attending the meeting. 'The number of ... singular verb)
36. The number of people attending the meeting are small. (say ... is small)
37. Neither of the pens are good. (say ... is good)
38. Every employee and every officer are expected to be present. (say: ... is expected to be present)
39. The judge disposed off the suit. (say ... disposed of the suit)
40. He has washed his hands off the unfair dealings. (say: ... hands of ...)
41. The train just arrived. (say: The train has just arrived) 'Just' is not used with the past tense .Eg; The train arrived.
42. I did not see you for the last three months. (say: I have not seen you for the last three months)
43. I did not go home since we met last time. (say: I have not gone home since we met last time.)
44. I have been here since two weeks. (say: I have been here for two weeks)
45. Study well lest you should not fail. (say; ... lest you should fail. (or) Study well lest you fail.)
46. I am searching for my pen since last Monday. (say: I have been searching for ...)
47. He is bed- ridden since three days. (say: He has been bed ridden for three days.)
48. He did not know that what they wanted. (say ... know what they wanted.)
49. He hanged the picture on the wall. (say: He hung ...)
50. He lied on the bed. (say: He lay on the bed.)
51. The hen lay an egg. (say: The hen laid an egg.)
52. I was writing a letter when the postman came. (say: I had been writing…..)
53. He could lift the weight easily. (say: He was able to lift ...)

    But: He could not lift the weight easily (correct.)

54. You had better to do it. (say: You had better do it.)
55. He is to be blamed for that. (say; He is to blame for that.)
56. He died with fever. (say: He died of fever.)
57. It is hard to be taken. (say: It is hard to take. (accept))
58. I prefer to learn than teaching. (say: I prefer to learn than teach.)
59. I cannot help to laugh . (say; I cannot help laughing)
60. He persisted to do the work. (say: He persisted in doing ...)
61. I am confident to succeed in the exam. (say: I am confident of succeeding ….)
62. He prevented me to do the work. (say: He prevented me from doing the work.)

Or

He prevented my doing the work.

'The police prevented the demonstration.' (correct)

Chapter 12 THE SEQUENCE OF TENSES

12.1 TENSE AND EVENTS (GENERAL)

Do not change tenses when two or more events happen at the same time. Change tenses only when one event precedes or follows another.

For Example:

1. He went and shouts at his neighbour.(wrong)

   He went and shouted at his neighbour.

   Here, both the events happened at the same time in the past.

2. When I reached the station, unfortunately for me, the train left.

   Here, the train left before I reached the station.

   Since the leaving of the train precedes my reaching the station, a change of tense is necessary to indicate this fact clearly.

   The sentence may, therefore, be recast as follows:

   When I reached the station, unfortunately for me, the train *had* left (change from past to past perfect to indicate the first event.)

3. By the time I reach the station, the train will leave.

   There are two future events in the above sentence.

   As it stands, the sentence gives the wrong idea that both the events happen at the same time in the future. Correct it as follows:

   By the time I reach the station, the train will have left.

   The future perfect clearly indicates that the leaving of the train will happen before my reaching the station.

12.2 SEQUENCE OF TENSES

The sequence of tenses is the principle according to which the tense of a subordinate clause must follow the tense of the main clause with certain exemptions detailed below. This is necessary to give clear ideas of the events described in the clauses, thereby avoiding any possible confusion or problem. To ensure this, the tense of the verb in the subordinate clause is required to be compatible with the tense of the verb in the main clause.

For Example:

He told me that he is not well.

Here a past tense in the main clause is followed by a present tense in the subordinate clause. Both the events happened in the past and, therefore, both the verbs should be in the past tense.

As the sentence stands, it is not clear whether he was not well only at the time of speaking or is not well still. This confusion can be avoided if the sentence is recast as follows:

He told me that he was not well. (both the verbs in the past tense)

The following rules should be observed in this regard:

(*i*) If the verb in the Principal Clause is in the Past tense the verb in the subordinate (or dependent) clause is normally in the Past tense.

For Example:

When I *reached* the Railway station the train *had left.*

He *told* me that he *would come* the next day.

I *saw* that the *boys were* playing.

He *said* that he *had been working* for the whole day.

He *said* that he *might come.*

He *told* me that *he had lost* his pen.

Exception:

(*i*) A past tense in the principal clause is followed by a simple present tense in the subordinate clause to express some universal truth or habitual facts; as,

For Example:

The teacher said that the sun rises in the East. (universal truth)

His father said that his son takes bath every day. (habitual fact)

She said that she comes to the office by bus everyday. ("   )

(*ii*) If a subordinate clause begins with some conjunction of comparison (*e.g.,* than, as well as, etc.) it can be in any tense irrespective of the tense of the verb in the Principal clause; as,

He hated you more than he hates me.

He hates you more than he hated me.

He has hated you more than he hated me.

He will hate you more than he hated me.

He will hate you more than he has hated you.

He hates you more than he hates me.

He hates you as well as he hates me.

He hated you as well as he hates me.

Note. If after the *conjunction* of comparison (*i.e.,* 'than' or 'as well as') the verb is understood in the subordinate clause then the tense of the verb is that of the verb in the Principal clause; as,

He liked me more than her.

i.e., He liked me more than (*he liked*) her.(Past tense in the principal clause)

He will hate you as well as me.

i.e., He will hate you as well as (*he will hate*) me.(Future tense in the principal clause)

(*iii*) A present or future tense in the Principal clause can be followed by any tense as required by the sense in the dependent clause.

For Example:

He believes that he is innocent.

He believes that he was innocent.

He believes that he will be innocent.

He will believe that he is innocent.

He will believe that he was innocent.

I shall give you the book if you will pay for it.(meaning ' if you are willing to pay for it')

But, if the subordinate clause in a sentence expresses a purpose the verb must be simple present expressed by the auxiliary 'may' even if the verb in the principal clause is present or future. If the principal clause is in the past tense 'might' must be used in the subordinate clause; as,

I study hard so that I may pass the examination creditably.

I shall do exercise every day so that I may become healthy.

She is working hard that she may get a first class.

He will be going to Chennai that he may get a job.

He studied hard that he might pass the examination creditably.

I lent some money to my friend that he might improve his business.

But, whenever the conjunction 'lest' is used to introduce a subordinate clause, either the infinitive without 'to' or the auxiliary 'should' must be used irrespective of the tense of the verb in the main clause. (The only auxiliary verb that can be used after 'lest' is 'should'.). As 'lest' is already negative, 'not' should not be used again; as,

He looked after his parents very well lest he *should fail* in his duty.

Or

He looked after his parents very well lest *he fail* in his duty. (not: fails)

(Meaning: He looked after his parents very well that he might not fail in his duty.)

He looks after his parents very well lest he should fail in his duty.

Or

He looks after his parents very well lest he fail in his duty. (not: fails)

(Meaning: He looks after his parents very well that he may *not* fail in his duty.)

He will look after his parents very well lest he should fail in his duty.

Or

He will look after his parents very well lest he fail in his duty.

(Meaning: He will look after his parents very well that he may *not* fail in his duty.)

Note. The changes of tenses in the subordinate clause are not obligatory if the facts in the reported clause are still valid.

For Example:

'He said he will come.' This is not *illogical* if he has not come yet.

She said, "I shall speak to you later."

'She said she will speak to me later' is not *incorrect* if she has not spoken to me at the time of reporting.

EXERCISE

Correct the following sentences:

1. He said that he has come yesterday.
2. He reached after the train had left.
3. Teacher told me that the earth was round.
4. Ramu told me that he is innocent.
5. Come early least you may miss the train.
6. He will come by the time I reach there.
7. When I will come to Kochi I shall come to your house.
8. When I reached the office the officer stood in front of my table.
9. I was so weak that I cannot walk.
10. She said that Raju is absent.
11. He told me that he will come tomorrow.
12. I was sorry that I gave him the wrong address.
13. He asked me why I want to go so early.
14. It is long time since I had left that place.
15. I finished me work before he came.
16. I advised him when he starts neglecting his studies.
17. He told me that honesty was the best policy.
18. He said that he may come to see me tomorrow.
19. He says that he might go to Chennai.
20. The teacher taught me that water was produced when oxygen combined with hydrogen.

Chapter 13 DEGREES OF COMPARISON

13.1 COMPARISON OF ADJECTIVES OR ADVERBS

There are three degrees of comparison:

(*a*) The Positive degree

(*b*) The Comparative degree

(*c*) The Superlative degree

The Positive Degree:

The positive degree of an adjective shows absolute or simple quality.

For Example:

Ramu is a *clever* boy.

Chandni is a *beautiful* girl.

It is used for comparison of equals. There are two types under this category:

(*i*) The Positive Comparison : ...... as + adjective + as construction.

(*ii*) The Negative Comparison : ...... not so + adjective + as

Or

not as +adjective + as construction

Ravi is as tall as Rahim. (same height) (positive comparison)

Ravi is not *so* tall *as* Rahim. (different heights)

Or

Ravi is not *as* tall *as* Rahim. (negative comparison)

Note: Either 'so.....as' or 'as......as' can be used in negative comparison.

In the positive comparison we use a qualitative adjective after the first 'as' and a qualifying prepositional phrase or clause after the second 'as' depending upon the second 'as' is treated as a preposition or a conjunction respectively. We can also use a noun group beginning with the indefinite article *'a'* or 'an', depending upon the noun used, after the qualitative adjective and before the second 'as' without altering the meaning.

For Example:

He is as good *as* his father. (the second 'as' is used as a preposition)

He is twice as tall as his younger brother.

(We can use 'half, twice, thrice, etc before the first 'as'.)

He is just as tall as his friend.

(We can use 'just, nearly, almost, quite' etc before the first 'as'.)

This is as tall *a man* as that one.

(Using a noun group. This is equivalent to saying 'This man is as tall as that one'.)

This is as big *an angle* as that one. (*i.e.* This angle is as big as that one.)

He is not as honest a man as you think. (*i.e.* He is not as honest as you think.)

The picture was not as (so) bad *as* I thought it would be.

(the second 'as' is used as a conjunction)

Note: If the prepositional phrase consists of only 'as' and a pronoun, the latter should be in the objective case (*e.g.*, him, her, me, etc.) If the second 'as' is followed by a clause, the pronoun becomes the subject of the clause and hence it should be in the subjective case.

She is as intelligent as *me.* (Not: I)

Or

She is as intelligent as *I am.* (Here 'as' is a conjunction.)

Note: In negative comparison, 'not' is used before 'as......as' or 'so....as'

For Example:

He is not as (so) intelligent as his brother. (Meaning: He is less intelligent than his brother.)

The Comparative Degree:

The Comparative degree is used when two persons or things are compared. The comparative degree of an adjective shows a higher degree of quality than the positive degree does. It denotes a comparison of two *unequal* things/persons. It is usually followed by 'than'.

For Example:

Ramu is *cleverer* than Mohan.

Radha is *more beautiful* than Meera.

Note: When not two different things are compared at different times the 'than' clause is usually omitted.

For Example:

Education is more expensive now. (than it was)

Information technology is becoming more sophisticated. (than it was)

Note: If we repeat the comparative word with 'and' we can convey the idea of continuing change. Here 'than' cannot be used.

For Example:

He is becoming more and more worried. (increasing)

The crowd is becoming smaller and smaller. (decreasing)

There are two types under the comparative degree:

(*i*) The Positive comparison: Comparative adjective + than; as,

This book is *better than* that one.

(*ii*) The Negative Comparison: not + comparative adjective + than; as,

She is not *more beautiful than* her sister.

Note: The Comparative degree is used when two persons or things are compared.

The Superlative Degree:

The superlative degree of an adjective shows the highest quality.

Use 'in' with the name of the group in which the comparison is made.

Ram is the *cleverest* boy in the class.

Radha is the *most beautiful* girl in the college.

Note: The Superlative degree is used when more than two things or persons are compared. It is usually preceded by the Definite article 'the'. (the + superlative degree)

For Example:

He is the *best* boy in the class.

It was the *most* splendid idea.

Note: The superlative is sometimes used to indicate 'very high degree'.

For Example:

This is an electronic meter with the highest precision.

He undertook the work with the greatest pleasure.

If the worst comes to the worst I will resign my job.

(If the situation becomes too difficult or dangerous I will resign my job.)

Note: The superlative 'most' is sometimes used before an adjective to mean 'very or highly'.

For Example:

He is a most respected leader. (Here 'most' is not a real superlative)

The author is most famous. (Here 'most' is not a real superlative)

She is best suited for this role.

Note: The following constructions using possessive pronouns, genitives, adjectives and relative clauses with superlatives may be noted.

He is my worst enemy. (with possessive pronoun 'my'; not 'the my worst enemy')

This is the world's greatest show. (with genitive 'world's')

It was the greatest tragic event. (with the adjective 'tragic')

That is the most wonderful show we have ever seen.

(with the relative clause 'we have ever seen')

Note: The definite article 'the' is sometimes omitted.

When the superlative forms part of the predicate, 'the' is omitted.

For Example:

I am one among those who hated him most (or the most).

He is a mediocre singer at best. (The best opinion you can have about him.)

When the superlative forming part of the predicate is preceded by the preposition 'at', 'the' is omitted.

For Example:

He can reach Mumbai before Monday at best.

(In any case he can reach Mumbai before Monday.)

When a possessive pronoun referring to the subject precedes the superlative, 'the' is omitted.

For Example:

He helped him his best.

When the superlative is preceded by 'at' and a possessive pronoun referring to the subject, 'the' is omitted.

For Example:

He was at his best today.

Note: 'of + plural/abstract/material/collective noun' may be used after a superlative to indicate a very high degree of quality. Similarly, 'of + a phrase containing a superlative' may also be used to indicate a very high degree.

For Example:

Gandhiji was the kindest of men.

He was in the finest of forms.

He took the best of food.

He made the most of his trip abroad.

He is the bravest soldier of the Indian army.

His performance was of the finest.

13.2 INTERCHANGE OF DEGREES OF COMPARISON

It is possible to change the degrees of comparison of an adjective or an adverb in a sentence without changing its meaning.

There are three different ways in which sentences can be compared according to the number of persons or things included.

Type I:

1. He is the *tallest boy* in the group. (superlative degree)

Or

He is the *tallest of all boys* in the group.

2. He is taller than *any other boy* in the class. (comparative degree)
3. *No other boy* in the group is so tall as he. (positive degree)

Type II:

1. He is *one of the best boys* in the class.
2. He is better than *most other boys* in the class.
3. *Very few boys* in the class is as good as he.

Type III:

1. Rani is *not the smartest of all the girls.*
2. Rani is not smarter than *some other girls.*
3. *Some girls are at least* as smart as Rani.

Note: When we compare two qualities in two different persons or things, we use the 'er' form.

For Example:

Ramu is *cleverer* than Mohan.

Note: But, when we compare two different qualities in one person/thing, we do not use the 'er' form. Instead, we use the positive degree with the word 'more' placed before it.

For Example:

Ramu is *more clever* than cunning. (right)

Ramu is cleverer than cunning. (wrong)

Note: When two things are compared with each other, the word 'other' should be used to exclude the first person or thing from the other.

For Example:

Ramu is cleverer than *any other* boy in the class.

Gold is more precious than *any other* metal.

Here, the comparison is between gold and all other metals taken as one set. If we say "Gold is more precious than any metal", gold is also included in the expression "any metal". So, to exclude gold from the other group of metals we should use 'other' which means 'any other metal than gold'.

Hint (1). *When two persons or things are compared only positive and comparative degrees are possible.*

(*a*) If it is 'as....as' positive form, interchange the persons or things and use 'not + comparative form' of the adjective to form the comparative degree.

For Example:

He is as clever as she. (positive)

She is not cleverer than he. (comparative)

(*b*) If it is 'not so....as' positive form, interchange the persons or things and use the comparative form of the adjective to form the comparative degree of the sentence ; as,

For Example:

He is not so clever as she. (positive)

She is cleverer than he. (comparative)

Hint (2). *'Few or very few' in the positive degree, ' most other' in the Comparative degree and 'one of the' in the superlative degree of a sentence will serve as 'tips' for conversion;* as,

(*a*) Few cities in Kerala are as big as Kochi. (positive)

Kochi is bigger than most other cities in Kerala. (comparative)

Kochi is one of the biggest cities in Kerala. (superlative)

(*b*) Trivandrum is one of the biggest cities in Kerala. (superlative)

Trivandrum is greater than most other cities in Kerala. (comparative)

Very few cities in Kerala are as big as Trivandrum.

Hint (3). *'No other' in the positive degree, 'any other' in the comparative degree and the 'superlative of the adjective alone' in the superlative degree of a sentence will serve as 'tips' for conversion*

(*a*) Kochi is bigger than any other city in Kerala. (comparative)

Kochi is the biggest city in Kerala. (superlative)

No other city in Kerala is as big as Kochi. (positive)

Hint (4). *'some .....at least' in the positive degree, 'some other' in the comparative degree and 'not the +superlative of the adjective' in the superlative degree will serve as 'tips' for conversion; as,*

(*a*) Trivandrum is not the biggest of all cities in Kerala.

Some cities in Kerala are at least as big as Trivandrum.

Trivandrum is bigger than some other cities in kerala.

Hint (5). *'not so........as some other' in the positive degree, 'some' in the comparative degree and 'not one of' in the superlative degree will serve as 'tips' for conversion.*

(*a*) Kottayam is not one of the biggest cities in Kerala.

Some cities in kerala are greater than Kottayam.

Kottayam is not so big as some other cities in Kerala.

1. The Comparative and superlative degrees are formed by adding '– er' and '– est' respectively to their positive forms .

fat	-	fatter	-	fattest
large	-	larger	-	largest
bold	-	bolder	-	boldest
clear	-	clearer	-	clearest
broad	-	broader	-	broadest
great	-	greater	-	greatest
small	-	smaller	-	smallest
sweet	-	sweeter	-	sweetest

tall	-	taller	-	tallest
young	-	younger	-	youngest

2. In adjectives ending in consonants, the last letter is doubled before adding '– er' and '– est' respectively.

thin	-	thinner	-	thinnest
fat	-	fatter	-	fattest
big	-	bigger	-	biggest
hot	-	hotter	-	hottest
red	-	redder	-	reddest
sad	-	sadder	-	saddest

3. In adjectives ending in '– *y*' the '*y*' is changed into '– ier' and '– iest'.

busy	-	busier	-	busiest
easy	-	easier	-	easiest
happy	-	happier	-	happiest
holy	-	holier	-	holiest
heavy	-	heavier	-	heaviest
merry	-	merrier	-	merriest
pretty	-	prettier	-	prettiest
busy	-	busier	-	busiest
ugly	-	uglier	-	ugliest
wealthy	-	wealthier	-	wealthiest
gloomy	-	gloomier	-	gloomiest.

4. When the adjectives have more than one syllable, the comparative and superlative degrees are formed by adding 'more' and 'most' respectively.(Syllable- A syllable is a unit of pronunciation having one vowel sound and usually one or more consonants and forming all or part of a word. *e.g.*, at, it, act, boy, etc are mono syllabic words because each contains only one syllable; before, befit, better, etc contain two syllables each; beautiful, cowardly, courageous, etc are words containing three syllables.)

beautiful	-	more beautiful	-	most beautiful
splendid	-	more splendid	-	most splendid
adventurous	-	more adventurous	-	most adventurous
courage	-	more courageous	-	most courageous
cowardly	-	more cowardly	-	most cowardly
careful	-	more careful	-	most careful
carefree	-	more carefree	-	most carefree
doubtful	-	more doubtful	-	most doubtful
difficult	-	more difficult	-	most difficult

industrious	-	more industrious	-	most industrious
interesting	-	more interesting	-	most interesting
agreeable	-	more agreeable	-	most agreeable
learned	-	more learned	-	most learned
proper	-	more proper	-	most proper

5. When the adjectives end in '– *e*', the comparative and superlative degrees are formed by adding '– *r*' and '– *st*' respectively.

large	-	larger	-	largest
able	-	abler	-	ablest
brave	-	braver	-	bravest
fine	-	finer	-	finest
sure	-	surer	-	surest
nice	-	nicer	-	nicest
noble	-	nobler	-	noblest
white	-	whiter	-	whitest
wise	-	wiser	-	wisest
severe	-	severer	-	severest

6. The comparative and superlative degrees of the following adjectives are not formed from their positive degrees:

bad/ evil/ ill	-	worse	-	worst
good/ well	-	better	-	best
late	-	later	-	latest/ last
many (countable)	-	more	-	most
much (uncountable)	-	more	-	most
little	-	less	-	least
far(distance)	-	farther	-	farthest
far (time)	-	further	-	furthest
fore	-	former	-	foremost / first
old	-	older	-	oldest
old	-	elder	-	eldest
in	-	inner	-	innermost
up	-	upper	-	uppermost
out	-	outer /utter	-	outermost /utmost.

Comparison Using Nouns

Comparison can be made by using *more of a, less of a, enough of a, much of a,* etc. with nouns like *fool, success, coward, man, etc.*

For Example:

He is more of a fool than she thought.

She is enough of a woman to face the situation.

It was as much of a victory as I expected.

He is too much of a coward to go to the police station.

He is less of a man than I thought.

Examples

I. 1. Raju is as fat as Pradeep. (positive)
Pradeep is not fatter than Raju. (comparative)
2. Money is as important as education. (*p*)
Education is not more important than money. (*c*)
3. This stick is not as long as that stick. (*p*)
That stick is not longer than this stick. (*c*)
4. Hira is as beautiful as Meera. (*p*)
Meera is not more beautiful than Hira. (*c*)

II 1. They are not so rich as the Nairs. (*p*)
The Nairs are richer than them. (*c*)
2. Ammu is not as tall as Anu. (*p*)
Anu is taller than Ammu. (*c*)
3. Ravi's picture is not so attractive as Raju's. (*p*)
Raju's picture is more attractive than Ravi. (*c*)

III 1. Veena is the prettiest of all girls. (*s*)
Veena is prettier than any other girl. (*c*)
No other girl is so pretty as Veena. (*p*)
2. Kolkata is the most thickly populated city in India. (*s*)
Kolkata is more thickly populated than any other city in India. (*c*)
No other city in India is so thickly populated as India. (*p*)
3. Binu is the cleverest in the group. (*s*)
Binu is cleverer than any one else in the group. (*c*)
No one else in the group is so clever as Binu. (*p*)
4. This is the finest material in the shop. (*s*)
This material is finer than any other material in the shop. (*c*)
No other material in the shop is so fine as this. (*p*)

IV 1. Mr.Raj is one of the wealthiest people in India. (s)
Mr. Raj is wealthier than most other people in India. (c)
Very few people in India are as wealthy as Mr. Raj. (p)
2. Mahatma Gandhi is one of the most well known personalities. (s)
Mahatma Gandhi is more well known than most other personalities. (c)
Very few personalities are as much well known as Mahatma Gandhi. (p)
3. English is one of the easiest languages. (s)
English is easier than most other languages. (c)
Very few languages are as easy as English. (p)

V 1. Madhavi is not the shortest of all girls. (s)
Madhavi is shorter than some other girls. (c)
Some girls are at least as short as Madhuri. (p)
2. Hritik Roshan is not the most handsome of all actors. (s)
Hritik Roshan is not more handsome than some actors. (c)
Some actors are at least as handsome as Hritik Roshan. (p)
3. Shakespeare is not the most popular of all writers. (s)
Shakespeare is not more popular than some writers. (c)
Some writers are at least as popular as Shakespeare. (p)

EXERCISE

I. Change into other degrees of comparisons.

1. Joseph is better than any other boy in the class.
2. No other flower smells as sweet as rose.
3. Nothing is as important as character.
4. Sanil works harder than any other man.
5. You can read better than I.
6. Australia is the smallest continent in the world.
7. No other airport in India is so modern as Nedumbasseri.
8. Prevention is better than cure.
9. Shakespeare is greater than most other writers.
10. The climate of Kerala is better than that of Andhra Pradesh.
11. No other leader is as humorous as E.K.Nayanar.
12. My sister draws as gracefully as her master.
13. I cannot listen to him as keenly as you.
14. Aravind is fatter than Anil.
15. There was no greater autocrat than Hitler.
16. She draws better than I.
17. Experience is the best teacher.
18. Maniratnam is one of the best directors in Tamil.
19. Painting is more difficult than drawing.
20. Cochin is one of the busiest cities in Kerala.
21. No other disease is so fatal as Aids.
22. The dog is the most faithful of all animals.
23. Gold is not as useful as iron.
24. Very few men are as rich as Mr. Birla.

25. The rocket is swifter than the aeroplane.
26. The lion is the most ferocious of all animals.
27. Rahim is not as strong as Karim.
28. He is one of the most intelligent boys in the class.
29. I am not so clever as John.
30. Sleep is at least as necessary as food.

II Change into positive degree:

1. The French are better than the Americans.
2. We are far more interested in studies in games.
3. Bombay is better than Koltata.
4. He is the best student of the year.
5. Thanu is richer than Aruna.
6. It is easier to preach than practise.

III Change into superlative degree:

1. Madhu's shirt is better than any other dress.
2. Very few mothers are so caring as my mother.
3. No other building is as big as this.
4. Very few monuments in the world are as splendid as the Taj.
5. No other virtue is so valuable as self confidence.

IV Change into comparative degree:

1. The Amazon is the widest river in the world.
2. Mridula was born two years as Akhila.
3. Germany is as beautiful as Switzerland.
4. Beena is the best tutor.
5. Sarojini Naidu was one of the greatest freedom fighters.

1. **Use of 'so....that' in place of the adverb 'too.....to'.**

   (*i*) He is too weak to do any work.

   He is so weak that he cannot do any work.

   (*ii*) The news is too good to be true.

   The news is so good that it cannot be true.

   (*iii*) He is too young to marry now.

   He is so young that he cannot marry now.

2. **Use of 'so.....that' in place of 'too.........not to'.**

   (*i*) He is too clever not to think of the consequences.

   He is so clever that he can think of the consequences.

   (*ii*) He was too strong not to face his enemy boldly.

   He was so strong that he faced his enemy boldly.

3. **Use of 'so.....that' in place of 'too' when 'too' modifies adjectives of quality like proud, gentle, honest, generous, etc.**

   (*i*) He is too gentle to pick quarrel with anyone.

   He is so gentle that he will not pick quarrel with anyone.

   (*ii*) He was too generous not to grant any request.

   He was so generous that he would grant any request.

   (*iii*) She is too proud to sing.

   She is so proud that she will sing.

4. **Use of 'so....that' instead of 'too.......for'.**

   In this case the sense is important and hence the conversion is carried out by using suitable words.

   (*i*) This question is too difficult for her.

   This question is so difficult that she cannot answer it.

   (*ii*) He is too junior for promotion.

   He is so junior that he cannot be promoted.

   (*iii*) The shirt is too big for me.

   The shirt is so big that it is not suitable for me.

Chapter **14**

Transformation of Simple, Complex, Compound and Multiple Sentences

14.1 TRANSFORMATION OF SENTENCES

The changing of a sentence from one grammatical form to another without altering its sense is called the Transformation or conversion of sentences.

Direct to Indirect narration is a typical example of the Transformation of sentences. It is an exercise worth learning as it enables us to use variety of expression in writing the English language.

The following cases of transformation may be noted carefully.

Interchange of the Affirmative and Negative sentences.

(*a*) As soon as I reached the Railway Station the train had left.
No sooner did I reach the station than the train had left.

(*b*) He is sometimes foolish. He is not foolish always. He is cleverer than she.
She is not as clever as he.

(*c*) Everyone makes mistakes sometimes.
Everyone does not make mistakes always.

Interchange of the Interrogative and Assertive sentences.

(*a*) Who does not like milk?
Everyone likes milk.

(*b*) Why advise him?
It is futile to advise him.

(*c*) When will they be reasonable?
They will never be reasonable.

(*d*) What though he rejects the offer?
It does not matter if he rejects the offer.

(*e*) What if he fails in the exam?
It does not matter if he fails in the exam.

Interchange of the Exclamatory and Assertive sentences

(*a*) How foolish he is!
He is very foolish.

(*b*) What a wonderful sight it is!
It is really a wonderful sight.

(*c*) O that I were you!
I wish I were you.

(*d*) What a piece of work is man!
Man is a wonderful piece of work.

(*e*) Alas he has passed away!
It is sad that he has passed away.

Use of one part of speech for another.

In this section we will learn how nouns, verbs, adjectives and adverbs are changed in a sentence without its meaning.

1. **Use of nouns in place of verbs.**

(*a*) He sympathized with him.
He had sympathy for him.

(*b*) He replied politely.
He gave a polite reply.

(*c*) She apologized to him.
She asked for his apology.

(*d*) He is proud of his family.
He takes pride in his family.

(*e*) His teacher advised him.
His teacher gave him advice.

(*f*) He resembles his father.
He has resemblance to his father.

2. **Use of verbs in place of adverbs.**

(*a*) He is apparently innocent.
He appears to be innocent.

(*b*) He regretfully noted the lapses.
He regretted the lapses.

(*c*) He successfully completed the course.
He succeeded in completing the course.

3. **Use of verbs in place of adjectives.**

(*a*) Smoking is injurious to health.
Smoking injures health.

(*b*) He was joyful to receive the guest.

He enjoyed receiving the guest.

(*c*) He was not obedient.

He disobeyed.

4. **Use of nouns in places of verbs.**

(*a*) He consented to marrying her.

He gave his consent to marrying her.

(*b*) He intended going.

He had intention of going.

(*c*) The book costs Rupees two.

The cost of the book is Rupees two.

(*d*) He arrived at the airport very late.

His arrival at the airport was very late.

5. **Use of nouns in place of adjectives.**

(*a*) He was generous to the poor.

He showed generosity to the poor.

(*b*) He was free to act.

He had freedom to act.

(*c*) He was regretful.

He was full of regret.

6. **Use of adjectives in place of adverbs.**

(*a*) He runs slowly.

He is a slow runner.

(*b*) He speaks distinctly.

His speech is distinct.

(*c*) He works silently.

He is a silent worker.

7. **Use of adjectives in place of nouns.**

(*a*) He is a man of honesty.

He is an honest man.

(*b*) He comes to me everyday.

He comes to me daily.

(*c*) The statement is full of facts.

The statement is factual.

(*d*) His mind is full of anxiety.

He is anxious.

8. **Use of nouns in place of adverbs.**

(*a*) He is waiting for his promotion eagerly.

He is waiting for his promotion with eagerness.

(*b*) He did his work carefully.

He did his work with care.

(*c*) He replied arrogantly.

He replied with arrogance.

14.2 SIMPLE, COMPLEX, COMPOUND AND MULTIPLE SENTENCES

Sentences are generally classified into Simple, Complex, Compound and multiple according to the number of clauses they consist of.

Clause: A group of words which forms part of a sentence and which has a subject and a predicate is called a clause.

Simple Sentence: A simple sentence is one which has only one finite verb.

Or

A simple sentence is one that has only one Subject and one Predicate.

In other words, a simple sentence contains only one clause.

For Example:

I met my friend last week.

The sun rises in the east.

It is raining. (Here 'It' is the formal subject.)

An excellent player, he was included in the team.

Working hard, he passed the exam.

In spite of illness, he attended the interview.

Notwithstanding (despite) his hard work, he did not pass the exam.

Complex Sentence: A complex sentence consists of one Principal or Main clause and one or more subordinate clauses. In other words, a complex sentence contains one or more than one member that is subordinate to the other.

Note: A Principal clause is one which makes complete sense and is independent of any other clause or clauses.

For Example:

(*i*) This is the man who came to see me yesterday.

This is the man – principal clause

Who came to see me yesterday–subordinate clause

(*ii*) Even if you send him to me I cannot help him because I am leaving for Madras this evening.

I cannot help him – principal clause

Even if you send him to me – subordinate clause

Because I am leaving for Madras this evening – subordinate clause.

(*iii*) The fact is, the book is missing. (That the book is missing is the fact.)

(*iv*) The reason was, he had lost her address. (That he had lost her address was the reason.)

Compound Sentence: A compound sentence consists of two or more principal clauses (or Main clauses or Co-ordinate clauses). It may or may not have any subordinate clause or clauses.

For Example:

(*i*) He asked me to explain the matter and I did so but he was not satisfied with my explanation. (Three principal clauses)

(*ii*) When my friend came to my shop I was not there but I was able to meet him outside. (Two principal clauses and one subordinate clause)

Double Sentence: A double sentence has only two principal clauses.

For Example:

He went to the railway station and waited for a long time.

I went to the airport to receive my friend, but he did not come.

Double Complex Sentence: A double complex sentence is one which consists of two principal clauses and one or more than one subordinate clause.

For Example:

I went to Chennai to meet my friend, but I could not meet him because he was away on tour.

Multiple Sentence: A multiple sentence consists of more than two principal clauses.

For Example:

He went to Delhi, met his friends and returned.

(*i.e.*, He went to Delhi; he met his friends; he returned.)

Multiple Complex Sentence: A multiple complex sentence consists of more than two principal clauses and one or more than one subordinate clause.

For Example:

The police officer came to the spot where the accident had taken place and made enquiries about the cause of the accident which had resulted in the death of three people and left for the hospital where the dead bodies were kept.

Note: When *who, which, but (all relative pronouns), whose (relative adjective), when and where(relative adverbs) etc.*, are used in a continuative sense (not in a restrictive sense) to join two clauses to form a sentence, a continuative clause is always preceded by a 'comma'. Such clauses are coordinate or main clauses and the whole sentence is a double sentence.

For Example:

He is my friend, who is a doctor. (Here who= and he)

I went to Delhi, where I met my friend. (where=and there)

There are few people, but agree with him. (but=who do not)

He is my friend, whose wife is a doctor. (whose=and his)

Contracted Sentences: Double sentences are very often contracted when

(*a*) there are two verbs or predicates to the same subject.

For Example:

He came and met me.

(He came and *he* met me–'he' omitted–same subject–contracted form.)

I went to his office and discussed the matter with him.

(I went to his office and *I* discussed the matter with him – 'I' omitted–same subject–contracted form.)

(*b*) there are two subjects to the same verb or predicate.

For Example:

He as well as they was present. – contracted form

(He was present as well they were present.)

Either he or his parents can attend the meeting.–contracted form

(Either he can attend the meeting or his parents can attend the meeting.)

He is old, but very active.–contracted form (He is old, but he is very active.)

Either he received the money or his wife.–contracted form

(Either he received the money or his wife received the money.)

1. Conversion of Simple sentences into Compound sentences.

Simple sentences can be converted into compound sentences by expanding words or phrases into co-ordinate clauses by using conjunctions like 'and', 'both.....and', 'either......or', 'not only......but also', 'yet,' 'or' and 'nevertheless'.

(*a*) You must study well to get a first class.(simple)

You must study well and get a first class.(compound)

(*b*) Working hard, he achieved the target.

He worked hard and achieved the target.

(*c*) He received help and encouragement.

He was both helped and encouraged.

(*d*) Besides learning Hindi, he learned music.

He not only learned Hindi but also studied music.

(*e*) In spite of being rich he is humble.

He is humble nevertheless he is rich.

(*f*) Notwithstanding her beauty she did not succeed in the beauty contest.

She was beautiful yet she did not succeed in the beauty contest.

(*g*) You must surrender to avoid execution.

You must either surrender or face execution.

2. **Conversion of Compound sentences into Simple sentences:**

(*a*) He came home and changed his dress.
Having come home he changed his dress.

(*b*) He not only admitted his mistake but also corrected it.
Besides admitting his mistake he corrected it.

(*c*) He rose from the seat and offered it to his teacher.
Having risen from the seat he offered it to his teacher.

(*d*) He was admitted to hospital and the doctor got his blood tested.
He being admitted to hospital the doctor got his blood tested.

(*e*) He was weak and so he took medicine.
Being weak he took medicine.

3. **Conversion of Simple sentences into Complex sentences:**

(*a*) He seems to be confused.
It seems that he is confused.

(*b*) We heard of his accident.
We heard that he had met with an accident.

(*c*) In the absence of proper vigilance corruption will thrive.
Unless there is proper vigilance corruption will thrive.

(*d*) He confessed his guilt.
He confessed that he was guilty.

(*e*) I bought my neighbour's house.
I bought the house which belonged to my neighbour.

(*f*) Only members are admitted.
If you are not a member you cannot be admitted.

4. **Conversion of Complex sentences into Simple sentences:**

(*a*) He does not know where he lives.
He does not know his address.

(*b*) He informed his officer that he was ill.
He informed his officer of his illness.

(*c*) They know that he is guilty.
They know his guilt.

(*d*) He asked why they came.
He asked the reason for their coming.

(*e*) I do not know when I shall return.
I do not know the time of my return.

(*f*) Those who are absent will miss the class.
Absentees will miss the class.

(*g*) The boy who was mischievous was dismissed.

The mischievous boy was dismissed.

5. Conversion of Compound sentences into Complex:

(*a*) Study well and you will pass.

If you study well you will pass.

(*b*) Study hard or you will fail.

If you do not study hard you will fail.

(*c*) He studied hard but he failed.

Although he studied hard he failed.

(*d*) He met his friend and gave the book.

When he met his friend he gave the book.

(*e*) Spare the rod and spoil the child.

If you spare the rod you will spoil the child.

6. Conversion of Complex sentences into Compound sentences:

(*a*) I am happy to know that he has passed.

He has passed and I am happy to know that.

(*b*) I got the book that I had misplaced.

I had misplaced a book but I got it.

(*c*) As soon as I reached the railway station the train had left.

He reached the station but the train had left.

(*d*) If I go home I shall meet him.

I may go home and in that case I shall meet him.

(*e*) Although he is illiterate he can speak well.

He is illiterate but he can speak well.

(*f*) Unless we work hard we cannot prosper.

Work hard and we will prosper.

Chapter **15** # ACTIVE AND PASSIVE VOICE

Voice is the form of a verb that tells us whether the person or thing denoted by the subject (active subject) does something or something is done to the person or thing (inactive or passive subject).

Examine the following sentences:

John killed a rat. ...(*i*)

Who killed a rat? John.

John is the subject of the sentence because he did the act and rat is the object. John is the *doer* of the action. Hence, the first sentence is an example of the Active voice because the subject is the doer of the action 'killed', *John* is therefore the *active subject*.

Examine the following sentence now:

A rat was killed by John.

In this case something was done to the subject 'rat' (object of the sentence at (*i*) above) by the doer John (subject of the sentence at (*i*) above). This is therefore an example of the Passive voice. Here, the object 'rat' is the receiver of the action by the subject John. The sentence, therefore, is in the passive voice because the subject (rat) is passive. It received or suffered some action. 'Rat' is therefore the *passive subject*.

There are two kinds of voice:

(1) The Active voice or simply the Active.

(2) The Passive voice or simply the Passive.

1. **The Active Voice:** It shows that the subject has done something.

   Here the subject is the agent or doer.

   For Example:

   Rama killed Ravana. (Subject- Rama)

2. **The Passive Voice:** It shows that something has been done to the subject.

   Ravana was killed by Rama.

Note: The object of the verb in a sentence in the active voice becomes the subject of the verb in the sentence in the passive voice.

Why is the Passive Required?

We can express one and the same idea in two different ways in the English Language. They are the active and the passive. The passive is often formed with the appropriate form of the auxiliary 'be' or sometimes with those of 'get' or 'become'. The two forms are used to shift emphasis from one person or thing to another whenever required. The verbs in some cases are therefore put in the active and in others in the passive.

For Example:

The court sentenced him to death. (Active voice)

He was sentenced to death (by the court).

(Passive voice- Here, the emphasis is on the action. In such situations the passive is preferred as the active subject 'court' is not very important.)

The passive is mainly used

(*i*) when it is unnecessary or undesirable to mention the active subject which may be unknown or cannot be specified.

For Example:

He was wounded in an accident.

The meeting was well attended.

Further details will be notified in newspapers.

He was drowned in the river.

(*ii*) where the passive subject assumes more importance.

For Example:

The house was gutted by fire.

She was bitten by a snake.

(*iii*) when the action is more important.

For Example:

He was arrested.

A meeting has been convened to discuss the matter.

***Rules* for changing the active to the passive:**

1. The object of the Active verb becomes the subject of the Passive verb.

Note: *Only transitive verbs and prepositional verbs (intransitive verbs made transitive by adding a preposition to them e.g. look into, laugh at, etc., where look, laugh, etc, are intransitive verbs) are used in the passive. An intransitive verb can be used in the passive if it takes a cognate object (a noun the meaning of which is partly implied in the intransitive verb itself.)*

For Example:

He *laughed* a hearty *laugh*. (laughed- intransitive verb; laugh- cognate object)

She *died* a miserable *death*. (died - intransitive verb; death- cognate object)

2. The preposition 'by' is usually added to the doer (*i.e.*, the object in the passive voice).
3. The past participle form of the verb is used.
4. The form of the verb is changed according to the number of the subject.
5. The different forms of 'be' are used according to the tense of the verb – be, is, was, are, were, being, been etc.
6. The auxiliary verbs in the sentence (can, may, will, shall) do not undergo any change.

Note: In some cases the object in the passive voice is preceded by the preposition *to, with, at* or *in* instead of the usual preposition 'by'.

For Example:

1. I know them. (Active voice)

   They are known *to* me. (Passive voice) (Not 'by' me)
2. This reply will not satisfy the officer. (Active voice)

   The officer will not be satisfied *with* this reply. (Passive voice) (Not 'by' his reply)
3. His act displeased me.

   I was displeased *at* his act. (Not 'by' his act)
4. This did not interest me.

   I was not interested *in* this. (Not 'by' this)

There are twelve tenses in the Active Voice as indicated below (four each for the three main tenses namely the present, the past and the future).

1. Simple Present
2. Present Continuous
3. Present Perfect
4. Present Perfect Continuous (no passive)
5. Simple Past
6. Past Continuous
7. Past Perfect
8. Past Perfect Continuous (no passive)
9. Simple Future
10. Future Continuous (no passive)
11. Future Perfect
12. Future Perfect Continuous (no passive)

Out of this, only eight tenses can be changed into the Passive Voice.

The rest four namely Present Perfect Continuous, Past Perfect Continuous, Future Continuous and Future Perfect Continuous do not have passive forms.

I. Affirmative Sentences : (Assertive or Declarative)

(They simply affirm or deny something. They are classed as statements)

1. She writes a letter. (Simple Present, singular object)

   A letter is written by her.

2. She writes letters. (Simple Present, plural object)
Letters are written by her.
3. She is writing a letter. (Present Continuous, singular object)
A letter is being written by her.
4. She is writing letters. (Present Continuous, plural object)
Letters are being written by her.
5. She has written a letter. (Present Perfect, singular object)
A letter has been written by her.
6. She has written letters. (Present Perfect, plural object)
Letters have been written by her.
7. I gave him a book. (Simple Past, singular object)
A book was given (to) him by me.
8. I gave him books. (Simple Past, plural object)
Books were given (to) him by me.
9. I was giving him a book. (Past Continuous, singular object)
A book was being given (to) him by me.
10. I was giving him books. (Past Continuous, plural object)
Books were being given (to) him by me.
11. I had given him a book. (Past Perfect, singular object)
A book had been given (to) him by me.
12. I had given him books. (Past Perfect, plural object)
Books had been given (to) him by me.
13. They will give him the money. (Simple Future)
The money will be given (to) him by them.
14. They will have given him the money. (Future Perfect)
The money will have been given (to) him by them.

Note: The above sentences are correct even without the preposition 'to' given within brackets. (The indirect object 'him' without 'to' is common in American English.)

II . Negative sentences :

1. She does not write a letter. (Simple Present, singular object)
A letter is not written by her.
2. She does not write letters. (Simple Present, plural object)
Letters are not written by her.
3. She is not writing a letter. (Present Continuous, singular object)
A letter is not being written by her.
4. She is not writing letters. (Present Continuous, plural object)
Letters are not being written by her.

5. She has not written a letter. (Present Perfect , singular object)
   A letter has not been written by her.
6. She has not written letters. (Present Perfect, plural object)
   Letters have not been written by her.
7. She did not write a letter. (Simple Past, singular object)
   A letter was not written by her.
8. She did not write letters. (Simple Past, plural object)
   Letters were not written by her.
9. She was not writing a letter. (Past Continuous, singular object)
   A letter was not being written by her.
10. She was not writing letters. (Past Continuous, plural object)
   Letters were not being written by her.
11. She had not written a letter. (Past Perfect, singular object)
   A letter had not been written by her.
12. She had not written letters. (Past Perfect, plural object)
   Letters had not been written by her.
13. She will not write a letter/ letters. (Simple Future)
   Letters/ a letter will not be written by her.
14. She will not have written a letter/ letters. (Future Perfect)
   A letter/ letters will not have been written by her.

III. Interrogative Sentences : (Questions)

1. Does he write a letter? (Simple Present, singular object)
   Is a letter written by him?
2. Does he write letters ? (Simple Present, plural object)
   Are letters written by him?
3. Is he writing a letter ? (Present Continuous, singular object)
   Is a letter being written by him?
4. Is he writing letters ? (Present Continuous, plural object)
   Are letters being written by him?
5. Has he written a letter ? (Present Perfect, singular object)
   Has a letter been written by him?
6. Has he written letters? (Present Perfect, plural object)
   Have letters been written by him?
7. Did he write a letter? (Simple Past , singular object)
   Was a letter written by him?
8. Did he write letters? (Simple Past, plural object)
   Were letters written by him?

9. Was he singing a song? (Past Continuous, singular object)
   Was a song being sung by him?
10. Was he singing songs? (Past Continuous, plural object)
    Were songs being sung by him?
11. Had she written a letter? (Past Perfect, singular object)
    Had a letter been written by her?
12. Had she written letters? (Past Perfect, plural object)
    Had letters been written by her?
13. Will he write a letter / letters? (Simple Future)
    Will a letter / letters be written by him?
14. Will he have written a letter / letters? (Future Perfect)
    Will a letter / letters have been written by him?
15. Did you call me?
    Was I called by you?
16. Does he read newspaper?
    Is newspaper read by him?
17. Am I reading a book?
    Is a book being read by me?
18. Who has made it?
    By whom has it been made?
19. What will she do?
    What will be done by her?
20. Whom do you like?
    Who is liked by you?
21. Why have you done it?
    Why has it been done by you?
22. When will they give the money?
    When will the money be given by them?
23. How did he spend his holidays?
    How were the holidays spent by him?

IV. Imperative Sentences : (They contain commands, requests or wish)

(A) Using 'Let':

1. Shut the door.
   Let the door be shut.
2. Open the book.
   Let the book be opened.
3. Send the application.
   Let the application be sent.

4. Send him in.

   Let him be sent in.

5. Stop smoking.

   Let smoking be stopped.

(B) Imperative moods express requests, orders, or commands. In imperative sentences the subject 'You' is usually understood.

Note : A sentence expressing a wish is called an Optative sentence.

For Example:

I wish I were you.

Form: You + are + asked/ requested/ commanded/ ordered/ implored/ begged/ advised/ told + to + verb. ('Passive voice form')

1. Please give me the book.

   You are requested to give me the book.

2. Don't be late.

   You are advised not to be late.

3. Get out.

   You are ordered to get out.

4. Show mercy on him.

   You are begged to show mercy on him.

5. Help the poor.

   You are asked to help the poor.

6. Keep your word.

   Your word should be kept.

V. When transitive verbs are followed by two objects. (The direct object and the indirect object)

Here either of the two objects can be used as the subject in the passive voice.

Usually the indirect object is used as the subject of the passive sentence. A few verbs having two objects are given below:

tell, show, teach, give, offer, pay, grant, write.

A sentence containing a direct and an indirect object can have two passive forms ; as,

She told *me a story*. (Active voice) (me-indirect object; a story – direct object)

I was told a story by her. (Passive Voice) ...(*i*)

A story was told (to) me by her. (Passive Voice) ...(*ii*)

Note: Since there are two objects in the Active two Passive forms are possible, the one with the direct object and the other with the indirect object as the subject. The passive form with the indirect object as the subject, as in (*i*) above, is usual. The direct object is the answer to the question 'what?' or 'whom' and the indirect object is the answer to the question 'to whom' or 'for whom'. In the example above 'She told— what? a story—direct object;' 'She told the story—to whom? me- indirect object'.

For Example:

1. She gave me an apple.

   An apple was given me by her.

   Or

   An apple was given to me by her.

   I was given an apple by her.

Note: The preposition 'to' is optional.

2. The Principal granted me leave.

   Leave was granted (to) me by the Principal.

   I was granted leave by the Principal.

3. He wrote me a letter.

   A letter was written (to) me by him.

   I was written a letter by him.

4. Some one has written him a complaint.

   A complaint has been written (to) him by some one.

   He has been written a complaint by some one.

5. They offered him an award.

   An award was offered (to) him by them.

   He was offered an award by them.

6. She taught him computer programming.

   He was taught computer programming by her.

7. They paid us our wages.

   Wages were paid (to) us by them.

   He was paid his wages by them.

8. The officer granted her leave.

   Leave was granted (to) her by the officer.

   She was granted leave by the officer.

VI. Use of Prepositions:

The preposition used after the verb in the Active should be used in the Passive too.

1. They looked after our children.

   Our children were looked after by them.

2. She laughed at the servant.

   The servant was laughed at by her.

3. A lorry ran over the beggar.

   A beggar was run over by a lorry.

4. He sent for the doctor.

   The doctor was sent for (by him).

VII. Omission of the subject in the Passive:

In some cases, importance is given to the action and not the doer. Hence, it is not necessary to mention the agent of the action. Transitive verbs can be used in the passive without mentioning the doer.

1. The police arrested the thief.
   The thief was arrested.
2. One should do one's duty.
   Duty should be done.
3. A storm wrecked the ship.
   The ship was wrecked.
4. Some one cleaned the board.
   The board was cleaned.

VIII. Changing sentences with 'infinitive' (to + bare form of the verb)

1. I want her *to sing* a song.
   I want a song to be sung by her.
2. She has a lot of work *to do.*
   She has a lot of work to be done.
3. They have no time *to waste.*
   They have no time to be wasted.
4. You expect him *to look after* the children.
   You expect the children to be looked after by him.

IX. Sentences beginning with 'It is / It was':

It is / It was + for + object + to be + past participle of the verb. (Passive voice form)

1. It is time to start the talk.
   It is time for the talk to be started.
2. It was time to close the shop.
   It was time for the shop to be closed.
3. It is time to start painting.
   It is time for the painting to be started.
4. It was time to call the doctor in.
   It was time for the doctor to be called in.

X. Sentences with object complement:

(Complement = that which completes)

1. They elected me chairman. (Here, chairman is the complement of the object 'me')
   I was elected chairman.
2. I consider her intelligent.
   She is considered intelligent.

3. She called him master.

   He was called master.

XI. Sentences with verbs denoting the senses. (There are five verbs denoting the five senses, namely see, smell, taste, feel, touch)

1. The fruit tastes sweet.

   The fruit is sweet when tasted.
2. The flower smells sweet.

   The flower is sweet when smelt.
3. That place smells bad.

   That place is bad when smelt.
4. The cloth feels rough.

   The cloth is rough when felt.
5. They saw him dancing.

   He was seen dancing.

XII. Sentences with auxiliaries: (can, could, may, might, shall, should, will, would, must, need, ought, do and did)

1. We can win the match.

   The match can be won by us.
2. We could meet him at the office.

   He could be met at the office.
3. They may bring the book.

   The book may be brought by them.
4. You must call him at once.

   He must be called at once.

6. I should do it for him.

   It should be done by me for him.
7. We ought to respect elders.

   Elders ought to be respected.
8. You need not help him.

   He need not be helped by you.

XIII. With changes of construction:

(*a*) Believe, claim, consider, find, know, say, suppose and think when used in the passive voice are followed by a 'to-infinitive'.

1. They say he is a liar.

   He is said to be a liar.
2. They say he was a spy.

   He is considered to have been a spy. (Past tense; hence 'was' became 'to have been')

3. He believes (that) his neighbour is a fraud.
   His neighbour is believed to be a fraud.
4. They claim (that) they are tourists.
   They are claimed to be tourists.
5. He finds that the work is very difficult.
   The work is found to be difficult.
6. They know (that) he is a pickpocket.
   He is known to be a pickpocket.
7. We suppose (that) he is a gentleman.
   He is supposed to be a gentleman.
8. They think (that) he is good.
   He is thought to be good.

(*b*) 'Subject + be supposed + infinitive' gives an idea of duty, especially when the subject is 'you'. ('Passive form')

1. It is your duty to obey me.
   You are supposed to obey me.

(*c*) Get + object + past participle of the verb.

1. Get someone to do it.
   Get it done.

(*d*) Conversion of sentences beginning with the words *how, when, what, where, which, why, who, whose and whom* in the active voice into the passive voice:

For Example:

How can I teach you?
How can you be taught by me?
When will he teach you?
When will you be taught by him?
What will he teach you?
What will you be taught by him?
Where will he teach you?
Where will you be taught by him?
Which subject will he teach you?
Which subject will you be taught by him?
Why should he teach you?
Why should you be taught by him?
Who will teach you?
By whom will you be taught?

Whom did you teach?

Who was taught by you?

Whose book have you taken?

Whose book has been taken by you?

XIV. Double passive voice

Consider the following sentence:

The king ordered the robber to be executed. (Active voice)

The robber was ordered to be executed (by the king.) (Passive voice)

Note: Only one transformation is possible in this case because we cannot have another transformation with 'to be executed' which takes the place of the indirect object.

EXERCISE

Transform the following sentences from the Active voice to the Passive voice:

1. Mother dresses the baby everyday.
2. They are giving a party in her honour.
3. The LTTE killed Rajiv Gandhi.
4. I was reading a book last night.
5. They will congratulate the winner.
6. Shut the door.
7. He gave me a good book.
8. The authorities prohibit smoking.
9. Please lend me your pen.
10. My father allows me fifty rupees.
11. He struck me on the head.
12. Respect your teachers.
13. He told us a horror story.
14. Let him go.
15. He was doing his duty.
16. He rang the bell.
17. What do you want?
18. People call him Big Mouth.
19. Who sent that message?
20. Why didn't you tell me?
21. Don't permit that.
22. Has someone posted that letter?
23. We will prosecute trespassers.
24. They are repairing my piano at the moment.
25. They haven't stamped the letter.
26. She didn't introduce me to her brother.
27. A frightful sound wakened me at 4p.m.
28. They threw away the rubbish.
29. We can't repair your clock.
30. An earthquake destroyed the town.
31. Candidates may not use dictionaries.
32. You need not type this letter.
33. Nobody has used this room for ages.
34. They brought up their in Italy.
35. Someone broke into their house and stole a lot of things.
36. We have warned you.
37. A lorry knocked him down.
38. The Government has called in the troops.
39. Fog held up the trains. (Agent unnecessary)
40. We called in the police.
41. They didn't look after the children properly.
42. Everyone looked up to him. (Agent needed)
43. All ministers will see him off at the airport. (Agent needed)
44. We can build no more rooms.
45. No one has taken out the cork.
46. People must hand in the weapons.

47. You must keep dogs on guard in the garden.
48. They are demolishing the entire block.
49. Why didn't nobody inform me of the plan?
50. The people cheered the leader.
51. I am employing a man to clean the toilet.
52. Someone seems to have made a terrible mistake.
53. It is your duty to make tea at 4 O'clock.
54. People know that he is armed.
55. Someone saw me pick up the gun.
56. Don't touch this switch.
57. It is impossible to do it.
58. Someone is following us.
59. He doesn't like people laughing at.
60. You don't need to wind this watch.
61. Who has done it?
62. Whom did you give the pen?
63. How can he do it?
64. What are you writing?
65. Where will you buy it?

Chapter 16 DIRECT AND INDIRECT SPEECH

There are two ways of reporting what a person has said.

1. Direct speech (Direct narration)
2. Indirect speech (Indirect narration)

In Direct Speech we repeat the actual words and tone of the speaker. Inverted commas are used to mark off the exact words of the speaker; as,

Father said, "I am late." ...(*i*)

In Indirect speech or Indirect narration the substance of what was said is reported, without quoting the actual words ; as,

Father said that he was late.

The verb used to introduce the reported speech is called the reporting verb.

In the above example, the word 'said' is the *reporting verb* and "I am late" is the *reported speech.*

A distinction must be made between Indirect speech and Reported speech. In the example above, "I am late" is the Reported speech while 'Father said that he was late' is the Indirect speech or narration of the direct speech at(*i*) above and *not the Reported speech of it.*

Changes that occur while converting Direct speech into Indirect speech.

1. The inverted commas are removed.
2. There is no comma after the introductory verb (Corresponding to the reporting verb) which forms an integral part of a single sentence.
3. Sometimes the reporting verb too changes according to the tone of the speech.
4. The tense of the verb changes.
5. The pronoun undergoes change.
6. All the punctuations are removed. (Including question and exclamation marks.)
7. The tense of the reporting verb never changes.

8. When the person addressed is mentioned by the speaker the pronoun *you* in direct speech is changed into the corresponding pronoun in the indirect speech.

For Example:

The lawyer said to his client, " *You* can come to my office and discuss the matter."

The lawyer told his client that *he* could come to his office and discuss the matter.

(The verb 'come' in direct speech does not always become 'go' in indirect speech. Sometimes the change depends upon the sense of the sentence.)

When the person addressed is not mentioned by the speaker in direct speech the pronoun *you* used therein is changed into *I/me* or *we/us* in indirect speech.

For Example:

" You can do it" said the officer.

The officer said that *I* could do it.

Note: When *you* is used as an impersonal pronoun *one* may be used in indirect speech.

For Example:

The teacher said to the students, "You can't go into the forest because there are wild animals."

The teacher told the students that one could not go into the forest because there were wild animals. (one=you)

9. When a reporting verb comes after reported speech the subject is used after the verb if it is a proper noun.

For Example:

"I have to go to the market," said Ravi.

But, when the subject is a pronoun the reporting verb comes after it.

For Example:

"I have to go to the market ," he said.

Change in Pronouns:

Direct		*Indirect*
I	-	me
me/my	-	his/ her
mine	-	his/ hers
myself	–	himself / herself
we	–	they
our	–	their
ours	–	theirs
ourselves	-	themselves
you	–	he/ she/I/ they/we
your	–	his/ her/ my/ their

this	–	that
yours	–	his /hers/ mine /their/ theirs
just	-	then
here	-	there
thus	-	so
come	-	go
said	-	said
said to	-	told

Change in Auxiliaries:

Direct		*Indirect*
shall	-	should
will	–	would
may	-	might
can	–	could
has/ have	–	had
am /is/ are	–	was/ were
must	–	had to / would have to
must not	–	was (were) not to.
has been	–	had been
have been	-	had been
need not	–	did not /needn't

When the reporting verb is in the past tense, the tenses of the verbs in direct speech usually are changed into the corresponding past tenses thus:

(*a*) Simple present ⟶ Simple past

Ramu said, " I am very tired."

Ramu said that he was very tired.

Note: When the reported speech relates to some universal truth or habitual fact the simple present tense remains unchanged; as,

The teacher said, "The sun rises in the east."

The teacher said that the sun rises in the east.

He said, "Water consists of oxygen and hydrogen."

He said that water consists of oxygen and hydrogen.

She said to her son, "Honesty is the best policy."

She told her son that honesty is the best policy.

(*b*) Present continuous ⟶ Past continuous

He said, "I am painting a picture."

He said that he was painting a picture.

(*c*) Present perfect ⟶ Past perfect

She said, "I have seen him."

She said she had seen him.

(*d*) Present perfect continuous ⟶ Past Perfect continuous

"I have been teaching here for two years," said Mary.

Mary said that she had been teaching there for two years.

(*e*) Simple past ⟶ Past perfect. But, past tenses used in time clauses are normally unaffected. The verb in the main clause can remain unchanged or become the past perfect.

He said, " When I studied in England I visited my friend often."

He said that when he studied in England he (had) visited his friend often. Here ' When I studied in England' is the time clause and 'I visited my friend often' is the main clause.

Anil said , "Madhu won the match."

Anil said that Madhu had won the match.

He said, " I had my breakfast at 8."

He said that he had had his breakfast at 8.

Note: *Had* in direct speech changes to *had had* (the past perfect tense of *have* when it is used as a full verb- not as an auxiliary) in indirect speech.

(*f*) Past continuous ⟶ Past Perfect continuous. The rules relating to the past tense are applicable to this tense also.

He said, " When I was studying in England I visited my friend often."

He said that when he was studying in England he (had) visited his friend often.

Janu said to me, "I was waiting for my friend."

Janu told me that she had been waiting for her friend.

(*g*) Past perfect ⟶ No change.

He said, " Ramu had not gone to Chennai before."

He said that Ramu had not gone to Chennai before.

(*h*) Past Perfect continuous ⟶ No change.

He said, "She had been waiting for Ramu since this morning."

He said that she had been waiting for Ramu since that morning.

(*i*) Simple Future ⟶ Conditional tense.(The conditional tense is used to express a past equivalent of the future tense. *Shall/will* in direct speech is therefore changed into the past equivalent namely *should/would* in indirect speech.

1. The teacher said, "I shall tell you a story."
   The teacher said that he would tell me a story.
2. The students said, " We shall listen carefully."
   The students said that they would listen carefully.

(see the important note below.)

3. The little boy said, "I shall buy that toy."
The little boy said that he would buy that toy. } see the important note below.

Important: Note the change from 'shall' to 'would' in the indirect speech. The personal pronouns *I* and *We* have changed to 'he' and 'they' respectively in the indirect speech. Both 'he' and 'they' take 'will' in the future tense and 'would' in the past tense. Hence, the change from *shall* to *would* in the indirect speech above.

(*j*) Will –can – may – shall change into would- could- might- should.

1. Mother said, " It will be a holiday."
Mother said that it would be a holiday.
2. "You will get the money," said the manager.
The manager said that I should (would) get the money.
3. "You may do it," said the teacher.
The teacher said that I might do that.
4. " We can write that," they said.
They said that we could write that.

(*k*) Must ⟶ had to/must.

"You must come here now," he said.
He said that I had to go there then.

(*l*) Had better /Ought to/ Used to ⟶ No change.

Note: Sometimes there is confusion whether the pronoun 'he' in the reported speech stands for the person speaking or the person spoken to; as,

Ram said to John, "I am a fool."
Ram told John that he was a fool.

There is confusion as to whether 'he' in this sentence stands for Ram or John. To avoid this confusion use the name (in this case Ram) in brackets after 'he'; as,

Ram told John that he (Ram) was a fool.

Change in words expressing time, distance and measure:

Direct		*Indirect*
this	–	that
these	–	those
now	–	then
here	–	there
thus	–	so
next	–	following
ago	–	before
at once	–	just then
today	–	that day

tonight	–	that night
yesterday	–	last day/ the day before/ the previous day
tomorrow	–	the day after/ the following day/ the next day
the day after tomorrow	–	in two days' time
the day before yesterday	–	two days before
a year ago	–	a year before/the previous year
last (week, month, year)	–	the previous (week, month, year)
next (week, month, year)	–	the following (week, month, year)
hither	–	thither
hence	–	thence.

Use of *say, ask, tell, must* and *could* in direct and indirect narration

Say: The verb *say* may be used both in the direct and indirect narration with or without the person addressed. It is usually used in direct speech when the person addressed is not specified.

For Example:

He said, " I shall come tomorrow."

He said to me, " I am waiting for you."

Ask: The verb *ask* is usually used to ask questions with or without the person addressed (*i. e.*, the indirect object). It can be used with direct or indirect narration.

For Example:

" Will you come to my house tomorrow?" she asked (me).

He asked (me) for an umbrella.

He asked (her) the reason for her coming late.

Note: The indirect objects like *me, her* and *them* may be omitted in the examples given above.

The following use of *ask* normally requires the person addressed:

He said to me, " Please don't come again."

He asked me *not to* come again. (Without the indirect object 'me' the meaning is not clear.)

When *ask* is used as a reporting verb in direct narration it is usually placed at the end of it.

"Are you going to Chennai tomorrow?" she asked me.

She asked (me) whether I was going to Chennai the next day.

He said to them, " What are you going to do?"

He asked (them) what they were going to do.

Must: 'Must' normally remains unchanged in indirect speech.

But it changes to '*had to*' while reporting interrogative sentences.

Father said to me, "You must obey your teachers."

Father told me that I must obey my teachers.

"Must I come tomorrow?" she asked her boss.

She asked her boss whether she had to come the next day.

Could: When *could* is used for request or invitation the reporting verb changes to *ask* or *invite.*

"Could you come for the party tomorrow?" asked Seeta.

Seeta invited him to the party.

When *could* is used for permission it does not change in indirect speech.

"Could I see the chairman?" said the applicant.

The applicant asked if he could see the chairman.

Need: *Need* in questions changes to *had to* in indirect speech.

" Need I change my dress?" asked the girl.

The girl asked if she had to change her dress.

Needn't: *Needn't* normally remains unchanged in indirect speech. It can also take the form *didn't have to/wouldn't have to* as an alternative.

"You needn't see me again," said the officer.

The officer said that I needn't see him again.

Or

The officer said that I didn't have to see him again.

16.1 CONVERSION OF STATEMENTS INTO INDIRECT SPEECH OR NARRATION

In reporting statements, introductory verbs like *say, tell, answer, inform* and *agree* followed by the conjunction 'that' are used. It is used after the reporting verb when it gives more information in the form of an explanation or a complaint. 'That' is not used in this manner when it is used as a relative pronoun. It is often omitted when the reported speech is a simple fact or statement.

For Example:

He said, " Corruption in government offices is on the increase."

He said that corruption in government offices was on the increase.

She said, "The accident took place owing to negligent driving."

She explained that the accident had taken place owing to negligent driving.

He said, "I am going to the market."

He said he was going to the market.

When the verb 'say' is used it becomes say/ says/ said + *to* + noun / pronoun.

Sometimes the verb 'say' is changed to 'tell' – then it becomes tell/ told/ tells + noun / pronoun.

'Tell' is used in indirect speech when the person addressed is mentioned.

They said to *him* " ...." (Direct speech)

They told him that .... (Indirect speech)

(Do not say : They *told to* him. Because 'tell = say to')

Examples:

1. "The film is interesting," he said.
   He said that the film was interesting.
2. He says, "The book was interesting."
   He says that the book was interesting.
3. I said to her, "Your father may be waiting for you."
   I reminded her that her father might be waiting for her.
4. "I don't believe you," she said to the boys.
   She told the boys that she did not believe them.
5. He said, "It is time he stopped smoking."
   He said that it was time he stopped smoking.
6. She said, "I wish I got a job."
   She wished that she got a job.
   Note: Past tense used after 'It is time', 'wish' etc, does not change.
7. She said to me, " You had better do it."
   She said (that) I had better do it.
   Or
   She advised me to do it.
8. "I am sure I won't pass," she said.
   She did not think that she would pass.
9. John said, "You're right, it is not a good film."
   John agreed that it was not a good film.
10. The officer said, "I'd rather *she* came in the morning."
    (I'd rather = I would rather) (See the note below)
    The officer said that he preferred her to come in the morning.

Note: (*i*) Two different subjects can be used before and after 'would rather' to indicate that the first subject would prefer the second to do something. In such cases we use a past tense with a present or future meaning.

Note: (*ii*) *You had better, I had better* and *we had better* normally remain unchanged in the indirect speech.

For Example:

She said to me, " You had better leave the place."

She told me that I had better leave the place.

Or

She advised me to leave the place.

16.2 CONVERSION OF QUESTIONS INTO INDIRECT SPEECH

In reporting questions, the verb comes after the subject in indirect narration as in the case of statements. The conjunction 'that' is not used.

In Wh- questions (questions beginning with *who, which, where, when, what*) the question word serves as a link between the verb introducing the indirect narration and the indirect narration of the question itself.

In Yes – No questions, the conjunction 'if' or 'whether' is placed before the indirect narration of the question.

The reporting verb *say* in direct speech is changed into verbs like *ask, inquire* and *wonder* in indirect speech.

Examples:

1. They said, "Where is your house?"

   They asked me where my house was.(Not: where was my house. Here the question word 'where' links the reporting verb to the reported question.)

2. "How is your father?" he said.

   He enquired how my father was.('how' is the question word)

3. "Has he gone to the office?" Ram said.

   Ram wanted to know whether he had gone to the office.

4. Teacher said, "Why are you distracted, Ram?"

   The teacher asked Ram why he was distracted.

5. He said to me, "Can you read?"

   He asked (me) if I could read.

6. "Will they go to the cinema today?" I asked her.

   I asked (her) whether they would go to the cinema that day.

7. "Did you see him?" asked the girl.

   The girl inquired whether I had seen him.

   Note: Verbs like *inquire* and *wonder* will not take an indirect object.

8. The master said, "Were you present yesterday?"

   The master asked (me) whether I was present the previous day.

9. The doctor said, "Are you feeling better now?"
   "Yes" he said.
   The doctor asked him if he was feeling better then.
   (The doctor expected a positive answer. See the note below.)
   He replied that he was.
10. "What is going to happen?" she said.
    She wondered what was going to happen.
11. He said, "Would you accept this gift?"
    He offered me a gift.
12. She said, "Can I have your pen?"
    She asked for my pen.
13. The boy said, " Need I do the homework today?"
    The boy asked if he had to do the homework that day.
14. She said, " Would you mind giving your pen? "
    She asked for my pen.
    Or
    She asked if I would mind giving my pen.
15. He said, "Shall we go to the cinema?"
    He suggested going to the cinema.
16. He said to the shopkeeper, "Shall I make the payment by cheque?"
    He asked the shopkeeper if he should make the payment by cheque.
17. "Shall I bring you some sweets?" he said.
    He offered to bring me some sweets.

Note: The person addressed may be used or left out when we ***ask*** questions or ***ask for*** something.

Note: Use of ' if ' and ' weather ' : They are almost interchangeable.

However, the subtle difference between them is given below:

'If ' is usually used with an indirect question when a positive answer is expected.

For Example:

Call me if you need money.

' Whether (or not) ' is usually used with an indirect question when either a positive or a negative answer is expected.

It is more formal than 'if' and is used more in written English.

For Example:

He asked me whether (or not) I was going to Chennai.

16.3 CONVERSION OF IMPERATIVES [COMMANDS AND REQUESTS] INTO INDIRECT SPEECH

When Imperative sentences are converted into indirect speech, the reporting verbs are changed into verbs like ask, tell, request, beg, plead, order, advise, command and urge. The commanding or requesting mood of the reported verb is changed into the infinitive mood. (the 'to +verb' form)

For Example:

The teacher said to Ram, "Go to your class."

The teacher ordered Ram *to go* to his class.

(Subject + reporting verb + personal object + (not) to + verb).

The word 'don't' in direct speech becomes 'not to' in direct speech.

1. She said to me, "Stand up."
   She ordered me to stand up.
2. "Obey your parents," said the teacher.
   The teacher advised us to obey our parents.
3. "Don't shoot," the Commander said.
   The Commander commanded not to shoot.
4. Rema said, " Please help me."
   Rema begged to help her.
5. The headmaster said to me, "Stay here."
   The Headmaster ordered me to stay there.
6. The Principal said to the peon, "Let the door be shut."
   The Principal ordered the peon to shut the door.

Note: 'Let' is normally used as a verb though it has some special use as a noun. The verb 'let' has many meanings depending upon the context in which it is used.

(*i*) It is used to give an order or instruction; as,

" Let no one talk in the class," said the teacher.

The teacher ordered that no one should talk in the class.

(*ii*) Let's (let us) usually expresses a suggestion; as,

" Let's go for a picnic," said my friend.

My friend suggested that we should go for a picnic.

Or

My friend suggested our going for a picnic.

(*iii*) 'Let me' usually expresses our willingness/wish to do something; as,

My friend said, "Let me bring something to eat."

My friend offered to bring something to eat.

(*iv*) Let is used as an ordinary verb meaning 'allow or permit'; as,

"Let me use your pen," asked my friend.

My friend asked me to let him use my pen.

Note: 'Let' is always followed by the ' infinitive without to'.

Don't say: My friend asked me to let him *to use* my pen.

16.4 CONVERSION OF EXCLAMATIONS INTO INDIRECT SPEECH

Exclamations are transformed into statements in indirect speech. According to the sense, the reporting verbs are changed into *exclaimed, cried out, prayed, mourned, shouted with joy, with regret, with delight, with sorrow*.

Exclamation marks and words like *alas, oh* and *hurrah,* are omitted. The conjunction 'that' is used in indirect speech.

1. She said, "What a beautiful idea !"

   She exclaimed that it was a very beautiful idea.
2. She said, " How cold it is !"

   She exclaimed (cried out) that it was very cold.
3. Ram said, "Oh! I am a fool!"

   Ram mourned that he was a fool.
4. Raju said, "What a long time it lasted !"

   Raju wondered that it had lasted for a very long time.

Note: *Would, should, could, ought, might, had better and used to* in direct speech do not normally change.

He said, " I would like biscuits."

He said that he would like biscuits.

She said, " I might come there."

She said that she might go there.

He said, " I used to go to her house."

He said that he used to go to her house.

They said, " We could not meet the Minister."

They said they could not meet the Minister.

The teacher said to the boy, "You ought to obey your parents."

The teacher told the boy that he ought to obey his parents.

He said to me, " You had better meet the officer."

He told me that I had better meet the officer.

Or

He advised me to meet the officer.

Other Types

Type I : General

In the following examples and in such others avoid as far as possible verbs like *say, ask* and *tell* in indirect speech. Instead use – accuse, admit, advise, agree, beg, call, complain, congratulate, exclaim, explain, give, hope, introduce, offer, point out, remark, remind, suggest, thank, threaten, warn, wish, etc.

1. "Thank you," they said.
   They thanked me.
2. She said, "welcome."
   She welcomed me.
3. Madhu said, "Happy Onam."
   Madhu wished me a happy Onam.
4. "Let's go to the shore," I said.
   I suggested that we go to the shore.
5. "Would you help me please?" the boy said.
   The boy requested me to help him.
6. She said, "Will you lunch with me ?"
   She invited me to lunch with her.
7. "Good night , Ravi," Madhu said.
   Madhu wished Ravi good night.
8. "What a grave mistake I have committed !" he said.
   He exclaimed with regret that he had committed a grave mistake.
9. They said, "Let's take him to the doctor."
   They suggested taking him to the doctor.
10. He said, "Let's listen to the music."
    He suggested our listening to the music.
11. The secretary said, " Let them see the Manager."
    The secretary suggested that they should see the Manager.
12. He said, " I let my friend do the work."
    He allowed his friend to do the work.
13. "Let no one talk in the class," the teacher said.
    The teacher ordered that no one should talk in the class.
14. "The minister is in station. Why don't you speak to him about your problems?" said my neighbour.
    My neighbour informed me that the minister was in station and advised me to speak to him about my problems.

Type 2 : The reporting verb in the Present and Future tenses remains unchanged.

1. She says, " I have done my duty."
   She says that she has done her duty.
2. I shall say, " I cannot go there anymore."
   I shall say that I cannot go there anymore.
3. You will say to her, "Your father did not meet him."
   You will tell her that her father did not see him.

Type 3 : In some cases there is no change in the tense in reported speech even if the reporting verb is in the past tense.

They are:

(*a*) Universal facts

(*b*) Historical facts

(*c*) Habitual facts

1. "The earth moves round the sun," said the teacher.
   The teacher said that the earth moves round the sun.
2. My father said, "One and one make two." (Universal fact)
   My father said that one and one make two.
3. He said to me, " India got independence in 1947." (Historical fact)
   He told me that India got independence in 1947.
4. "I eat an egg daily," Rani said to Padma. (Habitual fact)
   Rani told Padma that she eats an egg daily.(If the practice still exists when the speech is reported.)
5. The book reads, " Shahjehan built Taj Mahal."
   According to the book Shahjehan built Taj Mahal.

Type 4 : Direct speech denoting past habits or customs is changed into Indirect speech as shown below:

1. "I went to church on Sundays," he said to me.
   He told me that he went to church on Sundays.
2. "We played football during the vacation," they said.
   They said that they played football during the vacation.

Type 5 : Improbable conditions are changed into indirect speech as shown below:

1. "If I were a bird, I would fly," I said to my friend.
   I told my friend that if I were a bird, I would fly.
2. "If you were my brother, I would be happy," Ravi said to Mani.
   Ravi told Mani that if he were his brother, he would be happy.
3. "If I had time, I would come," he said to me.
   He told me if he had time he would come.

Type 6 : In certain cases past and past continuous tenses used in direct speech are not normally changed.

1. "When I reached home, they were about to leave," I said to my father. (Both actions took place simultaneously)

   I told my father that when I reached home they were about to leave.

2. "She had died before the doctor arrived," said the servant.

   The servant said that she had died before the doctor arrived.

   (Since the meaning is very clear from the conjunction 'before' the tense of the verb 'arrived' has not been changed to past perfect tense as required by rule).

3. He said, " When she was playing she met with an accident."

   He said that when she was playing she met with an accident.

Type 7: When there are two or more sentences in direct speech, expressions such as *added, further said* and *continued saying* are used after the first sentence in indirect speech or narration.

Direct: "I am going to attend the meeting," said my friend. " Are you coming with me? The meeting will begin soon. Well-known speakers are expected to address the gathering. The Chief Minister will deliver the key-note speech."

Indirect: My friend told me that he was going to attend the meeting. He asked me if I was going with him. He added that the meeting would start soon and that well-known speakers were expected to address the gathering. He continued saying that the Chief Minister would deliver the key-note speech.

Type 8: Nouns in Vocative Case (the form of a noun when addressing a person or thing) in direct speech is made the object of the reporting verb in indirect speech; as,

Ramu said, " John, I am going to the market."

Ramu told John that he was going to the market.

She said, " Father, my friend is going to Mumbai."

She told her father that her friend was going to Mumbai.

EXERCISE

Change the narration:

1. "I have something to show you," I said to her.
2. "I'm going to tomorrow, mother," he said.
3. The bookseller says to me, "You are welcome to my shop."
4. The fox said to the crow, " I want to listen to your song."
5. She will say, "I did not know where he came from."
6. The man said, "I have completed my work."
7. The captain said to the team, "We do not want to let down our country."
8. "I wish my children would eat vegetables," she said.
9. "I wish you'd seen it," I said to her.

10. My mother said to me, " I did not go to the market."
11. "Which country do you come from?" I asked Bill.
12. " Could I use your telephone?" I asked him.
13. The child said, "Mother, may I have this book?"
14. "How long have you been here?" said Ann.
15. The lady said to the stranger, " Whom do you want?"
16. "Do you play rugby?" asked Peter.
17. The patient said to the doctor, "Does smoking cause cancer?"
18. I said to the stranger, "Who is there standing in the dark?"
19. The peon said to the Principal, "Sir, should I ring the bell?"
20. "Did you play for your school team?" said John.
21. "What happened to Mr. Raj?" said one of the men.
22. "Which one of his sons inherited his estate?" asked another.
23. "Who is going to live there?" said the man.
24. "Where is the office?" said Ravi.
25. "When does the train reach Delhi?" he asked.
26. "How much does a T.V. cost?" the customer said.
27. "Is your father alright?" said my friend.
28. "Do puppies travel free?" said a dog owner.
29. "Can you get coffee on the train?" said my father.
30. "Are there smoking compartments in the train?" said the man with a cap.
31. "Have you reserved the ticket?" I asked him.
32. The saint said to his disciples, "Truth is ever green."
33. The teacher said to the students, "Panipat is known for three historical battles."
34. Mary said to her friend, "I take one peg of whisky before going to bed."
35. Mother said to me, "The sun rises in the East."
36. The doctor said, "Unhealthy conditions lead to epidemics."
37. The sage said, "Time keeps changing."
38. I said, "Friends, let us have a walk."
39. The teacher said, "Time keeps changing."
40. The commander said, "Boys look here."
41. The poor man said, "Please lend me a hundred rupees."
42. The gardener said, " Do not pluck flowers."
43. The police said to the police, "Go away from here."
44. The student said to the teacher, "Please look at my project work, Sir."
45. The beggar said, " What an empty dream."
46. The old man said to the lady, " May you live long !"
47. The girl said, " What a charming sight."
48. The boy said, "How beautiful the moon is!"
49. The man said, " Good heavens ! What do I see before me !"
50. Grandmother said to her, "May God help you !"
51. He said, "O that I were king."
52. We said, " Let bygones be bygones."
53. He said, "Don't walk on the ice, it isn't safe."
54. He said, "Where there is will, there is a way."
55. "I won't answer any questions," said the arrested man.
56. "I wish it would rain," she said.
57. "I will wait for you, I promise," he said to me.

58. "Many happy returns of your birthday !" we said.
59. "Farewell, my friends," she said.
60. The priest said, "May god bless you !"
61. The poor lady said to her only son, "May god give strength to you to fight your disease."
62. The millionaire said, "What a precious gift!"
63. My grandfather said to me, " May you have a safe journey."
64. I said, "Let us visit the library."
65. She said to him, "Mind your own business."
66. The mother said, "Doctor please save my child."
67. Mother said, "My child, fish cannot live without water."
68. The boy said to his father, "I did not misbehave in the class."
69. The bride said, "What a precious gift !"
70. She says to me, "You are indeed very clever."

Chapter 17 ARTICLES

There are 5 vowels (*a, e, i, o, u*) and 21 consonants (*b, c, d, f, g, h, j, k, l, m, n, p, q, r, s, t, v, w, x, y, z*) in the English language.

a or *an* and *the* are called Articles. They are basically demonstrative adjectives and are referred to as determiners in Modern English. a or an is called the indefinite article. 'a' is actually the contracted form of 'an'. '*the*' is called the definite article.

a or an is called the indefinite article because it is used when we do not speak of a definite or particular person or thing. The person or thing remains indefinite- not specifically defined. It is the same for all genders and is always used before singular common nouns referring to people or things not already mentioned. It is also used before uncountable nouns (or uncount nouns) when they have an adjective before them or phrase following them. 'a' is used before words beginning with a consonant or a consonant sound and 'an' used before words beginning with a vowel or vowel sound.

For Example:

I saw a *monkey* and an *ox.*

It is *a* beautiful scenery.

(scenery – uncountable. Since the adjective 'beautiful' is used before it, the indefinite article 'a' is used.)

He showed *a* courage *deserving special mention.*

(courage– uncountable– a phrase follows it.)

'*the*' is called the definite article because it refers to some particular or definite person or persons, or thing or things. It is the same for all genders; as, the boys (the boys already referred to by the speaker or known to him), the men, the boxes.

For Example:

I met a few *boys* in the park. *The boys* were from a nearby college.

Articles are not used before singular common nouns used in their widest sense.

For Example:

Man is mortal. (Here 'man' represents all men. Don't use *the man* in this sense.)

Man is stronger than woman.

But: *The man* in the story (a particular man) is mad.

The Indefinite Article 'a' or 'an'

a or *an* is

1. used to represent 'one'.

For Example:

I have a dozen shoes. (a=one)

We saw an ugly frog. (an=one)

He waited for an hour.

He replied in a word. (a=one)

He will be absent for a day or two. (for one day or two)

The account is correct *to a* rupee. (a=one)

He comes here once a month. (not, once in a month)

Note the correct usage: once a day, once a week, once a year, once every six months etc.)

2. used before a singular countable noun(or count noun) when it is mentioned for the first time and does not refer to any particular person or thing.

(A countable noun has a plural form while an uncountable noun has no plural form.)

For Example:

I saw *a* boy and *a* girl on the beach. *The boy* ('boy' mentioned in the first sentence) was taller than *the girl.* ('girl' mentioned in the first sentence.)

This is *an* umbrella. This is *a* raincoat. *The umbrella* is not so useful as *the raincoat.*

He called me a fool. (or He called me fool) – don't say 'He called me as a fool.'

3. used before a singular countable noun to represent the whole class.

For Example:

A dog is a faithful animal. (All dogs are faithful animals. A dog=All dogs)

An umbrella is quite useful during the rainy season.

4. used in the expressions of speed and price; a or an is used to denote *per* , *each* or *every;* as,

For Example:

Ten kilometers an hour. (an = per)

Rupees five a dozen. (a = each)

Three times a day. (a = every)

Twelve kilometers a litre.

A student took me to the Principal.

(Not: 'One student took me to the Principal.' as 'a' means 'any' and 'one' means 'no more than one'.)

5. used before noun complements and names of professions.

For Example:

She is a doctor. (profession)

I am an electrician. (profession)

He is an intelligent boy. (noun complement)

6. used in the sense of 'any' or 'single'.

For Example:

He is an untidy beggar.

There was a man in the house.

7. used in exclamations where singular countable nouns are used.

For Example:

What a beautiful girl!

What an excuse! What an ugly girl!

8. used with numerical expressions.

a million, a dozen, a couple, a number of, a good deal of

For Example:

He has property worth a million. (= rupees, dollars etc.)

I bought a dozen oranges.

He was absent for a couple of days.

9. used before a Proper noun to make it a Common noun.

For Example:

He thinks he is a Shakespeare. (a great poet like Shakespeare.)

She is a Mother Teresa. (a great social worker like Mother Teresa)

He is a little Tata. (a millionaire like Tata.)

10. used in the following idiomatic expressions:

take an interest, have a mind, in a hurry, in a position, on an average, at a loss, a happy Onam, with a view to, etc.

For Example:

I took an interest in his studies.

I have a mind to go to the park.

He is in a hurry to go.

He is in a position to spend money.

There are on an average fifty visitors a day.

Wish you a happy Onam/Christmas/Diwali etc.

He has come with a view to meeting his uncle.

I am at a loss to understand the logic behind it.

11. used in sentences beginning with *however* and *how.*

The indefinite article comes after the adjective even though its natural position is before the adjective.

For Example:

How *such an* accident has happened, is a mystery.

However *clever a* student he is, he cannot neglect his studies.

Note: With *as, so, too* and *no less* the adjective comes before the indefinite article; as,

She is as clever a girl as ever studied in this school.

It is too difficult a problem.

It is no less a matter to be ignored.

This work cannot be done in so short a time.

12. The indefinite article is used between 'half' and a 'noun'; as,

I drank half a glass of milk.

He bought half a kilogram of butter.

I advised him at least half a dozen times.

13. The indefinite article should not be omitted from ' and a half' and 'and a quarter' when they are added to another numeral or its equivalent; as,

He came back after a year and a half. (not, a year and half)

She spent two and a half years in jail.

He finished his work in two and a quarter hours.

The time allotted to complete this work is an hour and a quarter.

14. Used with predicative nouns. (*i.e.,* with subject complement)

For Example:

He is a sailor.

('a sailor' refers to the subject 'He'. It is therefore the *subject complement*)

She is an actress. (an actress– subject complement)

Uses of *a*: It is used

1. before words beginning with a consonant or consonant sound.

For Example:

a boy, a monkey, a cassette, a young man, a human being, a horse, a one-rupee note.

A boy is standing under the tree.

2. before words like *university, unit, European, union, uniform* and *useful* which begin with vowels with a 'y' sound (a consonantal sound); as, a useful thing, a university, a unit, a European, a uniform, a union.

For Example:

TV is a *useful* thing. (not, an useful thing)

He is a *university* college student. (not, an university student)

3. before words beginning with a 'wu' sound.

For Example:

word 'one' – when sounded 'wu' and pronounced 'wun'

a one-rupee note, a one-eyed man, a one-way traffic, such a one, a one-man tribunal.

I gave him a one-rupee note. (not an one-rupee note)

He is a one-eyed man etc.

4. before 'few' and 'little'

For Example:

a few –Used with countable nouns to mean a small *number*;

few – not many (It has a negative meaning);

a little – a small *quantity* or amount ; little – not much (It has a negative meaning.)

A few people attended the meeting. (a small number)

Few people attended the meeting. (not many – negligibly small number)

There is a little milk in the pot. (a small quantity)

There is little milk in the pot. (not much- practically nothing)

Note: 'little' is adjective in the following example:

A little boy came to me. (little = small – adjective)

5. before Mr/Ms +surname to mean a stranger.

For Example:

a Mr Murthy, a Mr Menon, a Ms John etc.

Note: The word 'one' is sometimes used as the indefinite article in place of 'a' for emphasis to mean 'a single' or 'just one'.

For Example:

There is *only one* way to escape.

(Don't say: There is only a way to escape. This is the difference between 'a' used to mean 'any' or 'every' and the numeral 'one')

6. in such word groups as *a lot of, a large number of, a great number of, a great deal of, a good deal of,* etc.

For Example:

He has a lot of friends.

A large number of people *have* attended the meeting. (plural)

He spent a good/great deal of money.

A great many of them *are* unemployed.

7. to mean 'the same' after the prepositions 'of' and 'at' in phrases like 'all of a size' (all of the same size), 'two at a time' (two at the same time).

   For Example:

   All the boys are of a size.

   He took two books at a time.

8. after the word many, quite, such and rather.

   For Example:

   Many a mistake was committed by him. ('many a' is singular)

   He is quite a stranger.

   It is such a pity that he is dead.

   He is rather a poor boy.

   What a wonderful opportunity he has lost! (after exclamatory 'what')

   Note: When the word 'great' is used before 'many', the word order changes.

   He collected a great many old stamps. (not: great many a)

   A great many people were affected by the earthquake.

9. after an adjective preceded by as, too, so, how, quite.

   For Example:

   He is as bright a boy as you are.

   This is too big a task for me to undertake.

   He is not so big a politician as you think.

   How important a matter it was nobody realized.

   Note: The phrase 'to a degree' means ' to a high degree or extremely'.

   For Example:

   His behaviour was rude to a degree. (=....was rude to a high degree)

10. after exclamatory 'what'

   For Example:

   What a wonderful scenery !

Uses of *an*: It is used

1. before words beginning with a vowel (a, e, i, o, u) or vowel sound.

   For Example:

   an ox , an egg, an owl, an idiot, an honest man.

   He bought an ox.

   He is an idiot.

   He bought many an apple.

2. before words beginning with a silent 'h'.

   For Example:

   an hour, an honest boy, an heir.

   I reached the office an hour before him.

3. before consonants beginning with vowel sounds.

   For Example:

   an M.A., an S.P., an L.L.B., an M.B.B.S.

   He is an M.A. etc.

4. after exclamatory 'what' , but not in questions.

   For Example:

   What an arrangement you have made!

   What arrangement have you made for the journey? (question)

Omission of the Indefinite article *a* or *an*:

1. Not used with plural nouns.

   For Example:

   Cats, boxes, girls. (not: a cats, a boxes, etc)

2. Not used with uncountable or mass nouns.

   advice, baggage, information, luggage, furniture, scenery, machinery, imagery, poetry, knowledge, work, business, experience are examples of uncountable nouns.

   Don't say: I gave him an advice. or He left a baggage etc.

But, we can use *some, any, a little, a lot of, a piece of, a bit of, an item of, etc.* with these words as shown in the examples given below

I gave him some advice.

He gave me a piece of advice.

A word of advice. Don't smoke.

Is there any news?

He gave me a piece of information.

I did not buy a particular item of furniture.

We received a lot of information about the incident.

He left a piece of luggage.

He was carrying a lot of baggage.

Note: Although the word 'knowledge' is uncountable it takes the article when used in a particular sense; as,

A knowledge of/English/Hindi/German/French is very essential. (Particular knowledge)

3. Not used with material nouns when used in the general sense.

For Example:

water, paper, sugar, glass, bread, wheat, coffee, milk, stone, wood, iron etc., are examples of material nouns.

We cannot live without water.

We use paper to write on.

Sugar is sweet etc.

But: I drank a glass of water. (particular use)

I bought an electric iron. (particular use)

He gave me a coffee. (a cup of coffee)

4. Not used with abstract nouns.

For Example:

happiness, beauty, love, pleasure, courage, hope, wisdom, affection, intelligence, fear etc, are examples of abstract nouns.

Happiness in life is our aim.

Beauty is skin deep.

He is in love with his classmate etc.

But an abstract noun, when qualified by an adjective or an adjectival phrase or clause, may take an article.

For Example:

The beauty of Cleopatra is famous.

(particularized. Qualified by the the phrase 'of Cleopatra'.)

He showed a courage worthy of a prince.

5. Not used with names of meals.

For Example:

Dinner, supper, lunch, breakfast.

Dinner starts at 8 p.m.

We take lunch at noon.

I had breakfast at 7 a.m. etc.

But: (*a*) Used with them when they are preceded by an adjective.

For Example:

I had a light breakfast this morning.

I had a heavy dinner.

(*b*) Used with special meals; as

They invited me to a dinner on his birthday.

6. Not used before predicative nouns; as,

   John is Principal of the college. (not: a Principal)

   Raju became president of the club. (not: a president)

   It has become part of history. (The predicative noun 'part' is used in a general sense.)

7. Not usually used before a noun indicating a profession, office, etc., preceded by 'as', which is normally held at a time by one person only.

   For Example:

   As president of the club he was a failure. ('a' before 'president' is usually omitted)

   As adviser he did his best.

8. Not used with words like title, office, post, rank etc., after the partitive-of.

   (Partitive: A word or phrase that shows a part or quantity of something.)

   He was given the title of *Padmashree.* (Padmashree–title. 'a' is not used before it.)

   John was given the post of *inspector* in the office of the Commissioner.(not: an inspector)

   He was promoted to the rank of *Inspector General.* (not: an Inspector General)

9. Not used with predicative nouns when a contrast between different capacities is made: as,

   He is poet first, novelist next. (not: a poet, a novelist)

   The book makes a study of Nehru as politician and statesman. (not: a politician, a statesman)

10. Not used before a noun phrase after *turn* and *go*: as,

    Hitler turned dictator. (when speaking disparagingly)

    He has gone communist/socialist. (mostly when speaking about political allegiance)

Use of the Definite Article 'the':

The definite article 'the' is the same for singular and plural nouns.

For Example:

the boy- the boys, the teacher- the teachers,

the woman- the women, the child- the children.

The definite article 'the' is

1. used before a common noun that is already known or mentioned.

   For Example:

   There is a boy in my class. *The* boy is very mischievous. (boy mentioned in the first sentence)

   He went to *the* park. (park already known to him)

   My neighbour has two boys and a girl. *The* boys are very intelligent and *the* girl is very hard-working.

2. used before great epics, sacred books, newspapers and names of important events.

   For Example:

   the Ramayana, the Mahabharata, the Bible, the Koran,

   the Hindu, the Times of India, the French Revolution etc.

   Note: 'the' is not normally used before magazines and periodicals.

   For Example:

   Week, Observer, Illustrated weekly of India, Blitz, etc.

3. used before a common noun to give it the emphasis of a superlative.

   For Example:

   He is the man of the match. (the best player)

4. used before common nouns made specific by location or association. (persons, places, or things known to the speaker.)

   For Example:

   The children are playing on *the* ground. (specific ground known to the speaker *e.g.,* school ground)

   They sent for *the* doctor. (particular doctor *e.g.,* family doctor)

   He went to *the* market. (market he frequently visits)

5. used before superlatives.

   For Example:

   the best, the most courageous, the tiniest, etc.

   He is the best student in the class.

   He is the most courageous man I have ever seen.

But most people (or most of the people), most of the cases, etc. (When 'most' represents majority 'the' is omitted)

(Not: the most people etc.)

I knew most of the people who assembled there. (meaning 'majority of the people')

Most of my friends agreed to attend the meeting.

6. used before ordinals (like first, second, third,..........) and the word 'next'.

   For Example:

   She was the first to talk.

   I was the fifteenth in the list.

   He is the next candidate.

Note: We do not normally use 'the' before ordinals when we are talking about prizes in competitions; as,

He won first prize in the chess competition.

She won second prize in the music competition.

7. used before 'only' when used as an adjective or a pronoun.

   For Example:

   He is the *only* son of a rich man. (adjective)

8. used before some comparatives involving only two things or persons.

   For Example:

   Ram is the better of the two boys.

9. used before comparative degrees as adverbs , when there is a sense of proportion.

   The deeper, the cooler;

   The taller, the better; etc. (double comparatives)

10. used with singular common nouns to represent a whole class .(generic nouns) . This is called the 'generalizing the'.

   For Example:

   The rose is a lovely flower. (meaning ' All roses are lovely flowers'.)

   The camel is the ship of the desert. (meaning ' All camels are ships of the desert'.)

   Can the leopard change its spots? (Can all leopards change their spots.)

   The cow is a useful animal. (All cows are useful animals.)

   Exception: Man is mortal.

   God created man and woman.

   Man is majestic.

(Here 'man' is used to mean all human beings. Hence man and woman are exceptions. 'the' is not used before man and woman in the generic sense, but it is used before them when used in a particular sense.)

For Example:

This is the man whom I saw yesterday.

11. used before names of rivers, gulfs, seas, oceans, valleys, mountain ranges, bays, deserts, forests, group of islands., straits.

   Rivers: the Ganga, the Cauvery, the Amazon, the Periyar, the Pampa etc.

   For Example:

   The Ganga is a holy river etc.

   Note: The word 'river' is usually omitted from the names of rivers.

   Gulf: the Persian gulf

   The Persian Gulf is between the Arabian Peninsula and Iran.

   Seas: the Arabian sea, the Red sea

   The Arabian sea is one of our boundaries.

   Oceans: the Pacific ocean, the Indian ocean, the Arctic ocean.

   The Indian ocean lies in the east.

Valleys: the Silent valley

The Silent valley is a virgin forest.

Mountains: the Himalayas, the Alps

The Himalayas is always covered with snow.

Bays: the Bay of Bengal

Depression in the Bay of Bengal causes heavy rain.

Deserts: the Kalahari, the Sahara, the Thar. (meaning 'the Kalahari desert' etc.)

The Thar (desert) is in Rajasthan.

Forests: the Chambal forest, the Black forest.

The Chambal forest is in Madhya Pradesh.

Group of islands: the Andamans, the Lakshadweep, the West Indies.

The Lakshadweep is a group of Islands.

Straits: the Palk Strait, the Bering strait.

Can you locate the Palk Strait in the map?

Exceptions: 'the' is not used with names of individual mountain peaks, single mountains and single islands.

For Example:

Mount Everest, Mt.Etna, Kanchenjunga, Mt.Abu, Sri Lanka, Java.

Mount Everest is in the Himalayas.

Note: Not used with capes and lakes.

For Example:

Cape Comorin, Cape of Good Hope, Lake Sambar, Lake Vembanad.

Cape Comorin is the old name of Kanyakumari.

12. used before the names of trains, ships and aeroplanes.

    The Himsagar Express, the Madras Mail, the Titanic, the INS Vikrant, the Queen Victoria, the Meghdoot, the Boeing 707.

    For Example:

    The Madras Mail starts from Trivandrum.

13. used before the names of historical buildings.

    For Example:

    the Taj Mahal, the Qutab Minar, the White House, the Golden Temple, etc.

    The Taj Mahal is in Agra.

14. used before the names of countries having the words 'union' or 'united' (made up of smaller units or constituent parts),

    the USA, the UK, the UAE.

For Example:

The USA is the most powerful country in the world.

15. used before a few countries, provinces and proper nouns.

the Sudan, the Gambia, the Hague, the Balkan, the Deccan, the Punjab, the Netherlands, the Midlands, etc.

For Example:

The Punjab (meaning 'the land of five rivers') is near Delhi.

The Deccan (meaning 'the country in the south') is a plateau.

He went to the Netherlands.

16. used before the four directions when used as nouns.

the north, the south, the east, the west.

For Example:

In December cold winds blow from the north.

17. used before the names of unique objects, places, specific names or proper nouns etc.

For Example:

the earth, the sun, the moon, the sky, the north pole, the universe, the world, the Pope, the devil, the Atlantic etc.

For Example:

The earth goes round the sun.

But, 'the' is not used before *Heaven* (Note the capital 'H'–place where gods and angels live), Hell (capital 'H'– the place of punishment for the wicked), God (capital 'G'–the Creator and Ruler of the universe.)

For Example:

God dwells in Heaven while devils dwell in Hell.

Note: 'the' is used before 'hell' in certain expressions in informal style and in spoken English.

The expression 'to get the *h*ell out of here' means 'to leave the place very quickly'. (Note the lower case 'h' in the spelling.)

For Example:

They got the hell out of there. (meaning 'They left the place quickly.')

The expression ' just for the hell of it' means 'just for fun' or 'without any reason'.

For Example:

We quarrelled with him just for the hell of it.

(We quarrelled with him just for fun or for no reason.)

Note: 'the' is used before 'heavens' (small '*h*'- in certain expressions. 'the heavens' means 'the sky'.(literary style)

For Example:

The Moon looks down from the heavens.

Note: 'the gods' (British English) means the seats that are high up at the back of a theatre.

Note on 'earth'

(1) 'the' is used before 'Earth' when it is referred to as a planet; as,

The Earth is one of the planets. (Note the use of the capital letter 'E')

(2) 'on Earth' = on the planet Earth.

For Example:

Scientists studied the origin of life on Earth.

'the earth' = the land on which we live. (Only small letter '*e*' is used in this sense)

There are mountains and rivers on the earth.

She is the most beautiful woman on the earth.

'bring somebody back down to earth' means 'make somebody see the reality after a life of great happiness forgetting everything else'.

For Example:

The tragic death of his only son brought him back down to earth.

'come down to earth/come back to earth' means ' begin normal life after a period of excessive happiness'.

For Example:

Finally, he has come down/back to earth, thus starting a normal life.

'charge/cost/pay the earth' means 'to charge/cost/pay a large amount of money'.

For Example:

I would like to visit all the western countries, but that costs the earth.

'on earth' is used in negative and interrogative sentences for emphasis.

For Example:

No force on earth can prevent me from doing it.

Nothing on earth could dissuade him from meeting her.

What on earth is he writing?

How on earth is he going to do it?

Why on earth should I do it for him?

18. used with the names of musical instruments.

For Example:

the piano, the violin, the guitar.

He played the piano.

19. used with the names of works of references.

For Example:

the Atlas, the dictionary

The Atlas gives us a lot of information.

The dictionary is an important work of reference.

20. used with the names of municipal or government departments, shops, business houses, banks and industrial concerns when they do not begin with a personal name.

For Example:

The High Court, the Directorate of Higher Secondary Education, the Public Library, the Grand Hotel, the Army and Navy stores, the West Minster Bank, the White House, etc.

The High Court of Kerala is at Kochi.

The Grand Hotel is in (the) M.G.Road.

21. used before historical events.

For Example:

The Industrial revolution, the Renaissance.

During the Industrial Revolution machines began to be used.

22. used to show the period or quantity used for buying, selling or measuring.

For Example:

Eggs are sold by the dozen. (Not: by the dozens)(the=each) (quantity)

Cloth is sold by the metre. (the =each) (Note the singular form after 'the'.)

Sugar is sold by the kilogram.

He is paid by the hour. (period)

We hired the bus by the day.

23. used before titles.

For Example:

Akbar the Great (or the great Akbar); Alexander the Great (or the great Alexander).

Akbar the Great was a benevolent king.

24. used before divisions of time.

For Example:

In the morning, in the evening, all the night, all the week.

He came to my house in the morning.

25. used before an adjective to make it a noun in the plural to represent the whole class.

For Example:

The rich must help *the poor*. (Rich people must help poor people)

The educated should teach *the illiterate*.

26. used before dates, months and years.

For Example:

On the 15th of August, on the 1st of April, in the year 2000, in the May of 1990.

We celebrate Independence Day on the 15th of August.

Or

We celebrate Independence day on 15th August. (When the 'of' form is not used.) Similarly, in May 1990.

Note: 'On Monday' generally has relation to the present time and means 'next Monday' or 'last Monday'. Similarly, 'the next Monday', 'the last Monday', 'on a Monday' or 'on the Monday' has a relation to a remote time.

27. used before Proper adjectives, when 'people' or 'nation' is understood.

For Example:

The English often fought with *the French.*

(The English means the people of England or Englishmen.)

The Indians live in India.

But: When the word 'language' is understood 'the' is omitted; as,

French is more difficult to learn than English. (languages)

Or

(The French language is more difficult to learn than the English language.)

Always say: the English language (or English), the French language (or French), the Malayalam language (or Malayalam), etc.

Don't say: English language, French language, etc.

But, we usually say: Translated from the Malayalam/Hindi/Tamil etc.

This means ' from the Malayalam/Hindi/Tamil *version*'.

28. used before the adjective 'same' and after the adjectives 'both' and 'all'.

For Example:

Chip of the same block.

Both the pictures are good. ('Both pictures are good' is also correct.)

All the people mourned his death. ('All people mourned his death' is also correct.)

29. used before Proper, Material and Abstract nouns to make them Common nouns.

For Example:

Kalidas is the Shakespeare of India. (means Kalidas is the greatest dramatist of India.)

Bombay is the Manchester of India. (biggest cloth producing centre)

While Gandhi was the Buddha, Nehru was the Asoka.

Love is the dawn of marriage and marriage is the sunset of love.

30. used before parts of the body in place of Possessive adjectives.

For Example:

I caught him by the hand. (the=his)

He stabbed me in the back. (the=my)

He stared me in the face. (the=my)

31. used before plural common nouns when used in a particular sense.

For Example:

The horses of Arabia are famous all over the world. (particular horses)

The roses in my garden are very beautiful. (particular roses)

32. 'the' may be used in the following expressions with the names of the seasons:
For Example:

in the spring, during the winter etc. (in spring, during winter etc, are also correct.)

It is very cold in (the) winter.

Flowers bloom in (the) spring.

People wear woolen clothes during (the) winter season.

33. used before ordinal numbers written in letters.
For Example:

Edward VIII (read Edward *the eighth*) ,

George V (read *George the fifth*),

(When written in Roman notation, no article is used.)

34. used before special meals given to honour somebody or celebrate something.
For Example:

The dinner he served yesterday was very good.

I attended the lunch arranged in honour of the Minister.

35. used before adjectives to make them nouns to denote particular part of something.
For Example:

I like the white of an egg, but I don't like the yellow part.

The lion took shelter in the thick of the forest.

36. used before adjectives and singular common nouns to express an abstract idea.
For Example:

The mother in her took pity. (motherly feelings)

The rebel in him raised his voice. (rebellious attitude)

He is groping in *the dark.* (darkness)

He played *the fool.* (To behave in a foolish manner.)

37. used before a noun to indicate a profession.
For Example:

Members of *the* Bar and *the* Bench were present. (lawyers and judges.)

The church will oppose the bill. (the clergy)

38. used before a common noun followed by a proper noun that identifies it.
For Example:

The novel 'Wreck' was written by *the* poet Rabindranath Tagore.

39. used when nouns expressing trades or professions follow the proper nouns.
For Example:

I know Mr. Raj, the Principal of the college.

40. used with nouns in apposition.

For Example:

Delhi, *the capital of India*, is a metropolitan city.

Sri A.P.J. Abdulkalam, the president, is a well-known scientist.

Or

President Abdulkalam is a well-known scientist.

(No article is used before a title when it is followed by a proper noun.)

41. used with idiomatic phrases; as, on the contrary, in the light of, off the mark, in the long run, on the spur of the moment, on the whole, on the way, the right hand man, etc.

For Example:

I expected him to be angry with me. On the contrary, he welcomed me with a smile.

In the light of clear evidence he was punished.

42. When two or more connected nouns refer to the same person or thing the article is used before the first only.

For Example:

The Principal and Manager of the school is on leave. (One person)

43. When two or more connected nouns refer to different persons or things, 'the' is used before each.

For Example:

The Principal and *the* President of the school are on leave. (Different persons)

44. used before a plural formed of a proper noun/name(referring to a whole family).

For Example:

The Ramans (all the members of Raman' s family), the Guptas, the Nairs.

The Ramans were invited to the party.

Note: Sometimes 'the + name' is used to identify a person. This is the Ram Gopal I spoke to you about.

45. 'the' is used in the following expressions:

All the morning, all the afternoon, all the evening, all the week, all the month etc.

He was playing all the morning/all the evening etc.

Note: 'the' is not used in the expressions 'all day' and 'all night'.

For Example:

He worked all day.

They did not sleep all night.

46. 'the' is used before 'university' named after a place if the place name comes after it.

For Example:

The university of Kerala , the University of Calicut, etc.

But, if the place name comes before it 'the' is omitted.

For Example:

Kerala University, Calicut University, etc.

He is a student of the university of Kerala.

Or

He is a student of Kerala University.(Don't say: He is a student of the Kerala University.)

In the case of a university named after a person 'the' is not used before it. It has only one form.

For Example:

Kamaraj University, M.G.University, etc. (Don't say: The University of Kamaraj, or The Kamaraj University, The University of Mahatma Gandhi, or the M.G. Univerasity, etc.)

47. 'The' is used before the names of political parties.

For Example:

The Indian National Congress, The Communist Party of India etc.

48. used in the following phrases:

On the whole, on the increase, in the wrong, in the right etc.

The price of gold is on the increase.

The car driver was in the wrong.

He knew that he was in the right.

On the whole, her performance was good.

49. used before a noun which is made specific by the addition of an adjectival(defining)clause or phrase.

For Example:

The dog that bit me.

The dog in the kennel is a special variety.

The boy who came here yesterday is dead.

50. used with an adjective before a proper name to identify two or more persons of the same name; as, the younger Nair, the elder Nair, etc.

For Example:

He went to see the younger Nair.

51. used before certain honorific titles showing respect for the person addressed to;

For Example:

The Honourable Chief Minister of Kerala state, the Right Honourable Srinivasa Sastry etc.

52. used before an adjective preceding a *countable* noun to particularize it.

For Example:

The tall boy standing there is her brother. (the *tall boy* particularizes the boy from other boys.)

Note: An adjective before an *uncountable* noun does not normally take *the* before it.

For Example:

Hot milk is better than cold milk.

But, 'The hot milk in that glass is for you'. (Uncountable noun particularized – hot milk in *that glass.*)

53. 'the' is used before 'same' to form the pronoun of identity.

'the same' means ' not different or exactly something mentioned or referred to immediately before or stated in what follows.'

For Example:

I and my friend were travelling on/by the same train. (not different)

He left Chennai in 2000. I too left it in the same year.

Wish you a happy Onam. Wish you the same.

This is the same man whom I met yesterday.

54. 'the' or 'a/an' is used with the count noun subject (complement) and object complement. 'a/an' is used with indefinite reference; as,

He is a reporter. ('reporter' – subject complement. The sentence means 'he is one belonging to the category of reporters'. This holds good in the following examples too.)

She considered him a hero. ('hero' – object complement)

They took him for a professor. ('professor' – object complement)

Note: 'the' is used with specific reference; as,

He is the reporter. (of a particular newspaper–specific)

Note: He is reporter. (means ' reporter of the particular newspaper we are talking of '. This holds good in the following examples too.)

She considered him the hero of the novel. (of a particular novel)

They took him for the professor of English. (of English–specific)

55. 'the' is used only once with two or more parallel words closely connected.

For Example:

The Malayalam and Tamil languages.

Through the length and breadth of the country.

The long and short of the matter, etc.

Omission of articles

The function of the article is to individualize the noun to which it is added.

The rules are: 'the' is

1. not used before a noun when it is considered to be in a general and indefinite sense and not in a particular and limited sense.

For Example:

A man came to see me. *The* man looked worried. ('man' mentioned in the first sentence.)

But when used without the article the noun 'man' is general and used in the widest sense.

For Example:

Man is mortal.

2. not used before Proper, Material and Abstract nouns.

For Example:

Midas longed for *gold*. (Midas–Proper noun, gold–Material noun)

Maya learns dance and *Rema* painting. (Proper nouns)

Milk is good for health. (Material noun)

Beauty is skin deep. (Abstract noun)

Honesty is the best policy. (Abstract noun)

Delhi is the capital of India. (Proper noun)

3. not used before the names of festivals, months and days of the weak.(Onam, Holi, Christmas, Easter,.... ; January, February,.... Sunday, Monday,.......)

For Example:

January is the first month. (Proper noun)

Sunday is a holiday. (")

Onam is a national festival. (")

Christmas is in the month of *December*. (")

Easter is celebrated all over the world. (")

4. not *usually* used with the noun complement after linking verbs like 'be' and 'become' and naming verbs like 'elect', 'appoint' and 'declare'.

(These noun complements are predicative nouns that denote unique positions – only one person at one time.)

For Example:

He is (the) president of the club. ('is' – linking verb)

They elected him President of India.

('They elected him the President of India' is also correct.)

He was elected president.

The committee appointed him (as) (the) Secretary of the club.

('appointed as', 'elected as' are increasingly used in Modern English.)

Sri A.P.J. Abdulkalam became (the) President of India.

They crowned her (the) Miss Universe.

She was crowned Miss Universe.

They elected him (as) (the) President of India., etc.

But: He was appointed a secretary. (if there is more than one secretary.)

He was appointed secretary. (if there is only one secretary.)

5. not used before the plural nouns denoting a class.

For Example:

Children like to play. (all children)

Horses are very useful animals.

But, if they are particularized 'the' is used.

The children of the house are playing. (particular children)

The horses of Mr. John are very useful.

6. not used before the nouns singular in form, but plural in sense. Cattle, furniture, advice, information, equipment, luggage and baggage.

For Example:

Cattle are grazing in the field.

He asked his father for advice.

Furniture is very costly nowadays.

He left the room bag and baggage.

7. not used before the common nouns used in pairs:

For Example:

Hand in hand, face to face, from end to end, from beginning to end, to live from hand to mouth, from north to south, husband and wife, bag and baggage, man to man, between thumb and finger, body and soul, father and son etc.

Both husband and wife are in service.

We walked along the street hand in hand.

8. not used before the common nouns preceded by 'kind of'.

For Example:

What kind of flower is it? What kind of animal was that?

9. not used before languages, subjects and colours used as nouns.

For Example:

She does not know *English* but she knows *Malayalam*.

(But: She does not know *the* English *language* etc.)

Black and white are my favourite colours.

I hate Economics and Psychology.

10. not used before the names of diseases and regular meals.

For Example:

Fever, dysentery, cholera, typhoid.

But, the measles, the mumps.

Lunch, dinner, tea , breakfast. ('The' is used if it is special.)

He is suffering from fever /dysentery.

But, the measles/the mumps spreads very fast. (Uncountable nouns; hence singular)

For Example:

I take breakfast at 8.

It is time for dinner.

Have you taken tea?

At what time do you have lunch?

11. not used before titles if they are followed by names.

For Example:

Rev. Fr. Joseph was treated by Dr. Ram.

Advocate Gopi has taken up the case.

Col. Krishna talked to Cap. Rahul.

12. not used before abstract nouns.

For Example:

A flower is a thing of *beauty*.

But when used in a particular sense 'the' is used.

He was attracted by the beauty of the flower.

13. not used before plural nouns used in a general sense.

For Example:

Teachers shape the future of the country.

Books are not cheap these days.

14. not used after a noun in the possessive case.

For Example:

This is Reghu's book. (not: Reghu's the book)

15. not used before the words 'nature' (usually 'Nature' in the sense 'the whole world as it exists') and 'society' (uncountable) (in the sense 'people living together in communities').

For Example:

We should maintain the balance of Nature.

Society is created for the welfare of man.

But, when 'nature' means characteristics it takes 'the'.

I was confused over the nature of the work.

Note: A society that does not look after the welfare of its members is no society. (a=any)

16. 'the' is used before the word 'society' when it means 'association'; as,

The society of working journalists decided to boycott the Chief Minister.

17. (*a*) not used before words like home, church, hospital , temple, school, college, market, court, prison, work, sea, bed when they are visited *for their primary purpose.*

For Example:

I go to bed early. (to sleep)
We go to church every Sunday. (to pray)
Ram is admitted in hospital. (for treatment)
I go to school regularly. (to study)
His father has gone to market. (for shopping)
Dr. went to hospital. (for treatment)
They have decided to go to sea. (as sailors)
The thief was sent to prison.

But, when we visit these places for other than their primary purpose we use 'the'.

For Example:

We went to the church to attend a wedding. (not: to pray)
He has made the beds. (to arrange it)
The police went to the market in search of a criminal.
I went to the hospital to visit my friend.
My father came to the school to pay the fees.
He was at the sea. (at the sea side)
He went to the prison to see his relative.

Exceptions: Use always *the temple, the mosque, the office (to work), the cinema, the theatre* (for entertainment).

For Example:

He goes to the temple every day. (to pray)
I did not go to the office yesterday. (to work)
We will go to the cinema tonight. (to see a film)

(*b*) Not used with the means of transport after 'by'.

For Example:

He went by bus/train etc. (not: by the bus)

18. not used before descriptive nouns when used appositionally (in apposition to).

For Example:

Pope John, St.Joseph, Sister Anne, Prime Minister Vajpayee.

(The name 'John' is in apposition to the Pope)

Note: We can say: The Pope, John, is in Rome.

The Prime Minister, Mr Vajpayee, left for the USA.

19. No article is used before 'home' when used alone.

For Example:

I went home.

The children came home in time.

He arrived home late.

But, when 'home' is preceded or followed by a descriptive word or phrase 'the' is used.

For Example:

I shall visit the home *of my ancestors.*

A shattered hut was the only home they had.

For quite some time this was the home *of my family.*

20. No article is used before 'Parliament'.

For Example:

He is a member of Parliament. (not the Parliament)

21. No article is used

(*a*) before the common noun in certain idiomatic phrases with transitive verbs.

For Example:

To catch fire, to send word, to leave school, to set sail, to set foot, to lose heart, to give ear, to strike root, to take breath, to shake hands, to follow suit, to leave school etc.

The house caught fire. (not: caught a/the fire)

He sent word to his father. (not: sent a/the word/words)

The plant struck root into the ground. (not: the roots/roots)

We should not give ear to rumours. (not: the ears/ears)

(*b*) before the common noun in certain prepositional phrases .

For Example:

at home, in hand, on foot, at ease, at arm's length, by day, at night, by water, by land, what on earth, in heaven, by name, at noon, at lunch, at tea, at sea, at bottom, at last, in fact, on shore, on top of, on account of, make one's hair stand on end, go to press, on shore, in course of time, loose heart, weigh anchor, etc.

When my friend came I was at home. (not at the home)

I do not have any money in hand. (not: in the hand)

I went to the park on foot. (not: on the foot)

He went to Delhi by land. (not: by the land)

Nothing on earth can prevent me from going there. (not: on the earth)

He called me by name. (not: by the name)

(*c*) in phrases consisting of two or more parallel members:

For Example:

from beginning to end, hand in hand, end to end, man to man,

from hand to mouth, look right or left, arm in arm, face to face, father and son, keep body and soul together, husband and wife, etc.

He read the book from beginning to end. (not: from the beginning to the end)

He arranged the benches end to end.

They stood hand in hand.

He discussed the matter with his friend man to man.

They lived from hand to mouth.

22. No article is used before the names of games.

For Example:

Cricket, tennis, chess, football etc.

Cricket is a popular game. I like to play chess.

23. No article is used before the names of colours.

For Example:

White represents purity. Green is associated with prosperity.

24. No articles is used before the names of seasons, days and months.

For Example:

May is the hottest month of the year.

I like to go to Munnar in winter.

Sunday comes before Monday.

25. No article is used before the names ending in Street, Lane, Avenue etc.

For Example:

His shop is in Mather Street.

The college is in Park Avenue.

He has a shop in College lane.

Note: 'the' is optional before a name ending in Road if 'Road' forms part of the name of the road.

For Example:

He has a shop in the M.G.Road. or He has a shop in M.G.Road.

If the word 'road' means the road leading to a particular place 'the' must be used; as,

He was driving along the Ernakulam road. (the road leading to Ernakulam)

26. No articles is used before the names of festivals, days of national importance etc.

For Example:

Independence Day, Republic Day, Christmas, Onam, Diwali, New year's Day etc.

Our college celebrated Independence Day. (not, the Independence Day)

27. 'the' is not used before the word 'town' in idioms like *to town, in town out of town, stay in town, go to town, return from town* etc.

They mean the place we live in or the place we are talking about.

For Example:

He went to town yesterday.

He is in town.

He will be out of town tomorrow.

Don't say: 'He went to city yesterday' etc., in this sense.

But, if a town is mentioned incidentally the article is used; as,

He went to the town yesterday.

28. 'the' is not used with an adjective before an uncountable noun;_as,

For Example:

White *bread* is good for the health. (Not: The white bread...... uncountable noun)

Fried *chicken* is very tasty. (uncountable noun)

29. No article is used before the common noun in the following prepositional phrases indicating the mode of conveyance.

For Example:

by bus, by road, by train, by air, by car etc.

He came by car/by bus/by train/by air etc. (Not: by the car/by the train etc.)

Note: He went to Trivandrum in *the* car (his own car).

30. Articles are deliberately omitted in newspaper headlines, telegrams and notices and labels.

For Example:

TN Assembly passes Anti-Conversion Bill

(The Tamil Nadu Assembly passes the Anti-Conversion Bill.)

CONFERENCE POSTPONED STOP NEXT DATE INTIMATED SOON

(The Conference has been postponed. The next date will be intimated soon.)

DON'T PLUCK FLOWERS

(Don't pluck the flowers.)

31. No article is used before the common nouns *father, mother, brother, uncle, aunt, baby, nurse, cook* where particularization is self-evident; as,

For Example:

Father got angry with me when I disobeyed him. (*father=my father*)

Mother gave me food. (*mother=my mother*)

Similarly, cook=our cook or my cook, nurse=our nurse or my nurse etc.

32. No article is used before an adjective followed by a proper noun; as,

For Example:

Immortal Valmiki, Immortal Shakespeare, Rare Ben Jonson, etc.

(not the Immortal Valmiki, etc.)

33. No article is used before the word 'space' when it is used in relation to astronomy and space science.

The astronaut floated in space.

34. When radio and television are used in the general sense, 'the' is not used before them.

Radio and television have become part of our life.

But: I saw the news on television. (no 'the' before television)

I heard the news on *the* radio. ('the' before radio)

Repetition of the Article

1. When two or more adjectives qualifying the same noun are connected by 'and' the article is used before the first adjective only.

For Example:

I have a black and white dog. (only one dog partly black and partly white)

This is an English and Malayalam dictionary. (only one)

I brought the brown and white saree. (only one)

2. When two or more adjectives qualifying different nouns are connected by 'and' the article is used before each adjective.

For Example:

I have a green and a red saree. (I have two sarees; one is red and the other is green.)

We saw the first and the second hen. (Two hens)

The first and the second scene. (Two scenes)

Note: Repetition of articles can be avoided by using two or more parallel words of similar category. (In such cases the article need be placed only before the first noun.)

For Example:

The first and second poems are interesting. (This actually means 'The first poem and the second one (poem) are interesting' .)

The red and green sarees are good.

The Telugu and Tamil languages are easy to learn.

The first and second scenes.

Through the length and breadth of our country.

The king and queen of England. (The king and the queen of England)

The punctuality, sincerity, and perseverance with which he studied made him pass the exam with flying colours.

Note: Examine the following sentence:

The red and green sarees are good.

From the above sentence it is not clear whether the reference is to only two sarees or more than two.

If it is to *only two* sarees we can recast the sentence as shown below to remove the ambiguity:

The red and white saree are good.

The plural verb 'are' indicates that there is more than one saree while the singular name 'saree' implies that there are two sarees, one red and the other blue.

3. When two or more nouns connected by 'and' refer to the same person or thing, the article is used before the first only; as,

For Example:

The chairman and Managing director is present.

(one person occupying both the positions.)

The owner and manager of the shop is known to me. (one person)

But, when they refer to different persons or things or different contrast, the article is used before each noun.

For Example:

The Principal and the Secretary do not agree on this point. (two persons)

4. In expressing a comparison:

If two nouns refer to the same person or thing, the article is used before the first noun only; as,

For Example:

Nehru is a greater scholar than administrator. (one person)

He is a better musician than actor. (one person)

But, if they refer to different persons or things, the article must be used before each noun; as,

He is a better musician than an actor. (different persons)

He is a better writer than a speaker. (different persons)

5. The article must be repeated if two or more statements of equal importance are connected together; as,

For Example:

She is a good mother, a good housewife but a bad teacher.

Errors in the use of Articles:

1. There is watchman at the gate. (say: a watchman)
2. I told man to go out. (say: the man)
3. The honesty is the best policy. (say: honesty –omit 'the')
4. We get the milk from the cows. (say : milk from cows)

5. He is Kalidasa of Kerala. (say: the Kalidasa.)
6. Bharathapuzha is the longest river in Kerala. (say: The Bharathapuzha)
7. The Mount Everest is the highest mountain in the world. (say: Mount Everest)
8. The Prime Minister Vajpayee is taking a tough stand against terrorism. (say: Prime Minister Vajpayee.....) (or) The Prime Minister Mr.Vajpayee ....
9. Ramayana is an epic. (say: The Ramayana, the Bible, the Koran etc.)
10. The Ceylon is an island in Indian Ocean. (say: Ceylon is....the Indian Ocean.)
11. The wisdom dawned late on him. (say: wisdom)
12. Wisdom of Ramu is well-known. (Say : The wisdom...)
13. The Minister shook hand with the Major.
    (say: Shook hands with. The phrase is 'to shake hands with'.)
14. There was depression in Bay of Bengal. (say: The Bay of Bengal)
15. The Mount Everest is in the Himalayas. (say: Mount Everest ...the Himalayas)
16. There are so many wonderful things in the Nature. (say: in Nature)
17. The gold is a precious metal. (say: Gold is a ......)
18. He told me lie. (... a lie)
19. Do not make noise. (..... make a noise)
20. He is a honourable man. (..... an honourable man)
21. He is sixth in the list. (say: ..... the sixth)
22. He was appointed the president. (appointed President)
23. English language is not easy to learn. (say: The English language (or) English)
24. Pandit Jawaharlal Nehru was a historian. (say: The Pandit Jawaharlal)
25. I bought a black and a white dog. (say: I bought a black and white dog)
    (I bought a black and a white dog means 'two dogs – one black and the other white.)
26. He is the Professor and the Principal. (say: He is the Professor and Principal – one man)
27. We went out without eating the breakfast. (say: ...eating breakfast)
28. Mathrubhumi is a Malayalm daily. (say: The Mathrubhumi..)
29. As sky was cloudy moon was not visible (wrong).
    (say: the moon, the sun, the stars, the universe, the sky etc.)
30. They went by the land. (say: by land)
31. They went by the water. (say: by water)
    Note: Use always by sea, by bus, by air, by train etc., whenever the mode of transport is thought of.

EXERCISES

Fill in the blanks with 'a', 'an' or 'the'

1. Will you close ...... door, please?
2. We live in ...... small flat near ...... centre of ...... city.
3. We went out for ...... meal last night ......
4. ...... Restaurant we went to was good.
5. Did ...... police find ...... person who stole your bicycle?
6. Has your house got ...... garden?
7. In ...... morning I had ...... boiled egg and ...... glass of milk.
8. ...... President of the United States visited India last year.
9. I got ...... ten rupee note from ...... pavement.
10. " Have you driven ...... car ?" "No, I've never driven ...... car in my life .
11. Can you turn off ...... light please ?
12. Where is ...... toilet, please ?
13. John isn't well . He has gone to ...... doctor. (his doctor)
14. Last night we went for ...... meal in ...... hotel.
15. I wrote my name at ...... top of ...... page.
16. ...... moon goes round ...... earth every 27 days.
17. Did you see ...... movie on ...... TV or at ...... cinema ?
18. After ...... lunch, we went for ...... walk by ...... sea.
19. Raj lives in ...... small town in ...... country.
20. I never listen to ...... radio. In fact I haven't got ...... radio.
21. It was ...... beautiful day. .....sun shone brightly in ...... sky.
22. What is ...... highest mountain in ...... world?
23. Can you turn ...... TV , please ?
24. Why do ...... English think they are great ?
25. ...... Piano is my favourite instrument.
26. ...... rose is my favourite flower.
27. The man is collecting money for ...... blind.
28. Did you like ...... coffee she gave us ?
29. The workers went to ...... church to repair its roof .
30. Manu went to ....jail to visit his brother.
31. Joseph goes to ...... church every Sunday.
32. How many people go to ...... University in your country?
33. Sherin reads ...... Malayala Manorama but his wife reads ...... Indian Express.
34. During ...... rainy season you must keep ...... umbrella with you.
35. Kashmir is in ...... North of India.
36. ...... Mount Everest is ...... high peak.
37. ...... Bay of Bengal lies to ...... south east of India.
38. Please draw ...... map of India.
39. Iron is ...... useful metal.
40. ...... Taj is ...... historical building.
41. It is half ...... hour past five.
42. Brutus is ...... honourable man.
43. ...... sun rises in the East.
44. Sanskrit is ...... difficult language.
45. Yesterday ...... European called at my office.
46. ...... lion is ...... king of beasts.
47. French is ...... easy language.
48. You are ...... fool to say that.
49. He returned after ...... hour.
50. ...... honest man always speaks ...... truth.
51. ...... abbey is ...... collection of buildings where monks live under ...... charge of abbots or sometimes, where nuns live under ...... charge of ...... abbess.
52. ...... Foot throttle of ...... motor vehicle such as ...... car, is called ...... Accelarator because when ...... driver steps on it, ... speed of ...... vehicle increase. This increase of speed in ...... given time is called acceleration.

53. ...... Philippines are in ...... Pacific.
54. ...... man is ...... second Hitler.
55. ...... virtuous are happy.
56. What ...... fool are you?
57. Which is ...... stronger, iron or stone ?
58. ...... Burmese are ...... Buddhist.
59. He has too high ...... opinion about himself.
60. Never tell ...... lie.
61. Durgadas was ...... historian.
62. ...... Sun and ...... Moon are lamps of heaven.
63. ...... Ganga is ...... sacred river of ...... Hindus.
64. ...... wise pity ...... foolish.
65. English is ...... language of ...... English.
66. He is ...... Indian and she is ...... European.
67. ...... one-eyed man live there.
68. ...... friend of mine wants to be ...... doctor.
69. ...... queen's daughter is called ...... princess.
70. ...... children wished their mother ...... Happy Birthday.
71. We visit ... ...old shop near ...... temple.
72. Open .... book and read ..... first line.

Chapter **18**

PUNCTUATION

Punctuation is the system of correctly putting stops and marks in writing.

Punctuation helps us make the meaning of a passage clear. These stops and marks divide one sentence from another or one part of a sentence from another.

Just as we use pauses and intonation while speaking to make our meaning clear, we use punctuation marks in writing to help the reader understand the meaning.

The principal marks of punctuations are:

(*i*) **Marks of 'Ending Punctuation' :** (Usually occur at the end of sentences.)

Full Stop (.) – Mark indicating a complete stop.

Interrogation mark (?) – Mark placed at the end of a question.

Exclamation mark (!) – Mark of an expression of sudden emotion.

(*ii*) **Marks of 'Internal Punctuation' :** (Occur in the middle of a sentence.)

Comma (,) – Mark indicating a very short pause.

Colon (:) – Mark indicating a list of something that is to follow especially after a statement using the words 'as follows', 'these', 'the following' .

Semicolon (;) – Mark indicating longer pause than the comma does. They are mainly used to separate main clauses not joined by coordinating conjunction such as 'and, but, for, yet, or, nor'.

Dash (-) – Mark indicating an abrupt pause.

Parentheses/Brackets [()] – Mark setting apart the enclosed material.

(*iii*) **Marks of 'Word Punctuation' :** (Concerned with the formation or construction of words.)

Capital letters – A, H, T, U.

Apostrophe (') – Mark showing omission of letters in a word.

Quotation marks or Inverted commas (" ….") –Mark indicating the beginning and end of the exact words of someone else quoted by another.

Single Inverted commas ('.....') – To indicate a quotation within a quotation.

Hyphen (_) –Mark which connects two parts of a word.

Oblique or Virgule (/) – To show choice.

Punctuation depends upon grammar. We cannot punctuate correctly until we understand how one part of the sentence is related to another.

1. **Full Stop (.)**

Full stop represents the longest pause. While speaking, we pause regularly and naturally. The pause in speaking has its counterpart in writing in the form of full stop.

All sentences – whether affirmative, negative or imperative – except the exclamatory and interrogative sentences– end with a full stop.

Even the exclamatory (!) and interrogative (?) signs have full stops under their respective signs.

(*a*) Used at the end of declarative and imperative sentences even though the sentence may contain only one word.

Kerala is the most literate state in India.

I know his house. No. Please sit down.

(*b*) Used to make abbreviations and initials.

M.A., Ph.D., M.B.A., M.Ed., B.Sc.

(*c*) Used when abbreviations consist of the first few letters of a word.

Capt., Col., Prof., Adv.

But, when the abbreviation is formed by the first and last letters of a word, the full stop is often omitted.

Dr (doctor), Mr (mister), Jr (junior), St (street), St (saint).

Note: When a series of abbreviation is used in a sentence or with a name, a comma is used after every abbreviation, but there is no need to use another full-stop (.) with the last abbreviation if a sentence or name ends with such a series.

Ms Bindu, L.L.B.,Ph.D. (Don't put another full-stop after 'D.')

2. **Interrogation mark (?)**

The question mark has more than the effect of a full stop.

It shows a certain quality of the sentence.

(*a*) It is used after a direct question.

What are you writing? Who was that? How is he?

Note: (*i*) Interrogation mark is not used after an indirect question.

I want to know what he said.

He asked where they lived.

(*ii*) When a question is reported (indirect speech) no question mark is used.

The teacher asked him why he was late.

(*iii*) Interrogation mark is not used after a polite request.

Would you mind coming with me.

Could you post this letter for me.

Will you kindly lend me the books.

3. **Exclamation mark (!)**

(*i*) Used strictly after words or sentences or phrases conveying sudden emotions like horror, contempt, amazement, happiness, wish or any other strong feelings.

Oh! , Alas !, Bravo !, Hurrah !, Heavens !, Stop !, Hush !,

How strange!, What a beauty !, How mighty! ,

What a pity!, Amazing !, Oh darling !, Hello !

(*ii*) Used after short orders.

Shut up ! Look here ! Stop there ! Go ! Get out !

4. **Comma (,)**

The comma is the shortest pause. Its use mainly depends upon the sense of a sentence.

Note: 'And' is not generally used after a comma.

(*a*) Used to separate more than two words of the same part of speech coming together in a sentence.

Noun: I saw Ravi, Rema, Jaya and Radha buying chocolates, ice-creams and cakes. (separating nouns)

Verb: He came, bathed , dressed and left. (separating verbs)

Adjective: She is beautiful, rich, humble and good-natured. (separating adjectives)

Adverb:Teacher taught us clearly, carefully, convincingly and effectively. (separating adverbs)

Note: This is sometimes known as 'serial comma'.

(*b*) Used when pairs of words connected by 'and' are to be separated.

big and small, rich and poor, high and low, strong and weak, kings and subjects.

(*c*) Used between nouns or pronouns in apposition.

Ramayana, a great epic, was written by Valmiki.

Gandhiji, the Father of our nation, died in 1948.

Rose, the queen of flowers, is loved by all.

Cochin, the queen of the Arabian sea, is in Kerala State.

(*d*) Used to separate the nominative of address from the rest of a sentence.

Raj, please do it for me.

Get out of the class, boys.

O God, give us strength. (Raj, boys and O God are nominatives of address.)

(*e*) Used after adverbial phrases of absolute construction.

The sun having set, darkness enveloped the world.

The meeting having finished, all left.

(*f*) Used before and after a participial phrase provided that the phrase might be expanded into a clause and is not used *in a merely qualifying sense.*

Caesar, having defeated his enemies, returned in triumph to Rome.(Having defeated means 'after he had defeated'.)

Asoka, having won the Kalinga war, decided to fight again. (Having won means 'after he had won'.)

(*g*) Used before and after an adjectival phrase formed with a participle.

Madhavi, having completed her studies, decided to get married.

(*h*) Used to separate words, phrases, and clauses inserted into the body of a sentence.

For Example:

of course, indeed, therefore, no doubt, in fact, as a matter of fact, for example, for instance, at best, at length, sooner or later, in the long run, after all, at last, all the same, on the whole , moreover, nevertheless, however, consequently, well, on the contrary, on the other hand, etc.

Well, what are you doing now?

The result, on the whole, was good.

You are, indeed, lucky.

Madhu is, after all, poor.

(*i*) Used to avoid repetition of a verb.

I gave her a flower, and him a watch.

Rahim is a pilot and Ram, a teacher.

Manoj joined the Medical College and Ravi, the Arts College.

Ravi got the first prize, Praveen the second.

(*j*) Used to separate a subordinate clause from the Principal clause when a sentence begins with a subordinate clause.

When he was a bachelor, he lived alone.

When the sun rises, the farmers go to the field.

If you go for the wedding, please let me know.

Where there is a will, there is a way.

(*k*) Used to separate a short co-ordinate clause in a compound sentence.

He came, he saw, he conquered. (three main or co-ordinate clauses)

Men may come, men may go, but I go on forever. (Tennyson)

The crowd shouted, waved and cheered the champion.

I went to the park, and my friend went to the cinema.

But when these main clauses are closely linked, no comma is used.

For Example:

I gave him a piece of advice and he followed it strictly.

(*l*) Used to separate a noun clause from the rest of a sentence.

Who we are and why we are, we do not know.

That he is an honest man, is beyond doubt.

Why I behaved like that, is not clear.

(*m*) Used to separate two clauses containing adjectives or adverbs in the comparative degree.

The higher we go, the cooler it is.

The more, the better.

(*n*) Used to break up groups of figures into

(*i*) millions and thousands

(*ii*) crores, lakhs, thousands and hundreds.

For Example:

(*i*) The population of Kerala is 13,254,325.

(*ii*) The population of Kerala is 1,32,54,325.

(*o*) Used after yes, no, well etc., when they come at the beginning of a sentence.

(*i*) Yes, I know that. No, he wasn't there.

(*ii*) Well, come in.

(*p*) Used before quotation marks in direct speech or quotation.

"Please listen to me", he said.

She said to Ram, "Where is he?"

(*q*) Used before coordinating conjunctions when a pause is needed.

To behave thus is not wisdom, but folly.

I had known him earlier, for he was my neighbour.

He came very late, but stayed till the end.

(*r*) Used before question tags.

He hasn't come, has he?

Let us go to the shore, shall we?

(*s*) Used to separate explanatory phrases.

The room was big, 6 feet in length, 4 feet in breadth.

To be very frank, I don't have any money with me.

(*t*) In letters, the comma is used after *Sir, Dear sir, Dear brother, Dear Mary, etc.*, and after *Yours faithfully, Yours obediently,Yours sincerely, Your loving brother, Sincerely yours, etc.*

(*u*) Used to separate phrases containing words like 'not', 'unlike' etc.

Our staple food is wheat, not rice.

Unlike the Indians, the Americans eat a staple diet of meat and wheat.

The golden rule about using commas is that it can be used wherever the writer thinks that a pause is required to make the meaning of a sentence clear.

Omission of Commas

(*i*) No comma is generally used before 'and'.

I saw Maya, Meera and Manu.

(*ii*) When only two words or phrases are connected by 'and'/'or' no comma is used.

You can come by car or bus.

Hari and Rahul are neighbours.

I met a lame man and a deaf man.

(*iii*) No comma is used before the first and last members of a series.

He reads newspapers, magazines and novels.

She likes short, vivid, exciting tales.

(Here, no commas are used before 'newspapers' and after 'exciting'.)

(*iv*) No comma is used between month and year in dates.

3 March 2006, but the use of comma is correct in 'March 3, 2006', 'Monday, November 6, 2006', 'March to May, 2006', etc.

(*v*) No comma is used between house No. and address.

His address is: 145 Town hall Road, Ernakulam.

5. Semi-Colon

The semicolon is half way between the comma and the full stop. It has a longer pause than the comma. It is usually followed by conjunctions like or, and, or but

(*a*) While comma with the briefest possible pause separates the individual items in a series, the semicolon separates different group or items.

For Example:

The visiting room has two sofas, one showcase, one table; the dining room has one table, five chairs, a washbasin; in the bed room were two cots, one chair, a table and few books.

(*b*) To separate the clauses of a compound sentence when they contain commas.

My uncle is an uneducated, honest and a simple man; but I love him.

She was a kind, generous lady; we all honoured her.

(*c*) To break up a long sentence into parts, each part having the same subject matter.

Ram was a naughty boy who often quarrelled with his classmates, in this quarrel, he sometimes broke others' limbs, but often got his own limbs broken, for his such acts of mischief, his parents were tired of him; to them he was a problem child.

(*d*) Clauses showing strong contrast are separated by the semicolon.

He is better yet; the doctor is not happy.

(*e*) Used to separate a series of loosely related clauses.

Reading maketh a full man; conference a ready man; writing an exact man.

Man is born; he lives for some years; and then dies; this is in brief, the history of man.

(*f*) Used between independent clauses when joined by conjunctions– besides, however, for example, that is, but etc.

People say that Munnar is a hill station; however, I have never gone there.

In childhood man is innocent and free; but in youth he learns the lesson of deceit and concealment.

6. **Colon (:)**

Colon demands a longer pause than the semicolon. (Sometimes it is represented by the sign :)

(*a*) Used to introduce a list of items, similar objects or ideas.

I can't bear: pudding, barking dogs and oily food.

Boys should bring: bedding, a pair of socks, a mug and a plate.

He subscribes to the following magazines: The Blitz, The Sunday, The Illustrated Weekly of India.

(*b*) Used to introduce a quotation.

John Keats says: A thing of beauty is a joy forever.

Aristotle said: Man is a social animal.

(*c*) Used before examples

There are three kinds of tenses: Past, Present and Future.

(*d*) Used to separate two sentences of which the second explains fully the meaning of the first.

I have made a timetable: For the first two days I shall study English, then for the next four days mathematics, science and social studies and for the last day Hindi.

The reason for my delay is this: I did not get up early today.

(*e*) Before a phrase or a sentence which sums up explanatory examples.

He works hard, he respects his parents and teachers, he has a good character, he maintains good health: these are qualities of an ideal student.

Honesty, truthfulness, bravery: this sums up character.

(*f*) To introduce a comment, a reason etc.

I can't go there: I have no time.

He left early: I suppose he was tired.

(*g*) To separate minutes from hours while denoting time.

3:30 a.m., 1:00 p.m., 11:14 p.m.

7. **Dash(–)**

The dash acts as an indicator of interruption .

(*a*) Used when there is an abrupt change, stop or break of thought.

If my daughter were here now – but why wish ?

I have been waiting for–ah, there he is!

Should I tell you the whole story – but no why should I?

(*b*) Used to summarize a scattered subject.

Friends, relatives, companions and health – all deserted me .

(*c*) Used to introduce dramatic anti climax in a sentence.

I tell you the name of your enemy – he is Raju.

He knows what he should do – send a telegram.

(*d*) Used to indicate hesitation.

Well–you know I feel shy.

(*e*) Used after a quotation.

Child is the father of man–Wordsworth.

8. **Parentheses (Brackets)( )**

(*a*) Used to separate an afterthought or aside from a sentence.

All members of Raj's family (excluding his youngest son) are well placed.

(*b*) Used to give sharp dramatic contrast to the portion enclosed.

For three long years (though he never knew it) Rema worshipped him.

(*c*) Used to explain exact meaning of abbreviations.

I know the S.I.(Sub Inspector of Police) of this area.

He is an ornithologist. (Lover of birds)

Square Brackets[ ]

The straight bracket/square brackets are used to indicate that a writer is adding something to clarify, correct or amplify something that he has already written.

They are, sometimes, used within the round brackets.

Mohan has a special taste for fiction (fiction [novels, short stories etc.] was the subject of his study).

9. **Capital Letters:**

Capital letters are used

(*a*) at the beginning of the first word of every new sentence.

He is a man. Who is that? I am Raju. How beautiful.

(*b*) to start each line of a poem.

(*c*) to begin all proper nouns and the adjectives derived from the respective proper nouns.

India – Indian, Shakespeare – Shakespearian, Britain – British, Jew – Jewish.

(*d*) For names of people, places, mountains, oceans, rivers, peaks, lakes, islands, seas, parks, planets.

(*e*) For nations and their adjectives showing nationality.

America – Americans, Egypt – Egyptians.

(*f*) For names of days, months, festivals, historical events, important documents and eras.

Monday, Friday, May, Onam, Independence Day, French Revolution, Romantic period, the Middle Ages, Magna Carta.

(*g*) For names of books, plays, essays, poems, articles (published), work of art, magazines, newspapers, buildings, streets, organizations etc.

The Ramayana, The Taj Mahal, The Red Fort, The Indian Express, Paradise Lost, The Tempest, King Lear, The India Today, Lamb's Essays, Daffodils, M.G.Road, Motilal Street, Krishi Bhavan, Vidhan Sabha.

(*h*) First letters of titles of people and names of things.

Padma Bhushan, Bharat Ratna, The President of India, The Golden Fleece, the Eternal City, The White Continent, The Chief Minister of Kerala, Asoka the Great, His Majesty.

(*i*) For all words and pronouns related to God.

God, Him, Lord, Allah, Almighty, Shiva.

(*j*) To write the pronoun'I' and the interjection 'O'.

O Lord, save me! I 'm dying.

(*k*) For academic degrees and abbreviations.

M.A., Ph.D., M.Phil., MBBS., B.Sc., UNESCO , M.P. etc.

(*l*) For the first and last words of salutations and greetings in a letter.

Dear Sir, My dear Father, Hai! Raj, My dear Madam.

(*m*) Used only for the first letter of the first word of the complimentary close (subscription) at the end of a letter.

Yours faithfully, Yours obediently.

(*n*) For names of firms or trade names.

The Hindustan Latex, Amul, Kissan, HMT.

(*o*) For names of geographical directions.

North, South, East, West.

(*p*) Names of religions.

Hinduism, Buddhism, Islam.

(*q*) For names of political parties.

Indian National Congress, Bharathiya Janta Party, Communist Party of India, Janta Dal.

(*r*) For titles of honours.

Sir, Reverend, Mahatma.

(*s*) To begin a quotation or a direct speech.

Teacher said, "Let's forgive him."

10. **Apostrophe (')**

Apostrophe is used

(*i*) with names of countries, ships, boats etc.

India's pride, Titanic's crew.

(*ii*) for phrases of time.

Today's timetable, yesterday's work, five- week's time,

Twelve- minute's walk.

(*iii*) in compound words and phrases 's is added to the last word.

My brother -in-law's house.(singular)

My brothers - in -law's house.(plural)

The American President's visit.

(*iv*) to denote the omission of a letter from words.

I'll , I'm , You 're, You've , haven't , Let's.

(*v*) to write plural forms of letters and figures.

Mind your p's and q's. Three 5's make fifteen.

in the late 80's after 30's

Count the number of 3's and 8's in the figures.

11. **Quotation Marks /Inverted Commas ["........"'.........']**

(*a*) Used to give exactly the words spoken by a person.

Teacher said, "You get out."

"Yes", said the boy, "I shall go there."

"Oh God!" the lady exclaimed.

However lengthy the quotation is, it should be strictly followed that, the quotation marks are to be used at the beginning of the first sentence and at the end of the last.

All other punctuations like the exclamation mark, comma, full stop etc, should come within the quotation marks.

Double inverted commas are used to quote proverbs and words of celebrated men.

He said, "Time and tide wait for no man."

I remember the saying, "Barking dogs seldom bite."

Single Inverted commas are used to enclose a quotation within a quotation.

Rema said, " I can never forget the person who said 'Child is the Father of man' ."

12. **Hyphen (-)**

Hyphen is shorter than the dash in length.While the dash indicates a break-off , the hyphen acts as a link.

(*a*) Used to join two or more words to form the compound words.

Father-in-law, day-break, self-reliant, gold-plated, simple-minded, tooth-brush, passer-by, happy-go-lucky man, self-addressed envelope, get-together, black-out, kick-off, now-a-days.

(*b*) Used to connect parts of a word divided at the end of a line for want of space. (Words should be broken only at the end of syllables. Monosyllables are not divided.)

(*c*) Used in compound numbers and in fractions.

twenty-five rupees, three-fourths, seventy-six per cent.

(*d*) Used between a stressed prefix before a proper noun and with prefixes like Ex-, Pro-, Vice-, Anti- etc.

Pre-degree, Ex-MLA, Anti-clockwise, Vice-President.

(*e*) Used after syllables Co and Pre where a vowel follows.

Co-operation, Pre-eminent, Co-ordinate.

13. **Oblique(/)**

(*a*) Used to represent abbreviations .

A/c (account), C/o (care of), S/o (son of), D/o (daughter of).

(*b*) Used to indicate two or more possibilities.

The boy/s who comes/come late will be punished.

He/She should do his/her duty properly.

Chapter 19 QUESTION TAGS OR TAG QUESTIONS

Question Tags or Tag Questions are forms of questions used in conversation. These are like Yes–or–No questions. We usually make statements in our conversation and ask for confirmation (agreement) from the listener. This makes conversation interesting, lively and personal.

For Example:

It is raining , isn't it ?

You have seen him, haven't you?

The snake hadn't disappeared, had it?

These shortened forms of questions added to the end of statements to give them added force are called 'Question Tags' or 'Tag Questions'. The subject of a Question Tag is always a pronoun and never a noun.

Punctuations for a Question tag

A comma (,) is put after the statement and the tag begins with a small letter. The negative tag should take the ' n't ' form of ' not '. A question mark is essential after the tag. The general pattern is given below:

Statement, verb (positive/negative) + pronoun ?

For Example:

Rahim is a doctor, isn't he?

Rules:

1. If the given statement is positive (affirmative) the question tag should be negative.

If the given statement is negative, the question tag should be positive (affirmative). That is,

Negative sentence >>> Positive tag.

Positive sentence >>> Negative tag.

2. Sentences with *no, not, never, n't* are negative. Words like none, nobody, seldom, scarcely, hardly, hardly any, rarely, few, little are semi-negative and take positive tag. But, *a few* and *a little* are positive and always take negative question tags. Note carefully the question tags in the following examples.

   For Example:

   Everyone was silent, weren't they?
   None of us kept quiet, did we?
   Few people knew the answer, did they?
   It has made little progress, has it?
   I have few friends, have I?
   I could scarcely see him, could I?
   She seldom goes out, does she?
   No one is ready to go, are they?

3. The auxiliary verb of the statement should be repeated in the question tag.

   For Example:

   She can do it, can't she?
   She won't attend the function, will she?

But, in some cases the statements appear without the auxiliary verbs.

In such cases *do, does, did* should be used in the question tags depending on the tense and number of the verb.

For Example:

She writes neatly, doesn't she?	(simple present–singular verb)
You eat fast, don't you?	(simple present–plural verb)
He cried loudly, didn't he?	(simple past)
I gave it, didn't I?	(simple past)
They worked well, didn't they?	(simple past)

Note: In the past tense, the number of subject never matters. We can always use 'did'. But in the simple present tense *plural subjects* take 'do' and *singular subjects* take 'does' in the question tags.

4. The subject of a question tag will be the subject of the statement.

   (*a*) If a personal pronoun is the subject of a statement, then the same personal pronoun is repeated as the subject of the tag.

   He went out, didn't he?

   (*b*) If a noun is the subject then the tag takes *he, she, it* or *they*.

   Ram and Rahim were absent today, weren't they?
   India is a great country, isn't it?
   She is a clever girl, isn't she?

But, if 'one', the generalizing pronoun, is the subject then 'one' alone should be used in the question tag.

One must do one's duty, mustn't one?

5. Subjects like *anybody, somebody, someone, everybody* and *everyone* form tags with the pronoun 'they'.

   Somebody knocked at the door, didn't they?

   Everyone (Everybody) was happy, weren't they?

   Someone came to see me, didn't they?

6. Negative words like nothing and nobody take positive tags.

   Nothing can happen to them, can it?

   Nobody shall stop him, shall they?

Note: The pronoun 'it' is used for nothing and 'they' for nobody. 'This' and 'that' take 'it' in the tag. But, 'there' remains unchanged.

That is Seeta, isn't it?

That is not Seeta, is it?

There is something in it, isn't there?

7. Question tag for 'used to' is 'didn't.'

   I used to visit him daily, didn't I?

8. *None, most, and some* if followed by *us, them, you* or *a plural noun* the question tags take *we, they, you or they* respectively.

   Note: 'None' being negative takes a positive tag while 'some' being positive takes a negative tag.

   For Example:

   None of us have gone there, have we?

   Some of us have gone there, haven't we?

   None of the teachers attended the meeting, have they? (plural noun)

   Some of the teachers attended the meeting, haven't they? (")

   Most of the teachers attended the meeting, didn't they? (")

9. (*a*) When simple requests are made irrespective of their being positive or negative the tag is always 'will you'.

   Please don't shout, will you?

   Please go away, will you?

   (Here the subject 'you' is understood.)

   (*b*) When they (requests) are invitations or suggestions the tag can either be 'will you' or ' won't you '.

   Go through this book, will you /won't you?

But, when the suggestions are to be obeyed or strictly followed, 'won't you' is used. It shows urgency.

Be careful when you cross the road, *won't you*?

Remember to take the medicine, *won't you*?

(*c*) When they are orders or expressing impatience we use 'can't you?'

Keep quiet, *can't you*?

Stand up, *can't you*?

Don't make a noise, can you?

10. Suggestions beginning with 'Let's (Let us)' take the question tag 'shall we'.

'Let's go to the seashore, shall we?

11. The question tag for the positive statement 'I am…' is 'aren't I?' .

But when the statement is negative it is 'am I?'.

I am right, *aren't I*? (not: amn't I)

I' m not right, *am I*?

12. Use of 'had better' and 'would rather'.

You *had better* go to his office, hadn't you?

Ram *would rather* remain at home than go for a movie, wouldn't he?

13. Neither…….. nor, either….or etc.

Neither Ram *nor* Rahim has seen it, have they?

Either Ram *or* Rahim has seen it, haven't they?

14. 'Used to' takes didn't as the question tag.

You *used* to come to our house, didn't you?

15. When *need* and *dare* are used in a positive sense they are like ordinary verbs. Then they take negative tags.

For Example:

You need to talk to him, don't you?

He dares to come before me, doesn't he?

Subjects and how they change

He/She/They	_	He/She/They
The boy	_	He
The girl	_	She
Noun (singular)	_	He/ She
Noun (plural)	_	They
Singular (inanimate)	_	It
Plural (inanimate)	_	They

Everyone	-	They
Everybody	-	They
None of us/Some of us	-	We
None of you/Some of you	-	You
None of the students	-	They
Let us	-	We
One	-	One

Negative Forms of Auxiliaries

is	-	isn't
are	-	aren't
am	-	aren't (not, amn't)
was	-	wasn't (was not)
were	-	weren't (were not)
has	-	hasn't (has not)
have	-	haven't (have not)
had	-	hadn't (had not)
do	-	don't (do not)
does	-	doesn't (does not)
did	-	didn't (did not)
can	-	can't (can not)
could	-	couldn't (could not)
will	-	won't (will not)
would	-	wouldn't (would not)
may	-	mayn't (may not)
might	-	mightn't (might not)
shall	-	shan't (shall not)
should	-	shouldn't (should not)
must	-	mustn't (must not)
need	-	needn't (need not)
dare	-	daren't (dare not)
used	-	didn't (did not)
ought	-	oughtn't (ought not)

EXAMPLES

1. He is here, isn't he?
2. He is not here, is he?
3. You will come, won't you?
4. You won't tell him, will you?
5. He came yesterday, didn't he?
6. He didn't go, did he?
7. You need to come earlier, don't you?
8. I am, aren't I?
9. I used to go, didn't I?
10. He lives in London, doesn't he?
11. Stop that noise, will you?
12. Let us go for a walk, shall we?
13. Let me tell him, shall I?
14. You had better say, hadn't you?
15. You would rather go, wouldn't you?
16. Everybody cannot do it, can they?
17. Pass me the book, will you?
18. Have another cup of tea, won't you?
19. None of the workers came for work, did they?
20. Some of us are learning, aren't we?
21. Some of us wanted to go , didn't we?
22. We must not be late, must we?
23. Be careful when you cross the road, won't you?
24. Remember to take the book , won't you?
25. She is ill, isn't she?
26. She won't be late, will she?
27. The man does not drink tea, does he?
28. He ought to have appeared for the post, oughtn't he?
29. You need another cup of tea, don't you?
30. They visited his uncle last month, didn't they?

EXERCISE

Add question tags to the following:

1. You are tired after the journey, ...
2. I am a student, ...
3. You are a doctor, ...
4. We know the way, ...
5. He can sing, ...
6. They adopted the child, ...
7. A sincere prayer may work wonders, ...
8. Let us begin the work, ...
9. He didn't ask for your help, ...
10. You never thought of this before, ...
11. You have met him already, ...
12. Remani must be here, ...
13. His son qualified as a lawyer, ...
14. You haven't got a car, ...
15. They came by car, ...
16. Tom won't be late, ...
17. They don't like us, ...
18. Ann will be here soon, ...
19. Tom should pass his exam, ...
20. Let's go out for a walk, ...
21. Open the door, ...
22. Don't be late, ...
23. I 'm late, ...
24. Tom was very angry, ...
25. You weren't listening, ...

26. You have got a camera, ...
27. There are a lot of people here, ...
28. I am too fast, ...
29. Listen, ...
30. I shouldn't have got angry, ...
31. Don't drop it, ...
32. They had to go home, ...
33. He'd never seen you before, ...
34. It's very expensive, ...
35. Ann's on a holiday, ...
36. He won't mind if I go early, ...
37. You haven't got a cigarette, ...
38. Tom should pass the exam ......
39. This chair is new , ...
40. The apples are ripe , ...
41. Those girls talk German, ...
42. The men have gone, ...
43. You should be rude, ...
44. The peons need not wait, ...
45. Your friends did not like it, ...
46. They do not often see films, ...
47. Ramu hasn't got a car, ...
48. Neither she nor her mother had done it, ...
49. Everyone attended the meeting, ...

Chapter 20 COMPREHENSION

Comprehension means the ability to understand the content especially of a given passage. This ability is tested by setting questions on a passage and asking the students to answer these questions.

The following hints on comprehension may be borne in mind:

1. Read the passage carefully and patiently to get the general idea of the passage.
2. Read it a second or third time in order to get at the meaning of the difficult words, phrases and expressions.
3. Now read the questions and understand them thoroughly before start answering them.
4. The answers should neither be too long nor too short – nothing more, nothing less.
5. Be careful not to add any new ideas of your own unless asked to comment.
6. Use simple, correct, forceful language of your own. The answers should be in complete sentences unless asked to write single words or phrases.
7. When asked to explain some words, phrases or expressions the one should be exact and to the point.
8. Revise the answers to see that they are complete and exact.
   Correct all mistakes including spelling, grammar and punctuation.
9. The heading, if asked to give one, should be expressive but not too long.
   It should refer to the central theme of the passage.

20.1 COMPREHENSION—EXERCISE

Write a précis on the following passage reducing it to a third of its length. Give a suitable title.

Answer the questions given below.

PASSAGES

Read the following passage:

1. A great part of Arabia is a desert. Here, there is nothing but sand and rock. The sand is so hot that you cannot walk over with your bare feet in the day time. Here and there in the desert are springs of water that come from deep under the ground – so deep that the sun cannot dry them up. These springs are few and far apart, but wherever there is one, green grass very soon covers the ground all around it. Soon fig trees and palm trees grow tall and graceful, making cool, shady place around the spring. Such a place is called an oasis.

The Arabs who are not in the cities live in the desert all the year round. They live in tents that can be put up and taken down very easily and quickly, so that they can move from one oasis to another, seeking grass and water for their sheep, goats, camels and horse. These desert Arabs eat ripe sweet figs, and also the dates that grow on the palm trees; they dry them too and use them as food all the year around.

These Arabs have the finest horses in the world. An Arab is very proud of his riding horse, and loves him as much as he loves his wife and children. He never puts heavy loads upon his horse, and often lets him stay in the tent with his family.

(Answer the following questions based on the above passage, each in not more than two sentences.)

1. How does an Arab treat his horse ?
2. What do the nomadic Arabs eat ?
3. What sort of place is Arabia ?
4. What sort of life do the Arabs lead ?
5. What is an oasis ?

Read the following passage:

2. Nations , like individuals, derive support and strength from the feeling that they belong to an illustrious race, that they are the heirs of their greatness, and ought to be perpetuators of their glory. It is of momentous importance that a nation should have a great past to look back upon. It steadies the life of the present, elevates and upholds it, and lightness and lifts it up, by the memory of the great deeds , the noble sufferings, and the valorous achievements of the men of old.

The life of nations, as of men, is a great treasury of experience, which wisely used, issues in social progress and improvement; or misused, issues in dreams , delusions and failure. Like men, nations are purified and strengthened by trials . Some of the most glorious chapters in their history are those containing the record of sufferings by means of which their character has been developed . Love of liberty and patriotic feeling may have done much, but trial and suffering nobly borne have done more than all.

(Answer the following questions based on the passage above, each in not more than two sentences.)

1. What duty is cast on a nation with a glorious past?
2. How is it important for a nation to have a great past?
3. What things in the past of nation help the life in the present?
4. How does a nation gain by wise use of its experience during the ages past?
5. What does a nation gain from trial and suffering?

Read the following passage:

3. There are in the world some 3,000 languages and dialects. This did not matter in the Middle ages, when communication between different parts of the globe was slow and difficult and when in Europe at least all educated men spoke Latin. Things have changed completely in our time. While few can now speak Latin, the telegraph and radio have made it possible to talk directly between continents, and a journey which might have then taken several weary months can now be achieved in a few hours by air.

It is not surprising, then, that, man have increasingly felt the need for a common language, and during the last century , various solutions of the problem have been put forward. The first of these was the creation of a completely artificial tongue, quite unconnected with any existing language. Although such a tongue must be difficult for people to learn, it at least had the advantage that everybody started on an equal footing.

The second solution was the invention of a synthetic language based on natural language, but without their numerous irregularities. Such languages as Esperanto, Volapuk, and Interlingua belong to this category and, since they are related to existing languages, are easier to learn for European speakers. The two remaining solutions to the problem of international language are either to adopt as a world auxiliary some existing language already spoken by a large number of people or peoples (such languages as French, Spanish or Russian would be suitable), or to create a simplified version of one of these languages , in which the vocabulary and grammatical forms would be reduced to a minimum. An example of this is "Basic English".

(Answer the following questions based on the passage above, each in not more than two sentences.)

1. What special advantage have the European speakers if Esperanto is made the common language?
2. What has caused the recent demand for a common language?
3. Why was the need for an international language not felt in the Middle Ages?
4. What is "Basic English" ?
5. What advantage does a completely artificial language have?

Read the following passage:

4. Nowadays life in cities has become dangerous for various reasons. First of all, it is dangerous to walk about in cities because always various kinds of vehicles keep moving at terrific speed. The smoke released by them poisons the atmosphere; consequently , it is dangerous to breath in this polluted air. The food that we get in cities also lack in purity. Nowadays everything is grown with chemical fertilizers which may cause danger to the consumers to fruits, vegetables and other things grown. Thus we do not get anything that is absolutely pure. The water also is sometimes contaminated. Hence, it is better to get out of cities at least for somedays every month; and to eat food, which is not contaminated; and to breath in fresh air which conduces to excellent health.

(Answer the following questions based on the passage above, each in not more than two sentences.)

1. Why have cities become dangerous these days?
2. What causes air pollution?
3. What makes the food in cities impure?
4. What does the passage suggest to city dwellers?
5. What are the advantages of going out of cities?

Read the following passage:

5. Our present cities are growing every year. This growth will almost certainly continue, and the cities of the future will be much bigger and far more complicated than those of today. Many problems will arise which will have to be solved. The solutions will undoubtedly change the face of the city and the life of its inhabitants. It is quite possible that the future city will have no traffic at all . H.G. Wells , in his book "The Sleeper Awakes", tells of man who slept for hundreds of years, and awoke to a very different world from that which he knew before. In the streets of that future London, there were no animals, carriages, motor-cars or tram-cars. The city was provided with moving roads, and therefore no longer needed the vehicles to which we are accustomed. One side of the road travelled in one direction; that his destination. He did not need to wait for a tram or a bus.

The moving way was always at his service, always moving silently along, always ready to take him to his destination. That city of the future had no traffic problems.

(Answer the following questions based on the passage above, each in no more than two sentences.)

1. How will the cities of the future appear?
2. What will be quite unique about the future city?
3. What did the sleeper in Wells' book find when he woke up?

4. How would the traffic problems of the future London be solved?
5. Use the words "undoubtedly" and "accustomed" in sentences of your own.
6. Why does the author say that the cities of the future will be much bigger than that of today?

Read the following passage:

6. It is physically impossible for a well- educated , intellectual or brave man to make money, the chief object of his thoughts, just as it is for him to make his dinner the principal object of them. All healthy people like the dinner, but their dinner is not the main object of their lives. So all healthy minded people like making money – ought to like it and enjoy the sensation of winning it; it is something better than money. A good soldier for instance, mainly wishes to do his fighting well. He is glad of his pay – very properly so, and justly grumbles when you keep him ten years without it – still, his main notion of life is to win battles, not to be paid for winning them. So of clergymen. The clergy man's object is essentially baptize and preach, not to be paid for preaching. So of doctors. They like fees no doubt , ought to like them; yet if they are brave and well-educated, the entire object of their lives is not fees. They, on the whole, desire to cure the sick; and if they are good doctors, and the choice were fairly put to them would rather cure their patient and other side moved the opposite way. Anyone who wanted to go to another part of the city stepped on the moving "way" and sat on one of the seats until he arrived lose their fee than kill him and get it. And so with all the other brave and rightly trained men; their work is first, their fee second – very important always, but still second.

(Answer the following questions based on the passages above, each in not more than two sentences.)

1. What is the chief object of life of a well educated man?
2. Who are the people mentioned in the above passage?
3. What does a good doctor prefer to do?
4. Who is clergy man and what is his object of life?
5. What do we learn from the above passage?

Read the following passage:

7. I stand before you as an individual being tried for certain offences against the state. But I am something more than an individual also. I too, a symbol of the present moment, a symbol Indian nationalism, resolved to break away form the British empire and achieve the independence of India. It is not me that you are seeking to judge or condemn but rather the hundreds of millions of the people of India and that is a large task even for a proud empire. Perhaps it may be that, though I am standing before you on my trial, it is the British Empire itself which is on trial before the war of the world. There are more powerful forces at work in the world than courts of law, there are elemental argues for freedom and food and security which are moving vast masses of the people and history is being moulded by them. The future record of this history might well say that in the hour of supreme trial the government of Britain failed because they could not adapt themselves to the changing world. (Pandit Nehru)

(Answer the following questions based on the passage above, each in not more than two sentences.)

1. Who is being tried here?
2. Why does he claim that he is more than an individual?
3. What , according to Nehru, are more powerful in the world today than courts of law?
4. What does the Indian national Movement stand for?
5. The future recorder of the history might say that the government of Britain failed. Why?

Read the following passage:

8. The position that Indian women occupy today is very largely the result of a little more than a century of earnest endeavour on the part of the social reformers, educationalist and political leaders; for it was the twentieth century that really ushered in an era of dynamic change and new concepts which fundamentally affected the status of woman, giving it a fresh dignity and importance. In India because of her political subjection at the time progressive movements had a political tinge and were the reflections of the people's determination to throw off all shackles of bondage. The women's movement was no exception to the rule. Therefore it was only when India gained political freedom and emerged as an independent sovereign republic that women truly came into their own as equal partners with men. The principle of equity was incorporated in the Objective Resolution of Free India in 1947 and was later elaborated in the Constitution of the India Republic.

(Answer the following questions based on the passage above, each in not more than two sentences.)

1. Whose earnest efforts have been responsible for the present position of Indian women ?
2. What changes in the women's status were introduced in the twentieth century?
3. What was the common feature of all progressive movements in India before independence?
4. How did the achievement of independence affect the status of women in India?
5. Use the words "endeavour" and "ushered" in sentences of your own.

Read the following passage:

9. Energy utilization has become the modern key to human progress. Nations show wide variation in their patterns of energy consumption and standard of living, as of Europe, the United States, Japan, Hong Kong and Singapore, for example have much greater per capita energy consumption than the agricultural nations of India, Bangladesh, Indonesia and Ethiopia, and they also have a higher standard of living in terms of housing, education, medical care, labour saving machines, leisure time and recreations opportunities. It cannot mean that they have a higher quality of living for this is a more subjective matter. Standard of living is an economic term, whereas quality of life is a value judgement. The urban dweller in an industrial nation pays for his physical comfort, labour saving devices and entertainment by his daily contact with crowding, noise, crime, pollution and separation from nature. Hence, his high standard of living may or may not involve a higher quality of life, depending on his own values and priorities.

(Answer the following questions based on the passage above, each in not more than two sentences.)

1. State the relationship between energy consumption and standard of living.
2. What does a higher standard of living imply?
3. What essentially is the difference between "Standard of living" and quality of life ?
4. What does the writer mean when he says that an urban dweller in an industrial nation pays for his physical comforts?
5. Bring out the central idea in the passage.

Read the following passage:

10. We sometimes think it would be very nice to have to work to do. How we envy rich people who do not have to work for their living but can do just what they please all the year round; yet when we feel like this, we make a mistake . Sometimes rich people are not as happy as we think they are, because they are tired of having nothing to do. Most of us are happy when we have regular work to do for our living, especially if the work is what we like to do. The first thing work does is give us happiness. Then work gives us self-respect. The idler, however rich he is , lives on the work of others. He is like the beggar in the street who takes money of the others who have had to toil for it. Such people do not live independently, and ought to feel ashamed of themselves. But the honest worker who earns his living by useful toil can hold up his head and respect himself. Lastly regular work helps to build up character. It teaches us such good habits as punctuality, as a rule, develops the best character.

(Answer the following questions based on the passage above, each in not more than two sentences.)

1. When are most of us happy?
2. What are the advantage of work?
3. In what way is the idler like the beggar in the streets?
4. How does regular work build up character?
5. Suggest a suitable title for the passage.

Read the following passage:

11. Democracy in the modern age requires planned central direction as well as decentralization of political and economic power. It should ensure safety of the state efficient production and cultural progress of the community as a whole. The smallest territorial unit should be able to have effective control over its corporate life by means of a popularly elected panchayat. In so far as it is possible, national and regional economic self sufficiency in the essential of life should be aimed at. In the case of industries, which in their nature have to be run on the large scale and on centralized basis, they should belong to the community, and they should be so organized that workers become not only co-sharers in the projects but are also increasingly associated with the management and administration of industry. Land, with its mineral resources, and all other means of project as well as distribution and exchange must belong to and be regulated by community in its own interest. Our aim should be to evolve an economic structure which yield maximum production without the creation of private monopolies and concentration can provide an alternative to the project making economy of private capitalism and the regimentation of a totalitarian stage.

(Answer the following questions based on the passage above, each in not more than two sentences.)

1. How can economic self sufficiency be achieved?
2. What should control corporate life?
3. What is required in the present democracy?
4. Which type of economic structure should be aimed at?
5. How should industries be organized?

Read the following passage:

12. The art of living deserves a place among the fine Arts. It is the art extracting from life its highest enjoyments and through it of reaching its height results. It finds delight in the performance of common duties, faithfully and honourably fulfilled. Take two men of equal means – one of whom knows the Art of Living and the other who does not. The one has seeing eye and intelligent mind. Nature is ever new to him, and full of beauty. He can live in the present, rehearse the past, or anticipate the glory of the future. His hand never tired of charity , his mind is never weary of sensitivity. His greatest monument is the good deeds he has done, and the beneficent example he has set before his fellow creatures. The other has little pleasure in life. Money has done everything that it could for him. Yet he feels life to be vacant and cheerless, "pleasure" soon tire him and he grows weary day by day. There is nothing left for him to relish in old age. Though he does not enjoy life. Yet he is terrified to leave it. Life has been a failure , for he has not known the Art of living.

(Answer the following questions based on the passage above, each in not more than two sentences.)

1. What is the art of living?
2. What does the man who knows the art of living find joy in?
3. What is the greatest monument of the man who knows the art of living?
4. What is the experience of the man who does not know the art of living?
5. What is the central idea of the passage?

Read the following passage:

13. The effect produced on the mind by travelling depends entirely on the mind of the traveller and the way in which he conducts himself. The chief idea of one very common type of traveller is to see as many objects of interest as he possibly can. If he can only, after his return home, say that he has seen such and such a temple, castle, picture gallery, or museum, he is perfectly satisfied. Therefore when he arrives at famous city, he rushes through it so that he may get over as quickly as possible, the task of seeing its principal sights, enter them by name in his note book as visited or in his own phraseology 'done' and then hurry on to another city which he treats in the same unceremonious way.

Far different is the effect of travel upon those who leave their native country with minds prepared by culture, to feel intelligent admiration for all the beauties of nature and art to be founding foreign lands. Their object is not to see much, but to see well. They find it more profitable and delightful to settle down for a week or stop at centers of great historical and artistic interest or of remarkable natural beauty, than to pay short visits to all the principal cities that they pass by. In this way, they gain refreshment and rest for their minds, intellectual joy, artistic delight and increased knowledge of the world and its inhabitants.

(Answer the following questions based on the passage above, each in not more than two sentences.)

1. What is the main idea of the common type of traveller?
2. How does the common type of traveller behave when he arrives at a famous city?
3. How does the genuine traveller arrive in foreign lands?
4. What are the benefits that the genuine traveller derive from travelling?

5. What is the chief difference between the genuine traveller and the common type of traveller?

Read the following passage:

14. One of the defects of our civilization is that it does not know what to do with its knowledge. Science has given us powers fit for the gods, yet we use them like small children. This fact is evident in our daily lives. For example, we do not know how to manage our machines. Machines were made to be man's servants; yet he has grown so dependent on them that they are in a fair way to become his masters. Already most men spend most of their lives looking after and waiting upon machines. And the machines are very stern masters. They must be fed with coal, and petrol to drink and oil to wash with, and they must be kept at the right temperature. And if they do not get their meals when they expect them, they grow sulky and refuse to work, or burst with rage, and blow up and spread ruin and destruction all round them. So we have to wait upon them and do all that we can to keep them in good temper. Already we find it difficult to work or play without the machines, and a time may come when they rule us altogether, just as we rule the animals.

(Answer the questions based on the passage given above, each in not more than two sentences.)

1. What is the great defect of our civilization?
2. What example does the passage offer to prove that man is unfit for scientific knowledge?
3. In what way are machines stern masters?
4. How does man employ the time and energy that machines have given him?
5. What is the ideal way to use the time and energy that machines have given man?

Read the following passage:

15. Students should devote the whole of their vacation to village service. To this end, instead of taking their walks along beaten paths, they should walk to the villages within easy reach of their institutions as study the conditions of the village folk and befriend them. This habit will bring them in contact with the villagers when the students actually go to stay in their midst, will by reason of the previous occasional contact, receive them as friends rather than as strangers to be looked upon with suspicion. During the long vacation the students will stay in the villages and offer to conduct classes for adults and to teach the rules of sanitation to the villagers and to attend to the ordinary cases of illness. They will also introduce the spinning wheel amongst them and teach them the use of every rare minute. In order that this may be done, the students and teachers will have to revise their ideas of the uses of vacation. Often thoughtless teachers prescribe lessons to be done during the vacation. This is a vicious habit. Vacation is just the period when students' mind should be free from routine work and be left free for self-help and original development. The village work I have mentioned is easily the best form of recreation and light instruction. It is obviously the best preparation for dedication to exclusive village service after finishing studies.

(Answer the following questions based on the passage given above, each in not more than two sentences.)

1. What is the method suggested for building devotion to village work?
2. What should students do during the vacation?
3. What is the vicious habit referred to?
4. What is the writer's view of vacations?
5. Suggest a title for the passage?

Read the following passage:

16. The cinema is an outstanding wonder of the modern age. It is not only a means of entertainment, but it is also in many ways an education in itself. The cinema is a very valuable teaching aid. Historical film help the teacher of history. A couple of hours spent in the company of historical characters dressed in the costumes of the period can teach us far more than we can learn from a whole week's study of a history book.

Science can be taught very effectively through films. There are educational film companies which devote the time to the filming of the habits and customs of animals , insects, fish, germs and numerous other branches of scientific life. We can see the hatching of the eggs of fish and the gradual development into large fish, we can watch the increasing activity of many kinds of germs and their effect on water, milk or blood. We can watch the opening and closing of flowers and leaves, and the growth of grass and weeds. All these actions and movements are greatly magnified on the screen. Such pictures are intensely interesting and are a very great help in the cause of education.

(Answer the following questions based on the passage above, each in not more than two sentences.)

1. What are the two great advantages of the cinema?
2. How do historical films help the teacher of history?
3. How can science be taught very effectively?
4. What do educational film companies do?
5. How are the actions and movements of animals and insects shown on the screen?

Chapter 21 PRECIS-WRITING

Precis (pronounced *pressee*) comes from the word 'precise' which means abstract or summary. A good précis is a reproduction of a piece of writing in a concise form, incorporating all the main ideas contained in the original passage. It is written in a minimum number of words and in such way that the chain of thought is not broken. (*i.e.*, the order of ideas must be strictly followed.)

A précis should be clear and brief; it should be easily understood.

Precis writing demands three things : Concentration, Comprehension and Condensation.

How to Write a Good Précis:

1. Keep in mind that the length of a précis should be approximately one third of the original passage.
2. Read the passage carefully and find out what it is about. If required read it several times till you understand the meaning clearly.
3. Find out the essential points and underline them. Make notes if needed. Unimportant points can be shortened considerably or left out. Repetitions should be omitted.
4. Count the number of words in the original passage. One-third of that number should be the length of the desired précis.
5. Prepare a rough draft. Avoid, as far as possible, words from the original text.
6. Revise the draft. Make a fair copy. Without missing any point or changing the meaning cut it short to the required length. It should be a single unified whole.
7. Count the number of words in the precis and write it in brackets on the right hand side at the end of the précis.
8. Give a suitable title to your précis.

Points to Remember:

1. Do not attempt to reduce the given passage to a précis of one-third by deleting a few words or phrases here and there from the original passage.
2. Nothing should be added from outside – no examples or comments. Never bring in your own ideas into the précis. Try to use one-word substitutes for phrases and clauses.
3. Omit quotations, proverbs, similes, poetic expressions, anecdotes , if any.
4. Direct speech should be changed into Indirect speech.
5. Write in your own words.
6. Use simple and clear language.

21.1 SPECIMEN

Democracy in the modern age requires planned central direction as well as decentralization of political and economic power. It should ensure safety of the state, efficient production and cultural progress of the community as a whole. The smallest territorial unit should be able to have effective control over its corporate life by means of a popularly elected panchayat. In so far as it is possible, national and regional economic self- sufficiency in the essentials of life should be aimed at.In the case of industries, which in their nature have to be run on the large scale and on centralized basis, they should belong to the community and they should be so organized that workers become not only co-sharers in the projects but are also increasingly associated with the management and administration of industry. Land, with its mineral resources, and all other means of project as well as distribution and exchange must belong to and be regulated by community in its own interest. Our aim should be to evolve an economic structure which will yield a maximum production without the creation of private monopolies and concentration can provide an alternative to this. (291 words)

21.2 FUNCTIONS OF DEMOCRACY

In democracy there should be decentralization of political and economic power. The smallest unit in democracy should have elected panchayat for effective control. Democracy must aim at national and regional self-sufficiency. Large-scale industries should be run centrally with the employees' participation in the management.Land should be utilized by community in its own interest. Democracy should evolve an economic structure with maximum productivity, without creating monopolies. (66 words)

EXERCISE

1. The position that Indian women occupy today is a very largely the result of a little more than a century of earnest endeavour on the part of social reformers, educationalist and political leaders: for it was the twentieth century that really ushered in an era of dynamic change and new concepts which fundamentally affected the status of woman, giving it a fresh dignity and importance. In India, because of her political subjection at the time progressive movements had a political tinge and were the reflections of the people's determination to throw off all shackles of bondage. The women's movement was no exception to the rule. Therefore it was only when India gained political freedom and emerged as an independent sovereign republic that women truly came into their own as equal partners with men. The principle of equity was incorporated in the Objective Resolution of Free India in 1947 and was later elaborated in the Constitution of the Indian Republic. (158 words)
2. Energy utilization has become the modern key to human progress. Nations show wide variation in their patterns of energy consumption and standard of living, as the latter is conventionally defined. The industrial nations of Europe, the United States, Japan, Hong Kong and Singapore, for example have much greater capita energy consumption than the agricultural nations of India, Bangladesh, Indonesia and Ethiopia, and they also have a much higher per capital income. This implies that they have a higher standard of living in terms of housing, education, medical care, labour saving machines, leisure time and recreational opportunities. It cannot mean that they have a higher quality of living for this is a more subjective matter. Standard of living is an economic term, whereas quality of life is a value judgement. The urban dweller in an industrial nation pays for his physical comfort, labour saving devices and entertainment by his daily contact with crowding, noise, crime, pollution and separation from nature. Hence, his high standard of living may or may not involve a higher quality of life, depending on his own values and priorities. (180 words)
3. We sometimes think it would be very nice to have work to do. How we enrich people who do not have to work for their living but can do just what they please all the year round; yet when we feel like this, we make a mistake. Sometimes rich people are not as happy as we think they are, because they are tired of having nothing to do. Most of us are happy when we have regular work to do for our living, especially if the work is what we like to do. The first thing work does is give us happiness. When work gives us self-respect, the idler, however rich he is, lives on the work of others. He is like the beggar in the street who takes money of others who have had to toil for it. Such people do not live independently, and ought to feel ashamed of themselves. But the honest worker who earns his living by useful toil can hold up his head and respect himself. Lastly regular work helps to build up character. It teaches us such good habits as punctuality, as a rule develops the best character. (195 words)

4. The art of living deserves a place among the Fine Arts. It is the art extracting from life its highest enjoyments, and through it of reaching its highest results. It finds delight in the performance of common duties, faithfully and honourably fulfilled. Take two men of equal means – one of whom knows the Art of Living and the other who does not. The one who has seeing eye and intelligent mind, nature is ever new to him, and full of beauty. He can live in the present, rehearse the past, or anticipate the glory of the future. His hand is never tired of charity, his mind is never weary of sensitivity. His greatest monument is the good deeds he has done, and the beneficent example he has set before his fellow creatures. The other has little pleasure in life. Money has done everything that it could for him. Yet he feels life to be vacant and cheerless. "Pleasure" soon tires him and he grows weary day by day. There is nothing left for him to relish in old age. Though he does not enjoy life. Yet he is terrified to leave in it. Life has been a failure, for he has not known the Art of Living. (About 206 words)

5. We should face facts as they exist. We are multilingual, it is true, and a very poor country too. The fear of getting employment or not getting employment springs, out of the poverty of ours. But once we took courage in both our hands and began to work, poverty would vanish, and then those languages which have created a narrow regional spirit instead of being the curse that they seem to us today, would function as magnificent vehicles of expression for the rich variety of cultural patterns and modes of living and thought that we have developed. Let us hope that day dawns very soon. A regional language as the medium of instruction can facilitate the process of education. It helps the child to learn with ease and interest. But if it is thrust on an unwilling minority used to another allied language it can vitiate the very process of education. It is supposed to help and would create difficulties of a socio-political nature. (165 words)

6. The test of a great book is whether we want to read it only once or more than once. Any really great book we want to read the second time even more than we wanted to read it the first time; and every additional time that we read it we find new meanings and new beauties to it. A book that a person of education and good taste does not care to read more than once is very probably not worth much. But we cannot consider the judgement of a single individual infallible. The opinion that makes a book great must be the opinion of many. For even the greatest critics are apt to have certain dullness, certain in appreciations ....A man must be many sided to utter a trust-worthy estimate of many books. We may doubt the judgement of the single critic at times. But there is no doubt possible in regard to the judgement of generations. Even if we cannot perceive anything good in a book which has been admired and praised for hundreds of years, we may be sure that by trying, by studying it carefully, we shall at last be able to feel the reason of this admiration and praise. The best of all libraries for a poor man would be a library entirely composed of such great works only, books which have passed the test of time. (About 232 words)

7. If by some magic you could be granted one quick wish, perhaps you might wish to be popular. Being popular means being liked by a lot of people instead of just a few close

friends and that is a big wish. All the same you, too, can be well liked if you are willing to be on guard against the perils of popularity.

Let us consider some of these. You cannot be polite and friendly to some and not to others without the word getting around as to what kind of person you really are. When you are considering other people , take time to be friendly with the folks older than you are– your neighbours, teachers, parents and other relatives. If you treat them with respect, they are going to think of you as a likeable person, not as a good for nothing boy. And do not forget to be kind to the little kids too. Again you must think of others and consider their wishes. A majority wins, you know, and if you are out voted in the discussion of what to do and where to go, remember that being a good sport is another way to help your popularity. A good lover does not complain when the plans do not go his way. At the same time do not be afraid that you are risking your popularity to stand up for what you think is right. It takes courage to say so, and is appreciated. (245 words)

Chapter 22 INDIANISM

22.1 COMMON MISTAKES COMMITTED BY INDIAN SPEAKERS IN ENGLISH

The use of the English language by Indian speakers is influenced to some extent by the mother tongue or the vernacular of Indian speakers. This very often happens when they try to translate certain English usages into the mother tongue. An example of this is given below.

These slippers are too tight for my legs.

In most of the Indian languages leg also means 'foot'. But in the English language legs and feet are differently spoken of. Hence the sentence should be written; as,

These slippers are too tight for my feet.

The most commonly used Indianisms (I) (incorrect) and their corrections (C) are given below.

1. You are writing a book, isn't it? (I)
   You are writing a book, aren't you? (C)
2. He is a mischievous boy, isn't it?
   He is a mischievous boy, isn't he?
3. What all did he do?
   What did he do?
4. Who all were present?
   Who were present?
5. All the my family members.
   All the members of my family.
6. He is my cousin brother /sister.
   He is my cousin.
7. He told me everything in details.
   He told me everything in detail.

8. He gave me less than ten mangoes.
   He gave me fewer than ten mangoes.
9. He gave a speech.
   He made a speech.
10. The marriage was attended by my all friends.
    The marriage was attended by all my friends.
11. He has just taken his meals.
    He has just taken his meal.
12. I was standing at the back side.
    I was standing at the back.
13. He was keeping quiet.
    He was unemployed.
14. He availed of leave.
    He availed himself of leave.
15. There was pin-drop silence in the auditorium.
    There was complete silence in the auditorium.
16. He gave key to the clock.
    He wound up the clock.
17. He called me as a fool.
    He called me a fool.
18. He will do the needful.
    He will do what is necessary.
19. He resigned from his job.
    He resigned his job.
20. He died from small pox.
    He died of small pox.
21. He picked up quarrel with me.
    He picked quarrel with me.
22. He is a good fellow.
    He is a good man.
23. He is keeping good health.
    He is enjoying good health.
24. He had no alternative than death.
    He had no alternative to death.
25. They are not on talking terms.
    They are not on speaking terms.

26. There is no space in this hall.
    There is no room in this hall.
27. He bought a floor-carpet.
    He bought a carpet. (carpet = woollen or artificial fabric used as floor covering.)
28. He married with Sita.
    He married Sita.
29. We are pulling on.
    We are getting on.
30. It is the first time.
    This is the first time.
31. He is a family man.
    He is a man with a family.
32. The President convened an emergent meeting.
    The President convened an emergency meeting/ urgent meeting.
33. We were travelling in the female compartment.
    We were travelling in the women's compartment.
34. He has thoroughly enjoyed in the music.
    He has thoroughly enjoyed the music.
35. The details are as follow.
    The details are as follows.
36. I obliged him. There was no other go.
    I obliged him. There was no alternative.
37. He was sick for a few days.
    He was ill for a few days.
38. He has disposed off his land.
    He has disposed of his land.
39. He has wished his officer.
    He has wished good morning/good afternoon etc., to his officer.
40. He took leave from his father.
    He took leave of his father.
41. He died due to illness.
    He died owing to illness.
42. He is our mutual enemy.
    He is our common enemy.
43. He bought both shirts as well as pants.
    He bought both shirts and pants.
44. He ordered for three books.
    He ordered three books.

45. He refused the allegation.
    He denied the allegation.
46. He knows singing.
    He knows how to sing.
47. He discussed about the matter.
    He discussed the matter.
48. It is a word by word translation.
    It is word for word translation.
49. He did not honour his words.
    He did not honour his word.
50. He is using a red bed sheet.
    He is using a red sheet. (sheet= bed sheet)
51. I do not know what to do.
    I do not know what I am to do (or) what is to be done.
52. There are twenty female members in our club.
    There are twenty women members in our club.
53. I bought a match box.
    I bought matches.
54. The bucket has full of water.
    The bucket is full of water.
55. He read pages after pages.
    He read page after page.

    Or

    He read pages and pages.

Chapter 23 WORDS CONFUSED AND MISUSED

About and On

About is used to suggest something general while 'on' is used to suggest something serious and in-depth.

For example:

He wrote a book on the computer. (a serious book)

He wrote a book about the computer. (a general book)

Above and Over

Both these words can be used to describe a place or position higher than something.

For example:

Can you see the moon above/ over the tree.

They can also mean 'more than'. Above is used with reference to a minimum level or fixed point.

For example:

The temperature is ten degrees above zero.

The quality of this rice is above average.

This place is thousand feet above sea level.

'Over' is used with numbers, age, money and time.

For example:

The man worked over two hours.

He is over sixty.

The umbrella costs over hundred rupees.

According to

We use 'according to' to refer to something stated or reported by somebody or something.

For example:

According to history Asoka was a benevolent king.

According to the Minister the officer is corrupt.

But don't say: According to me he is a scoundrel. (wrong)

According to his opinion I am a total failure as a Police officer. (wrong)

Say: In my opinion he is a scoundrel.

In his opinion I am a total failure as a Police officer.

Note: When referring to one's opinion or view we must use only 'in my opinion' / 'in his opinion' and *not* ' according to me/according to his opinion'.

Along and through

He walked through the road. (wrong)

He walked along/across the road.

The word 'through'is related to 'inside' or 'in'.

He walked through the forest.

I went through the gate/tunnel.

Along is used with nouns related to a thin, long shape – like road, line, rivers etc.

Alternate and alternative

When two things happen one after the other regularly we say they are alternate.

For example:

He comes on alternate days.

This means he comes on one day and does not come the other day and this cycle is repeated.

If we use one thing instead of another, we say that we have an alternative. This word is usually followed by the preposition 'to'.

For example:

There is no alternative solution to this problem.

Nobody suggested an alternative to his opinion.

Note: Avoid saying " He has no alternative but to obey the orders". (wrong)

Say: He has no alternative to obeying the orders.(right)

(After the word 'to' the gerund 'obeying' is used because 'to' is a preposition.)

Arise and Rise

'Arise' is used to mean to happen or to occur. It is used usually with abstract nouns such as problems, discussions, difficulty, doubt etc.

For example:

A doubt has arisen about the genuineness of his identity.

A problem has arisen about its availability.

'Rise' is used to mean going higher–come up, go up, increase, etc.

For example:

The sun rises in the morning.

The prices are rising everyday.

During the rainy season water level in wells rises.

Arouse and Rouse: Both these words convey the same meaning.

'Arouse', a transitive verb, is usually used to mean 'to cause an emotion or feeling or attitude, to wake up somebody from sleep.

For example:

His behaviour aroused considerable suspicion in their minds.

The way she dressed has aroused sexual excitement in him.

The noise aroused him from sleep.

'Rouse' is used to mean 'to wake up' from sleep, 'to excite', etc.

It is a transitive verb.

For example:

She rouses her child in the morning.

His speech roused little interest.

He was roused to action by his leader's speech.

He can be easily roused. (excited)

At Onam and On Onam

We use 'at' to indicate the entire period of public holidays; as, at Christmas, at Onam, at New Year, at Easter etc.

For example:

I shall go to my native place at Onam.

We shall go to Trivandrum at Easter.

We use 'on' to indicate a day of the period of holidays.

For example:

I shall go to Sabarimala on Onam day.

We have good feast on Easter day.

We use 'in' to indicate Onam week, Onam month, Easter Week, etc.

For example:

There are various celebrations in Onam week.

The accident occurred in Easter month.

Accept / Except:

Accept – receive or take willingly.

He accepted a gift from us.

Except – exclude.

All have passed except Ramu.

Access/Accession:

Access – approach

He has access to the Minister.

Accession – the act of becoming a ruler.

His accession to the throne marked the beginning of an era of peace.

Adapt / Adept / Adopt:

Adapt – adjust

We must adapt ourselves to the situations.

Adept – skilled

He is an adept in the art of photography.

Adopt(v) – to choose, to take somebody else's child and become its legal parents.

He adopted a new course of action.

They adopted a girl child.

Accident / Incident:

Accident – disaster

He met with an accident.

Incident – event

Getting an award for excellence is an important incident in my career.

Advice (noun)/Advise (verb):

Advice (n) – He acted upon my advice.

Advise (v) – He advised me to take up higher studies.

Affect/Effect

Affect – influence

Frequent changes in climate will affect cultivation.

Effect – result

The medicine has good effect on the patient.

Allusion / Illusion:

Allusion – reference to

He made an allusion to Shakespeare's 'Othello'.

Illusion – apparition or imaginary appearances.

He saw a ghost coming towards him. It was only an illusion.

Altar/Alter:

Altar – a holy flat-topped stone block or table in a church or temple for the devotees to place their offerings to deity.

He placed the offerings on the altar.

Alter – change

He did not alter his plans.

Apposite/Opposite:

Apposite – appropriate or useful to the occasion.

His remarks on the occasion were not very apposite.

Opposite – diametrically different.

His views are the opposite of mine.

Artist / Artiste /Artisan

Artist – one skilled in fine arts.

A painter is an artist.

Artiste – (usually theatrical), a professional actor, singer, dancer etc.

She is a famous artiste.

Artisan – a craftsman, a skilled workman

A carpenter is an artisan.

Alternate/Alternative:

Alternate – (of two things) happening or following one after the other regularly.

They play hockey and tennis on alternate days.

Alternative – one or the other of two courses.

There is no alternative to his proposal. (always followed by the preposition 'to')

Ascent /Assent:

Ascent – going up

The ascent of the mountain was not difficult.

Assent – agree to a proposal.

He gave his assent to the proposal.

Avenge / Revenge:

Avenge –To punish someone on behalf of a person who is hurt or oppressed. To avenge is unselfish.

To avenge is to inflict just punishment upon a person for a wrong or injury done to us (ourselves) or to someone else. It does not imply any personal feeling of anger or malice. To avenge a man is *to punish his enemy* who deserves punishment.

An avenger is a noble-minded person.

For example:

He wants to avenge the poor for the ill treatment meted out to them.

(He wants to punish those who have ill treated the poor.)

He avenged his father. (He punished his father's offender.)

He avenged his father's death. (He punished his father's murderer.)

I will avenge the wrongs done to the poor.

(I will punish those who have done wrongs to the poor.)

He avenged his son's murder.

Revenge - Revenge as a noun means something that you do to punish someone for their wrongs. The phrase is 'to take revenge on somebody'.

As a verb it means to punish someone for personal satisfaction because they have hurt you or someone.

'To revenge oneself on somebody for something' or 'be revenged on someone' is to punish for a wrong or injury they have done to oneself. It always implies a personal feeling of animosity or anger.

'Vengeance' (noun) implies punishment inflicted on someone because they have done something wrong to you. The phrase is 'to take vengeance on/upon somebody'.

For example:

(*a*) He revenged himself on his colleague who had once insulted him in public.

To revenge himself = to take revenge (noun) on someone.

(*b*) She took revenge on her classmate who had ridiculed her.

(*c*) I revenged myself on my neighbour for the insult.

(*d*) He took revenge on the man who had insulted him.

(*e*) He could not rest until he had his revenge.

(*f*) He decided to be revenged on his enemy.

(*g*) She took vengeance on her colleague for the nasty remarks.

But,'*with a vengeance*' is used for laying emphasis on something that happens more vigorously than usual.

For example:

After her failure in the exam she started studying with a vengeance.

Avocation / Vocation / Vacation:

Avocation –Occupation usually pursued by someone for pleasure in addition to their usual work.

For example:

Gardening is his avocation.

Vocation -regular pursuit or job.

Business is his vocation.

Vacation –a fixed period of time when an educational institution or a court of law is closed.

When does the summer vacation begin.

Apprise / Appraise:

Apprise – to inform

The Collector apprised the Minister of the situation arising out of the employees' strike.

Appraise – to evaluate

The income tax authorities appraised the property.

Allay /Alley/ Ally:

Allay – to remove

The teacher allayed the fears of the student.

Alley – a narrow passage between houses or other buildings.

Our office is situated in the alley near the market.

Ally – friend or partner.

France was an ally of England in the second World War.

Amicable / Amiable:

Amicable – friendly

The striking labourers finally reached an amicable settlement with the management .

Amiable – pleasant

He has an amiable character.

Agony / Anguish:

Agony – pain

When he lost his job he was in great mental agony.

Anguish – sorrow

When he lost his father he was in great anguish.

Anonymous / Unanimous:

Anonymous – unknown

He received an anonymous letter.

Unanimous – with one voice.

He was unanimously elected President.

Action / Auction:

Action – deed

He took action on the complaints.

Auction – bidding

Our old furniture was sold in auction.

Admission / Admittance:

Admission – entry

He has got admission to the course.

Admittance – entry (more formal)

No admittance without permit.

Antic / Antique:

Antic – usually used in the plural – strange laughable movement especially by a clown in circus.

We enjoy the antics of the clown in the circus.

Antique – old fashioned.

He deals in antique furniture.

Barbarism / Barbarity:

Barbarism –uncultured state

Barbarism should not find a place in modern society.

Barbarity –cruelty

Killing animals is a barbarity.

Bear / Bare

Bear – endure

I could not bear his sufferings.

Bare – uncovered

He went bare-footed.

Beneficial / Beneficent

Beneficial – (is applied to things), advantageous

His acts were beneficial to the poor.

Beneficent – kind

Asoka was a beneficent king.

Beautiful / Handsome / Pretty

Beautiful – of beauty of women.

She is a beautiful girl.

Handsome – of pleasing appearance (of men)

He is very handsome.

Pretty – charming.

She is a pretty girl.

Begin / Commence:

Begin – to start doing something

He began doing his work.

Commence – Official beginning (formal)

The government has commenced welfare measures.

Start – I started for Madras at 8 p.m.

Break / Brake:

Break – to cause to come into pieces.

He was about to break the glass.

Brake – stopping device.

We apply brake to stop vehicles.

Berth / Birth:

Berth – sleeping place in a train.

Three tier berths are now available in all trains.

Birth – Coming to life.

The birth of a son is always celebrated.

Bridal / Bridle:

Bridal – relating to bride or wedding

The bridal ceremony was grand.

Bridle – headgear of harness including rein.

The bridle was put on the horse.

Bail / Bale:

Bail – money that somebody agrees to pay if a criminal does not appear in court for trial.

The court granted bail to the murderer.

Bale – bundle of goods

We have received a number of bales of cloth.

Canvas / Canvass:

Canvas – coarse cloth

The tent is made of canvas.

Canvass – solicit votes, seek

They went to canvass for the candidate.

Casual / Causal:

Casual – occasional

He made a casual remark.

Causal – relating to cause and effect between two things, where one causes the other to happen.

There is a causal relationship between food and health.

Ceremonial / Ceremonious:

Ceremonial – relating to ceremonies

There was a ceremonial parade on Independence Day.

Ceremonious – showing excess formality.

He was rather ceremonious on the occasion.

Cession / Cessation:

Cession – the transfer of territory by one country to another.

The cession of Goa to India took place long back.

Cessation – ceasing (stopping)

The cessation of hostilities between India and Pakistan is necessary.

Cheque/ Check:

Cheque – a mode of money transaction

I paid the dues by cheque.

Check – restraint

Government should have a check on its expenditure.

Please check the bills.(verb-to verify)

Childish / Childlike:

Childish – Used in a bad sense

His manners were so childish that everyone ridiculed him.

Childlike – He has childlike simplicity. (Used in a good sense)

Cite / Site:

Cite – quote

He cited two lines from Shakespeare.

Site – ground for building.

The site for the building was inspected by the Engineer.

Compliment / Complement:

Compliment – regard or courtesy

Please pay my compliments to your wife. (Please convey my regards)

Complement – that which completes.

What I have done is the complement of his work.

Comprehensive / Comprehensible:

Comprehensive – extensive

Literature is a comprehensive subject.

Comprehensible – understandable

His speech was not at all comprehensible.

Cast / Caste:

Cast – throw

The tree has cast its shadow.

Caste – The caste system prevailing in India must go.

Ceiling /Sealing:

Ceiling – inner side of the roof

The ceiling of the building is made of wood.

Sealing – affixing seal

When I received the letter the sealing was intact.

Collision / Collusion:

Collision – hitting against one another

In the collision between a car and a bus three persons were killed.

Collusion – secret understanding

The opposition in collusion with some independent members toppled the govt.

Coma / Comma:

Coma – unnatural deep sleep, usually from injury or disease.

The patient is in a coma now.

Comma – mark of punctuation

Comma is one of the punctuation marks.

Confidant / Confident:

Confidant – noun, a person entrusted with the knowledge of one's private affairs.

The officer gave all the secret files to his steno who is his confidant.

Confident – fully assured.

He is confident of his success.

Council/ Counsel:

Council – Committee

The Municipal council meeting was held yesterday.

Counsel – used as a noun and a verb, meaning advice and advise respectively.

(*a*) He counselled her to lead a clean moral life.

(*b*) He could not tolerate the counsel of the Priest.

(*c*) The counsel (advocate) engaged by the Govt. did not present the case properly before the judges.

Conscious / Conscientious:

Conscious – aware

He is conscious of his responsibilities.

Conscientious – scrupulous

He is a conscientious worker.

Canon / Cannon:

Canon – General standards or principles by which something is judged

We must follow the canons of good conduct.

Cannon – gun

A cannon is a large mounted gun.

Contemptible / Contemptuous:

Contemptible – mean, vile, base, deserving contempt

He is a contemptible cheat.

Contemptuous – showing contempt

He wrote a contemptuous letter to his boss.

Continual / Continuous:

Continual – frequent occurrence

There is continual flow of water. There was continual rain.

Continuous – uninterrupted

It was raining continuously.

Continuance / Continuation:

Continuance – the act of remaining for some time in the same state

His continuance as collector is doubtful.

Continuation – extension of something incomplete

This letter is in continuation of my previous one.

Corporal / Corporeal:

Corporal – relates to the body

Corporal punishment is cruel.

Corporeal – physical or material as opposed to spiritual

God is not a corporeal being.

Course/Coarse:

Course – line of action

The course of action chosen by him is defective.

Coarse – rough

Coarse cloth is cheaper than fine cloth.

Credible/ Credulous:

Credible -believable

The news is credible.

Credulous – ready to believe things

(*a*) Illiterate people are always credulous.

(*b*) He was so credulous that he readily believed me when I said that I had seen a ghost.

Crime / Sin:

Crime – offence punishable by law

Murder is a heinous crime.

Sin-violation of divine law

Cruelty to fellow beings is a sin.

Custom / Habit:

Custom – usual practice prevailing in society

There are many strange customs among tribals.

Habit – settled tendency or practice of a man

He is in the habit of getting up early in the morning.

Corps / Corpse:

Corps – pronounced core (a large unit of army)–plural: Corps

An army corps was deployed in the troubled area.

Corpse – dead body of human being

A corpse was found in the forest.

Considerable / Considerate:

Considerable – much

He has got considerable experience in the field.

Considerate – sympathetic

He is always considerate to his employees.

Cool / Cold:

Cool – as opposed to warm

The atmosphere is cool now.

Cold – as opposed to hot

I took bath in cold water.

Confirm / Conform:

Confirm – establish firmly

He told me that he would confirm his arrival.

Conform – comply with

This conforms to the specifications.

Complaisant / Complacent:

Complaisant: polite/obliging

He has a complaisant nature.

Complacent – over pleased, self satisfied

He has a complacent side.

Cymbal/Symbol:

Cymbal – a kind of musical instrument

I like the sound of cymbals.

Symbol – representative of something

The red triangle is the symbol of family welfare.

Career/Carrier:

Career – profession

Nowadays it is difficult to get a suitable career.

Carrier – one who carries or that which carries

We engage carriers to transport goods.

Cell / Sell:

Cell – underground room

He kept his valuables in the cell.

Sell – dispose of for a price

He sells ice-cream.

Deceased / Diseased:

Deceased – dead

The deceased has left no will.

Diseased – affected with a disease

The diseased man was admitted to hospital.

Decent / Descent / Dissent:

Decent – proper

I expected decent behaviour from him.

Descent – downward slope

It was a steep descent.

Dissent – disagree

One of the judges dissented from others.

Deny / Refuse:

Deny – declare untrue, repudiate

(*a*) He denied that he was a thief.

(*b*) He denied his word.

(*c*) He denied having signed.

(*d*) He denied the existence of God.

Refuse – not to accept

He refused to do the work.

He refused to carry out the orders of his boss.

He refused to accept the offer.

Dependent / Dependant:

Dependent – depending on, subordinate, subject

We are dependent upon foreign aid.

Dependant – one who depends on another for support

All his brothers and sisters are his dependants.

Discover/ Invent:

Discover – find or detect something which existed before

Columbus discovered America.

Invent – find or detect something which did not exist before

Watt invented the steam engine.

Disinterested / Uninterested:

Disinterested – unbiased, free from personal or selfish motives

A judge must be disinterested in cases.

Uninterested – lacking in interest

He is uninterested in music.

Draft / Draught :

Draft – rough copy

The clerk put up the draft of the letter.

Draught – amount of liquid drunk at a time, current of air

(*a*) He drank a draught of medicine.

(*b*) If you sit outside you will get a draft.

Dairy / Diary:

Dairy – where milk is kept and butter made.

We live near Milma Dairy.

Diary – a book for daily records of events.

I bought a diary yesterday.

Drown / Sink:

Drown – relating to animate objects

He was drowned in the river.

Sink – relating to both animate and inanimate objects

The ship sank into the sea.

The patient is sinking.

My heart sank as heard the unpleasant news.

Difference / Deference:

Difference – dissimilarity

There is a lot of difference between the two persons.

Deference – respect

He welcomed the stranger with deference.

Defer / Differ:

Defer – put off / disagree

He decided to defer the meeting to a future date.

Differ – disagree

I differ with you on these points.

Defective / Deficient:

Defective – faulty

The clock is defective.

Deficient – wanting

His food is deficient in vitamins.

Dependence / Dependency:

Dependence – reliance

Our overdependence on the World Bank will land us in trouble.

Dependency – a subject country (a country that is controlled by another country)

India is not a dependency of England now.

Desirable / Desirous:

Desirable – that which is desired

He has all the desirable qualifications.

Desirous – longing

He is desirous of going to the cinema.

Discreet / Discrete:

Discreet – prudent or judicious

We must be discreet in our dealings.

Discrete – separate

The medicine consists of discrete chemical elements.

Discrete mathematics deals with the digits '0'and '1'.

Desert/ Dessert:

Desert – a waste tract of sandy land

The Thar desert is in Rajasthan.

Dessert–fruit served after dinner

The dessert served in the dinner was liked by all.

Duel / Dual:

Duel – a fight between two

Ramu defeated Raju in a duel.

Dual – double

He has a dual role to play.

Dye / Die:

Dye – colour

I have decided to dye my gray hair.

Die–expire

People die of hunger.

Dose / Doze:

Dose – quantity of medicine administered at a time

He took the usual dose of medicine.

Doze –to sleep lightly for a short time

He dozed till 8 in the morning.

Doze off – to sleep during the day

He dozed off after lunch.

Effective/Efficient /Efficacious:

Effective – having a high degree of effect

The new taxation measures are very effective.

Efficient – capable, competent

He is an efficient officer.

Efficacious – producing the desired effect

The new medicine is very efficacious.

Elemental / Elementary:

Elemental – pertaining to the elements - earth, air, fire and water

Air can be called an elemental substance.

Elementary – primary, simple, dealing with the elements or first principles of a subject

He has written a book on elementary physics.

Elicit / Illicit :

Elicit – to draw out

The police elicited important information from the culprit.

Illicit – unlawful

Illicit liquor is available everywhere.

Emigrant / Immigrant:

Emigrant – one who leaves his country to settle in another

He is an emigrant from England.

Immigrant – one who comes to live in a foreign country

Immigrants are respected in our country.

Eminent / Imminent:

Eminent- distinguished

He is an eminent professor.

Imminent – impending (likely to happen very soon).

He is aware of the imminent danger.

Envious / Enviable:

Envious – feeling envy

I am envious of his position.

Enviable – arousing envy

His position in the government is enviable.

Eruption / Irruption:

Eruption – outbreak of volcano, war, passion, disease, etc.

The volcanic eruption destroyed the whole city.

Irruption – invasion

There were many foreign irruptions in our country.

Fetch / Bring:

Fetch – go for and bring back a person or thing

Please fetch the book.

Bring – please bring your book. (Please come with your book)

Facilitate / Felicitate:

Facilitate – make easy

Modern inventions facilitate housework.

Felicitate – congratulate

They felicitated him on his success.

Elusive / Illusive:

Elusive – difficult to find

There is an elusive fault in our TV.

Illusive – deceptive

His appearance is illusive.

Faint/ Feint:

Faint – to swoon, not clear

When he saw blood he fainted.

He has a faint voice.

Feint – pretence

He made a feint of doing the work. But he was not sincere.

Fare/Fair:

Fare – cost of passage

The fare for the journey by train is considerable.

Fair – lovely, just, a show

She is a fair girl.

He is fair in his dealings.

We went to the fair yesterday.

Feat / Feet:

Feat – an exploit

It was a brilliant feat of skill.

Feet – a part of the body

He hurt his feet.

Forego / Forgo:

Forego – go before

This point was mentioned in the foregoing paragraph.

Forgo – give up

You must forgo pleasures in order to become a saint.

Foul / Fowl:

Foul – dirty, unfair

He adopted foul means to earn money.

Fowl – a bird

Fowls are seen in the forest.

Gait / Gate:

Gait – manner of walking

I can recognize her by her gait.

Gate – please open the gate.

Graceful / Gracious:

Graceful – elegant

She was graceful in her dress.

Gracious – courteous

The king was gracious to his subjects.

Goal / Gaol:

Goal – aim

We should aim at a noble goal.

Gaol – jail

The thief was put in gaol.

Honorary / Honourable:

Honorary – conferred as a honour, serving without pay

He received an honorary degree.

Honourable – worthy of honour

He is an honourable man.

Human / Humane:

Human –of man

Human nature is unique.

Humane – benevolent, compassionate

He is a man of humane character.

Humiliation / Humility:

Humiliation – lowering of one's dignity

He suffered great humiliation.

Humility – humbleness

Humility is a virtue which everybody should practise.

Imaginary / Imaginative:

Imaginary – fictitious , existing only in the imagination

The Phoenix is an imaginary bird.

Most of your problems are imaginary.

Imaginative – having a higher degree of imagination

He is writing ghost stories because he is highly imaginative.

Industrial / Industrious:

Industrial – relating to industry

Industrial policies of the Government are quite encouraging.

Industrious – diligent, active, hardworking

He is very industrious.

Ingenuous/Ingenious:

Ingenuous – simple, natural, frank, open

He is ingenuous. His was an ingenuous smile.

Ingenious – cleverness and skill of a person

He has an ingenious mind.

Jealous / Zealous:

Jealous – envious

He is highly jealous of his neighbours.

Zealous – full of enthusiasm

He is a zealous worker in the cause of education.

Judicial / Judicious:

Judicial – legal, impartial, unprejudiced

Ramu is a judicial officer.

A judge must adhere to judicial ethics.

Judicious –sensible , discreet

He made a judicious selection of books.

Liberty / Freedom:

Liberty – being free from imprisonment , slavery, undue authority

The prisoner was set at liberty.

Freedom – personal liberty, independence

India got freedom in 1947.

You have to choose between freedom and liberty.

Literal / Literacy:

Literal – corresponding exactly to the original

This is a literal translation of the original in Hindi.

Literacy –of literature or authors

Malayalam is a literary language.

Loose / Lose:

Loose (loosen) – to unfasten, release, set free etc.

Wine loosed his tongue.

Lose – to part with something involuntarily

He was careful not to lose his purse.

He loses his temper.

Loveable / lovely:

Loveable – worthy of love

The child has loveable features.

Lovely – beautiful

She is a lovely girl.

Luxuriant / Luxurious:

Luxuriant – prolific, thick, strong in growth, abundant

There is luxuriant vegetation on the compound.

Luxurious – very comfortable

It is a luxurious hotel.

Memorable / Memorial:

Memorable – worth remembering

Marriage is a memorable event.

Memorial – a statue, festival etc, serving to commemorate, statement of facts as the basis of a petition.

A memorial to Mahatma Gandhi was built before the Indian Parliament.

The employees submitted a memorial to the Minister.

Momentary / Momentous:

Momentary – lasting for a moment

The lightning was momentary.

Momentous – of great importance

It was a momentous decision.

Negligent / Negligible:

Negligent – careless

He is a negligent boy.

Negligible – unimportant

It is a negligible amount.

Notable / Notorious:

Notable – worthy of being noted (in good sense)

He is a notable citizen.

Notorious – infamous

He is a notorious man.

Observance / Observation:

Observance – the practice of observing

We must be strict in our observance of the road rules.

Observation – the habit of observing

His observation about her was not correct.

Oar / Ore:

Oar – a pole with a flat blade used for rowing in water

The boatman started rowing the boat with an oar.

Ore – metal ore

Iron ore is mined in Bihar.

Official /Officious:

Official – connected with an office

He received me in his official capacity.

Officious – giving advice or offering help that is unwanted

He is officious by habit.

Peaceable / Peaceful:

Peaceable – tending to peace

He has a peaceable disposition.

Peaceful – state of peace

He is leading a peaceful life.

Persecute / Prosecute:

Persecute – harass, punish unjustly

Many people were persecuted during the freedom struggle.

Prosecute – institute legal proceedings against

Trespassers will be prosecuted.

Pitiable / Pitiful / Piteous:

Pitiable – arousing pity

The condition of the patient is pitiable.

Pitiful – feeling pity

He prayed to God to be pitiful.

Piteous – calling for pity

He told us a piteous story of her sufferings.

Plain / Plane:

Plain – simple to see or understand

He is a man known for his plain speaking.

The plain fact is that he has deceived us.

Plane – level

He is on the same plane as we are.

Popular / Populous:

Popular – liked and admired

He is a popular artiste.

Populous – thickly populated

India is a populous country.

Practical / Practicable:

Practical – as opposed to theoretical

He has a practical knowledge of everything.

He was fond of practical jokes.

Practicable –feasible, that which can be done

Your suggestion is not practicable.

Practice / Practise:

Practice – noun – habit – repeated exercise

It is his practice to take bath in the morning.

Practise – verb- to do frequently, carry out in action

She practises dance everyday.

We must practise what we preach.

Pray / Prey:

Pray – He prays to God everyday.

Prey – He fell a prey to red tape.

Physique / Physic:

Physique – bodily structure

He has got a good physique.

Physic – medicine

A dose of physic will cure the disease.

Quiet / Quite:

Quiet – calm

He has a quiet nature.

Quite – He is quite sure of his success.

Principal / Principle:

Principal – Chief

He is the Principal judge of the court.

Othello is the principal character in Shakespeare's 'Othello'.

Raju is the present Principal of the college.

The Principal clause is the main clause.

Principle – fundamental truth, general law, personal code of right conduct

Newton formulated the principles of conservation of momentum.

Coming late to the office is against his principles.

Regretful /Regrettable:

Regretful – feeling regret

He is regretful of his misdeeds.

Regrettable – feel sorry

It is a regrettable incident.

Respectable / Respectful:

Respectable – worthy of respect

He is a respectable man.

Respectful – full of respect

We should be respectful to our teachers.

Reverend / Reverent:

Reverend – deserving reverence (respect)- adjective used only before noun- the title of a member of the clergy

He spoke to the Reverend Father John.

Reverent – feeling or showing reverence

He is reverent to his superior.

Route / Root:

Route - way

Columbus discovered a new-sea route to America.

Root – part of a plant

The most important part of a tree is its root.

Sensitive / Sensible:

Sensitive – quickly or easily receiving impressions

The eyes are sensitive to light.

Sensible – showing or having good sense

She is a sensible woman.

Sensual / Sensuous:

Sensual – given up to sexual enjoyment

He leads a sensual life.

Sensuous – appealing to the senses

Keats was a sensuous poet.

Great poetry must be sensuous.

Social / Sociable:

Social – concerning to society

Eradication of illiteracy is a social obligation.

Sociable – fond of company

Man is sociable.

Spirituous / Spiritual:

Spirituous – alcoholic

We should abstain from spirituous drinks.

Spiritual – of spirit as opposed to matter

We believe in a spiritual life.

Stationary / Stationery:

Stationary – fixed

A lorry hit against a stationary car.

Stationery – this store deals in items of stationery

(plural: items of stationery ; not stationeries)

Statue / Statute:

Statue – sculptured or cast or moulded figure of a person or animal

The president unveiled the statue of Mahatma Gandhi.

Statute –a written law of a legislative body (e.g., Act of Parliament)

These statutes are no longer in force.

Stimulant / Stimulus:

Stimulant – that which excites artificially

Some tonics are stimulants.

Stimulus – something that stimulates

People work harder under the stimulus of praise.

Sew / Sow:

Sew – pronounced 'so'(e.g., sewing machine)

She knows how to sew.

Sow – putting seeds

As you sow, so you shall reap.

Tamper / Temper:

Tamper – meddle with

He has tampered with the electric connections.

Temper – modify , mitigate

Justice should be tempered with mercy.

He never lost his temper.

Temporal / Temporary:

Temporal – of this physical life as opposed to spiritual life

As head of the Vatican state the Pope has temporal powers.

Temporary – short living

This medicine gives only temporary relief.

Union / Unity:

Union – being united

Union is strength.

Unity – oneness

He worked all his life for Hindu-Muslim unity.

Chapter 24 MISCELLANEOUS

Errors in the use of verbs

1. I am twenty years old and she sixteen. (wrong)

   I *am* twenty years old and she *is* sixteen.

   Here, the verb 'am' is made to serve two subjects namely 'I' and 'she'.

   This is wrong. Hence the correction.

2. I have never and I will never call him fool. (wrong)

   I have never called and I will never call him a fool.

   Here, two auxiliaries are made to agree with the verb "call". This is wrong because the correct form of call after 'have' is 'called' and not 'call'. Hence the correction. This wrong sentence can be corrected as follows.

   I have never called him a fool and I will never.

3. Ten M.L.As have attended the meeting and one boycotted it. (wrong)

   Ten M.L.As have attended the meeting and one has boycotted it.

   Here plural and singular nouns are made to agree with the same Auxiliary verb 'have'. Hence the correction.

4. These points were discussed in the meeting and a decision taken . (wrong)

   Here 'were' is made to agree with both 'points' (plural) and 'decision' (singular). It may be corrected as follows:

   These points were discussed in the meeting and *a decision was* taken.

   Or

   These points were discussed in the meeting and *decisions* taken.

Correct use of Superlatives

1. Raju's the youngest brother is a student. (wrong)

   Raju's youngest brother is a student.

2. His the youngest sister is a lawyer. (wrong)

   His youngest sister is a lawyer.

   But: She is the youngest sister of Raju.

'the' should not be used before the superlatives if the nouns are in the possessive case or they are preceded by possessive adjectives. (e.g., my, our, his, her, your etc.)

Use of 'by far'

After 'by far' the superlative degree should be used; as,

It is by far the safest way.

He is by far the youngest student.

Wrong use of the Present Perfect

I have done the work yesterday. (wrong)

I did the work yesterday.

The Present Perfect Tense should not be used to indicate an action at a definite time in the past. In such cases we should use only Simple Past Tense.

I have passed the SSLC exam in 1992. (wrong)

I passed the SSLC exam in 1992.

Or

I have passed the SSLC exam. (right because it has no reference to the time of passing)

Examine the following sentences:

1. I have met him this year.

This sentence is correct because the adverb of time (this year) is not over at the time of speaking. The action is well within the period. In other words such adverbs are partly past and partly future. Today, this week, this month, this year etc. come under the category of this kind of adverbs.

Now consider this sentence: I met him this year.

This is correct because this action took place in the past which is part of this year that is not still over.

Q: What is the difference in meaning between the following sentences?

1. He has done business for a year.
2. He has been doing business for a year or for the last one year.

The first sentence conveys the meaning that he continued the business up to the present time but does not clearly convey the meaning that he still continues the business while the second sentence tells us beyond doubt that he still continues the business and may continue in the future too.

Q : What is the difference in meaning between the following sentences ?

1. He has been absent.
2. He has been absent for the last one month.

The first sentence contains no adverb of time (adverbial expression) and hence it suggests that he is not absent now (a finished event) while the second sentence suggests that he is still absent (an unfinished event). It acquires this meaning because it contains the adverb of time 'last one month'.

Note: Although the present perfect tense conveys almost the same meaning as the present perfect continuous tense does, it does not categorically tell us that the activity still continues. But the present perfect continuous tense ensures that the activity still continues. The word 'for' is always followed by an adverb of time (adverbial expression).

Adverb clause indicating futurity:

If the main clause in a complex sentence is in the future tense the present tense is usually used in an adverb clause subordinate to it to indicate futurity.

For Example:

I will do the job if you tell me.	(Not: If you will tell me.)
I shall not do it unless you tell me.	(Not: unless you will tell me.)
Unless you go there, they will not come here.	(Not: unless you will go there ......)
If he comes, I shall meet him.	(Not: If he will come ......)
I shall not go to the office if my friend comes.	
I shall inform him as soon as he comes.	
We are going to Bombay next week if the tickets are available.	

Words ending in 'ly' used as adjectives and adverbs

Only, cowardly, daily, early, hourly, leisurely, weekly, yearly, monthly, fortnightly etc, can be used as both adjective and adverb.

This is the only book I have read.	(adj.)
I only saw Ramu.	(adv.)
It was a cowardly act.	(adj.)
He acted cowardly.	(adv.)
It is a daily newspaper.	(adj.)
He does it daily.	(adv.)
It was an early decision.	(adj.)
He came early.	(adv.)
We hear hourly news.	(adj.)
We rated his performance hourly.	(adv.)
It is a leisurely job.	(adj.)
He did the job leisurely.	(adv.)

We came by the fortnightly express.

The magazine is brought out fortnightly.

Note: The following words which end in 'ly' can be used only as adjectives.

Homely, timely, brotherly, godly, goodly, likely, lonely, lovely, gentlemanly, manly, motherly, womanly, unseemly etc.

For Example:

It was homely food.

He gave me timely news.

He showed a brotherly attitude.

It was a godly act.

He gave his sister many goodly things.

She is a likely choice for her.

He went for a lonely walk.

She has a lovely face.

He has a gentlemanly behaviour.

She has a manly appearance.

She has all the womanly qualities.

He has an unseemly behaviour.

24.1 DIFFERENCE BETWEEN FAIRLY AND RATHER

Fairly is used before adjectives and adverbs which are positive to express a desirable situation.

Rather is used with adjectives and adverbs which are either positive or negative to express an undesirable or desirable situation.

For Example:

The speech was fairly good.

(Don't say): The speech was fairly bad.

But we can say: The speech was rather bad. (undesirable)

The speech was rather good. (desirable)

Other uses of 'rather':

(a) It is used in comparisons.

For Example:

It is rather a better choice.

He went rather hurriedly.

(b) 'Rather' is used to indicate a state of mind or attitude.

It is rather a shame that he made fun of you. (before a noun)

It is rather a pity that you did not pass the exam. (before a noun)

I rather hate him. (used as an adverb)

I would rather wish that I were you.

Mistakes in reporting questions in the Indirect Speech;

1. He asked me where was my house. (wrong)

   He asked me where my house was.

2. They asked him what was he doing. (wrong)

   They asked him what he was doing.

Difference between 'used to' and 'be used to':

'Used to' is used to show a habit or custom.

For Example:

I used to swim while I was young.

'Be used to' means 'accustomed to'.

A noun, pronoun or a gerund is used after this.

For Example:

He is not used to *drinking* liquor.

The boy is not used to beggars.

You should get used to travelling by bus.

Difference in meaning between 'certainly' and 'of course':

'Of course' means 'as a result' and *not* 'certainly'.

For Example:

He is getting married and is of course happy.

(as a result of his getting married he is happy.)

He stands first in the exam and is of course very happy.

His father died and he was of course very sad.

Will you please give me your umbrella? Certainly I will. (Don't say: 'Of course I will'.)

Did you fare well in the exam? Certainly I did. (Don't say: 'Of course I did'.)

Use of 'could have':

'Could have' is used to express a past possibility that was not tried.

For Example:

He could have saved his life if he had taken the proper medicine.

(This means: He did not take the proper medicine and he died.)

I could have given him the book if he had asked for it.

(He did not ask for the book and so I did not give it.)

EXERCISE

I. Subject and Predicate:

Separate the subject and the predicate in the following sentences:

1. He is a clever boy.
2. My sister is weak in Mathematics.
3. We could not go to school yesterday.
4. All that glitters is not gold.
5. They went to Delhi by air.
6. He is a man of character.
7. Please help that poor man.
8. Is he going to school today?
9. Don't do that.

II. Parts of Speech:

Name the parts of speech of each underlined word in the following sentences:

1. *Ramu* is clever boy.
2. The river *flows* into the sea.
3. The boys are playing *on* the ground.
4. He *and* his brother are playing together.
5. He *ran* quickly.
6. Sometimes we have to take *quick* decisions.
7. He *still* works in that office.
8. This is the house he lives *in*.
9. They ran *after* the thief.
10. The city buses were *off* the road last Monday.
11. Chinnu is an intelligent girl. She is always first in the class.
12. You must do your homework before you go to bed.
13. Good Heavens !

III. The Noun-Kinds of Nouns:

Point out the kinds of nouns in the following sentences:

1. Ramu is a good boy.
2. Honesty is the best policy.
3. The committee has decided to meet next Monday.
4. The Ganges is the biggest river in India.
5. Health is wealth.
6. Gandhiji won freedom for India.
7. The lion is the king of animals.
8. Nepolean was a dictator.
9. His innocence was proved beyond doubt.

IV. From abstract nouns:

1. From the following common nouns :

   For Example:

   priest - priesthood.

   Child, mother, friend, man, woman, patriot, beggar, hero, boy, pilgrim.

2. From the following adjectives:

   For Example:

   deep - depth.

   Strong, long, young, dark, vacant, poor, free, high, cruel, humble, wise

3. From the following verbs:

   For Example:

   serve - service

   Obey, laugh, know, please, believe, move, free, see, punish.

V. Gender:

Form the Feminine gender of the following nouns:

1. *For Example:*

   Husband – wife

   [boy, cock, brother, bullock, dog, drake, father, gentleman, horse, uncle, lord, lion.]

2. *For Example:*

   Host - hostess

   [author, host, lion, manager, mayor, poet, priest]

3. *For Example:*

   actor - actress

   [conductor, actor, instructor, prince, tiger, waiter, master, murderer, hero, administrator, sultan, fox.]

4. *For Example:*

   man servant – maid servant

   [Bull calf , man servant , landlord, milkman, grandfather, washer man.]

VI. Number:

Form the plurals of the following nouns:

Box, class, match, buffalo, mango, hero, dynamo, radio, photo, army, lady, wolf, city, chief, grief, proof, belief, tooth, man, woman, mouse, foot, swine, sheep, deer, son-in-law, daughter- in-law, commander-in-chief, maid-servant, step-daughter, passer-by, index, radius, formula, memorandum, axis, crisis, basis, analysis, hypothesis, phenomenon, criterion, madam, ox, child, spoonful, handful, woman-servant.

Correct the mistakes if any in the following sentences:

1. I gave him many advices.
2. He gave me a lot of informations about the accidents.
3. Ramu bought many furnitures.
4. I have got a nice scissor at home.
5. His trouser is dirty.
6. Mumps are rare diseases.
7. He made these amends.
8. Summons were issued by the court.
9. The peasantry was made to suffer.
10. There are twenty six alphabets in English.
11. The scenaries of Kerala are fine.
12. The poetries of Vallathol are famous.
13. He hurled much abuses at me.
14. The couple has no issues.
15. My neighbour has three offsprings.
16. There are many sheeps gracing in the field.
17. There are two deers in the zoo.
18. They bought two kilograms of fishes.
19. I bought six dozens of mangoes.
20. I lived there three scores of years.
21. He had two pair of shoes.
22. Measles were not a dreadful disease.
23. Many a man were present.
24. More than one persons were present.
25. There are lots of milk left.
26. Two-thirds of paddy were sold.
27. A number of members was absent.
28. The number of students absent were small.
29. His sons-in-laws came yesterday.
30. The plural of Commander-in-Chief is Commander-in- Chiefs.
31. There were three maids – servant in that house.
32. There are many man-servants in that house.
33. She gave two spoonsful of milk to the child.
34. I drank two mouthsful of water .
35. There is heaps of time before the exam begins.
36. The house is under repairs.
37. She has beautiful hairs.
38. He is building his house with bricks and stones.
39. I took my meals at 2p.m.
40. He kept his words.
41. The wages of penance is heaven.
42. The gallows are visible from a distance.
43. Politics are an integral part of Democracy.
44. The police has come to his rescue.
45. The M.G.Road was once called Seventy Feet Road.

46. I bought a spectacle.
47. He played billiard.
48. Bread and butter were served for the party.
49. Rice and curry are our food.
50. There are 140 MLAs in our Assembly.
51. It is a six storeys building.
52. I lost a ten rupees note.
53. He is a sixty years old man.
54. They are brothers in the teaching profession.
55. He has put on his new cloths.
56. They did not file their annual return.
57. We use sands to build our houses.
58. We use irons to make agricultural instruments.
59. He is staying in the Government quarter.
60. He took pain to explain the matter.
61. The house with its premise was sold.
62. They went into the wood.
63. Our thanks is due to the Press.
64. Gulliver's Travels are a good book.
65. I have put my sign on the document.

VII. Noun – Case:

Correct the following sentences:

1. He wrote to him a letter.
2. He wrote him.
3. He is studying in the Boy's school.
4. He is a member of the Merchant's Union.
5. He sacrificed everything for Jesus' sake.
6. My table's leg are made of steel.
7. The road's safety is at peril.
8. I met him at the Woodland's Hotel.
9. His daughter's friend's son lives in the city.
10. your's faithfully, your's sincerely.
11. We went to see the Childrens' play.
12. One of the member's identity card was lost.

VIII. The Adjective:

Correct the following sentences:

1. He did not give him some food.
2. He did not have some food.
3. He has given him any food.
4. Everyone of the two brothers is happy.
5. Each one of the huge crowd was shouting.
6. Every one of the five students is intelligent.
7. It occurred after each thirty minutes.
8. Either person died in the shoot out,.
9. The tank overflowed on both sides.
10. You may take both sides.
11. You may go to both ends.
12. He can use both hands.
13. The three men quarreled each other.
14. The two boys quarreled one another.
15. You should not reach neither end.
16. He is the cleverest of the two.
17. He is a best boy.
18. He is a worst boy.
19. Wheat is superior than rice.
20. Orange is inferior than apple.
21. he is senior than Ramu.
22. She is junior than Manju.
23. Which is the most famous brand ? Sony /Akai.
24. Ramu is more intelligent than any boy in the class.
25. Ramu is as intelligent as any boy in the class.
26. He is the most intelligent of all other boys in the class.
27. Diamond is the strongest of all other metals.

28. The population of Kochi is greater than Trivandrum.
29. The drivers of Kochi are more safety conscious than Trivandrum.
30. Raju is the most cleverest of all boys in the class.
31. Wheat is more cheaper than rice.
32. Kochi is one of the largest and populous cities in Kerala.
33. Taj Mahal is the most unique of all monuments in the world.
34. This is the most perfect work of arts.
35. This is quite ideal.
36. This practice is the most universal.
37. He is more equal than the rest.
38. He is my older brother.
39. He is elder than his sister.
40. Not less than twenty people were rescued.
41. No fewer than ten measures of rice was sold.
42. Jain and Sekhar are mutual friends.
43. He appeared in both verbal and written exam.
44. This is the latest item in the list.
45. Ramu had given the book to Meenu. The last kept it in her cupboard for a week.
46. People want these kind of foreign goods.
47. It is difficult to deal with these sort of customers.
48. His the eldest son is a lawyer.
49. The rich people are reluctant to help the poor people.
50. Little money does not make a man rich.
51. He lost the little money he had.
52. He took few days leave.
53. It is a worth viewing serial.
54. Much thanks for your timely help.
55. The minimum passing marks is forty.
56. We prefer TV than radio.
57. We shall discuss few points..
58. Rich are generally unhelpful.
59. He is older than me.
60. He likes Raju more than me.
61. Bombay is the biggest of any city in India.
62. Both the boys did not come.
63. Sugar tastes sweetly.
64. Ramu is enough rich to help him.
65. He is becoming weak and weak.
66. He is a coward fellow.
67. Please open your text to page ten.
68. He is the chiefest Financial officer of the company.
69. This is the most excellent work he has done.
70. Raju gave him a little amount.
71. The number of members attended the meeting was a very little.
72. He is a miser fellow.
73. He came here on last Friday.
74. The marriage will be on next Friday.
75. Thousands of civilians were injured in the attack.
76. This is the only one of his proposals that is worth considering.
77. On the way he met with a minor accident which made him apply for leave.
78. He lost his child which made him sad.
79. He bought a car which was in good condition and which was owner driven.

IX. The Adverb:

Correct the following sentences:

1. We are pleased highly with your performance.
2. He loudly spoke.
3. He bravely faced the situation.

4. They finally reached the destination.
5. He meets me often.
6. He goes to the office always early.
7. We eat non-vegetarian food sometimes.
8. We go to the cinema rarely.
9. He goes out usually in the morning.
10. We visit our neighbours frequently.
11. The floor is enough hard to withstand the pressure.
12. Sugar tastes sweetly.
13. The book was too interesting.
14. He was very thrilled at the sight.
15. They could not help not crying at the tragedy.
16. I am much glad to welcome you.
17. He seldom or ever takes liquor.
18. They behaved cowardly.
19. Both he as well as his friends were present.
20. The exam was very difficult for me to pass.
21. I study on the eve of the exam only.
22. He scarcely makes mistakes.
23. We should be much thankful to our teachers.
24. The faster you walk earlier you reach.
25. They saw him going angrily .
26. He explained as to why they were caught.
27. That is the reason because I failed.
28. He is too intelligent.
29. He is too happy.
30. I did not do my homework. My friend also did not do his.
31. I don't think like they do.
32. He fought as a soldier.
33. He carefully conducted his experiment.
34. We should have not written to him.
35. I met him today morning.
36. I will go to the cinema today night.
37. I went to meet him yesterday night.
38. You are requested to attend the meeting on 10th September 2001 at 8 O'clock in the evening.

Insert the adverbs or adverb phrases (given in brackets) in their proper positions:

1. We are glad to welcome him. (very)
2. I have guessed that. (already)
3. I shall come to your place. (tomorrow evening)
4. We shall go to the cinema. (this noon at Sridhar)
5. I am lucky to have him here. (enough)
6. He has completed the work. (just)
7. We play tennis. (seldom)
8. He comes home. (always)
9. He goes to the temple. (rarely)
10. I visit my uncle. (often)
11. He tells a lie. (never)
12. He smokes. (sometimes)
13. He is confident. (quite)
14. They will come tomorrow. (perhaps)
15. We have to handle it. (carefully)
16. I paid him two rupees. (only)
17. Admission restricted to pass holders. (only)
18. The police can arrest him. (only)

Agreement of the verb with the subject.

Correct the following sentences giving justification for the correction :

1. Late news are stale news.
2. Every man and every woman were present at the meeting.
3. Five and five makes ten.
4. A large number of students was present.
5. The number of participants were very small.

6. The quality of these things are to be ascertained first.
7. Either her children or her husband were invited.
8. The news about the recent earthquake were disturbing.
9. Every boy and every girl were unhappy.
10. Raju along with his parents were present in the meeting.
11. Neither the parents nor their son were permitted to go.
12. Either of the boys were very rude.
13. Neither of the speakers were clear about the objectives.
14. Both the boys did not come.
15. He is one of my friend who have helped me.
16. One of the boys who has helped me were my neighbour.
17. The long and (the) short of the matter are this.
18. My neighbour with his children have gone to Bombay.
19. Many a men were arrested by the police.
20. The police has warned him.
21. The jury was not unanimous in its decision.
22. The majority of people attended the meeting was men.
23. Ramu together with his sisters have gone to Madras.
24. Hundred Rupees are not a big amount.
25. The Manager and the Publisher are going to cinema today.
26. Law and order are state subjects.
27. I wish I am a millionaire.
28. Raju as well as his brother have come.
29. Both Raju as well as his brother came.
30. Neither he or his friend was present.
31. She has neither got the bag nor umbrella.

Fill in the blanks with the appropriate verb given in brackets:

1. I as well as my friends ...... come. (has, have)
2. Bread and butter ...... my food. (is, are)
3. The Principal and Head of the Department ...... present today. (is, are)
4. Each of the boys ...... present. (are, is)
5. Five hundred rupees ...... a big sum. (make, makes)
6. One of the boys who ...... filed is leaving the school shortly. (has, have)
7. I who ...... director is responsible for the administration. (is, am)
8. The jury ...... divided in the decision. (was, were)
9. The crew ...... seen roaming around. (was, were)
10. Neither he nor I ...... angry. (is, am, are)
11. Many a man ...... present on the scene. (was, were)
12. One of his children ...... done it. (has, have)
13. Two thirds of the mangoes ...... bad. (was, were)
14. Three-fourths of the bread ...... eaten by him. (was, were)
15. The cost of sugar, rice and pulse ...... (are, is) steady.
16. Three Musketeers ...... good novel. (is are)
17. Your house and mine ...... destroyed. (were , was)
18. Time and Tide ...... for no man. (waits, wait)

19. Truth and honesty ...... the best policy. (is, are)
20. Ram in addition to his friends ...... ready to do the work. (are, is)
21. The Gullivers Travels ...... a good book. (is, are)
22. The blue and red car ...... good. (is, are)
23. A group of people ...... assembled there. (has, have)
24. The poultry ...... us eggs and meat. (give, gives)
25. The crew ...... of twenty five sailors. (consist, consists)
26. A large quantity of rice ...... distributed among the poor. (was, were)
27. The quality of these mangoes ...... poor. (is, are)

Transformation of Sentences

Rewrite the following sentences removing the adverb 'too' without changing the meaning.

1. She is too weak to do any work.
2. The load is too heavy to lift.
3. He is too clever to be cheated.
4. He is too inexperienced for a teacher.
5. The work is too heavy to do it.
6. It is never too late to mend.
7. He was too late to attend the class.
8. Ramu was too intelligent not to do the problem.
9. The teacher was too fast to be followed.
10. The shirt is too cheap to be good.
11. The news is too good to be ignored.
12. He is too cautious not to guard against frauds.

Change the degrees of comparison without changing the meaning.

1. He is as rich as his brother.
2. Iron is cheaper than gold.
3. Gold is the most sought after metal.
4. Walking is the best exercise.
5. Platinum is the hardest metal.
6. Some countries are at least as large as India.
7. Very few countries are as large as Russia.
8. Raju is one of the tallest boys in the class.
9. There are few countries in the world as large as Africa.
10. She is more beautiful than any other girl in the class.
11. It is better to do some work than sit idle.
12. Madras is one of the biggest cities in India.
13. He does his work as well as I do.
14. There is nothing so useful as a coconut tree.
15. He does his work as well as I do.
16. Some actors are at least as famous as Mohan Lal.
17. She looks after all her sons equally well.
18. He was the first man to call on the president.
19. Trivandrum is not the biggest city in Kerala.

Change from Interrogative to assertive:

1. Can any one hate his mother ?
2. Who would not love his motherland ?
3. Can the leopard change its spots ?
4. What is the use of quarreling ?
5. Does any one hate his country ?
6. Can anyone forget God?
7. Shall we forget the past ?

Change from Affirmative to Negative :

1. As soon so the train reached he got into it.
2. He is a clever boy.
3. He broke his promise.
4. I am hopeful of the results.
5. I am suspicious of his movements.
6. He wanted only his blessings.
7. The minister declined to comment upon the news.
8. We respect our leaders.
9. Ramu is taller than his friend.
10. As soon as I saw him I hugged him.
11. Every one is likely to make mistakes.
12. She is ugly.
13. He will admit that he made a mistake.
14. He is angry sometimes.

Change from Exclamatory to Assertive:

1. How ignorant he is !
2. What a fool he is!
3. How beautiful she is !
4. O that I were with you !
5. O what a fall was there my country men!
6. What a piece of work is man !
7. O for a glass of wine !
8. O what a sight it is !
9. O what a shame my friend !

Parts of Speech

Change from one part of speech to another:

Use the noun forms of the underlined words in the following sentences :

1. They received the news of his achievement joyfully.
2. Smoking is injury to health.
3. He replied to his letter.
4. Handle it carefully.
5. The soldiers fought bravely.
6. He resigned from the post.
7. He goes to school daily.

Use the adjective forms of the underlined words in the following.

1. He is a teacher with experience.
2. He entered the room with a smile.
3. He is a knowledgeable person.
4. There is influence in his lecture.
5. He hopes that he will pass.
6. Handle with care.
7. The President absented himself from the meeting.
8. He performed poorly.
9. He works slowly.
10. We were waiting for him with anxiety.

Replace the Adverbs by verbs in the following sentences:

1. He successfully completed his exam.
2. I regretfully admit my mistake.
3. This is admittedly the first book on the subject.
4. His case was apparently overlooked.
5. He forcibly made her dance.

Replace the adjective forms by noun :

1. The play was quite amusing.
2. He does not know that she was dismissed.
3. He draws charmingly.
4. He travels by bus.
5. He is a diligent worker.
6. His body grow up gradually.
7. He was defeated suddenly.
8. He replied angrily.
9. They treated me respectfully.
10. We encouraged them.

Simple, Complex and Compound Sentences:

Change the following sentences into compound sentences ;

1. In spite of hard work he could not pass.
2. Notwithstanding repeated reminders they did not pay the dues.
3. Owing to pain he was screaming.
4. In addition to financial help she recommended their case to Minister.
5. Having completed his studies he went abroad.
6. After leaving the office I go to the temple.
7. He being a bachelor they gave him only a room to live in.
8. His father having died he inherited the whole wealth.
9. Besides being rich he is generous.
10. With death of his father he has to look after the entire family.
11. We eat to live.
12. Going along the road he met with an accident.
13. We must work hard to earn a livelihood.
14. Being a blind man, he is not free to move about.

Change the following Compound sentences into Simple sentences :

1. The bell had rung and the class started.
2. He had finished his work and went home.
3. You must not make mistake or you will be sent out.
4. He came late and the train had left.
5. Do your work quickly or else you will not be able to complete it.
6. She came and the baby cried for milk.
7. I went to him for help but he did not respond.
8. Not only did he quarrel with her but also he beat her up.
9. Either he was angry with him or he did not want to speak to him.
10. He neither cleared the dues nor turned up.
11. He is a rich man but he is generous.
12. He as well as his wife was present in the hall.
13. He is very intelligent but absent minded.
14. He went to Madras but could not attend the interview.
15. He was ill so he could not attend the office.
16. He bribed the police or else he will be arrested.
17. He has lost everything in the earthquake yet he is hopeful.
18. He was ill and so he could not go to the office.
19. He has not agreed to our proposal and so we are disappointed.
20. The minister arrived and the meeting began.

Change the following Simple sentences into Compound sentences :

1. I am sure to pass.
2. We came to know of his success.
3. He pleaded guilty.
4. His absence in the meeting was noticed.
5. We must hope for a better tomorrow.
6. His walk out from the meeting shows his protest.
7. The thief entered the house by the back door to avoid seeing by anyone.
8. Nobody can guess the price of this diamond.
9. We know the author of the book.
10. They were stated to have arrested by the local police.

11. It was a mistake to be overlooked.
12. Their interpretation of the rule is not correct.
13. He, an agent of the CIA , is in possession of the information.
14. It was the adventure of the hero.
15. He is too clever to be deceived.
16. Being a victim of the recent earthquake he got financial assistance from the government.
17. I request your guidance.
18. Tell me the facts.
19. I pray to God for your happiness.
20. He was the first to witness the accident.
21. The man sitting beside me is the Secretary.
22. The formerly reader of Mathematics is our Professor now.
23. On being selected he felt happy.
24. Owing to bad weather he cancelled his tour.
25. He felt sorry for having been deceived.
26. He was unhappy at being insulted.
27. With a new to meeting his friend Raju went to his office.
28. After having completed his studies he left London.
29. He may prove his innocence.
30. There is none to question my authority.
31. The news is too good to be true.
32. A drowning man will catch at a straw.
33. With all his problems he is always worried.
34. It is too early for breakfast.
35. He informed me of his inability to attend the meeting.

Convert the following Complex sentences into Simple sentences:

1. The court ordered that he be relieved.
2. He asked me why I came late.
3. They do not know when the Minister will come.
4. We hope that the better sex will prevail.
5. Whoever comes here is welcome.
6. I will not do this unless I get permission from my superiors.
7. I do not know where he resides.
8. He confessed that he had committed the offence.
9. This is the pen that I lost week.
10. Please tell me when and where I can meet you.
11. They do not know where he resides.
12. They did not believe what he said.
13. He explained to his officer why he quarreled with his colleague.
14. They do not know where he is.
15. He does not when he will come back.
16. The Police Commissioner has instructed the sub-inspector that the pickpocket be apprehended.
17. That you will meet him gives me peace of mind.
18. This is the house where we reside.
19. He completed his primary education in the town where he was born.
20. He was so tired that he fell asleep.
21. As he was ill he could not attend the meeting.
22. No sooner did he reach the railway station the train had left.
23. You will succeed if you try.
24. As soon as he left I started my studies.
25. I will write the report as well as I can.
26. I used to smoke when my father was away.
27. They swam as fast they could.
28. He insisted that I should leave the place.

Conversion of Compound sentences to Complex.

1. Ask him for the book and he will give it.
2. He saw the danger signal and stopped the vehicle.
3. He fell down but nothing happened.
4. Be careful or you will regret.
5. Read well or you will fail.
6. He wanted to pass the Exam and so studied well.
7. Spare the rod and spoil the child.
8. He was a rich man but he was unhappy.
9. He was very intelligent and therefore he passed the exam.
10. Give me the files concerned and I will prepare the statement.
11. He is blind and yet he is able to read and write.
12. He is very strict but honest.
13. Weather was bad , nevertheless we went out.
14. He is very cruel and therefore I hate him.
15. He is very intelligent and so he does not need tuition.
16. I was late, so I did not go to office.
17. Either he or she will attend the meeting.

Conversion of Complex sentences to Compound;

1. He has told me that he will do it.
2. I got the pen that I had lost.
3. I shall go out when she returns.
4. As soon as I got the message I started.
5. Unless we go there they will not give us the book.
6. He lost more than he anticipated.
7. If you do not go now you will miss him.
8. He works hard in order that he may get a first class.
9. He is more a coward than a hero.
10. You should not go to the office till you recover.

Miscellaneous examples

Rewrite the following sentences as directed.

1. As soon as the chairman came the meeting started. (Change to a Simple sentence)
2. He was too late to go to the office. (Change to a Complex sentence)
3. Work hard or you will fail. (Change to a Complex sentence)
4. I do not know when and where from he will depart. (Change to a Simple sentence)
5. They proved that he was innocent. (Change to Simple sentence)
6. Having done my work I went to the Cinema. (Change to Compound)
7. Notwithstanding my ailment, I used to attend my tuition classes. (Change to a Complex sentence)
8. Being ill I took leave for five days. (Change to Compound sentence)
9. He is poor but he is honest. (Change to Complex sentence)
10. He came out of his house and got into the car. (Change into Complex)
11. He has got his lost pen. (Change into Complex)
12. I know the time of his departure. (Change into Complex)
13. I know his nativity. (Change into Complex)
14. She is so proud that she will not beg. (Rewrite using too…to)

15. He was so late that he could not attend the office. (Replace 'so' by 'too')
16. The problem is too difficult for her to solve. (Replace 'too' by 'so')
17. She is too unsuitable for him. (Replace 'too' by 'so')
18. Can I carry this heavy bag ? (Change into Assertive)
19. Shall we go to the cinema ? (Change to Assertive)
20. Is there any point in your agreement ? (Change to assertive)
21. No sooner did he reach the station than the train left. (Change to Assertive)
22. He is not always reasonable. (Change into Assertive)
23. What a wonderful show it is ! (Change into Assertive)
24. The train started as soon as I reached the station. (Use 'sooner')
25. Shut the door. (Change the voice)
26. He reported the matter to the Police. (Change the voice)
27. They say that he is rogue.
28. He proved that he was innocent. (Use 'innocence')
29. The officer was ill and so he could not go to the office. (Combine into a Simple sentence)
30. He is too old to do any work. (Replace 'too' with 'so')
31. Very few cities are as big as Bombay. (Use the other two degrees)
32. They made fun of him. (Change the voice)
33. When he saw the scene of accident he could not but cry. (Use 'help' instead of 'but')
34. Bombay is at least as big as any other city in India. (Use the other degrees of comparison)
35. Some other cities in India are at least as big as Bombay. (Use the other degrees of comparison)
36. Delhi is one of the biggest cities in India. (Use the other degrees of comparison)
37. He is a very cruel man. (Change into Exclamatory)
38. What a wonderful idea it is ! (Change into assertive)
39. India is bigger than Pakistan. (Use the other degrees of comparison)
40. He is better of the two. (Correct the mistake, if any)
41. He is too foolish not to trouble you.
42. He is too intelligent not to do this work. (Use 'so')
43. He is so stupid that he can be easily cheated. (use 'too')
44. The train reached so late that I missed it. (Use 'too')
45. This hall is too big for him to sweep every day . (Use 'to')
46. My heart is too full for words. (Use 'so')
47. He is too junior for promotion.
48. Spare the rod and spoil the child. (Change to Complex)
49. Please do not say like that. (Correct the mistake) – Omit 'like'

Chapter 25 CORRECTIONS

25.1 MISCELLANEOUS CORRECTIONS

1. I saw a slim and young woman. (wrong)

   I saw a slim young woman.

   (when there are two or more adjectives before a noun 'and' is not usually used to separate them.)

   But: I saw a black and white picture. (When two or more adjectives of colour are used the last two adjectives are separated by 'and')

   I saw a black, white and blue bird.

2. I have more time than they.

   This sentence is grammatically correct but the following construction is better.

   For Example:

   I have more time than they have.

   So also, 'He is more intelligent than she is' is a better construction than

   'He is more intelligent than she.'

   It is always better to repeat the verb after than/as, if they are followed by a third person pronoun.

   But the verb is usually omitted if they are followed by a first or second person pronoun.

   For Example:

   She is as beautiful as you. He is more intelligent than I.

3. The student, who stands first in the class, will get the prize. (wrong)

   In this sentence the clause, 'who stands first in the class' is a *defining relative clause* because it actually defines the student. If we omit this relative clause it is not clear who will get the prize. It is therefore essential to use a clause of this type to make the meaning clear.

If a defining relative clause is used, *no comma* should be used between the noun and the relative clause. The correction therefore is:

The student who stands first in the class will get the prize.

4. My father who is God-fearing has advised me to be kind to the poor. (wrong)

   In this sentence the relative clause 'who is God-fearing' is a non-defining relative clause because even if we omit this clause the meaning of the sentence is complete. It only gives additional information about the subject. Such clauses are called *non-defining relative clauses* and they should always be separated by commas. Hence, the given sentence may be corrected as shown under:

   My father, who is God-fearing, has advised me to be kind to the poor.

   The officer, who is incorruptible, refused to accept the gift.

Errors in the use of Nouns

1. My sister lives in a boarding. (wrong)

   My sister lives in a boarding house. (say always: boarding house)

2. We had a visitor today morning.

   We had a visitor *this* morning. (say: this morning, this evening, this afternoon)

   We shall go to the cinema today night. (wrong)

   We shall go to the cinema *tonight.*

   We went to the picture yesterday night. (wrong)

   We went to the picture *last* night.

3. We cook vegetable every day. (wrong)

   We cook *vegetables* everyday.

4. We are living in my brother's quarter. (wrong)

   We are living in my brother's *quarters.* (say always: quarters in this sense)

5. My house is under repairs. (wrong)

   My house is under *repair.*

   This house is built of bricks and mortar. (wrong)

   This house is built of *brick* and mortar.

   Note: Brick here means the material and not the number of bricks.

6. I got my hairs cut. (wrong)

   I got my hair cut. (Hairs means individual stands of hair)

   For Example:

   A number of hairs were found in the food.

7. I have received all the informations about the matter. (wrong)

   The noun 'information' is uncountable and hence has no plural form. (Only countable nouns have plural forms). It is made plural by adding either 'pieces of' or 'items of' before it.

   For Example:

   I have received many pieces/items of information about the matter.

8. I am very particular about keeping my words. (wrong)

   The phrase is: to keep one's word.

   For Example:

   I am very particular about keeping my word.

9. He died without issues. (wrong)

   'Issue' in the sense 'children' will not take the form 'issues'.

   He died without *issue.*

   He died leaving behind two *issue.* (two children)

10. Two-third of the cake was eaten. (wrong)

    Two-thirds of the *cake* was eaten. (Single cake and hence singular verb)

    Two-thirds of the boys were absent. (Boys plural or countable and hence plural verb)

11. I have a hundred-rupees note. (wrong)

    I have a hundred-rupee note (or)

    I have hundred rupees with me.

    In 'hundred-rupee note' *hundred rupee* is functioning as an adjective qualifying 'note'. Use always 'hundred-rupee note', 'two hundred-rupee note', etc.

    So also, seventy-foot road, hundred-foot tower, three thousand–foot mountain etc.

    (Not seventy-feet road, hundred-feet tower etc.)

12. Kerala is full of beautiful sceneries. (wrong)

    'Scenery' is an uncountable noun (meaning that it has no plural form).

    The correction therefore is:

    Kerala is full of scenery. **(or)** Kerala is full of scenes.

13. He has to do many works. (wrong)

    Work in the sense of job is uncountable and hence has no plural form.

    He has to do many jobs.

    Or

    Say: He has to do many items of work. (or) He has to do much work.

    Note: 'Works' means factory or place of work.

14. Our cat has three offsprings. (wrong)

    Offspring means children. It does not have a plural form.

    Same word is used in both the singular and the plural.

So the correction is:

Our cat has three offspring.

15. It is a beautiful poetry. (wrong)

It is a beautiful poem.

'Poetry' means a collection of poems. It may also mean poems in general.

We can say: It is a beautiful piece of poetry.

16. There are twenty six alphabets in English. (wrong)

There are twenty six letters in the English *alphabet.*

'Alphabet' is a set of letters in a specific order used in a language.

For Example:

He has learnt the *alphabets* of English, French and Spanish.

Note: Alphabet of one language but alphabets of many languages.

17. He went for higher study. (wrong)

He went for higher studies.

'Study' means the activity of acquiring knowledge through books etc.

'Studies' means the activity of acquiring knowledge by a person at a college or university.

18. His father died last week. Under the *circumstance* he could not go to work. (wrong)

His father died last week. In/Under the *circumstances* he could not go to work.

(Use always 'circumstances' in such contexts. Here this plural form means 'conditions'.)

19. He paid ₹ 500 for boarding and lodging. (wrong)

He paid ₹ 500 for board and lodging.

'Board' means the cost of daily meals in a lodge.

We can say: There is a boarding house or boarding school.

Errors in the use of Cases

1. My wife's neighbour's son is an intelligent boy. (wrong)

The son of my wife's neighbour is an intelligent boy.

Note: Use of double possessive should be avoided.

2. He reached the mountain's top.

He reached the top of the mountain.

Normally/Usually possessive forms of inanimate things are not used.

Use, instead, the 'of' form.

3. Between you and I there is no dispute. (wrong)

Between you and me there is no dispute.

Here 'between' is a preposition. Use only the objective case of a personal pronoun after a preposition.

(The objective case of 'I' is 'me')

Errors in the use of Prepositions

1. The clerk availed leave for two days. (wrong)

   The clerk availed himself of leave for two days.

   (The phrase is 'avail oneself of' something. It means make use of something.)

2. We enjoyed in the party. (wrong)

   We enjoyed ourselves in the party.

   'To enjoy' is a transitive verb requiring an object.

   For Example:

   We enjoyed the music. (or) We enjoyed ourselves.

3. The population of India is greater than Pakistan. (wrong)

   The population of India is greater than that of Pakistan.

   In the first sentence population is compared with the country 'Pakistan'. The writer means that the population of India is greater than the population of Pakistan and not Pakistan itself.

   For Example:

   The climate of Delhi is hotter than Kochi. (wrong)

   The climate of Delhi is hotter than that of Kochi.

4. Raju absented from the class. (wrong)

   Raju absented himself from the class.

   'To absent' is a transitive verb and hence it requires an object to complete the meaning.

5. Ramu prided on his achievement. (wrong)

   Ramu prided himself on his achievement.

   'To pride oneself on something' is the phrase.

   Or

   Ramu took pride in his achievement.

   'To take pride in something' is the phrase.

Errors in the use of Adjectives

1. He is taller than any person. (wrong)

   He is taller than any other person.

   (The first sentence means that he is taller than any person including himself. This is absurd and hence the correction.) Use 'other' after positive and comparative when two things of the same kind are compared.

2. Milk is superior than water. (superior to water)
3. Rich should help poor. (The rich.........the poor)
4. Rice is preferable than wheat. (preferable to wheat)
5. I drank little milk I had. (the little milk I had)

6. He is the most wise man of all other men.
(wise man of all-'other' should not be used after superlatives in comparison)
7. I did not bring some money. (say: any money)
8. Please give me any food to eat. (say: some food)
9. He gave me few books to read. (say : a few books)
10. Give me little water to drink. (say : a little)
11. He has a little time to waste. (say : little)
12. Give me few mangoes. (say: a few)
13. The three brothers quarrelled with each other. (say: one another)
14. Ramu is the cleverest of the two bothers. (say : the cleverer of the two brothers)
15. Rani is cleverest of all other girls. (say : the cleverest of all girls)
16. He is my the greatest friend. (say: my greatest friend).

When possessives like my, his and our are used before a superlative, do not use the definite article 'the' before them. When the superlative is used to indicate 'majority' do not use 'the' before it, as ;

Most of the boys were present.

(**Do not say** ; The most of the boys were present.) (say: Most of the.........)

The most of the ice melted. (say: Most of the most ice melted)

17. He is the cleverest boy. (say: He is a very clever boy. There is no comparison involved)
18. She is one of the best and beautiful actresses. (wrong)

She is one of the best and the most beautiful actresses.

(If the first of the two or more adjectives is a superlative the others should also be superlative.)

19. He occupies the most unique position. (say : a unique position)

Adjectives like unique, perfect, complete, extreme, chief, ideal do not admit of any comparison because they stand for the ultimate or absolute.

20. He is my older brother. (say: elder.)

When members of the same family are referred to 'elder' and 'eldest' are used and they are applied only to persons . Do not use 'than' after 'elder'. 'Older' and 'oldest' are used when 'age' is referred to. They are applied to both things and persons.

21. We should help poor. (say: the poor = poor people)
22. He left India for the good. (say: for good or for good and all. This means forever – never to return.) 'for good and all' and 'for good' are interchangeable.

Errors in the use of Articles

1. There is watchman at the gate. (say: a watchman)
2. I told man to go out. (say: the man)
3. The honesty is the best policy. (say: honesty –omit 'the')
4. We get the milk from the cows. (say : milk from cows)

5. He is Kalidasa of Kerala. (say: the Kalidasa.)
6. Bharathapuzha is the longest river in Kerala. (say: The Bharathapuzha)
7. The Mount Everest is the highest mountain in the world. (say: Mount Everest)
8. The Prime Minister Vajpayee is taking a tough stand against terrorism.
(say: Prime Minister Vajpayee) (or) (The Prime Minister Mr.Vajpayee etc.)
9. Ramayana is an epic. (say: The Ramayana , the Bible, the Koran etc.)
10. The Ceylon is an island in Indian Ocean. (say: Ceylon is ......the Indian Ocean.)
11. The wisdom dawned late on him. (say: wisdom)
12. Wisdom of Ramu is well-known. (Say : The wisdom......particularized)
13. The Minister shook hand with the Major.
(say: Shook hands with. The phrase is 'to shake hands with'.)
14. There was depression in Bay of Bengal. (say: the Bay of Bengal)
15. The Mount Everest is in the Himalayas. (say: Mount Everest......the Himalayas)
16. There are so many wonderful things in the Nature. (say: in Nature)
17. The gold is a precious metal. (say: Gold is a ......)
18. He told me lie. (......a lie)
19. Do not make noise. (......make a noise)
20. He is a honourable man. (.....an honourable man)
21. He is sixth in the list. (say: ......the sixth)
22. He was appointed the president. (appointed President)
23. English language is not easy to learn. (say: The English language (or) English)
24. Pandit Jawaharlal Nehru was a historian. (say: The Pandit Jawaharlal)
25. I bought a black and a white dog.
(say: 'I bought a black and white dog' if he bought only one dog)
I bought a black and a white dog means 'two dogs – one black and the other white)
26. He is the Professor and the Principal. (say: He is the Professor and Principal– one man)
27. We went out without eating the breakfast. (say: …eating breakfast)
28. Mathrubhumi is a Malayalm daily. (say: The Mathrubhumi.)
29. As sky was cloudy, moon was not visible (wrong)
(say: the moon, the sun, the stars, the universe, the sky etc.)
30. They went by the land. (say: by land)
31. They went by the water. (say: by water)
Note: Use always by sea, by bus, by air, by train etc. whenever the mode of transport is thought of.

Errors in the use of Verbs and Tenses

1. The murderer was hung. (say: hanged)
2. I am forty and my wife thirty five. (say: my wife *is* thirty five)

3. Thirty students are present and one absent. (say: one *is* absent)
4. They never have and will never admit their lapses. (say: They never have admittedand never will admit......)
5. He had met with an accident. (say: He met with......)
6. He said that he will come the next day. (say: ......that he would come the next day.)
7. Much water has flown under the bridge. (say: has flowed)
8. The canal has over flown its banks. (say; over flowed......)
9. He awaited for the train. (say: awaited the train (or) He waited for the train.)
10. He told that he would go to Bombay shortly. (say: He said that......(or) He told me that he......)
11. Poet Vallathol has founded the Kalamandalam. (say: Poet Vallathol founded)
12. The festival has ended yesterday. (say; The festival ended)
13. I am reading this book for the last one hour. (say; I have been reading)
14. He has been punished in a criminal case two years ago. (say: He was punished)
15. Go to eat your breakfast. (say; Go and eat your breakfast)

    Note: In imperative sentences of this type , do not use the 'to' infinitive.
16. He addressed to the main issue. (say: Addressed the main issue)

    (or) He addressed himself to the main issue.
17. He avenged on his brother's wrongs. (say: He avenged his brother's wrongs. Meaning; "He took vengeance for the wrongs done to his brother.)
18. He avenged his father's murder. (say: He avenged his father's murderer– meaning he took vengeance on his father's murderer)

    Note: Take vengeance on somebody or take vengeance for something.
19. The train left when I reached the station. (say: the train had left ......)
20. Columbus had discovered America. (say: Columbus discovered America.)
21. He asked me to do next work. (say: ......the next work)
22. This is not a thing to play. (say: ......thing to play with.)
23. There is no chair to sit. (say: There is no chair to sit on/in.)
24. This is the house I am living. (say: ......I am living in)
25. Crossing the road a car hit me. (say: While I was crossing the road......)
26. Being a rainy day we did not go out. (say: It being a rainy day......)
27. It is I who is responsible for this mishap. (say: It is I who am......)
28. It is you who is to blame. (say: It is you who are......)
29. He was to immediately come to me. (say: He was to come to me immediately.)
30. He never has and never will do that. (say: He never has done and never will do that.)
31. The students availed of the concessions. (say: The......availed themselves of the concessions.)
32. I want to know where is he going. (say: I want to know where he is going.)
33. Do you know who are they ? (say: Do......who they are ?)
34. How you know he is innocent ? (say: How do you know he is innocent ?)

35. A large number of people is attending the meeting.
(say......are attending the meeting. 'The number of ......singular verb)
36. The number of people attending the meeting are small. (say: ......is small)
37. Neither of the pens are good. (say: ......is good)
38. Every employee and every officer are expected to be present.
(say: ......is expected to be present)
39. The judge disposed off the suit. (say: ......disposed of the suit)
40. He has washed his hands off the unfair dealings. (say: ......hands of......)
41. The train just arrived. (say: The train has just arrived) 'Just' is not used with the past tense. E.g; The train arrived.
42. I did not see you for the last three months. (say: I have not seen you for the last three months.)
43. I did not go home since we met last time. (say: I have not gone home since we met last time.)
44. I have been here since two weeks. (say: I have been here for two weeks.)
45. Study well lest you should not fail. (say: ....lest you should fail. (or) Study well lest you fail.)
46. I am searching for my pen since last Monday. (say: I have been searching for......)
47. He is bed- ridden since three days. (say: He has been bed ridden for three days.)
48. He did not know that what they wanted. (say: ......know what they wanted.)
49. He hanged the picture on the wall. (say: He hung......)
50. He lied on the bed. (say: He lay on the bed.)
51. The hen lay an egg. (say: The hen laid an egg.)
52. I was writing a letter when the postman came. (say: I had been writing.....)
53. He could lift the weight easily. (say: He was able to lift......)
But: He could not lift the weight easily (correct.)
54. You had better to do it. (say: You had better do it.)
55. He is to be blamed for that. (say: He is to blame for that.)
56. He died with fever. (say: He died of fever.)
57. It is hard to be taken. (say: It is hard to take. (accept))
58. I prefer to learn than teaching. (say: I prefer to learn than teach.)
59. I cannot help to laugh. (say; I cannot help laughing.)
60. He persisted to do the work. (say: He persisted in doing......)
61. I am confident to succeed in the exam. (say: I am confident of succeeding......)
62. He prevented me to do the work. (say: He prevented me from doing the work.)
Or
He prevented my doing the work.
'The police prevented the demonstration.' (correct)

Errors in the use of Adverbs

1. I have money enough to buy the book. (say: I have *enough* money......adjective.)
2. I am enough strong to face the enemy.

   (say: I am strong *enough* to face the enemy - adverb.)
3. He is fluently speaking. (say: He is speaking fluently.)

   When the verb is intransitive the adverb is placed after the verb.
4. He fluently spoke English. (say: He spoke English fluently.)

   When the verb is transitive the adverb is placed after the object.
5. He fortunately escaped unhurt. (say: Fortunately, he escaped unhurt.)

   When the adverb modifies the whole sentence place it at the beginning.
6. He goes to church seldom. (say: He seldom goes to church.)

   Note: When the adverb of time like always, often, never, rarely, sometimes, seldom, ever and frequently are used in a sentence they are placed before the verb.

   For Example:

   He often makes mistakes. He frequently goes to Madras.
7. I am mistaken very often for my brother.

   I am very often mistaken for my brother.

   (When adverbs are used in sentences containing auxiliary verbs they are placed immediately after the auxiliary.)
8. He swiftly ran . (say: He ran swiftly.)

   (When adverbs of manner such as swiftly, slowly, gently, softly and fluently are used they are placed after the verb they modify.)

   For Example:

   He walked slowly.
9. He went soon there. (say; He went there soon.)

   When adverbs of time and place are used in a sentence, the time should be used only after the place.

   For Example:

   He reached there quickly.
10. You are kindly requested to attend the function.

    (say: You are requested to attend the function. Both 'request' and 'kindly' are not required as both stand for 'politeness'.)
11. The court united the couples together.

    (say: United the couples...... because 'united' means brought together.)
12. He is considered as an expert. (say: He is considered an expert.)

    Or

    He is considered to be an expert.

    (When we think of somebody or something in a special way we should not use 'as' after the verb 'consider'.)

13. Ramu was appointed as Managing Director. (say:......appointed M.D.)
14. She is both intelligent as well as hardworking.

    (say: She is both intelligent and hardworking. (or) She is intelligent as well as hardworking. The word 'both' is always followed by 'and' and not 'as well as'.
15. This machine is rather unique.

    (say: This......is unique. The word 'unique' is absolute and does not admit of comparison.)
16. He is too angry. (say; He is very angry.)

    Do not use 'too' to mean very. It is used with adjectives and adverbs to indicate a higher degree or in the sense 'more than is desirable or allowed'.

    For Example:

    He is too cruel to show any mercy.
17. His negligence cost him dearly.

    (say: His negligence cost him dear. The idiom is 'cost somebody dear' meaning to make somebody suffer.)
18. I am too happy to welcome you. (say: I am very happy to welcome you. The given sentence means,' I am so happy that I cannot welcome you' which is meaningless.
19. He went directly to his office. (say: He went direct to his office.)

    Directly means straight (in a line or manner). Direct means without any interruption or without any one in between.

    For Example:

    I will deal with him direct. (without any body in between or personally)

    The two buildings are directly opposite.
20. Ration was distributed freely to flood victims. (say: Ration was distributed free among the flood victims; 'freely' means liberally and 'free' means without cost. In American English 'for free' is used instead of 'free' ; as,

    Rice was distributed for free among the flood victims.
21. When he was attacked he behaved cowardly.

    (say; ......he behaved like a coward (or) in a cowardly manner.)
22. He is presently the Chairman of the Company.

    (say: He is currently the Chairman of the company.)

    'Presently' in British English means 'shortly'. In modern English, it is used to mean 'currently'.
23. This is comparatively a better choice. (say: This is a better choice.)

    'Comparatively' and 'better' mean the same. Hence, 'comparatively' is redundant. (repetition)
24. He not only was intelligent but also clever.

    (say: He was not only intelligent but also clever.) (or)

    He not only was intelligent but also was clever.

    Note: Not only......but also construction should always be balanced.

    In the given sentence 'was intelligent' comes after 'not only'.

So the construction after 'but also' should be similar to the one after 'not only'. So the sentence should be either " He was not only intelligent but also clever". Here the adjective 'intelligent' comes after 'not only' and the adjective 'clever' comes after 'but also', thus balancing the construction with the same part of speech after each part of the compound conjunction. (or) He not only *was intelligent* but also *was clever.*

25. The teacher wants to know as to why he had been absent. (say: The teacher wants to know why he was absent.)

"As to" means with regard to something or concerning something, as;

(1) As to the examination , his performance was very poor.

(2) Nothing is known as to his accident.

Errors in the use of Gerunds and Infinitive

1. Raju is interested to read novels. (say: Raju is interested in reading novels.)

   The phrase is 'interested in'. After the preposition use only a noun or gerund.

2. Would you mind to come with me.

   (say: Would you mind coming with me. Gerund should be used after the following verbs : enjoy, prevent, avoid, deny, stop, forgive, finish, consider, keep, delay, resist, postpone, resent, understand.

3. We have heard of him winning the award. (say: ....of his winning.)
4. I was delighted to see him. (say: I was......at seeing him.)
5. He was ashamed to come to me. (say:......ashamed of coming to me.)
6. We enjoyed to play the game. (say: We enjoyed playing the game.)
7. His hobby is to sing. (say: His......is singing.)
8. He aims to get a first class. (say: He aims at getting a first class.)
9. I insisted to see the officer. (say: I insisted on seeing the officer.)
10. He worked hard with a view to get a rank.

    (say: He......with a view to getting a rank. In Modern English 'with a view to get' is considered correct.

11. I am capable to do that job. (say: I am capable of doing that job.)
12. I am used to eat rice. (say: ....used to eating rice.)
13. He was busy to prepare for his exam. (say: He is busy preparing for his exam.)
14. The exhibition is worth to see. (say; The exhibition is worth seeing.)
15. We should avoid to smoke. (say: We should avoid smoking.)
16. I can't help to criticize. (say: I can't help criticizing.)

    Note: Verbs like enjoy, remember, avoid, stop, finish, hate and intend will take gerunds after them.

    The verbs begin, like and dislike can take either 'to–infinitive' or 'gerund' without change in meaning as;

He began to read. He began reading.

He likes to read. He likes reading.

He dislikes to read. He dislikes reading.

17. I have great pleasure to invite you to the party. (say: ......pleasure in inviting......)

18. He was desirous to go to Madras. (say: He......desirous of going......)

19. It is no use to cry over spilt milk. (say: ......use crying over......)

Note: Phrases like look forward to; to take pride in, bent upon, passion for, to charge with and persist in are always followed by gerunds.)

20. There is possibility of Ramu's being questioned. (say: There......of Ramu being questioned.)

Note: If a noun is used in the passive sense possessive form of the noun should not be used before the gerund.

21. The danger of a war's breaking out is remote.

(say: The danger......of a war breaking out.)

Note: If the name of an inanimate thing comes before the gerund, the possessive form of the name (noun) should not be used.

22. I don't remember to have seen you. (say: I don't remember seeing you.)

('seeing'- gerund)

Note: When you remember a past event use only the gerund form. If you want to draw the attention of a person what he has to do in the future, use 'to-infinitive' of the verb after 'remember', as;

Remember to do your homework.

Similar is the case with the following verbs; attempt, continue, forget, hate, intend, bear, love, prefer, regret, try, see, watch, allow, advise, forbid, start, stop, propose.

The following adjectives also follow the same rule; sorry, certain, interested, afraid, sure, used, accustomed.

For Example:

(1) say: Sorry to interrupt you. (We are apologetic about doing something.)

When we say "We are sorry for wounding your feelings." (or)

When we say; "We are sorry for having wounded your feelings" we mean we are apologetic about what we have already done.

(2) 'I like playing cricket' means I really enjoy playing cricket.

'I like to play cricket' means I prefer or choose to play cricket.

(3) I advise you to take a season ticket. ('you'-personal object)

I advise taking a season ticket.

In the first sentence there is a personal object. If there is a personal object we use the to-infinitive form of the verb 'advise'.

In the second sentence there is no personal object. If there is no personal object we use the 'ing' form of the verb.

The verbs *permit, allow,* and *forbid* follow the same rule.

(4) I heard him speaking.

(The present participle 'speaking' suggests that I heard only part of his speech and that the activity was incomplete.)

Note: When an activity is incomplete or in progress we use the 'ing' form (the present participle) of the infinitive.

I heard him (to) speak. (The infinitive 'speak' suggests that the activity is complete. The sentence means that I heard him from beginning till end.)

The verbs 'see' and 'watch' follow the same rule.

Chapter 26 STORY WRITING

Story writing is important to develop language skills. It requires some practice. A beginner may find it difficult to narrate story in an orderly manner. He may omit important details and give priority to comparatively minor details. This results in a story that is not readable. In the examination you may be given an outline story and asked to develop it into a readable story. The following points should be born in mind while writing a story.

1. As a first step try to have a clear grasp of the story before you start writing.
2. Read the given outline carefully and note all the important points.

   Do not change the order in which the points are given in the outline.

   Do not omit any points.
3. Then start writing the story in a simple and natural style. Write the story in the past tense even if the outline is in the present tense.

   Connect the points in such a way that it will read like a good story.
4. You may introduce dialogue or conversation to make the story read natural.
5. Go through what you have written and correct mistakes, if any.
6. Supply a suitable title to the story.

Specimen outline (1)

A thirsty crow ...... searching for water ...... sees a jug ...... water only at the bottom ...... trying to reach the water ...... but in vain ...... looks around ...... sees pebbles ...... picks one by one ...... drops into jug ...... water rising up slowly ...... reaches to the rim ...... drinking water ...... flies away.

26.1 COMPLETE STORY

The clever crow

A thirsty crow flew here and there in search of water. It saw a jug with some water at the bottom. The crow tried to reach the water but its efforts were in vain. It looked around and saw some pebbles lying about the jar. It picked the pebbles one by one and dropped them into the jug. The water in the jug slowly rose up and reached the brim. The crow drank the water and flew away.

Specimen outline (2)

A crow perching on a tree ...... holds a piece of meat in its beak ...... A fox sees it ...... wants to have the meat....plays a trick ...... praises the crow ...... asks her to sing...the proud crow singing ...... the meat falls down...fox eats it and goes away.

26.2 COMPLETE STORY

The foolish crow

A crow was perching on a tree. It was holding a piece of meat in its beak. A fox saw the crow. He wanted to eat the meat. Thought of a plan. He started praising the crow.

"You are very beautiful and your voice is musical too", said the fox.

He requested the crow to sing in her musical voice. Praised by the fox the foolish crow felt proud of her beauty and voice. As soon as it opened its beak to sing the meat fell down. The clever fox ate it and went away.

Construct a readable story from each of the outlines given below and give a suitable title:

1. Eccentric rich man ...... goes to town ...... wants to give a prize to the laziest man ...... reaches the beach ...... sees three beggars lying in the Sun ...... offers a gold coin to the laziest ...... two beggars jump to claim it ...... the third neither moves nor speaks.......too lazy even to claim the prize ...... gets the prize.
2. A milk maid with a can of milk on her head ...... imagines she will sell milk and save money.......will buy more cows........will become rich and build a mansion.....tosses her head in pride.....can of milk falls down......cries over spilt milk.
3. An old merchant ...... fond of jokes ...... wished to look younger......habit of dyeing his beard black ...... gray hair always covered with turban ...... attends dinner party......turban falls off ...... friends laugh ...... merchant explains ...... "hair twenty years older than beard".
4. Manager of the firm advertises for a night watchman ...... walk–in-Interview ......applicants present themselves ...... one man Masood, patiently waits his turn ......

manager questions him about his health ...... "nothing wrong Sir, except that I don't get sleep at night at all", says Masood ...... manager ...... appoints him.

5. A merchant and a farmer ...... merchant often away on business ...... once Entrusts gold coins to his farmer ...... friend ...... returns after a month ...... demands the coins ...... farmer says they consumed by rats ...... merchant pretends to accept the story ...... patiently waits ...... a chance comes ...... farmer plans a pilgrimage ...... leaves his son with merchant ...... comes back after a month ...... the son hidden ...... merchant reports his cat made a prey of him ...... farmer returns coins ...... boy returns home.
6. Sindbad tired of his idle life in Bagdad ...... put to sea a second time ...... Landed Sindbad on an island ...... no inhabitants ...... wandered about ...... had a good meal ...... fell asleep ...... on awakening ...... found ...... ship had left ...... cried in agony.
7. An old lady ...... blind ...... calls in a doctor ...... large fee if cured, but nothing. If not……doctor calls daily ...... covets lady's furniture ...... delays cure ...... everyday takes away some of her furniture ...... cures her ...... court case ...... judge asks lady ...... sight not restored ...... cannot see all her furniture ...... verdict in her favour.
8. Farmer daughter ...... with a pot of milk on head ...... going to market thinks ...... what she can buy with the price of milk. Dreams of ...... being rich and ...... refusing offers of marriage ...... tosses her head in pride ...... the pot falls ...... the shattering of all dreams.
9. Cap seller under tree ...... with ten red caps for sale ...... fall asleep….. when
He awakes caps gone ...... ten monkeys in the trees each wears a cap ...... he cannot catch them ...... despairs ...... snatches cap off his head and throws it down ...... monkeys do the same ...... imitation.
10. A king displeased with his court jester ...... passes death sentence ...... However one last merely shown ...... asks him what kind of death he wishes to die ...... the jesters calm and resourceful reply ...... we would die of old age ...... this saves himself from death.

Chapter 27 LETTER WRITING

A letter is a written communication or message. Letters are of different kinds. They may be roughly classified into two categories.

1. Social or private letters.
2. Business letters.

Social or Private letters are mostly personal. They include letters sent to friends and relatives, rivals and strangers, letters of invitation to parties and functions, congratulation, condolence, introduction etc.

Business letters are impersonal. They consist of letters addressed to or by persons or institutions and government offices in their official capacity, letters sent to or by business establishments, letters to newspapers, etc. They also include applications (for jobs, leave of absence, etc.), petitions, representations, etc..

27.1 GENERAL FORM OF A LETTER

The letter-form has five parts in common with all types of letters although each type has its own form.

(*a*) The Heading–This consists of the writer's address (without his name) and date. It is written at the top right- hand corner with the date below it.

(*b*) The Salutation or Greeting–The manner in which we address a person: Sir, Dear..., My dear, Madam, etc. (written on the left hand side of the letter)

(*c*) The Body–The message or the content of the letter.

(*d*) The Subscription–The polite leave taking that concludes the message.

(*e*) The Signature–The writer's signature with the name below it.

1. **The Heading.** The heading is written at the top right-hand corner of the page. The writer's full address omitting the name is written with the date below it; as,

Leela Nivas
Punnakkal Lane
Ernakulam
Kochi-682018
April 21,2002

Note: 1. Commas and full stop are not required in the address so written.

2. Date may be written in any one of the following forms:

April 21, 2002
April 21st 2002
21 May 2002
the 21st of April 2002
21st April, 2002

2. **Salutation or Greeting.** The form of salutation depends upon the relationship between the writer and the addressee. Below are given some familiar forms of salutation and the corresponding subscriptions:

(1) *Social or private letters*

(*a*) To members of the same family

Salutation	*Subscription*
My dear father/mother/son/daughter...	Yours affectionately/ Your affectionate son/ daughter/father/mother...
My dear Ravi/Sitha...	Your loving father/mother...

(*b*) To intimate friends

Dear/My dear Ravi...	Yours sincerely

(*c*) To persons of equal rank/acquaintances

Dear Mr Menon/Miss	Yours sincerely

(*d*) To one's teachers

Dear Sir or Madam	Yours obediently

(*e*) To strangers

	Yours faithfully
Dear Sir/Madam	Yours truly

3. **The Body.** The letter (body) should be written in a simple and natural style. Everything that we want to write should be included in the 'Body' so that we can avoid Postscript (P.S-This is what is written at the end of a letter after the subscription)

4. **The Subscription.** This is the polite leave-taking that concludes the letter.

The signature of the writer and his name are given below it in that order.

Note: In personal letters the following subscriptions are also used:

Yours very sincerely, Sincerely yours, Yours affectionately (to relatives),

Your loving daughter/son/father/mother/wife/etc (to close relatives)or

Your affectionate daughter/brother/sister/father/ mother, etc.

Note: The following courtesy expressions are sometimes used at the close of the body of the letter but before the Subscription:

With best wishes, With love, With regards, Wish you the best of luck, Hopping to hear from you soon, Looking forward to seeing you, etc

If the courtesy expressions start with a present participle, we must add phrases like 'I remain' or 'I am' just after them; as,

Looking forward to seeing you, (present participle) I am, Yours affectionately,	*Or*	*Wishing* you the best of luck, (present participle) I remain, Your loving brother,
Or		*Or*
Look forward to seeing you. Yours faithfully,		Wish you the best of luck. Your loving brother,

(2) *Business letters*

(*a*) Letters written to or by a person in his business capacity

Sir/Dear sir — Yours faithfully,

(*b*) Letters written to a company or firm

Sirs\Dear sirs\Gentlemen — Yours faithfully,

Name & Designation

(3) *Official letters*

Official letters are highly formal. They are written to or by some one in his official capacity. He may be representing some public office , Government office , etc. or holding some public Office Dear Sir/Dear Madam, With reference to your letter of......	 Yours faithfully, Name & designation

(4) *Demi-official letters*

'Demi' means half.

A demi-official letter is therefore partly official and partly personal. They are written to or by officers holding government or *public offices to draw personal attention to* some important matters requiring immediate action.

My dear X/Dear Mr X	Yours sincerely or
Thank you for your letter of...	Sincerely yours,
	Signature
	Name.
(5) *To newspapers*	Yours truly or
Sir/Madam	Yours faithfully,
	Signature
	Name

Note: The Salutation and the Subscription end with a comma.

Note: The writer must sign below the Subscription followed by his Name.

Note: In official letters (except Demi-official ones) only the official designation and no name is written below the superscription (address); as,

Official		*Business*
The Principal,	*Or*	Indian Telephone Industries
University College,		Bangalore.
Kochi-682018		

Note: If you are asked to write a letter in the examination, you may write the address on the left-hand side of the page at the bottom. You should not write your name but may write an imaginary name.

Note: Salutations like 'Respected sir' and 'Honoured sir' are Indianisms and therefore should be avoided.

Note: What has been stated above applies to the writing of formal letters only.

But, in our day to day life we write quite a few informal letters in which we often deviate from the *standard form.* Even in official correspondence this form is very often used. Take, for example, the case of a student writing a letter to the principal requesting him to grant leave of absence from the school. The student may write the letter as follows:

From

C.Chandni

Standard V B

Chinmaya Vidyalaya

Kochi-18

To

The Principal
Chinmaya Vidyalaya
Kochi-18

Sir,

(Body of the letter)

Ernakulam — Yours obediently,
26-11-2010 — (Signature)
C.Chandni

Note: Do not put apostrophe (') before the letter 's' in Subscriptions like 'Yours faithfully' 'Yours sincerely' and 'Yours obediently'.
Do not write 'Yours' in Subscriptions like 'Your loving brother' and 'Your affectionate father'.

27.2 THE SUPERSCRIPTION

The superscription (the address to which the letter is sent) must be written on the front side of the envelope.(In the case of the post-card the address must be written at the specified place).If the Superscription begins with the word 'To' no comma should be put after it.

Specimen Letters

1. Write a letter to your Headmaster/Headmistress requesting him/her to grant you leave for three days, *which you have already availed yourself of*

From

Name
Class

To

The Headmaster/Headmistress
School
Place

Sir,

As my grandfather passed away on 29.11.10. I was not able to come to school on 29.11.10 & 30.11.10.

I therefore request you to grant me leave of absence for those two days.

Place — Yours obediently,
Date — Signature
(Name)

2. Write a letter to the Headmaster/Headmistress of your school requesting leave for two days *to attend you brother's wedding.*

From

Name

Class

To

The Headmistress

School

Place

Madam,

As my brother is getting married on 01.12.10 at Trivandrum,

I request you to grant me leave for three days from 30.11.10 to 02.12.10 so as to enable me to attend the wedding.

Place — Yours obediently,

Date — Signature

(name)

3. Write a letter to the headmaster of your school *asking for a testimonial/certificate.*

From

Name

Address

Place

To

The Headmaster

School

Place

Sir,

I was a student (Science batch) of the school during the academic year 2008 – 2010. I passed the Higher Secondary Exam in March 2010. I was a member of the school football team at the State level. I was also a member of the N.C.C. At present I am looking for a job and called for an interview for the post of Assistant in a private firm. I have to produce my Conduct and Sport certificates at the time of my interview. You are therefore requested to issue me the above mentioned certificates at your earliest convenience.

Place — Yours faithfully,

Date — Signature

(Name)

4. Write a letter to the Postmaster of your Post Office informing him about the *change of your residence.*

From

Name

Address

Place

To

The Postmaster

.........Post Office

Place

Sir,

Sub : Change of residence.

I have shifted my residence to the following address:

'Nest',

P.T. Usha Road,

Ernakulam,

Cochin – 17.

I therefore request you to redirect my letters to the new address hereafter.

Place — Yours faithfully,

Date — signature

(Name)

5. Write a complaint to the Postmaster of your Post Office, about non-delivery of a Money Order/ letter sent by you.

From

Name

Address

Place

To

The Postmaster

.........Post Office

Place

Sir,

Sub : Non- receipt of Money Order.

I sent a money order for ₹ 1000/- to my sister at the following address:

Meera .S, Thundathil House, Fort , Trivandrum – 23.

It was sent on 09.11.10 from your post office. Unfortunately for me, the money order is yet to be delivered to my sister. It is more than two weeks now. The M.O. No. is 192.

A copy of the receipt is enclosed for ready reference.

Kindly look into the matter and let me know the present position.

Place: Yours faithfully,

Date: signature

(Name)

6. Write a letter to a Publishing Company placing orders for books.

From

Name

Address

Place

To

The Manager

M/s Prakash Publishing Co.

Delhi – 31

Sir,

Sub : Supply orders for books.

Kindly supply the following books by V.P.P. at your earliest convenience allowing the maximum discount admissible to students. Please enclose your latest catalogue too.

Your bill shall be paid promptly after its receipt:

1. The Web of Our Life - 10 copies
2. Surya's Super Quiz - 12 copies
3. Mental Maths (Shakuntala Devi) - 5 copies

Place Yours faithfully,

Date Signature

(Name)

7. Write to a sports company *ordering some sports* goods for your school.

From

The Physical Education Master
School
Place

To

The Manager
Messrs Addidas sports company
Chennai

Sir,

Kindly supply early the following sports goods to our school .

Please send the goods by Kerala Roadways Ltd. and the way bill through The South Indian Bank, Ernakulam.

1. Cricket Balls - 5 Nos
2. Cricket bats - 2 Nos.
3. Shuttle Cock - a dozen
4. Badminton net - 2 Nos.
5. Tennis racket - 6 Nos.

Please allow discount as usual. Your bill in triplicate may be sent to the Principal for prompt payment.

Place
Date

Yours faithfully,
Signature
(Name)

8. Write a letter to the P.R.O of a factory/company/diary asking his permission for a group of school students to visit the factory etc.

From

The Principal
School
Place

To

The Public Relations Officer
Milma Diary Products Ltd.
Place

Sir,

Sub: Grant of permission to visit your factory

The Higher Secondary students of this school propose to visit your factory as a part of their Study Tour. There are fifty students students accompanied by five teachers. You are requested to grant permission for the visit. It would be of great help if you could arrange one of your officers to take the team round the plant. A convenient date and time for the visit may kindly be intimated.

Any date during the first week of next month is preferred.

Place — Yours faithfully,
Date — signature
(name)

9. Write a letter to the Accountant General requesting him to be the guest of honour at the annual day function of your school.

From

The School Leader
School
Place

To

The Accountant General
Place

Sir,

Our school is celebrating its annual day on 24th December 2010.

The function is scheduled to begin at 4 p.m. As the School Leader of the school I have the privilege to invite you to be the Guest of honour.

You being an old student of our school we would feel elated to have you amidst us on that day. We would like to have you distribute the prizes to the winners of various competitions held in connection with the annual day celebrations

Please intimate your consent well in advance.

A self-addressed envelope duly stamped is enclosed.

Place — Yours faithfully.
Date — Signature
(Name)

10. Write a complaint letter to the Inspector of Police about a theft in your house.

From

Name
Address
Place

To

The Inspector of Police

Place

Sir,

Sub: Theft in my house

We had gone to Trivandrum on 21st November 2010 to attend my sister's wedding leaving home locked. We returned on 23rd November 2010 at about 7.30 a.m. On our return we found that someone had entered the house by breaking open the lock and stolen our T.V.(BPL), V.C.R (Sony) andTape recorder (Philips).The almirah in the bed room had been thrown open and ornaments worth ₹ 50,000/-and cash over ₹ 10,000/- missing.

Kindly do what is necessary in the matter immediately.

Place — Yours faithfully,

Date — Signature

(name)

11. Write a letter of complaint to the Asst. Executive Engineer, KSEB about the frequent failure of electricity in your locality.

From

Name

Address

Place

To

The Asst. Executive Engineer

KSEB

Sir,

Sub: Frequent failure of electricity at ...... (place)

I regret to inform you that a lot of inconvenience is caused to the people of this place owing to the frequent power failure and voltage fluctuation.

Most of us depend on electricity for cooking and washing other than lighting. Students especially those taking their Public exams are affected adversely. We are not able to watch TV and operate the computer. This frequent power failure has increased the incidence of thefts in this area. The summer heat and mosquitoes make the nights without electricity miserable.

We had complained several times to the officials at the local office but of no use. You are therefore requested to pay your personal attention to this matter and take necessary remedial action immediately.

Place — Yours faithfully,

Date — signature

(Name)

12. Write a complaint to the Municipal Commissioner drawing his attention to the insanitary condition of your locality.

From

Name

Address

Place

To

The Municipal Commissioner

Corporation of ....(place)

Sir,

Sub: Insanitary condition of our locality. (Place)

As a concerned resident of this locality I would like to draw your kind attention to the unhygienic condition prevailing in our area.

Garbage clearence has not been done for over a month as a result of which the whole area is stinking. Rains and stray dogs make the situation worse.

Drainage blocks are not attented to . I have informed the local muncipal authorities of this many times but nothing has been done yet. If remedial action is not taken forthwith contageous diseases like cholera might break out very soon in this locality.

I therefore request you to visit the place and see for yourself the unhygienic condition of the place.

Kindly do what is necessary in this matter immediately.

Place — Yours faithfully,

Date — Signature

(name)

13. Write a letter to the Librarian of your school about the loss of a book which you borrowed two months back.

From

Name

Class

To

The Librarian

School

Sir,

Sub: Loss of library book No: 376

I am sorry to inform you that the book titled " The God of Small Things"borrowed by me on 20 December 2010 has been missing for quite some time. Despite my best efforts I have not been able to trace the book. Please let me know the amount I have to remit towards the cost of the book. The inconvenience caused is regretted.

Place

Date

Yours faithfully,

signature

(Name)

14. Write a letter to the Police that your brother has not returned from school.

From

Name

Address

Place

To

The Inspector of Police

Place

Sir,

My brother Ravichandran has been missing since yesterday, the 11th of February 2010. As usual he went to school at about 8 a.m. He was in his school uniform. He used to come back by 4 p. m, but he has not returned yet. Either his Principal or his class teacher was not able to give any information on the matter.We searched all places where he was likely to go. I am sorry to say that we have not succeeded in tracing him.

I am very much concerned about him. He is fourteen and is six feet four inches.

There is black mole on his left cheek .A copy of his recent photograph is enclosed.

In the circumstances, I request you to do what is necessary in the matter and help us trace him as early as possible.

Ernakulam

12-02-2010

Yours faithfully,

Signature

Name

15. Prepare an application for the post of Clerk in a firm.

From

Name

Address

Place

To

The Manager
Meera Lab Agencies
Kochi

Sir,

Sub: Application for the post of Clerk.

In response to your advertisement in "The Hindu" dated 9th March 2010, I offer myself as a candidate for the post of Clerk in your firm.

I am twenty and have passed my Higher secondary Exam with a high first class. Currently I am doing B.A. in English Literature privately. I know typing and can type 40 words/minute in English. I have also passed the Postgraduate Diploma in Computer Applications.(PGDCA). I have been working as a Store Keeper in a local Co-operative store for the last two years. I have good knowledge in commercial practice and correspondence.

Two testimonials are enclosed, one from the Principal of my school and the other from the manager of the local co-operative store where I am working now.

If selected I assure you that I will discharge my duties earnestly and sincerely.

Place
Date

Yours faithfully,
signature
(Name)

27.3 INFORMAL LETTERS/ PERSONAL LETTERS

1. Write a letter to your brother thanking him for the birthday gift he sent you.

Address
Place
Date

My dear brother,

I received your gift and the letter. I was surprised to note that you had remembered my birthday. Thank very much you for the wrist watch you have sent me as your gift. It is really a beautiful watch.

I have been desirous of having a watch because all my friends have watches. During my recent exam I very badly felt the need for a watch. In the absence of it I was not able to allot time properly to each question resulting in the omission of certain questions. Now that I have received your watch , I am sure that I will be able to do better next time. I shall preserve it for a very long time as a token of your love affection.

Once more I thank you for the beautiful gift.

Hoping to see you early,

I am,

Your loving brother,

signature

Name &

Address

2. Write a letter to your father asking for his permission to go on an educational tour organized by your school.

Address

Place

Date

My dear Father,

I have received your letter. I am happy to know that Raj has fared well in his exam. I am studying well with a view to getting a rank in my exam.

Our school has organized an educational tour for the +2 students to a number of places in Karnataka next month. It is a three day trip and the expense will be ₹ 550/- including board and lodging. Our Principal and four teachers will accompany us. I have never gone on a tour outside Kerala.

Hence I too would like to join. The exact date of the tour has not been announced yet.

If you do not mind my joining the tour kindly send me ₹ 650/- by next week so that I can have a pocket money of ₹ 100/- .

Convey my regards to all at home.

Your loving daughter,

signature

3. Write a letter to your father requesting him to send you some money.

Address

Place

Date

My dear father,

I received your letter last week. I am happy to know that all are OK at home. Here I am quite all right. I am studying well with the aim of getting a distinction.

A book exhibiton will be held in our school next month. I have come to know that there will be some rare books which will be of great use to me. As I would like to buy some of these books please send me a sum of Rupees thousand.

Convey my love and affection to mom and sister.

Yours lovingly,

signature

4. Write a letter to your friend congratulating him/her on his/ her success in the Higher Secondary Examination.

Address

Place

Date

Dear Kripa,

Hearty congratulations on your creditable success in the Higher Secondary Examination. When I saw your photograph in the morning newspapers and on T.V. today, I was so much delighted. To secure a rank in the Higher Secondary Exam is really a creditable achievement. Only will hard work bring such a credit. You have brought honour to your school too. Above all, your efforts have been crowned with success.

My parents too join me in congratulating you on your creditable achievment. I am sure that this is only the beginning of your series of achievements. Write to me about your future programmes.

Hope to see you soon.

Yours sincerely,

S/d

5. Write a letter to your friend who has been admitted to hospital following an accident, wishing him speedy recovery.

Address

Place

Date

Dear Ravi,

I received your birthday greetings last week. which you send for me. But now I am shocked to hear that you met with an accident. It was your uncle who told me all the details – that you had been knocked by a car and has been in the hospital for the last five days. Thank God, I am glad to know that the worst is now over, and you are much better.

Actually I wanted to come over there immediately to see you. But my exams are quite near that I cannot spare even a day.

You must follow the doctor's advice and take enough rest. I wish you a speedy recovery. As soon as you can sit up and write, do write to me.

Convey my regards to your parents and sister.

Yours lovingly,

signature

6. Write a letter to your friend inviting him to join you on a tour during the Onam holidays.

Address

Place

Date

Dear Raju,

It's quite a long time since I heard about you. How are your parents and sister? I hope your annual exams are over. I am to write my exams next week. It will be over by the end of this month. Our Onam holidays start on 20 August.

Rahim, Binu, Neeraj and I have planned a five day trip to Ooty during the holidays. My uncle in Ooty has arranged for our stay and sight seeing. We leave on Thursday (26.08.2010) night at 8.30 p.m.by car. We would be happy if you could join us and make it a memorable trip. Don't forget to bring your woollen clothes. Please inform me about your plans as soon as you get this letter.

Convey my regards to all at home.

Yours lovingly,

signature